A Light to the Nations

A Light to the Nations

Explorations in Ecumenism,
Missions, and Pentecostalism

EDITED BY
Stanley M. Burgess
AND
Paul W. Lewis

FOREWORD BY
Byron D. Klaus

☙PICKWICK *Publications* · Eugene, Oregon

A LIGHT TO THE NATIONS
Explorations in Ecumenism, Missions, and Pentecostalism

Copyright © 2017 Wipf and Stock. All rights reserved. Except for brief quotations in critical publications or reviews, no part of this book may be reproduced in any manner without prior written permission from the publisher. Write: Permissions, Wipf and Stock Publishers, 199 W. 8th Ave., Suite 3, Eugene, OR 97401.

Pickwick Publications
An Imprint of Wipf and Stock Publishers
199 W. 8th Ave., Suite 3
Eugene, OR 97401

www.wipfandstock.com

PAPERBACK ISBN: 978-1-4982-3813-7
HARDCOVER ISBN: 978-1-4982-3815-1
EBOOK ISBN: 978-1-4982-3814-4

Cataloguing-in-Publication data:

Names: Burgess, Stanley M. and Lewis, Paul W., editors | Klaus, Byron, foreword

Title: A light to the nations : explorations in ecumenism, missions, and pentecostalism / Stanley M. Burgess and Paul W. Lewis, editors

Description: Eugene, OR: Pickwick Publications, 2017 | Includes bibliographical references and index.

Identifiers: ISBN 978-1-4982-3813-7 (paperback) | ISBN 978-1-4982-3815-1 (hardcover) | ISBN 978-1-4982-3814-4 (ebook)

Subjects: LSCH: Pentecostal churches—Relations—Catholic Church. | Pentecostal churches—Missions. | Pentecostal Churches—History. | Pentecostalism.

Classification: BX8762.A4 L35 2017 (print) | BX8762.A4 (ebook)

Manufactured in the U.S.A.   03/01/17

The works in this volume are in loving memory of,
appreciation of and gratitude for

Gary B. McGee (April 22, 1945–December 10, 2008)

father, husband, friend, colleague, and co-worker
and model *par excellence* of the Lord Jesus Christ

Contents

Foreword: Gary B. McGee and the "Radical Strategy" in Pentecostal Missions | xi
—Byron D. Klaus

Preface | xv
—Stanley M. Burgess and Paul W. Lewis

List of Contributors | xix

Introduction

Introduction | 3
—Stanley M. Burgess and Paul W. Lewis

1 Gary Blair McGee (1945–2008): A Lasting Legacy | 13
—Annette Newberry

Ecumenism, Roman Catholic-Pentecostal Engagement

2 The Contribution of Gary McGee to the International Roman Catholic-Pentecostal Dialogue | 37
—Cecil M. Robeck Jr.

3   The Significance of the Classical Pentecostal-Catholic International Dialogue: A Catholic Perspective | 54
    —John A. Radano

4   Revival and Renewal Revisited | 70
    —Peter Hocken

5   A Radical Reorientation: Missiology Following the Second Vatican Council | 83
    —Mary M. Motte, FMM

Missions, Missiology, and Missions History

6   An Overlooked Pillar: The Great Commission in Romans | 103
    —Benny C. Aker

7   Conversion and its Consequences: Nineteenth-Century Missionary Understanding | 126
    —Jonathan J. Bonk

8   The Holy Spirit and Christian Mission Today | 155
    —Stephen B. Bevans, SVD

9   Essential Characteristics of Pentecostal Mission | 170
    —Grant McClung

10 Pentecostal Church Mission and Social Ethics: Love, Justice, and Just Peacemaking | 192
    —Murray W. Dempster

Pentecostal Theology and History

11 Tongues as Evidence of the Character of the Spirit's Empowerment in Acts | 227
    —Craig S. Keener

CONTENTS

12 1 Corinthians 12:13 Revisited—A Pentecostal Reading | 239
—Donald A. Johns

13 Understandings of the Gift of Tongues in Reformation Protestantism and Catholicism | 256
—Gregory J. Miller

14 "This is Our Story": The Early Historiography of the Azusa Street Revival and the Spiritual Politics of Pentecostal Memory | 271
—Edward J. K. Gitre

15 Healing in the Early Pentecostal / Charismatic Tradition: A Historical Perspective | 286
—Vinson Synan

16 Pentecostal Origins in Scandinavian Pietism on the Great Plains | 301
—Darrin J. Rodgers

17 Power in your Mouth: Pentecostalism and Orality | 330
—Del Tarr

"Questions for Lazarus" | 349
Poem by Kilian McDonnell, OSB

Index of Authors | 351

Foreword

Gary B. McGee and the "Radical Strategy" in Pentecostal Missions

Byron D. Klaus

A FESTSCHRIFT IS AN attempt to steward the conceptual resources of a circle of friends to offer respect to someone who is loved and revered. That certainly would be the case with this attempt to honor Gary B. McGee. Colleagues, academics and former students from around the world have been joined together to demonstrate their gratitude for Gary; whose life was well-lived, with considerable influence, but sadly, was too short for this world.

As a scholar, Gary's historiographical assumptions clearly leaned toward the telling of the Pentecostal story through the lens of missions history. He became increasingly convinced that anyone attempting to understand Pentecostals needed to do so realizing that Pentecostals were not merely "doers", but actually very theologically reflective. His last volume, substantively completed just two weeks before his death in December 2008,[1] chronicled the theological and missiological reflection of incipient Pentecostals who were focused on how the world could be evangelized in the last days, before the imminent return of Jesus Christ. The narratives of these early Pentecostals were the repository of this very serious theological and missiological reflection. Gary's historiographical method unveiled that reflection in the focus on the characters of that era and the meaning of their lives and motivations.

The last decade of Gary's teaching and research clarified and expounded what I want to posit was his crowning contribution to the study of

---

1. McGee, *Missions, Miracles and American Pentecostalism*.

Pentecostal history: the development of the theme of the "*radical strategy.*" First seen in an article entitled, "The Radical Strategy in Modern Mission: The Linkage of Paranormal Phenomena with Evangelism,"[2] McGee's framing of the radical strategy was a critique of the Great Century of missions represented as the 19th century. While affirming the historical continuity between mission strategies of past centuries and Pentecostalism, he offered an alternative perspective. He argued that there was a unique and historical discontinuity between the Great Century's strategy of *Christianization by civilization* and the radical strategy seen in the missionary efforts of early Pentecostals. McGee essentially argued that the DNA of Pentecostalism was a fresh theological reflection and strategic critique of the assumptions of the Great Century. This radical strategy was actually a uniquely pneumatological approach to mission that affirmed a belief in the need for a subsequent spiritual empowerment that sent the recipient toward a destiny connected to the continuing redemptive mission of Jesus. The empowerment was for the purpose of world evangelism, was sourced by the Holy Spirit and accompanied by signs and wonders, thus energizing missionary efforts and hastening the return of Christ. The theme of the radical strategy was a clear response to the queries of the likes of the young and activist Student Volunteer Movement who were in a quest for how they could reach the world in their generation with greater speed and effectiveness. The essence of the radical strategy was also affirmed readily by those in the Holiness movement who already had been moved to missionary activity by their affirmation of a deeper life of the Spirit.

This Festschrift will reflect more than the theme I have suggested is at the heart of Gary McGee's corpus of work. His humble persona inspired students by the thousands. His personal piety was evident for all to see. The contributors are global and ecumenical from a variety of publics. But they reflect the broad sphere of the influence of Gary B. McGee, my friend and colleague. I think he would be intrigued by the corpus of this work and my guess is that, even with all the expertise reflected in these essays, he would still wield that infamous red pen of his on the content on the following pages.

—Byron D. Klaus

Past President, Assemblies of
God Theological Seminary
Springfield, Missouri

2. McGee, "The Radical Strategy in Modern Mission," 69–95.

Bibliography

McGee, Gary B. *Missions, Miracles and American Pentecostalism*. Maryknoll, NY: Orbis, 2010.
———. "The Radical Strategy in Modern Mission: The Linkage of Paranormal Phenomena with Evangelism." In *The Holy Spirit and Mission Dynamics*, edited by C. Douglas McConnell, 69–95. Pasadena, CA: William Carey Library, 1997.

Preface

Stanley M. Burgess
and
Paul W. Lewis

As we journey through life, there are a few men or women who make a lasting impact on us. It is not uncommon to clearly see the extent of their impact until after they are gone. Such is the legacy of Gary Blair McGee. While he truly was a great family man, wonderful friend, teacher, colleague, and follower of Christ, his legacy and influence is all the more keenly felt (and our awareness of them) since he passed away. In a very real sense, this volume not only demonstrates the breadth of this impact, it also highlights the arenas of his influence.

The origination of this volume stemmed from an accidental conversation between the two of us (Stan and Paul) after a Sunday School class that Stan was teaching. We had been talking about various projects that we were working on, and Stan noted that there had not been a memorial volume for Gary B. McGee. For Stan, he and Gary had been friends and colleagues in Springfield, Missouri for many years most notably jointly working on the *Dictionary of Pentecostal and Charismatic Movements*,[1] and had an ongoing friendship over the decades. Paul became acquainted with Gary McGee through his father, Terrance R. Lewis. Both men were teachers and colleagues at both Central Bible College and the Assemblies of God Theological Seminary. Further at both of these institutions as well as in Sunday School classes, Paul had been Gary's student. After contemplation, it seemed important that the impact of Gary B. McGee should be memorialized in a volume in his honor.

---

1. There are more details on elements of this in the *Introduction*.

Insofar as this volume was to be a reflection on the major areas of mind and heart of Gary McGee, the structure of the volume was to reflect these arenas. The sections highlight the combination of his own Christian tradition of Pentecostalism and its history, his irenic spirit working in the ecumenical dialogues (notably participating in the Roman Catholic-Pentecostal dialogues, both internationally and locally), and his heart for missions, notably Pentecostal missions (especially Assemblies of God (USA) missions). An apt description of McGee is that he "was a Pentecostal Erasmus: a man of even temper, ecclesial loyalty, critical mind and manifold intellectual interests–all in service to Christ."[2] This volume seeks to mirror his attitude, and his areas of influence—ecumenical interaction, missions, Pentecostal doctrine and history.

In order for this volume in honor of Gary B. McGee to take place, there has been many who have given support to this endeavor. First, was the then President of the Assemblies of God Theological Seminary (AGTS) (Springfield, Missouri), Byron Klaus, at the beginning of the project, and the family of Gary B. McGee—Alice McGee, his wife, and daughters, Angela and Catherine. They all provided suggestions and resources to the formulation of this volume. Further, there are many supporters who were colleagues of Gary McGee's from AGTS: Roger Cotton, Deborah Gill, James Hernando, Stephen Lim, Johan Mostert, Warren Newberry, Melody Palm, James Railey, DeLonn Rance, Charles Self (who followed Gary as the Church Historian at AGTS), Cheryl and Jay Taylor, Randy Walls, and the current President of AGTS Mark Hausfeld. There were many others who very supportive of this project, including Gerald Anderson, William Burrows, Rosalie Digenan, A. C. George, Bishop John Leibrecht, Myron Houghton, Martin Mittelstadt, Dana Robert, Ruth Tucker, Grant Wacker, and Wayne Warner, each expressing their appreciation for McGee's life, and the project. Further, there is a list of current pastors, chaplains, missionaries, and colleagues who expressed their indebtedness to McGee as their friend, teacher, colleague, mentor and example of Christ.[3] There were many more beyond this, who verbally or in writing noted their appreciation for the life and example of Gary B. McGee, and likewise supported the project in McGee's honor.

Alice McGee especially would like to articulate her heart-felt appreciation to all who contributed and expressed their support for this volume and for the legacy of Gary McGee. Since the passing of her husband on

---

2. Self, "The Intellectual Biography of Gary B. McGee," 76.

3. These notes were compiled for the funeral of Gary McGee, Dec. 2008. This compilation is held by his wife, Alice McGee.

December 10, 2008, there has been such a warm and whole-hearted support for her family.

There have been many hands who have worked on various aspects of this volume. We would like to express our gratitude for the technical help of Tammy Burnham, John Gresham, Jennifer Hall, Donald A. Johns, Rachel Harden, Susan Meamber, Anna Mitchell, and Lois E. Olena, the photographic help of Catherine McGee, and the assistance by the editorial staff at Pickwick Publishers, notably Brian Palmer, Chris Spinks, and Matthew Wimer. We would also like to express our gratitude for and appreciation of the support of our spouses, Ruth V. Burgess, and Eveline S. Lewis, respectively, and our families, without whose encouragement and allowance of time, this project would not have come to completion.

This volume is dedicated to Gary B. McGee—father, spouse, teacher, mentor, colleague, and model of a follower of Jesus Christ (April 22, 1945—December 10, 2008).

—Stanley M. Burgess and Paul W. Lewis

Bibliography

Burgess, Stanley M., Gary B. McGee, and Patrick H. Alexander, eds. *Dictionary of Pentecostal and Charismatic Movements*. Grand Rapids: Zondervan, 1988.

Self, Charles. "The Intellectual Biography of Gary B. McGee." *International Journal of Pentecostal Missiology* 4 (2015) 65–78.

Contributors

Benny C. Aker is Professor Emeritus of New Testament and Exegesis at the Assemblies of God Theological Seminary, Springfield, Missouri.

Stephen B. Bevans, SVD, is the Louis J. Luzbetak, SVD Professor Emeritus of Mission and Culture at Catholic Theological Union, Chicago, Illinois.

Jonathan J. Bonk is Director of the *Dictionary of African Christian Biography* (www.dacb.org) and Research Professor of Mission at Boston University School of Theology. He is also the Executive Director Emeritus of the Overseas Ministries Study Center.

Stanley M. Burgess is Professor Emeritus of Religious Studies at Missouri State University, Springfield, Missouri.

Murray W. Dempster is Distinguished Professor of Social Ethics and Co-Director of the Center for the Study of Global Pentecostalism at Southeastern University, Lakeland, Florida.

Edward J. K. Gitre is an Assistant Professor of History at Virginia Tech, Blacksburg, Virginia, and an Associate Fellow at the Institute for Advanced Studies in Culture at the University of Virginia.

Monsignor **Peter Hocken** is a Catholic priest, who is a specialist in Pentecostal-charismatic studies. Since 2002 he has been a resident in Austria.

Donald A. Johns is Professor in the Department of Bible and Theology at the Assemblies of God Theological Seminary at Evangel University, Springfield, Missouri.

Craig S. Keener is the F. M. and Ada Thompson Professor of Biblical Studies at Asbury Theological Seminary, Wilmore, Kentucky.

Paul W. Lewis is Professor of Historical Theology and Intercultural Studies at the Assemblies of God Theological Seminary at Evangel University, Springfield, Missouri.

Grant McClung is President of Missions Resource Group (www.MissionsResourceGroup.org) and Missiological Advisor to the World Missions Commission of the Pentecostal World Fellowship.

Kilian McDonnell, OSB, is Professor Emeritus of Theology at Saint John's School of Theology and Seminary, and is executive director and President of the Collegeville Institute for Ecumenical and Cultural Research at Collegeville, Minnesota.

Gregory J. Miller is Professor of History and Director of General Education at Malone University, Canton, Ohio.

Mary M. Motte, FMM, is a Missiologist and Director of Mission Resource Center-Franciscan Missionaries of Mary, North Providence, Rhode Island.

Annette Newberry is the Associate Professor of Pentecostal Church History and Missions (retired) at the Assemblies of God Theological Seminary, Springfield, Missouri.

Monsignor **John A. Radano** is currently an Adjunct Professor in the School of Theology, Seton Hall University, and formerly he served on the staff of the Pontifical Council for Promoting Christian Unity, Vatican City, 1984–2008.

Cecil M. Robeck Jr. serves as Professor of Church History and Ecumenics and is Director of the David du Plessis Center for Christian Spirituality at Fuller Theological Seminary, Pasadena, California.

Darrin J. Rodgers is the Director of the Flower Pentecostal Heritage Center, Springfield, Missouri.

Vinson Synan is Professor of Pentecostal and Charismatic History and Dean Emeritus of Regent University, Virginia Beach, Virginia.

Del Tarr is the past President, and Professor Emeritus of the Assemblies of God Theological Seminary, Springfield, Missouri, and currently is an Adjunct Professor at Northwest University, Sacramento Campus.

Introduction

Introduction

Stanley M. Burgess
and
Paul W. Lewis

THERE ARE A VARIETY of quotes about those who do not remember or learn from the past being doomed to repeat those same things. Whereas in a snippet sort of way this is true, it can be equally the case that those who are enmeshed in the past do not live in the present. The challenge is to be astute in the past and its lessons while living in the present and having a vision for the future. Gary B. McGee embodied this truism. As such, this volume conforms to this "ministry of remembrance"—remembering and learning from the past to let it inform present decisions and contexts while pointing to the future. These essays highlight the importance of remembrance, the significance in present understanding and dialogue as well as looking to the future in mission.

The "Ministry of Remembrance" in Three Parts: A Personal Reflection

Stan's interest in editing a reference work on modern Pentecostalism was first ignited in the period between 1970 and 1976, his last years on the faculty at Evangel College (now Evangel University), Springfield, Missouri. During that period, several seminal writings on various topics dealing with modern Pentecostalism appeared that spurred his imagination. These included Harold Vinson Synan's *The Holiness-Pentecostal Movement in the United States* (1971), William W. Menzies's *Anointed to Serve* (1971), and

Russell Paul Spittler's *Perspectives on the New Pentecostalism* (1976).[1] During this period, these very authors, together with several peers, founded the Society for Pentecostal Studies (1970) in Dallas, Texas. Stan was involved in the Society from 1972 onwards, offering a paper in that year on *glossolalia* as an aspect of medieval "Pentecostalism" to the meeting in Oklahoma City.

In 1976, Stan began a twenty-eight-year-long stint, first as a Visiting Professor of History (1976–1977) and then as a Professor of Religious Studies at Southwest Missouri State University (SMSU) (now Missouri State University) in Springfield, Missouri (1977–2004). No longer tied down with a huge committee load, Stan now found time to spread his wings as a researcher. He began to examine new possibilities for research and writing. Within a few years Stan became acquainted with Gary B. McGee, then a young Professor at Central Bible College in Springfield.

How the development of their friendship led to the editing of the original *Dictionary of Pentecostal and Charismatic Movements*[2] is described by McGee in a short article, "Prompted by the Spirit: How an Outstanding Reference Book Got Its Start over Slices of Pizza."[3] Together with their associate editor, Patrick H. Alexander, they met on a weekly basis to share fellowship and food at what was then McSalty's Restaurant adjacent to the SMSU campus (now Bambino's Café).

McGee relates that in the spring of 1984 he met with Stanley N. Gundry, an executive of Zondervan Publishing House, Grand Rapids, Michigan. Gundry was in Springfield, Missouri to discuss possibilities for collaboration with scholars in the area. Not expecting that the evangelical Gundry would consider a proposal for a reference work on modern Pentecostalism, both Gary and Stan were surprised when he "jumped" at the suggestion of publishing the *Dictionary of Pentecostal and Charismatic Movements*.

McGee recalled that they originally called the book the *Dictionary of the American Pentecostal and Charismatic Movements*, but decided to shorten the title by eliminating the word "American." There also was a discussion over whether to include "Charismatic Movements," although it was clear from the demographics that there were far more charismatics than Pentecostals worldwide. After debating the issue of scholarly objectivity, the team agreed to treat controversial issues in a non-defensive manner.

This volume came off the press in 1988 with a large early sales record. By the time they had decided on a revision, the original *Dictionary* had sold

---

1. Synan, *The Holiness-Pentecostal Movement*; Menzies, *Anointed to Serve*; and Spittler, *Perspectives on the New Pentecostalism*.

2. Burgess and McGee, *Dictionary of Pentecostal and Charismatic Movements*.

3. McGee, "Prompted by the Spirit," 18–20, 51.

around forty thousand copies. The downside came when critics began to describe the work as "limited," "one-sided" or overly Pentecostal, and clearly "American." One of the chief critics was the great father of Pentecostal historians, Walter Hollenweger, whom Stan met at the 1989 meeting of European Pentecostal Theological Association (EPTA) held in Utrecht, Netherlands. Although initially irritated by his comments, Burgess soon realized that Hollenweger was calling for an expanded version of the first edition. But being busy with other projects, including the second and third volumes of his trilogy on the Holy Spirit, the expanded version of the *Dictionary* waited until the other books were completed.

All of this changed in the summer of 1996, when Stan became critically ill and was not expected to live. Clearly God spared him, while questioning why he was not taken, again and again the revised dictionary version came to mind. Once again scheduling an appointment with Gary McGee at McSalty's, they discussed the possibility of working together again on the expanded project. To his surprise, his former colleague was not interested. McGee had committed himself to a new history of the Assemblies of God. Burgess began to feel somewhat like the apostle Paul, as he chose different partners for his several missionary journeys.

Shortly thereafter, an editorial assistant was contracted for the new task. At the suggestion of Stan Gundry, Burgess contacted Eduard van der Maas of Zondervan, who had done much of the publisher's editing for the original *Dictionary*. He pointed out that Ed now knew much of the material, and would be positioned to help Stan with the new project. Ed agreed to be the Associate Editor.

The New International Dictionary of Pentecostal and Charismatic Movements (2002) was to be both new and international. It fell to Burgess to direct the content changes. He chose to eliminate articles on books of the Bible from the original *Dictionary* in order to make room for country and regional coverage. The real challenge was to find scholars of Pentecostalism from around the world to handle the new content. Early on it became clear to him that, in many cases, such regional scholars did not yet exist. But it was obvious, from the criticisms of Hollenweger and others, that the editors could not depend on Americans or even Europeans to produce the new materials. In the end, Stan was able to marshal about 140 authors, although the new work did not represent scholars of Pentecostalism from Africa, Asia, and South America as fully as North America and Europe. However, the authors chosen did represent a wider denominational range than in the earlier work, most notably with additional Roman Catholic and secular scholars.

It was Stan's feeling that the original *Dictionary* did not clearly distinguish a taxonomy of classical Pentecostals and the various charismatics.

Using David B. Barrett's (with Todd Johnson) taxonomy of demographic information, Burgess chose to follow his three way division—(1) Classical Pentecostals, (2) Charismatics (within existing Christian denominations), and (3) Neo-charismatics (outside existing denominations). According to Barrett, in 2000 there were 65,832,970 Classical Pentecostals in the world; 175,836,690 Charismatics, including 119,912,200 Roman Catholics; and 295,405,240 Neo-charismatics. The total of all in the renewal in 2000 was 523,767,390 worldwide. It was clear that the third category was by far the largest. It included 18,810 independent, indigenous, and post-denominational groups that could not be defined as either Pentecostal or Charismatic, but they shared a common emphasis on the Holy Spirit, spiritual gifts, Pentecostal-like experiences, signs and wonders, and power encounters. In virtually every other way they were as diverse as the world's cultures they represented. Unfortunately, neo-charismatics were still the least understood, in large measure because they had not yet developed an adequate stable of reflective scholars, and had not yet been studied by observers from the outside.[4]

The *New International Dictionary of Pentecostal and Charismatic Movements* (*NIDPCM*) was organized into three sections. Part I is a Global Survey, an overview of the diverse groups by continent, region, and country (212 articles). Part II is a set of David B. Barrett's global statistics. Part III is the dictionary proper, containing around one thousand topical and biographical entries arranged alphabetically, with bibliographies attached whenever appropriate. Because of its size, the *NIDPCM* is indexed by personal names, countries and regions, groups and associations, relevant periodicals, and finally, a general index.

Burgess has long been convinced that the Holy Spirit has breathed upon each generation that has accepted Jesus as Lord and Savior. As a result the *New International Dictionary* includes a timeline for Pentecostals and Charismatics during the twenty-first centuries. This represents a full denial of cessationalism, which is the doctrine that the Holy Spirit had completed the divine task of giving spiritual gifts by the end of the first century. According to this belief, the divine third person of the Trinity then "took a vacation," with divine gifts suspended.

Because of the vastness of the subjects addressed in the *NIDPCM*, this volume became a collection of periscopes, or high points, rather than full treatments of the trans-spatial, trans-temporal, and trans-cultural natures of these movements. Obviously, there was no provision for updating these materials, and for filling in the many gaps remaining in the coverage.

4. See Barrett and Johnson, "Global Statistics," 286–89.

That opportunity came in the year 2014, when Mirjam Elbers, acquisition editor for Brill (Leiden) approached Stan at the Society of Pentecostal Studies meeting in Springfield, Missouri with the suggestion that they work together on developing a plan to update the *NIDPCM*. In addition, the latest version would include an on line version of the new *Brill Encyclopedia of Global Pentecostalism* (*BEGP*), in addition to a hard-copy reference work which would represent the Pentecostal/Charismatic world in 2017, when this the third reference work would be present.

The *BEGP* will place emphasis on Latin America, Africa, and Asia—where most Pentecostals and Charismatics are now located reflecting continuity and changes, while still including North America and Europe. Attempts were made to secure writers who share insider perspectives. Furthermore, *BEGP* will treat these movements from an anthropological or social scientific perspective, rather than from a merely historical approach. There will be no mini-biographies, as found in the first two reference works. Perhaps most importantly, the entire *BEGP* will be regularly updated on line—a feature considered vital in covering the vast and dynamic movement known as global Pentecostalism.

In this manner, the long-term influence of Gary B. McGee is seen. Furthermore, reference works such as those described herein, that are of such academic and popular value, must be updated regularly both in content and venue. In much the same way this "ministry of remembrance" is in three acts, and while Gary McGee is no longer with us, his fingerprints are all over all three works.

Summary of the Volume

The first essay in this volume is by Annette Newberry, a colleague of Gary B. McGee. She and her husband, Warren Newberry, were close friends with McGee and a great support for him in his last years as he battled cancer. Her essay, "Gary Blair McGee (1945–2008): A Lasting Legacy," is a historical biography of the life of Gary McGee, but with a personal component highlighting McGee's own reflections and memoirs of his life and ministry. Newberry incorporates both personal and public elements, allowing those who were most personally impacted by McGee's life to express themselves. She also provides a select bibliography to highlight the significant contributions of his scholarship.

The first section of this volume focuses on *Ecumenism, Roman Catholic-Pentecostal Engagement*. As an expression of this, the initial essay of the section written by Cecil M. Robeck, Jr., sets the tone for this volume. Robeck focuses specifically on the role and "The Contribution of Gary McGee to the International Roman Catholic-Pentecostal Dialogue." Within the broader contexts of the dialogue, Robeck focuses on the insights of McGee in his 1990 presentation to the dialogue participants on evangelism from a Pentecostal perspective as well as noting the Pentecostal view of Roman Catholics. Robeck likewise focuses on the Roman Catholic perspective propounded by Father Karl Müller, SVD. McGee's summary of the dialogue and his suggestions for the future were duly noted by Robeck. McGee's insights and presentation were pervasive for many years to come within the dialogue.

Monsignor John A. Radano follows with an explication of the significance of the International Roman Catholic-Pentecostal Dialogue highlighting its importance from a Roman Catholic perspective. He emphasized important and predominant aspects of the dialogue, including conversion, faith, Christian formation and discipleship, experience, and baptism in the Holy Spirit. While the essay clearly discusses the parameters of the dialogue, the benefits and value of the dialogue as greater understanding and, at times, commonality were highlighted, yet without diminishing some differences. The fruit of this and other dialogues, helped formulate the Global Christian Forum, which Monsignor Radano underscores as the Church looks toward the future.

The essay by Monsignor Peter Hocken looks at "Revival and Renewal" as a continuation of his original studies in 1980 and 1997. This work focuses on the developments on Revival and Renewal, especially among Roman Catholic and Pentecostal-Charismatic traditions. The renewal and new emphasis within the Catholic tradition highlighted Christocentric, Trinitarian, and ecclesial elements partially realized within ecumenical dialogue. In the discussion of the Pentecostal developments, Hocken notes the twin goals of revival and renewal, representatively seen through the Pentecostal, Catholic, and independent Charismatic lens. Ultimately, Hocken argues for a broader understanding of the Spirit's activity of restoration, revival, and renewal "across the whole *oikoumene*." Both revival and renewal are needed until the end of the age.

Mary Motte, FMM, focuses on the developments in missiology after Vatican II within the Roman Catholic Church. Motte notes the developing connection between missions and ecumenism, which included several official dialogues. The dialogues and joint ecumenical missiological groups are foundational to ongoing missiology development. Subsequent missiological developments noted through synods, papal addresses, encyclicals (namely from Popes Francis, John Paul II, Paul IV), and collective bishop expressions lead into a new paradigm, a move to a "new Pentecost."

The second section of this volume focuses on *Missions, Missiology and Missions History*. Benny C. Aker focuses his essay on the Great Commission, which he argues is found in the first seven verses of Paul's epistle to the Romans. Aker emphasizes that this has been a neglected perspective. Through this Pauline text, this missiological focus was embedded, emphasized, and assumed in Paul's communication. Therefore, the Great Commission, which is presupposed in this epistle, should not be overlooked nor neglected.

Jonathan Bonk unpacks the key missiological texts of the nineteenth century church. Bonk, summarizing the key works of William Warren, Thomas Laurie, John Liggins, and James Dennis from their own works, looks at the 1910 World Missionary Conference in Edinburgh and the missional aftermath of World War I. Underpinning the historical study is the progression of the understanding of "conversion." He emphasizes that the nineteenth century understanding of missions and "conversion" are antecedents to missiological methods and models today.

Steve Bevans's essay on "The Holy Spirit and Christian Mission Today" delineates the role of the Holy Spirit in mission. Bevans initiates his discussion with some key biblical texts and missiological statements by Roman Catholic Popes Paul VI, John Paul II, and the former Archbishop of Canterbury, Rowan Williams, among other thinkers. Bevans highlights six basic elements in Christian mission: witness and proclamation; liturgy, prayer and contemplation; justice, peace and the integrity of creation; interreligious and secular dialogue; inculturation; and reconciliation. He ultimately highlights, affirms, and emphasizes that the "Holy Spirit is the principle agent of Mission."

Grant McClung, in his essay, seeks to expound what he considers to be the "Essential Characteristics of Pentecostal Mission." McClung focuses on Pentecostal missions sensibilities as part of the Lausanne Congress, expressed in the joint statements: The Lausanne Covenant and the Manila Manifesto. McClung sees Pentecostal Mission as: experiential, exegetical, expressive, eschatologically urgent, exposure and confrontation, ecologically active, egalitarian in recruitment and leadership, and ecumenically interdependent. These are necessary for a fully developed Pentecostal missiology. The importance of these characteristics is for the global church to work together for the sake of the Christian mission.

The role of Pentecostalism's mission as part and parcel of social ethics is highlighted in the essay by Murray W. Dempster. He notes that various ongoing and historic compassion ministries within Pentecostal missions and ministry have been important to the transformation of societies. The Calcutta Mission of Mercy, Convoy of Hope, Latin America ChildCare, and Teen Challenge provide key examples. Dempster argues that love and justice should work together for social transformation, demonstrably in the "Memphis Miracle" that saw traditionally white and black Pentecostal denominations come together for repentance, forgiveness, and moving forward in unity. Dempster also argues for the importance of peacemaking for social transformation. Social action and social tranformation are part of Pentecostalism's missional task.

The section on *Pentecostal Theology and History* is opened by the essay by Craig Keener on "Tongues as Evidence of the Character of the Spirit's Empowerment in Acts." Keener, while looking through the lens of Lukan pneumatology, emphasizes the prophetic and cross-cultural inspired speech in Acts, and a demonstration that "tongues" is a sign of the universal mission (contra Babel). These observations have implications to Pentecostal theology and missions. So while providing careful caveats, Keener does argue for the Lukan highlighted importance of the tie of "tongues" to the missionary enterprise enabled and empowered by the Holy Spirit.

Donald Johns delves into 1 Corinthians 12:13 by providing a summary of the commonly held positions about the understanding of the text. Then, through careful exegesis, he argues for an exegetically sound reading of the text that has connections with and implications for a Pentecostal understanding of Paul's purpose in this text, including a Pauline expression of the "Pentecostal gift."

Greg J. Miller focuses on the understanding of "speaking in tongues" in the late Medieval and early Reformation era. Miller is selective (due to the need for brevity) of whom he interacts with in the Protestant and Roman Catholic persuasions during this period. He engages with Martin Luther and John Calvin on the gift of tongues, and specifically Luther on the Ephesians 5:18-20 and Romans 8:26 texts to see if he saw a linkage between these texts and speaking in tongues. Miller then looks at the contemporaneous understandings in Roman Catholicism, notably highlighting "Jubilation," and the lives of Philip Neri and Teresa of Avila. Miller argues that there is much for Pentecostals to learn from the pneumatologies of Luther, and especially, Calvin. Yet he also notes the differences between them and Pentecostals, which is contrasted with Roman Catholic expressions that had much in common with Pentecostals.

Edward Gitre delineates the early Pentecostal historiography in the Azusa Street Mission revival era in his essay entitled, "'This is our Story': The Historiography of the Azusa Street Revival and the Spirit Politics of Pentecostal Memory." He focuses on key historical descriptions about the founding and precursors of the revival. Gitre highlights the distancing of William J. Seymour and Charles Parham, and the resulting "Spiritual Politics of Pentecostal Memory." As such, Gitre notes that the history expressed was adjusted due to certain sensibilities.

"Healing in the Early Pentecostal/Charismatic Tradition: A Historical Perspective" is written by Vinson Synan to summarize the early modern Pentecostal Movement's understanding of healing. Important late nineteenth-century proponents of divine healing, such as Charles Cullis, Adoniram J. Gordon, and Alexander Dowie, provide the backdrop for Charles Fox Parham and William J. Seymour with the Azusa Street revival. Synan unpacks the tension in the fledgling movement between divine healing and the role of modern medicine. He further sees the blending of the extremes with the significance of Oral Roberts and his noted healing ministry with the building of the "City of Faith." This led to the more common balanced position that is seen in the movement today.

The extensive analysis of the origins of the modern Pentecostal movement in the upper Great Plains (USA) is presented by Darrin Rodgers. In his research, he demonstrates that the roots of the Pentecostal movement in the upper Great Plains was based on the roots of Scandinavian pietist revivals prior to the Azusa Street revival. Many of these forbearers were the earliest missionaries from this fledgling movement, and also would later become important in future Classical Pentecostal denominations. From this analysis, Rodgers calls for a revised historiography to correct the previously understood history to include this neglected Pentecostal antecedent.

The essay by Del Tarr, "Power in your Mouth," is a study of orality from a Pentecostal perspective. In this study, Tarr delves into the significance of the oral / aural. He likewise highlights that the biblical text strongly emphasizes oral communications, and articulates the cultural and psychological impact of oral communication and engagement. Tarr also notes the Western move toward literacy and the printed text (or borrowing from James K. A. Smith) with "the textualization of the faith."[5] As such, the differences between oral / aural, and the literate cultures is brought to the forefront. Tarr thereby presents a case arguing for the importance of orality biblically and culturally.

The volume concludes with a poem by Kilian McDonnell on "Questions for Lazarus." McDonnell was closely tied to the Roman Catholic charismatic movement and the Roman Catholic-Pentecostal dialogue. This poem is offered in honor of Gary B. McGee.

While these essays (and a poem) do demonstrate a diversity of topics, and a diversity across and within the sections (Ecumenism, Roman Catholic-Pentecostal Engagement; Missions, Missiology and Missions History;

---

5. Smith, "Closing of the Book," 49–71.

and Pentecostal Theology and History), they also have a unifying factor. Ultimately, all the articles reflect the interests, skills, and influence of Gary B. McGee, and his desire and passion to be *A Light to the Nations*.

Bibliography

Barrett, David B., and Todd Johnson. "Global Statistics." In *Dictionary of Pentecostal and Charismatic Movements*, 286–89. Grand Rapids: Zondervan, 2002.

Burgess, Stanley M., Elaine R. Cleeton, and Todd M. Johnson, eds. *The Brill Encyclopedia of Pentecostalism*. Leiden: Brill, 2017 (in preparation).

Burgess, Stanley M., Gary B. McGee, and Patrick H. Alexander, eds. *Dictionary of Pentecostal and Charismatic Movements*. Grand Rapids: Zondervan, 1988.

Burgess, Stanley M., and Eduard van der Maas, eds. *The New International Dictionary of Pentecostal and Charismatic Movements*. Grand Rapids: Zondervan, 2002.

McGee, Gary B. "Prompted by the Spirit: How an Outstanding Reference Book Got Its Start over Slices of Pizza." *Assemblies of God Heritage* 18 (1998–1999) 18–20, 51.

Menzies, William W. *Anointed to Serve: The Story of the Assemblies of God*. Springfield, MO: Gospel, 1971.

Smith, James K. A. "The Closing of the Book: Pentecostals, Evangelicals, and the Sacred Writings." *Journal of Pentecostal Theology* 11 (1997) 49–71.

Spittler, Russell P., ed. *Perspectives on the New Pentecostalism*. Grand Rapids: Baker, 1976.

Synan, Vinson. *The Holiness-Pentecostal Tradition: Charismatic Movements in the Twentieth Century*. Grand Rapids: Eerdmans, 1971.

1

Gary Blair McGee (1945–2008)

A Lasting Legacy

Annette Newberry

> "The heritage and vision of any movement cannot be adequately explained without looking at the lives of the people who made it happen. Their sacrifices and faithfulness, joys and sorrows, hopes and disappointments, are all parts of the larger story of Christians called to advance God's kingdom."[1]
>
> —Gary B. McGee

GARY BLAIR MCGEE EXPERTLY integrated fascinating stories about real people into his teaching and writings. The time has come to add his life to the larger story of the people of the Spirit who advanced the kingdom of God. Gary would be uncomfortable with the idea, yet his own story exemplifies his integration of stories in his teachings, writings, and life. While there have been several important biographies and reflections on Gary's life,[2] however, it was intentional that in order to honor him in this essay, this biography would be compiled from his own articulations and reflections.[3]

1. McGee, *People of the Spirit*, Kindle Locations 120–22.

2. E.g. Alexander, "McGee, Gary Blair," 854–55; and "Gary McGee: A Saintly Scholar," 58–62, 70.

3. Thus, this essay relies primarily on three sources in his own words: (1) a sermon, "The Gift of Teaching in a Pentecostal Context: A Personal Reflection," he delivered for an Assemblies of God Theological Seminary (AGTS) chapel service on September 19, 2001; (2) Gary McGee, "Living Dedication; a Lasting Legacy," a video interview conducted as an assignment for the course Assemblies of God History and Polity by Adam Trimbur and Natalia Guerreiro, Assemblies of God Theological Seminary

Birth and Early Childhood

Gary McGee's time on this earth began on April 22, 1945, in Canton, Ohio. He was the second of the five children born to Ronald and Velma McGee. During his childhood, he spent every summer in the home of his maternal grandparents, George and Lucille Hetzel, who lived next door to his parents. He enjoyed these experiences so much that he would cry when he had to return to his parents's house for school in the fall. Lucille, who had been converted in 1923 in an Aimee Semple McPherson's evangelistic campaign, influenced him with stories of early Pentecostalism and "often reminisced about the glory and power of God in Sister's ministry."[4]

When the McGee children were older, the boys helped their dad plaster old schools during the summer vacation. Ronald, the eldest brother, remembers Gary "beet red with sweat pouring down his face, complaining about having to lug plaster." Ronald also recalled looking for Gary to help with the chores and discovering him reading a book.[5]

Baptism of the Holy Spirit

Gary grew up in the Bethel Temple Assembly of God in Canton, Ohio, where both his grandparents and parents regularly attended services. His "dear Mother" and father, with their five children in tow, attended meetings five or six nights a week, which often lasted two or three hours plus "tarrying time." In Gary's young mind, tarrying was "hard work requiring confession of every known possible sin."[6]

He described his personal Baptism of the Holy Spirit as an "interesting process," which started when he was nine or ten years old during the tarrying service after a meeting held by two women evangelists. At some point, while people prayed on either side of him, he stuttered a few words, then someone declared, "He's got it." This created a dilemma for Gary because he knew he did not have "it." Six or seven years later, however, while standing with his hands upraised praising the Lord, English stopped and unknown

---

(AGTS) students, on April 13, 2007; and (3) a personal journal kept by Gary during a lectureship in Moldova (August 2–24, 1998); I would like to express a note of appreciation to Alice McGee. These three sources, and the numerous personal cards, notes, and writings were made available to me for this essay. These sources are found in her private collection unless noted otherwise.

4. McGee, "And Your Daughters Shall Prophesy"; if listed as McGee in this biography, it will refer to Gary B. McGee.

5. Ronald McGee, personal note card.

6. McGee, in "Living Dedication; a Lasting Legacy."

tongues started. "It was an easy transition and the most amazing experience. It was a reminder that God is the one who baptizes."[7]

Call to the Ministry and Central Bible Institute

Influenced by several outstanding teachers in his Junior and Senior High school, Gary wanted to teach. He also felt called to the ministry; a pastor advised him to enroll at Central Bible Institute (later Central Bible College) in the fall of 1963. Gary wrestled, however, with a common Pentecostal tension of the time: ministry versus teaching. At that time, "three vocations enjoyed the limelight: pastor, evangelist, and missionary . . . The calling into Christian higher education rested under a cloud of suspicion . . . because it appeared to be so far away from practical church work."[8] To resolve this dilemma, Gary sought the advice of Robert E. Cooley, a professor and Dean of Students at Central Bible Institute (CBI).[9] After hearing Gary's intentions to transfer to another college in order to pursue teaching, Cooley explained that teaching is a ministry in the Church. Since Cooley modeled this principle, Gary continued his education at Central Bible College (CBC).[10]

Open Bible College in Des Moines, Iowa (1967–1970)

Before graduating from CBC in 1967, Gary accepted a position as Dean of Men at Open Bible College (OBC)[11] in Des Moines, Iowa, a school sponsored by Open Bible Standard Churches. During the interview progress, the OBC committee revealed the college needed a Greek teacher. The first interviewee, a young man with only one semester of Greek under his belt, confidently affirmed he could teach the course because he could identify with the first year students. Gary who had studied two and a half years of Greek replied he did not feel qualified and nervously laughed at the idea. The OBC interviewer replied, "If you are hired, you will teach Greek." Gary was hired as Dean and also taught Greek among other courses.[12]

Gary enjoyed his experience at OBC and learned lifelong lessons:

7. Ibid.
8. McGee, "The Gift of Teaching in a Pentecostal Context."
9. Robert Cooley later became the president of Gordon Conwell from 1981–97.
10. McGee, in "Living Dedication; a Lasting Legacy."
11. OBC closed and merged with Eugene Bible College, Oregon, in 1986.
12. McGee in "Living Dedication; a Lasting Legacy."

> I worked hard in the three years I served on the faculty there before returning to CBC as an instructor. Nothing deterred me in my resolve to do the Lord's work—Not the time students threw a dead skunk [a welcoming gift] into my room in the dorm, . . . Nor the time the student chef cooked the garbage by mistake, and I ate a dish of it because I was a representative of the college administration and felt that I had to set an example.[13]

The skunk and the garbage provided him with more stories to tell. The hard work and experiences in a small Pentecostal school gave him a chance to view things from the other side—a valuable asset as his ministry as a church historian developed. The hardships he faced drove home the meaning of commitment in the face of adversity.[14]

Ministry Opportunities

In his tenure at OBC, Gary found ministry activities at the First Church of the Open Bible, a historic Midwestern Pentecostal church. He also worked at the First Assembly of God under Charles Crabtree (a future Assistant General Superintendent of the General Council of AG and President of Zion Bible College in Massachusetts). "Those were joyful years in many respects, crowned by ordination as a teacher by the Iowa District Council of the Assemblies of God in 1969."[15]

Return to CBC (1970–1984)

As Gary's own teaching style developed, he remembered his mentors and models.

> "Who will I be today?" I frequently wondered as a young Bible college instructor in the late 1960s. If well prepared for a lesson (perhaps on the threshold of being "profound"!), I might feel like Stanley Horton, one of my former professors at Central Bible College. When passionately explaining a point, I briefly fancied myself as William Menzies, another mentor. A profitable interchange of ideas with students over the Biblical text would transform me into Donald F. Johns. And if my Greek class went

---

13. McGee in "Living Dedication; a Lasting Legacy."
14. McGee, "The Gift of Teaching in a Pentecostal Context."
15. Ibid.

well, it would seem that Anthony Palma had addressed the students that day. But who was I as a teacher?[16]

When Gary returned to CBC in as a professor in 1970, he still struggled with the validity of teaching and scholarship as a ministry.[17] A few years into his teaching career, he read *The Christian Scholar in the Age of the Reformation* by E. Harris Harbison,[18] who "explained that great teachers of the faith from Augustine to Luther and Calvin viewed scholarship as a ministry and indispensable to the healthy growth of the church."[19] Gary later recalled this "aha" moment, "Although I could never be a Luther, or a Horton for that matter, I knew that God had called me as well to the ministry of teaching—to prepare God's people for works of service (Eph. 4:12). In time, I discovered my own gifts in the classroom."[20]

His gifts included a marvelous sense of humor. When a student challenged him concerning the interpretation of a passage of Scripture, he leaned back "on the heels of his wing-tipped shoes with crossed arms and one hand on his chin and relied 'Well, I guess you could make peanut butter out that passage if you tried hard enough.' Then, he let out his signature high-pitched laugh and completely disarmed his overconfident opponent."[21]

Marriage and Family life

Gary B. McGee and Alice F. Murray both attended CBC, but did not meet until after he returned to Springfield as a teacher at CBC. At 28 years of age, he rejoiced in finding Alice.[22] He sensed within himself "she was the one God had for him." Their first date was to the CBC Senior Banquet in April 1993. Alice stated it was not love at first sight, however, she saw in him the "qualities of someone [she] could love." He shyly asked her to attend another event in the September after he returned from a summer ministry trip to the West Indies. He communicated over the summer by sending postcards, but the dating process began in earnest in the fall.[23]

---

16. Ibid.
17. Ibid.
18. Harbison, *Christian Scholar*.
19. McGee, "The Gift of Teaching in a Pentecostal Context."
20. Ibid.
21. Mark T. Hendrix, personal letter to Alice McGee, December 15, 2008.
22. Ronald McGee, sympathy card to Alice McGee, December 2008.
23. Alice Murray McGee in "Living Dedication; a Lasting Legacy."

"Bone of My Bone"

After giving careful thought to the exact wording, he asked Alice to marry him on February 14, 1974. Befitting his position at CBC, and in consideration of his background in Pentateuch and Biblical Studies, he phrased the proposal in a biblical tone, "Will you be bone of my bone and flesh of my flesh?" She asked pointedly, "Are you proposing to me?" After he assured her it was a proposal, she responded, "Okay. Yes."[24]

They married on May 25, 1974. Their wedding gifts included one large bust of Martin Luther, which occupied a prominent place in his faculty office. Alice happily remembers those early years full of activity: preparing for lectures, teaching classes, pursuing higher education, and sharing the joys of serving the Lord in ministry.[25]

Children and Grandchildren

Their first daughter, Angela, was born in 1976. Exactly nine and one half years later to the day in 1986, the couple welcomed their second daughter, Catherine. Ronald McGee remembers Gary's bubbling joy and pride in both of the girls, "We both [Ronald and his wife Louise] thought [Gary] would actually bounce [Angela] so much she would twitch for the rest of her life."[26]

Their first grandchild, Bailey, arrived in 2003. Weighing only one pound and twelve ounces at birth, she spent her first three months of life in the neonatal intensive care unit. At high risk of infection, she had to be handled with care and could not go out in public for a year. She struggled for several months, but Bailey grew into an active little girl without any disabilities.

Marshall, her baby brother, was born in 2004. Gary's delight in both of his grandchildren was apparent, but he had a special bond with Marshall. At his baby dedication, the little boy, totally unimpressed with the ceremony, started to fuss and cry. He refused to be consoled by anyone until Gary took him in his arms. After the ceremony, the beaming grandfather carried "Bubbie" down the aisle and out to the church nursery.

After Bailey and Marshall joined the family, things changed around Gary's office. Pictures of the grandkids stood prominently among the curios and stacks of photocopies of research for his latest project. Dr. Gary McGee, distinguished professor of Church History and Pentecostal Studies, received

---

24. Ibid.
25. McGee, *People of the Spirit*, Kindle Locations 120–22.
26. Ronald McGee, sympathy card.

a new illustrious title: "Papa." He confessed it came with a price, because playing horsey strained the knees.[27] Alice shared, "The picture was pretty good before, but when the grandchildren came, it was like the final piece of the puzzle. Gary was a happy man."[28]

Hobbies

Gary listed two hobbies on his curriculum vitae: playing the piano and gardening.[29] He took piano lessons as a child, and later used this ability as a teaching tool. He loved the Reformation and Wesleyan hymns. Each semester, seated at the keyboard of the grand piano in the William J. Seymour Chapel at AGTS, he introduced many students to gospel songs and hymns that shaped the Protestant and Pentecostal traditions. After carefully explaining the theological meaning of words and phrases to the students, he led them with gusto in singing the songs of Zion.

He also enjoyed gardening. He sought out sickly-looking tomato plants and flowers from the nursery's discount rack and nurtured them back to life. His organically-grown produce often grew in unusual shapes and sizes because he did not spray with insecticide. One year, he bought two cherry trees which, incorrectly tagged, eventually produced apples. Like most things in his life, his gardening influenced the academic world. Through the years, the distribution outlet for extra produce became the AGTS Faculty Lounge.

More Education and a Terminal Degree

Before he married Alice, Gary completed a Master of Religious Studies at Concordia Theological Seminary in St. Louis, Missouri, in 1971. After their marriage in 1976, he finished a Master of Arts in Religious Studies at Missouri State University (MSU) in Springfield, Missouri. At MSU, he studied under James C. Moyer, a professor of Religious Studies. Gary credits Moyer as the person who influenced him in the development of his writing skills.

When Gary began a PhD in Church History at St. Louis University in 1978, two events helped affirm and direct the course of his dissertation. First, in 1978 while attending "The Messiah" in St. Louis, he met Roy Suelflow, a former professor of History of Missions from Concordia who enquired about the topic of his dissertation. When Gary replied he was considering

27. McGee, personal conversation with Annette Newberry, 2007.
28. Alice Murray McGee, phone interview by Annette Newberry.
29. McGee, AGTS Curriculum Vitae for Gary McGee, October 30, 2008.

the unwritten story of the Assemblies of God Foreign Missions, Professor Suelflow encouraged him to use that topic, "because it is the greatest thing taking place overseas right now."[30]

Second, in 1979, a full year before Gary could submit a proposal for a dissertation, he felt compelled to interview Noel Perkin, former Assemblies of God (AG) Foreign Missions Director (1927–1959). The subsequent interview provided him with the "real sense and feel of AG Foreign Missions" that guided his dissertation.[31] Several weeks later, after hearing that Perkin had passed away,[32] Gary realized how providential the timing had been.[33] From then on, he championed the idea that the AG must be viewed through the lens of its missions history.[34]

Gary's dissertation, *A History and Theology of Assemblies of God Foreign Missions to 1959*, was printed in 1986. A second volume, *A History and Theology of Assemblies of God Foreign Missions since 1959—Volume 2*, which was dedicated to J. Phillip Hogan who had highly commended the work, was published in 1989.[35] Afterward, McGee emerged as one of the most highly respected and loved educators in the Assemblies of God, as well as one of the most articulate voices concerning the history of Pentecostal missions.[36]

Assemblies of God Theological Seminary (1984–2008)

Upon completion of his doctorate, McGee began teaching at the Assemblies of God Theological Seminary. The hats, bells, and artifacts collected on his many lectureships, and numerous books reflecting his love of all church traditions filled his office. The bust of Martin Luther, prominently positioned, solemnly kept watch over all the activity. Students constantly added to his collection. "I bought you a little stick-on Virgin of Guadalupe at a Mexican grocery store. I thought it would give you a laugh."[37]

Every year at the AGTS Christmas Carol sing, he descended the stairs wearing a big smile and something Christmassy under his signature sweater

30. Gary McGee in "Living Dedication; a Lasting Legacy."
31. Ibid.
32. Perkin died on October 3, 1979.
33. Gary McGee in "Living Dedication; a Lasting Legacy."
34. Byron Klaus, remarks at memorial service.
35. J. Philip Hogan was Director of AG Missions (1959–1989).
36. Obituary for Gary B. McGee, Springfield (MO) News Leader, Dec. 12, 2008.
37. Crawford, personal note.

vest, while a favorite bell tinkled in his hand. Throughout the school year, other items were used creatively to teach classes. Few students, however, accepted the challenge to give their class presentations wearing the thick woolen hat from Eastern Europe and earn an "A" for the completion of the task.

He remembered and related minute details about his travels around the world. A student thanked him for sending her to the cathedral in Đakovo, Croatia, "It was my favorite church out of all the ones I saw in Croatia, Hungary, and Austria."[38] In 2001, Gary gave detailed instructions about this same cathedral to my husband and I when we went to Croatia and Bosnia Herzegovina.[39]

The price of taking a McGee course was much blood, sweat, and tears.[40] Students feared his examinations and tried, to no avail, to enlist his daughters to intercede for them.[41] To grade exams and papers, Gary retreated to his favorite Panera Bread restaurant where he had free refills of coffee and a freshly baked cookie when he answered the daily trivia question.

He presented colorful yet truthful accounts of people with their faults and failings but all part of Christ's Church and its beautiful and honorable history.[42] He respected all aspects of history, regardless of the church tradition from which they originated. He "saw larger than life characters of church history as real people, not mere objects of abstract conjecturing."[43] He told in detail the lives of preachers and priests, popes and ordinary people, the prophets of Zwickau, and many Pentecostal odd fellows. To Gary, nothing was trivial. Students often joked they prepared for his exams by "skipping major points and going straight to the fine print."[44]

His students had mixed feelings about being chosen to give a presentation or debate in class. If they paid the cost and participated well, however, they were rewarded with an A for the course. Most of the debates were done elaborately, with scripts and makeup. Subjects of the debates might be Martin Luther versus Ulrich Zwingli or John Wesley versus Phoebe Palmer. Visitors to AGTS were shocked to meet Anthony of the Desert or another historical figure in the halls of AGTS.

---

38. McDougall, personal note.
39. McGee, personal conversation with Annette and Warren Newberry, May 2001.
40. Morrison, personal comments.
41. Brim, personal letter.
42. Gale, personal comments.
43. Klaus, "Remembering Gary McGee," 61.
44. Annette Newberry, personal comments.

Excellence in the Classroom

Gary's colleagues and friends described him as "an exemplary teacher untouched by arrogance and deeply committed to students."[45] He began his classes with prayer and often included the song, "The Steadfast Love of the Lord." Even though one student said it "gave students the faith to stay in his class,"[46] it was part of his role to "inspire the younger generation with a past that is theirs too, even if it's not in their memory" and to "serve students in both spiritual and academic formation."[47] He taught what it truly meant to be Pentecostal—to live by the Spirit.[48]

"He strategically and intentionally desired that encounters with students would be filled with the extending of human dignity."[49] He sought out little known, but economical, places to have lunch with students. Much of his teaching, both spiritual and academic, took place in settings serving Indian, Thai, or Chinese food. According to the whim of the day, he might be found in a tiny Indian food restaurant attached to a Service Station/convenience store, Patrick's Thai Express, or another restaurant *du jour*.

Students loved his non-judgmental attitude and user-friendly style. The AGTS memory book and cards expressed their sentiments. "[Dr. McGee] like few other professors, understood my not-so-traditional frame of mind. [He] accepted, encouraged, and challenged me."[50] Another student thanked him for not judging her "tatts or lingo."[51] A female chaplain candidate simply said, "You da, man!"[52]

Gary modeled and taught that "being spiritual and intellectual is not an either/or proposition."[53] He was a pastor in academic garb with an open door policy for students. While teaching at CBC, he helped one Hispanic student improve his English and stay at CBC. Gary's family often helped him share in other ways, such as providing Thanksgiving dinner for students who were far from home.[54]

---

45. Spittler, sympathy card.
46. Morrison, personal comments.
47. McGee, *People of the Spirit*, Kindle Locations 162–63.
48. Morrison, personal comments.
49. Klaus, "Remembering Gary McGee," 61.
50. Hall, personal note.
51. Crawford, personal note.
52. Cochrane, personal letter.
53. Kitnoya, personal note.
54. Davis, personal letter.

In recognition of his excellent teaching, he received the "Missouri's Governor's Award for Excellence in Teaching" in 1999. Then, in 2001, he was honored with Distinguished Educator Award (Delta Alpha) by the Commission on Higher Education from The General Council of the AG.

Determined Researcher and Prolific Writer

Gary wanted "to help outsiders understand who Pentecostals really are."[55] He wrote readable books and articles that reflected detailed research from primary sources. A champion of the unsung heroes of the faith and a voice for the unheard, he was pleased to correct mistakes or oversights if possible. He tirelessly sought out information about little known Pentecostals such as Jennie Glassey, to whom he dedicated his last book. He mined nuggets of information from odd places and delighted in the search. The manager of the AGTS bookstore remembers his excitement when books for his research arrived.[56] He loved to receive the mail for the same reason, and often "beat the mailman"[57] to the post boxes.

He authored seven books, edited and contributed to three books, wrote chapters in fifteen books, penned over 185 published articles, contributed many essays for *Festschriften*, and frequently contributed to denominational publications as well as other Church History and Missionary journals and periodicals. He completed his last book, *Miracles, Missions, and American Pentecostalism*, just weeks before his passing away—diligently laboring over the manuscript to finish the draft before his death. This final book became the capstone of his work, reflecting his meticulous research methods and the culmination of ideas he had been working on most of his life.[58]

While he liberally applied colored ink to his students's papers, he also looked for budding talent and gave them a chance to be published with him. To many, he was the first person who ever encouraged them to write, and write well.[59] The *People of the Spirit*, his biographical history of the AG, showcases the research capabilities and creative talents of four graduates of AGTS in several sidebar articles.[60]

---

55. Gary McGee in "Living Dedication; a Lasting Legacy.".
56. Thomas, personal note.
57. Maempa, personal note.
58. Klaus, "Remembering Gary McGee," 59–60.
59. Triska, personal note.
60. The former students were Robert C. Phraner, Darrin J. Rodgers, Kenneth A. Worthley, and Annette Newberry. McGee, *People of the Spirit*, Kindle Location 109.

This Gospel Shall Be Preached to all the World
(Overseas Lectureships)

Gary, who was as often seen as a missiologist as well as a historian, traveled extensively in the United States and around the world lecturing at Bible Colleges, pastors conferences, and missionary retreats. He first lectured overseas for Peter Kusmič at Evangelical Theological Seminary in Osijek, Croatia (the former Yugoslavia). Later, at the invitation of David Grant, he travelled to India. Gary held a special place in his heart for India. He returned there to lecture several times and often sought out Indian students while they were in the USA. Through the years, his travels took him to Belgium, Costa Rica, Cyprus, Mexico, Moldova, Romania, Singapore, and Ukraine.

As early as 1989, Gary considered missionary appointment. He wrote to a colleague, "In regard to possible missions service, my wife and I are still praying about it and plan to meet with our European field director in April. I feel strongly inclined toward pursuing missionary appointment and I'll keep you informed about the developments."[61] While Gary did not pursue appointment, his burden for missions grew stronger. A journal entry from his trip to Moldova in 1998 reveals the impact of Moldova on his life and his passion for missions.

> I've only stayed here a week [Moldova] but I've wept several times about leaving . . . I've never wept over leaving a place. God has touched my heart for Moldova . . . Will I become a missionary? Probably not, I love my present ministry and the opportunities to serve in overseas schools in seminars. And yet something happened in my heart. . . . I think I wept because I felt that the Lord helped me to give of myself so deeply. Certainly the rational and the affective parts of who I am melted together as the Spirit anointed me.
>
> I weep for Moldova, for its poverty, for its potential, for leaving my newfound friends, but most of all because this is God's hour here for Moldova. I sense the rush of history here and God's mighty power at work. I weep because God has touched my heart in a new way here. . . . What does this mean? I don't know. But I intensely love God and know that if I follow him in faith that He will lead me on. I wept, Lord, I wept. What does it mean?[62]

---

61. McGee, personal communication with Gerald H. Anderson.
62. McGee, personal journal for trip to Moldova, August 14, 1998.

He prayed that the Lord would to show him how to "open his heart and mind to the Spirit's directives." Then Gary expressed joy in the experience of "the free-fall of dependence of God's leading. . . . No coincidences here. It's God. No place for anything else than humility and obedience!"[63]

Classical Pentecostal/Roman Catholic Dialogue

Kilian McDonnell describes Gary as "a great scholar, a great churchman, and a great friend. As an ecumenist, he was a supporting, weight bearing pillar of the International Classical Pentecostal/Roman Catholic Dialogue."[64] Gary was a member of this Dialogue from 1990–2006. He actively participated in the Fourth phase (1990–1997) "Evangelization, Proselytism and Common Witness" and presented a paper entitled, "Apostolic Power for End-Times Evangelism: A Historical Review of Pentecostal Mission Theology" at Emmetten, Switzerland, in 1990. He also attended meetings at Rocca di Papa, Italy (1992), Brixen, Italy (1995 and 1996), and Geneva, Switzerland (1997). He contributed to the final drafting and editing of the report of the Fourth Phase in 1997, and was a member of the drafting committee for the Report of the Fifth Phase of the International Dialogue (1998–2006).[65]

On February 16, 1997, Gary received a confirmation from the Spirit that this ecumenical dialogue was indeed God's will for him. He wrote on the back of a church bulletin,

> The Lord said he has sent his children out from Maryknoll, Nyack, CBI, AGTS and many other schools. His kingdom is far greater than any human organization/denomination. He has servants in the RCC [Roman Catholic Church], the Orthodox churches, and Protestant churches. The Lord said not to be afraid if He calls me to minister to a broader section of His church. Don't be afraid but follow.[66]

Gary co-chaired the local (unofficial) dialogue in Springfield, Missouri, between members of the AG and the Roman Catholic Diocese of Springfield and Cape Girardeau (Missouri) until his death (1985–2008),

---

63. McGee, personal journal for trip to Moldova, August 20, 1998.
64. Kilian McDonnell in "Gary McGee: A Saintly Scholar," 70.
65. "Report of the Fifth Phase of the International Dialogue."
66. Gary McGee, handwritten note on a church bulletin, February 16, 1997.

although not continuously. This dialogue is the only local meeting of its kind.[67] He tasked a friend[68] with the responsibility to see it continued.

A note should be added here about a harder element of this ecumenical spirit. Over the time that Gary taught at CBC and AGTS, sometimes due to his desire, willingness, and openness to have these dialogues, and engage the broader academic world, he was confronted by some denominational leaders. He endeavored to respond equitably, but the local dialogue stopped for a time, and he bore the weight emotionally. He never regretted his Pentecostal heritage, but saw the need for engagement in the broader Christian world. At times, the challenges took a toll—but students and all but those close to him would never know to what extent.

Professional Memberships, Service, and Awards

Gary formerly served as chair of the Dissertation Series Committee of the American Society of Missiology (ASM). In June 2008, he was elected to the office of Second Vice-President of ASM. His last book, *Miracles, Missions, and American Pentecostalism,* was published by Orbis Books for the ASM Series.

He was named Distinguished Professor of Church History and Pentecostal Studies at AGTS in 2006.[69] He was honored for his scholarly contributions to Pentecostal studies and his service in a variety of positions as a member of the Society for Pentecostal Studies (SPS).[70] On March 15, 2008, the Society awarded him its Lifetime Achievement Award while meeting at Duke University Divinity School. Posthumously, in April 2011, his final book received the Pneuma Book Award at the SPS meeting in Memphis, Tennessee.

In Sickness and in Health

Gary understood that serving God does not mean insulation from sorrow, pain, and sickness. Nor does it provide the answers to all our difficult

---

67. This group is the only existing local dialogue in the USA between the Classical Pentecostal and Roman Catholics.

68. Gary asked Warren Newberry to see that the dialogue continued. After a short hiatus, the dialogue continued to meet in Springfield, MO with strong AG and Roman Catholic involvement.

69. McGee, AGTS Curriculum Vitae.

70. "Gary McGee Honored for Lifetime Achievement by SPS."

questions. He expressed this sentiment in his book, *How Sweet the Sound: God's Grace for Suffering Christians* (1994).

Over the last ten years of his life, Gary suffered up and downs with bouts of arthritis and Non-Hodgkin's Lymphoma (NHL), yet he did not complain even when reduced to using a walking cane and foam pads on his desk to ease the pain in his arms. His attitude remained cheerful and optimistic, he "was always ready for a joke as well as a prayer,"[71] because God had given him the full assurance of His steadfast love and faithfulness. In a handwritten note on a church bulletin, Gary recorded that assurance:

> I am always near you. I will never leave you or forsake you. My grace makes up the difference where your strength ends. My grace is always sufficient for you. I am proud of your work because you are working for my glory and the building of my kingdom and not your own. Remember that despite your failures and feelings of unworthiness, I love you, am always near you, and will keep you.[72]

Gary underwent chemotherapy for NHL in 2001. After a four-year remission the disease returned, and he started the second series of chemo, which spanned several months in 2005. He shared the news in an email to several close friends and faced what would be his last battle.

> As you may know, while NHL is incurable, it is treatable. This will be the second series of chemotherapy . . . It has been God's blessing that I was in remission for so long. In hindsight, I realize that for the last several weeks the Lord has been preparing my heart for this. He has assured me of His strength and that His grace will be sufficient. Consequently, despite ups and downs of anxiety, there is a strong sense of peace in my heart. Yesterday morning in church, we sang the great 17th-century hymn, "Praise Ye the Lord, the Almighty." One verse read: "Ponder anew, what the Almighty may do, if with this love he befriends thee." Who could ask for better news?[73]

Last Days in the Hospital

Because of complications due to a bacterial infection and a weakened immune system because of his long battle with cancer, he entered the hospital

---

71. Wacker and Rodgers, "Remembering Gary McGee," 59–60.
72. Gary McGee, handwritten note, January 17, 1998.
73. Gary McGee, email message, May 2, 2005.

for the last time on November 13, 2008. During the last three weeks of his life, Gary took care of unfinished business, said his goodbyes, and planned his funeral with amazing peace and composure. Showing no anxiety or despair, he demonstrated how to live well and modeled how a man of God could die well. He constantly thought of others during this time. Byron Klaus, the President of AGTS, recalled their last meeting in the hospital. Gary prayed for him, then closed the prayer with this praise, "Oh, Creator of history, thanks for letting me write the story of your exploits among God's People."[74]

Death

A few days later, at home with his family around him, Gary's 63 years of life on earth ended shortly before noon on December 10, 2008. After his death, the family discovered a small card with a picture of Jesus and a poem, "Safely Home," printed on the back. It read: "I am home in Heaven, dear ones. . . . Jesus's love illuminated every fearful glade. . . . You must not grieve so sorely for I still love you dearly . . . There is work still waiting for you [and] when that work is all completed, He will gently call you home . . . Oh, the joy to see you come."[75]

Funeral and Burial

His funeral and celebration of his life took place at 1:00 p.m. on December 13, 2008, in the E. S. Williams Chapel at Central Bible College, where he began his ministry. The service, conducted by his pastor, Charles Arsenault of Evangel Temple Christian Center, Springfield, Missouri, followed the course Gary dictated during his last few days in the hospital. His body lay in a handmade coffin of red oak made by a Mennonite craftsman from Seymour, Missouri, which symbolized Gary's love for church history and all church traditions. He was buried in Springfield, Missouri, at Greenlawn Memorial Gardens, the last resting place of several of the people of the Spirit about whom he wrote. A few months later, he was awarded Professor Emeritus at AGTS posthumously (2009). The school also established a room in its library to house many of his personal books—the McGee Research Collection for Pentecostal Studies and Church History.

---

74. Klaus, remarks at memorial service.
75. Sacred Heart Monastery, "Safely Home."

"He Taught Us Well": A Lasting Legacy

The phrase, "He taught us well," printed on the front of the funeral program, summarized the tributes paid to Gary in dozens of cards, letters, entries in a memory book at AGTS, and at the funeral and memorial services. After his death, while the family members sorted through his papers and belongings, they discovered he had written the phrase, "A Saintly Scholar," in his Bible. While unsure of the reason behind this, it also encapsulates his life and ministry. In a sermon delivered at AGTS in September 2001, he expressed his philosophy that a teacher is not exempt from the "responsibility for the evangelization of the world and the advancement of the Kingdom of God." He suggested that Spirit-filled seminary professors use "their skills to weave a tapestry of Christian reflection and training that stretches from the classroom to the Sunday school room, a fabric that can withstand the tearing of the secularism that continually challenges our faith and witness." Acknowledging the lectern as sacred trust, he exhorted that the "leading of the Spirit should be welcomed in one's pedagogical work" for the spiritual insights and directions . . . so God is ultimately glorified and His kingdom advanced."[76]

With his characteristic skill with words, he challenged teachers and scholars to keep their hands in "the ecclesiastical sandbox" so that they would "have an accurate feel for the needs of the laity and clergy." He then closed with a thought that forms a fitting conclusion to this essay; I will let Gary have the last word.

> I am grateful to the Lord for His calling and blessing, to the wonderful teachers who prepared me, to the thousands of students that I have been privileged to teach at home and abroad, to my esteemed faculty and staff colleagues, and to past and present administrators of this Seminary . . . whose gifts of administration have enhanced my own gifts. On one occasion, Jesus remarked that "when you have done everything you were told to do, [you] should say, 'We are unworthy servants; we have only done our duty'" (Luke 17:10). I readily confess that I have only done my duty as a servant, but what a privilege it has been![77]

---

76. Gary McGee, "The Gift of Teaching in a Pentecostal Context."
77. Ibid.

Bibliography

Alexander, Patrick H. "McGee, Gary Blair (1945–)." In *The New International Dictionary of Pentecostal and Charismatic Movements*, edited by Stanley M. Burgess and Eduard van der Maas, 854–55. Grand Rapids: Zondervan, 2002.

Brim, Angela. Personal letter read at funeral read by Jennifer Gale, December 13, 2008.

Cochrane, Raylene. Personal letter to Gary McGee, October 12, 2002.

Crawford, Rebecca. Personal note in AGTS memory book, December 2008.

Davis, John. Personal letter to Gary McGee, 2008.

Gale, Jennifer. Personal comments at funeral, December 12, 2008.

"Gary McGee: A Saintly Scholar." *Assemblies of God Heritage* 30 (2010) 58–62, 70.

"Gary McGee Honored for Lifetime Achievement by SPS." http://www.agts.edu/news/press_releases/2008mcgee_sps_award.html. Accessed September 30, 2016.

Gary McGee. Obituary. Springfield (MO) News-Leader, December 12, 2008.

Hall, Jennifer. Personal note in the Assemblies of God Theological Seminary memory book for Gary B. McGee, December 2008.

Harbison, E. Harris. *The Christian Scholar in the Age of the Reformation*. New York: Scribner, 1956.

Hendrix, Mark T. Personal letter to Alice McGee, December 15, 2008.

Kitnoya, Dan. Personal note in the Assemblies of God Theological Seminary memory book for Gary B. McGee, December 2008.

Klaus, Byron. Remarks at memorial service at William Seymour Chapel, Springfield, Missouri, December 15, 2008.

———. "Remembering Gary McGee," *Assemblies of God Heritage* 30 (2010) 59–61.

Maempa, Jan. Personal note in the Assemblies of God Theological Seminary memory book for Gary B. McGee, December 2008.

McDougall, Christy. Personal note in the Assemblies of God Theological Seminary memory book for Gary B. McGee, December 2008.

McGee, Alice Murray. Phone interview by Annette Newberry, Springfield, MO, November 17, 2013.

McGee, Gary B. "And Your Daughters Shall Prophesy—The Revival Legacy of Aimee Semple McPherson." Accessed October 15, 2013, http://www.agts.edu/faculty/faculty_publications/articles/mcgee_aimee.pdf.

———. Curriculum Vitae, AGTS, 2008.

———. Email message to a group of friends and colleagues, May 2, 2005.

———. "The Gift of Teaching in a Pentecostal Context: A Personal Reflection." A sermon delivered at AGTS, September 19, 2001. Accessed November 1, 2013, http://www.agts.edu/resources/sermons/mcgee_9_19_2001.pdf.

———. Handwritten note on the back of church bulletin, January 17, 1998.

———. Handwritten note on a church bulletin, February 16, 1997.

———. *How Sweet the Sound: God's Grace for Suffering Christians*. Springfield, MO: Crism, 1994.

———. "Living Dedication; a Lasting Legacy." A video interview by Adam Trimbur and Natalia Guerreiro, April 13, 2007.

———. *People of the Spirit*. Kindle ed. Springfield, MO: Gospel, 2012.

———. Personal communication with Gerald H. Anderson, February 13, 1989.

———. Personal conversation with Annette and Warren Newberry, May 2001.

———. Personal conversation with Annette Newberry, 2007.

———. Personal journal for trip to Moldova, August 14, 1998.

———. Personal journal for trip to Moldova, August 20, 1998.

———. *This Gospel Shall Be Preached: A History and Theology of Assemblies of God Foreign Missions*. 2 vols. Springfield, MO: Gospel, 1986, 1989.

McGee, Ronald. Personal note card to Alice McGee, December 2008.

———. Sympathy card to Alice McGee, December 2008.

Morrison, Dan. Personal comments at AGTS memorial service, December 15, 2008.

Newberry, Annette. Personal comments at AGTS memorial service, December 15, 2008.

"Report of the Fifth Phase of the International Dialogue Between Some Classical Pentecostal Churches and Leaders and the Catholic Church (1998–2006)." Accessed November 1, 2013. http://www.vatican.va/roman_curia/pontifical_councils/chrstuni/eccl-comm-docs/rc_pc_chrstuni_doc_20060101_becoming-a-christian_en.html#Appendix_1:_PARTICIPANTS.

Sacred Heart Monastery. "Safely Home." Small card. Hales Corners, WI: n.d.

Spittler, Russell P. Sympathy card to Alice McGee, December 2008.

Thomas, Ashley. Personal note in the Assemblies of God Theological Seminary memory book for Gary B. McGee, December 2008.

Triska, Joel. Personal note in the Assemblies of God Theological Seminary memory book for Gary B. McGee, December 2008.

Wacker, Grant, and Darrin Rodgers. "Remembering Gary McGee." *Assemblies of God Heritage* 30 (2010) 59–60.

Select Bibliography of Gary B. McGee

Books authored/co-authored or edited/co-edited

Aker, Benny C., and Gary B. McGee, eds. *Signs and Wonders in Ministry Today*. Springfield, MO: Gospel Publishing House, 1996.

Burgess, Stanley M., Gary B. McGee, and Patrick H. Alexander, eds. *Dictionary of Pentecostal and Charismatic Movements*. Grand Rapids: Zondervan, 1988.

McGee, Gary B. *How Sweet the Sound: God's Grace for Suffering Christians*. Springfield, MO: Crism, 1994.

———. *Miracles, Missions, & American Pentecostalism*, American Society of Missiology Series 45. Maryknoll, NY: Orbis, 2010.

———. *People of the Spirit: The Assemblies of God*. Springfield, MO: Gospel, 2004.

———. *This Gospel Shall Be Preached: A History and Theology of Assemblies of God Foreign Missions*. 2 vols. Springfield, MO: Gospel, 1986, 1989.

McGee, Gary B., ed. *Initial Evidence: Historical and Biblical Perspectives on the Pentecostal Doctrine of Spirit Baptism*. Peabody, MA: Hendrickson, 1991.

McGee, Gary B., Randy Hedlun, and Annette Newberry. *Assemblies of God: History, Missions, and Governance. An Independent Study Textbook of Global University*. Springfield, MO: Global University, 2005.

Moreau, A. Scott, Gary R. Corwin, and Gary B. McGee. *Introducing World Missions: A Biblical, Historical, and Practical Survey*. Grand Rapids: Baker, 2004.

Essays or Articles

McGee, Gary B. "Assemblies of God: The Ideal of Worship." In *The Complete Library of Christian Worship*, vol. 3, *The Renewal of Sunday Worship*, edited by Robert E. Webber, 12–14. Nashville: StarSong, 1993.

———. "Assemblies of God Missions: Strategy on the Run." In *Working Together with God to Shape the New Millennium: Opportunities & Limitations*, edited by Gary Corwin and Kenneth B. Mulholland, 189–96. Evangelical Missiological Society 8. Pasadena, CA: William Carey Library, 2001.

———. "Assemblies of God: Worship and Related Ministries." *The Complete Library of Christian Worship*, vol. 7, *The Ministries of Christian Worship*, edited by Robert E. Webber, 13–14. Nashville: StarSong, 1994.

———. "Baptism of the Holy Ghost & Fire! The Mission Legacy of Minnie F. Abrams." *Missiology* 27, no. 4 (1999) 515–22.

———. "'Brought into the Sphere of the Supernatural': How Speaking in Tongues Empowered Early Pentecostals." *Pneuma* 30, no. 1 (2008) 108–35.

———. "The Calcutta Revival of 1907 and the Reformulation of Charles F. Parham's 'Bible Evidence' Doctrine." *Asian Journal of Pentecostal Studies* 6, no. 1 (2003) 123–43.

———. "The Dilemma Over the Apostolic Nature of Mission in Modern Missions." In *He Gave Apostles: Apostolic Ministry in the 21st Century*, edited by Edgar R. Lee, 47–66. Springfield, MO: Assemblies of God Theological Seminary, 2005.

———. "The Dilemma Over the Apostolic Nature of Mission in Modern Missions." *Encounter: Journal for Pentecostal Ministry* 2, no. 1 (2005). http://www.agts.edu/encounter/articles/2005_winter/mcgee.htm. Accessed September 30, 2016.

———. "A Dose of Truth." *Ministries Today* (2004) 32.

———. "From Azusa Street to the Ends of the Earth." *Christian History & Biography* (2006) 46–47.

———. "Historical Background." In *Systematic Theology*, edited by Stanley M. Horton, 9–37. Springfield, MO: Gospel, 1995.

———. "A Kaleidoscope of Pentecostalism: The Dictionary of Pentecostal and Charismatic Movements." *Missiology* 27, no. 1 (1999) 59–63.

———. "'Latter Rain' Falling in the East: Early-Twentieth-Century Pentecostalism in India and the Debate over Speaking in Tongues." *Church History* 68, no. 3 (1999) 648–65.

———. "The Legacy of Melvin L. Hodges." *International Bulletin of Missionary Research* 22, no. 1 (1998) 20–24.

———. "Levi R. Lupton: A Forgotten Pioneer of Early Pentecostalism." In *Faces of Renewal: Studies in Honor of Stanley M. Horton Presented on His 70th Birthday*, edited by Paul Elbert, 192–208. Peabody, MA: Hendrickson, 1988.

———. "'The Lord's Pentecostal Missionary Movement': The Restorationist Impulse of a Modern Mission Movement." *Asian Journal of Pentecostal Studies* 8, no. 1 (2005) 49–65.

———. "Miracles and Mission Revisited." *International Bulletin of Missionary Research* 25, no. 4 (2001) 146–56.

———. "'More Than Evangelical': The Challenge of the Evolving Identity of the Assemblies of God." In *Church, Identity, and Change*, edited by David A. Roozen and James R. Nieman, 35–44. Grand Rapids: Eerdmans, 2005.

———. "'More Than Evangelical': The Challenge of the Evolving Identity of the Assemblies of God." *Pneuma* 25, no. 2 (2003) 289–300.

———. "'Power from on High': A Historical Perspective on the Radical Strategy in Missions." In *Pentecostalism in Context: Essays in Honor of William W. Menzies*, edited by Wonsuk Ma and Robert P. Menzies, 317–36. Sheffield, UK: Sheffield Academic, 1997.

———. "Pentecostal and Charismatic Missions." In *Toward the 21st Century in Christian Mission*, edited by James M. Phillips and Robert T. Coote, 41–53. Grand Rapids: Eerdmans, 1993.

———. "Pentecostal Missiology: Moving Beyond Triumphalism to Face the Issues." *Pneuma* 16, no. 2 (1994) 275–81.

———. "Pentecostal Phenomena and Revivals in India: Implications for Indigenous Church Leadership." *International Bulletin of Missionary Research* 20, no. 3 (1996) 112–17.

———. "Pentecostal Strategies for Global Mission: A Historical Assessment." In *Called & Empowered: Global Mission in Pentecostal Perspective*, edited by Murray W. Dempster, Byron D. Klaus, and Douglas Petersen, 203–24. Peabody, MA: Hendrickson, 1991.

———. "Prompted by the Spirit: How an Outstanding Reference Book Got it's Start Over Slices of Pizza." *Assemblies of God Heritage* 18 (1998–1999) 18–20, 51.

———. "The Radical Strategy in Modern Missions: The Linkage of Paranormal Phenomena with Evangelism." In *The Holy Spirit in Mission Dynamics*, edited by C. Douglas McConnell, 69–95. Evangelical Missiological Society 5. Pasadena, CA: William Carey Library, 1997.

———. "The Saints Join Hands—90 Years Ago in Arkansas." *Assemblies of God Heritage* 24, no. 1 (2004) 4–13.

———. "The Story of Minnie F. Abrams: Another Context, Another Founder." in *Portraits of a Generation: Early Pentecostal Leaders*, edited by James R. Goff Jr. and Grant A. Wacker, 87–104. Fayetteville: University of Arkansas Press, 2002.

———. "Saving Souls or Saving Lives: The Tension Between Ministries of Word and Deed in Assemblies of God Missiology." *Paraclete* 28, no. 4 (1994) 11–23.

———. "Shortcut to Language Preparation? Radical Evangelicals, Missions, and the Gift of Tongues." *International Bulletin of Missionary Research* 25, no. 3 (2001) 118–23.

———. "Surprises of the Holy Spirit: How Pentecostalism Has Changed the Landscape of Modern Mission." In *Between Past and Future: Evangelical Mission Entering the Twenty-first Century*, edited by Jonathan J. Bonk, 51–65. Evangelical Missiological Society 10. Pasadena, CA: William Carey Library, 2003.

———. "Taking the Logic 'A Little Farther': Late 19th-Century References to the Gift of Tongues in Mission-Related Literature and Their Influence on Early Pentecostalism." *Asian Journal of Pentecostal Studies* 9, no. 1 (2006) 97–123.

———. "To the Regions Beyond: The Global Expansion of Pentecostalism." In *The Century of the Holy Spirit: 100 Years of Charismatic Renewal*, edited by Vinson Synan, 69–95. Nashville: Nelson, 2001.

———. "True or False?" In *Understanding the Five-fold Ministry*, edited by Matthew Green, 167–74. Lake Mary, FL: Charisma House, 2006.

———. "True or False?" *Ministries Today* (2004) 30–32, 35, 37.

———. "Where Did Modern Pentecostalism Begin?" In *Questions and Answers about the Holy Spirit*, edited by Hal Donaldson, Ken Horn, and Ann Floyd, 21–23. Springfield, MO: Gospel, 2001.

Ecumenism, Roman Catholic–Pentecostal Engagement

2

The Contribution of Gary McGee to the International Roman Catholic-Pentecostal Dialogue

CECIL M. ROBECK JR.

THE INTERNATIONAL ROMAN CATHOLIC-PENTECOSTAL Dialogue is now over forty years old. Begun in June 1972 when David du Plessis and Father Kilian McDonnell, OSB, gathered together two small teams and met in Zürich, Switzerland, it has produced five major reports.[1] Dr. Gary B. McGee joined this important dialogue in June 1990 when it began its fourth round

1. The first three reports of the International Roman Catholic-Pentecostal Dialogue of this Dialogue were published in *Pneuma* 12, no. 2 (1990) 85–142. See also Rusch and Gros, *Deepening Communion*, 367–422. The reports from the first four rounds of discussion may be found in Gros, Meyer, and Rusch, *Growth in Agreement II*, 713–79. They are also published in Vondey, *Pentecostalism and Christian Unity*, 101–98.
"Evangelization, Proselytism and Common Witness," 105–51; also in the Pontifical Council for Promoting Christian Unity's *Information Service* No. 97 (1998/I–II), 38–56, in *Pneuma* 21.1 (1999) 11–51. It has been published in French in the *Service d'information* No. 97 (1998/I–II), 38–57, as a Portuguese language booklet under the title *Diálogo Católico-Pentecostal: Evangelização, Proselitismo e Testemunho Comum* (São Paulo, Brazil: Paulinas, 1999), 77 pp; in Spanish in "Evangelización, Proselitismo y Testimonio Común," *Diólogo Ecuménico* 34, n. 108 (1999) 103–152, and in German with all previous reports in Norbert Baumert und Gerhard Bially, eds. *Pfingstler und Katholiken im Dialog: Die vier Abschlussberichte einer internationalen Kommission aus 25 Jahren* (Düsseldorf, Germany: Charisma, 1999), 59–95.
"On Becoming a Christian," was published in The Pontifical Council for Promoting Christian Unity's *Information Service* N. 129 (2008/III), 162–215; in French in *Service d'information* N. 129 (2008/III), 163–219; The English version is available in Vondey, *Pentecostalism and Christian* Unity, 95–216 and at: http://www.vatican.va/roman_curia/pontifical_councils/chrstuni/eccl-comm-docs/rc_pc_chrstuni_doc_20060101_becoming-a-christian_en.html, at: http://www.prounione.urbe.it/dia-int/pe-rc/doc/e_pe-rc_5-contents.html, and at: http://www.pctii.org/cyberj/cyberj18/2007RC_Pent_Dialogue.pdf;.

of talks in Emmetten, Switzerland, and over the next fifteen years he participated nine times. The interruptions in his participation were typically linked either to teaching commitments in one or another Assemblies of God schools somewhere in the world or increasingly, due to limitations of health. His position on the Pentecostal team was always a delicate matter. The Bylaws of the General Council of the Assemblies of God formally disapproved of ecumenical work at the time,[2] and McGee served as a professor at the Assemblies of God Theological Seminary in Springfield, Missouri, the primary historian for the Assemblies of God, and frequently taught in Assemblies of God schools around the world for Assemblies of God World Missions (USA). It was further complicated because, from the beginning, many Assemblies of God leaders were suspicious of this Dialogue with Catholics.

Part of that suspicion came from the fact that the Pentecostal cofounder of the Dialogue, David du Plessis, had been defrocked by the Assemblies of God in 1962 largely because of his refusal to cut his ecumenical commitments, and when the Dialogue began in 1972 he was still under sanction. He would remain under sanction until 1980 when his ordination was restored.[3] But part of the suspicion must also be linked to the fact that in many parts of the world, such as Italy and most of Latin America, Pentecostals often viewed Catholics as unbelievers and at times even as enemies of the Christian faith. For their part, Catholics viewed Pentecostals at best as unwelcome interlopers within their territory and treated them as "sects," a particularly pejorative term that allowed, if not encouraged, local priests and bishops to take actions that could make life extremely difficult for Pentecostals.[4]

For the most part, Pentecostals had long accepted the claims of the sixteenth-century Protestant Reformation regarding the Catholic Church. The Protestant narrative that had been passed along for generations contributed significantly both to Pentecostal ignorance and Pentecostal fears in their refusal to recognize the Catholic Church as a legitimately Christian church. Furthermore, Pentecostals had not paid much attention to the Second Vatican Council of the Catholic Church, held at the urging of Pope John XXIII between 1962 and 1965. Indeed, many Catholics were not yet sure of what the bishops actually meant in the various documents released in November 1964 by the Council, especially in their "Dogmatic Constitution on the

2. "Bylaws of the General Council of the Assemblies of God, Article IX.B," *Minutes of the 50th Session*, 131-32. The bylaw was changed in 2005. See, "Bylaws of the General Council of the Assemblies of God, Article IX.B," *Minutes of the 51st Session*, 125.

3. Ziefle, *David du Plessis and the Assemblies of God*, 67-101, 167-81.

4. Robeck, "Roman Catholic-Pentecostal Dialogue," 249-76.

Church" (*Lumen Gentium*) and the "Decree on Ecumenism" (*Unitatis Redintegratio*). But things had changed dramatically, and du Plessis was among the first Pentecostals to recognize this fact.

The International Roman Catholic-Pentecostal Dialogue had begun with little steps and it continued to stumble along through the second round of discussions. The first round was highly supplemented by Charismatic participants from Presbyterian, Lutheran, Baptist, Anglican, and Orthodox churches because du Plessis was unable to find a suitable slate of Pentecostals to form his team. While this matter was rectified in the second round, the Dialogue was nearly destroyed when Mary became the focus of international Pentecostal discussion in 1981. There was nothing in the Pentecostal paper offered by Assemblies of God missionary to Belgium, Jerry L. Sandidge, that year that should have been problematic for Pentecostals, but when some news outlets read the press release from the Dialogue, they claimed wrongly that the Pentecostal team had capitulated to Catholic teaching on the subject of Mary. A furor broke out that ultimately led to the loss of Sandidge's missionary appointment and a much more cautious approach to the content of press releases issued by the Dialogue until quite recently.[5] It was in its third round that the Dialogue seemed to find its voice for the first time. The release of its report "Perspectives on *Koinonia*" was well received by a range of Christian leaders, including some Pentecostals.[6]

At the end of its 1989 meeting in Rome, the steering committee for the Dialogue, Father Kilian McDonnell, the Catholic co-chair, Monsignor John A. Radano, Catholic co-Secretary, the Pentecostal co-chair, Rev. Justus du Plessis, Dr. Jerry L. Sandidge, Pentecostal co-Secretary, and Dr. Cecil M. Robeck, Jr., Pentecostal treasurer, met to discuss possible topics for the fourth round of the Dialogue. Sandidge lobbied strongly that the issue of proselytism should be addressed, indeed, from his perspective, this was *the reason* for the existence of the Dialogue. Justus du Plessis strongly agreed. Robeck was equally convinced that the time was not yet ripe for such a potentially damaging discussion. He argued that the topic was too contentious to be taken on by a Dialogue often misunderstood and still so fragile, given the hesitations and continuing opposition by most Pentecostal leaders at the time.

On the Catholic side, the Co-Secretary Radano thought that the issue of proselytism needed to be addressed because of complaints coming from

---

5. Sandidge, *Roman Catholic/Pentecostal Dialogue (1977–1982)*, I: 234–53, 305–12; II: 272–64.

6. See Robeck, "Catholic-Pentecostal Dialogues, 1972–1989," published the report as well as thirteen responses. See also Gusmer, "A Review/Appreciation of 'Perspectives on *Koinonia*,'" 192–96.

Latin America, while the Co-chair, McDonnell, was strongly opposed to pursuing the topic, fearing that the Dialogue would be destroyed because of suspicion from the outside and contention within. It was decided that all members of the Dialogue who were present in Rome at that time would be consulted. In the end there was near unanimous agreement to address this difficult issue. The sole exceptions were McDonnell and Robeck.

When the steering committee reconvened, it decided that the best way to address this topic would be to contextualize it as one of three related topics, "Evangelization, Proselytism and Common Witness." It was the intention of the steering committee that the discussion would run five years. In 1990, the Dialogue teams met in Emmeten, Switzerland at the Swiss Pentecostal Mission Hotel, SPM-Heimstätte, which also served as the headquarters for the Swiss Pentecostal Mission. Father Karl Müller, SVD, was invited to present the Catholic paper which he titled "A Catholic Perspective of Evangelization".[7] Dr. Gary McGee presented the Pentecostal paper titled "Apostolic Faith for End-Times Evangelism: A Historical Review of Pentecostal Mission Theology."[8] While their titles seem to suggest that they were going in very different directions, the papers and the discussion that followed their presentations over the next week brought a number of important issues to the fore.

Gary B. McGee and Karl Müller

McGee's entrance into the Dialogue came at a critical time in the history of the Dialogue. The 1990 session of the Dialogue began with introductions on Saturday evening, July 14. Following a worship service on Sunday, the Dialogue gathered in the afternoon to hear McGee's presentation. Professor McGee had received his PhD in Historical Theology from the University of St. Louis (Missouri), a Catholic institution. He began with an overview of Pentecostal history, noting the Pentecostal Movement cannot be understood apart from its commitment to missions. Because of its restorationist historiography, Pentecostals viewed their Movement as a harbinger of the

---

7. The paper presented by Karl Müller, "A Catholic Perspective of Evangelization," was twelve pages in length. To my knowledge, it has never been published. A copy of this paper may be found in the personal papers of Cecil M. Robeck Jr. His papers will eventually be placed in a personal collection housed within the David du Plessis Archive, at Fuller Theological Seminary, Pasadena, CA.

8. The paper presented by Gary B. McGee, "Apostolic Power for End Times Evangelism: A Historical Review of Pentecostal Mission Theology," was thirty-one pages in length plus twelve pages of endnotes. To my knowledge, it has never been published. A copy of this paper may be found in the personal papers of Cecil M. Robeck Jr.

"last days." Therefore, it seemed only appropriate that the earliest Pentecostals would ask, "How [can] the world be evangelized in the 'last days's before the imminent return of Christ?"[9]

Reference to this question opened up a longer discussion on the nature of Pentecostalism as a "restorationist" movement. While McGee pointed both to a Reformed type of evangelicalism and to the Wesleyan holiness movement as making contributions to the Pentecostal Movement, he cited several factors that had led Pentecostals to embrace its restorationist position. Among them were (1) their tendency toward biblical literalism, (2) the growing rumors of war on the international front, (3) the rise of Zionism with agitation for the return of Jews to Palestine, (4) the marginalization that early Pentecostals experienced, (5) a widespread move toward "premillennialism" coupled with (6) a general pessimism about the future. With the adoption of this restorationist approach came a trajectory that included concerns for (1) a baptism in the Holy Spirit with power to evangelize, (2) the expectation that signs and wonders had been given to validate the message of the Gospel, (3) the hope that the "gift of tongues" would shorten the time spent in missionary preparation and allow those with this gift to travel immediately to the foreign field for service in that language, and for some, (4) a return to apostolic life as described in the New Testament, complete with the five-fold offices of apostle, prophet, evangelist, pastor and teacher described in Ephesians 4:11 being restored.[10]

McGee made it clear that virtually all Pentecostals come to their concern for evangelization with the understanding that the sin of Adam has been imputed to all of humankind, thereby requiring an atoning sacrifice. God provided that sacrifice through His Son, Jesus Christ. With few exceptions,[11] people must hear the Good News of what God has accomplished in the death and resurrection of Jesus Christ so that they can accept God's action on their behalf. He described the belief that, while the Holy Spirit actively works in the world to help sinners recognize their sinfulness and their need for repentance, those who have not heard the Gospel will be lost, as a strong motivating factor for Pentecostal missions. A secondary motivating factor for Pentecostal missions, he contended, is compassion for the poor and marginalized.[12] Both of these aspects have found institutional locations within the Pentecostal Movement.

9. McGee, "Apostolic Power," 1.

10. Ibid., 2–10.

11. McGee cited Pearlman, *Knowing the Doctrines*, 355, as allowing for those who die in infancy to go directly into the presence of God.

12. McGee, "Apostolic Power," 14–15.

At this point, McGee offered a number of insights on the history of Pentecostal missions, beginning with the struggle between what he called "Spirit vs. Structure." He noted that the "appetite for personal direction from the Holy Spirit with its implicit distrust of ecclesiastical authority has generally remained characteristic of Pentecostalism."[13] He went on to note that the rise of para-church missionary organizations and claims that the offices mentioned in Ephesians 4:11 were now in place, only exacerbated the issue. He concluded that "the nature of spiritual authority and the unity of the Church" is a significant problem that Pentecostals must address lest they founder in competition.[14]

The Catholic team received an honest account of how many Pentecostals perceived the Catholic Church. McGee noted that Pentecostal missionaries in Latin America had often commented on the "distortion of the Christian Faith" that they saw in the Catholic Church, especially in its sacramentalism, its use of statues, and its veneration of Mary and the saints. He raised a common Pentecostal concern that many of those who had been baptized and claimed to be Catholics could not be described as anything more than "nominal" in their practice of faith and were in need of salvation, or at least a challenge to become spiritually transformed and integrated fully into the life of the Church.[15] As might be imagined, these criticisms became important talking points not only in 1990, but in subsequent years as the teams worked to understand one another and to reach agreement on these difficult claims.

Pentecostals, too, were subject to further criticism by McGee as he moved easily back and forth between a narrative of history and various theological concerns, while drawing his paper to a close. He noted that while the Pentecostal Movement talked a great deal about cooperation and the need to work together, their history pointed in a very different direction. While denominational missionary institutions talked a great deal about developing indigenous leadership and indigenous churches, they were often still far too paternalistic in their actions.[16] He pointed to the Catholic Charismatic Renewal as a sign of the Spirit's work in the Catholic Church and suggested that Pentecostals needed to re-evaluate the spiritual realities that they see in that Movement and ask themselves some fresh ecclesiological questions.[17]

13. Ibid., 16.
14. Ibid., 18.
15. Ibid., 18–20.
16. Hodges, *The Indigenous Church*.
17. For an up-to-date assessment of Catholic Charismatics in Latin America, for instance, which has seventy-three thousand members, see Cleary, *The Rise of Charismatic Catholicism*.

He made a strong appeal for a holistic approach to how the sovereignty of God is understood and how the Kingdom of God is manifested in the world at this time, including such overwhelming needs as poverty, various types of injustice, ethnic hatred, and hostilities without losing the commitment to proclamation.[18] He raised questions to those Pentecostals who were attracted to the idea that the offices of apostle and prophet were being restored to the Church, noting that they were in danger of forming a "new class of leaders" with an unwillingness to be accountable to the Church.[19] And he charged that the decline of eschatological expectations among many Pentecostals, attributable to "social lift," and the enthusiastic embrace of materialism apparent in some prosperity teachings,[20] put at risk the very call that it had embraced a century before, "that history is moving to a close and that all humankind must be reconciled to God through Jesus Christ (2 Cor 5:18–21)."[21]

The following afternoon, Monday, July 16, Müller presented his paper to the Dialogue. A gentle and humble member of the Society of the Divine Word, Müller was the initial drafter of the "Decree on the Church's Missionary Activity" (*Ad Gentes*) adopted December 7, 1965 by the bishops at the Second Vatican Council. A missiological heavyweight, Müller, who was then serving as the Director of the Missiological Institute in St. Augustin, Germany, opened his presentation by providing an overview of the various definitions that Catholic theologians had used for the term "evangelization." He argued that evangelization that leads to salvation is primarily God's work into which all Christians have been called to participate by proclaiming the "Good News" of the Gospel that Jesus Christ has paid for our salvation. God has offered this salvation to everyone, and once offered it is up to each individual to accept or reject it.

Müller drew heavily upon the Apostolic Exhortation of Pope Paul VI titled, "The Evangelization of the Men of our Time," (*Evangelii Nuntiandi*). It had been released in December 1975 on the tenth anniversary of *Ad Gentes*. In this exhortation Pope Paul VI reminded his readers that "To reveal Jesus Christ and His Gospel to those who do not know them has been, ever since the morning of Pentecost, the fundamental program which the Church has taken on as received from her Founder."[22] The Church is essential to the

18. Dempster et al., *Called and Empowered*.

19. See, for example, the claims in Wagner, *Apostles Today*, which has attracted a number of Pentecostals; see also Green, *Understanding the Fivefold Ministry*.

20. For a helpful series of discussions on this topic, see Attanasi and Yong, *Pentecostalism and Prosperity*.

21. McGee, "Apostolic Power," 31.

22. Paul VI, *Evangelii Nuntiandi*, 51. In this document His Holiness stated that the

proclamation of the Gospel message. Müller noted that with all the changes in modern culture, one can no longer look at a map of the world and denote some countries as those needing missionary work while others are denoted as spiritually mature. Indeed, he cited *Evangelii Nuntiandi* again, noting that Pope Paul VI held that it is for these reasons that mission work in today's world is "all the more urgent."[23]

Müller made the strong point that at the heart of all Christian evangelization and mission stands Jesus Christ. He surveyed what the New Testament had to say about the centrality that Christology and the Incarnation play throughout the Gospel, citing the Apostles John, Paul, and the writer to the Hebrews[24] before turning his attention to the pronouncement of *Ad Gentes*, which proclaimed:

> This missionary activity finds its reason in the will of God, who wishes all men to be saved and to come to the knowledge of the truth. For, there is one God and one Mediator between God and man, himself man, Christ Jesus, who gave himself a ransom for all.[25]

Müller then noted that the bishops wished to avoid "misunderstandings" and put "the missionary obligation into relief" by adding the following statement.[26]

> Therefore, though God in ways known to himself can lead those inculpably ignorant of the Gospel to that faith without which it is impossible to please him (Heb. 11:6), yet a necessity lies upon the Church, and at the same time a sacred duty, to preach the Gospel. Hence missionary activity today as always retains its power and necessity.[27]

With this citation, Müller stated the standard post-Vatican II Catholic interpretation on the application of Christ's atoning work.[28] He made it

---

proclamation of the gospel message was "not an optional contribution for the Church. It is the duty incumbent on her by the command of the Lord Jesus, so that people can believe and be saved. The message is indeed necessary. It is unique. It cannot be replaced. It does not permit either indifference, syncretism or accommodation. It is a question of people's salvation" (5).

23. Paul VI, *Evangelii Nuntiandi*, 14.

24. Müller cited John 1:16; Col 2:9; Eph 4:15; Heb 9:12, 10:10; and Rev 1:5, 22:14.

25. *Ad Gentes*, 7. *Ad Gentes* is also known as the "Decree on the Church's Missionary Activity."

26. Müller, "A Catholic Perspective on Evangelization," 6.

27. *Ad Gentes*, 7.

28. Since Vatican II, the Catholic Church has held that, in some mysterious way,

quite clear, however, that this did not mean that the Church's task was, for instance, to help make Hindus better Hindus as though their religion was in some way ultimately salvific, but that since all receive their lives from the One God who desires to save all, the spiritual quest in which all are engaged may hold clues to the riches of Christ in some mysterious way.[29]

Müller went on to address himself to the holistic understanding of contemporary mission work, bringing into the discussion the notion of inculturation. It is through culture that human society is organized, and culture enriches our lives together. Making the Gospel intelligible in various cultures carries with it both challenges that can lead to real breakthroughs in evangelization and risks that can obscure the essential nature of the Gospel itself. Inculturation of the Gospel demands that it take seriously such challenges as peace and justice in its many and varied forms. Using Latin America as a case in point, Müller noted the enormous social problems that many people face, problems such as economic disparity, unemployment, homelessness, migration, illiteracy, and political oppression, and he argued that in a 1971 Synod gathered in Rome, the bishops had declared that such things were "an essential component of the proclamation of the Gospel."[30]

If Jesus Christ stands at the center of mission, it follows that the mystery of His Incarnation is extremely important to the evangelizing task. Müller noted that Pope Paul VI had relied heavily upon Luke 4:18–19 as the basis for his thoughts in *Evangelii Nuntiandi*. The fact that Jesus acknowledged that it was because the "Spirit of the Lord" had come upon Him, led Müller to cite once again the Pope's Apostolic Exhortation. "Evangelization will never be possible without the action of the Holy Spirit," Pope Paul VI had noted, and as if in response to certain "Church Growth" theories of evangelization then popular in Pentecostal circles, the Pope had gone on to observe, "Techniques of evangelization are good, but the most advanced ones could not replace the gentle action of the Holy Spirit."[31] For Müller then, the Holy Spirit is the "Prime Mover of Evangelization."

God *may* be known in a way that preserves both his love, righteousness, and justice to apply the soteriological work of Christ in the atonement to those who are "inculpably ignorant" of the gospel. This idea shows up in *Ad Gentes*, 7.

29. This may be viewed as commentary on the work of the Holy Spirit in the world; cf. John 16:8–11.

30. Müller, "A Catholic Perspective on Evangelization," 10. This appears to be a less than subtle reference to Luke 4:18–19. It is interesting to note that, while Pentecostals tend to interpret the New Testament in a more or less literal sense than many other Christians, this is one passage where Pentecostal tend to adopt a spiritual reading of the text while most other Christians take a literal reading at this point.

31. Paul VI, *Evangelii Nuntiandi*, 75; Müller, "A Catholic Perspective on Evangelization," 11–12.

Gary McGee's Evaluation of the Discussion

Upon his return to the United States, Gary McGee wrote a letter to Loren Triplett, then serving as the Executive Director of the Division of Foreign Missions for the Assemblies of God. He thanked Triplett for permission to participate in the Dialogue, funded from his short-term mission account, and he described his impressions of the Dialogue. He began by apprising Triplett that Jakob Zopfi, then serving as Secretary of the Pentecostal World Conference and editor of the Conference's magazine, *World Pentecost*, had served as the Dialogue's host in Emmeten, Switzerland. Zopfi also served as the President of the Swiss Pentecostal Mission at that time and the SPM-Heimstätte where the Dialogue took place served as the Swiss Pentecostal Mission's headquarters. McGee went on to explain that those Pentecostals who were present at the Dialogue, some in an official capacity for their denominations, were drawn from the Apostolic Faith Mission of South Africa, the Pentecostal Assemblies of Canada, the International Church of the Foursquare Gospel, the Pentecostal Churches of Yugoslavia, and the Assemblies of God. The Catholic team, appointed by the Pontifical Council for Promoting Christian Unity included a number of well-known theologians and missiologists.[32]

McGee went on to inform Triplett that his paper had been well received, that he had found the climate of the Dialogue to be quite cordial, and that he had been pleasantly surprised at the amount of agreement that had surfaced on a number of issues during the discussion. He also noted that on the issues where differences were clear, the discussion was intensely theological in nature. These issues, he noted, would be further addressed in future sessions, among them the relationship between Gospel and culture, the question of proselytism, and the relationship between evangelization and social concern.

He was particularly interested to realize the extent of changes that had occurred within the Catholic Church that had come as a result of the Second Vatican Council. He noted his surprise to find the candor in the Dialogue that he witnessed, with no interest in playing what he called "word games that mask profound differences," and he was extremely pleased to see the genuine concern expressed by the Catholic team "to reach men and women for Christ."[33] He was also surprised to discover that local bishops

---

32. Gary McGee, Personal Correspondence to Loren Triplett.
33. Ibid., 1.

are allowed much more freedom to act, that "the Vatican has far less authority over local bishops" than he had previously thought.[34]

Of particular interest was McGee's account of what he believed to be the potential benefits of continued participation by the Assemblies of God in this dialogue. First, he noted that the Dialogue opened the door to greater understanding regarding the changes that had come in the Catholic Church since Vatican II and greater understanding regarding the commitments of both Pentecostals and Catholics on the subject of missions. Second, he noted that the Dialogue had the potential for the development of more positive feelings between the Pentecostal and Catholic traditions in such a way that it could result in the lowering of tensions between them and improve their relationship.

His third observation was perhaps his most insightful, and it held within it a challenge to the Assemblies of God and by association to the larger Pentecostal Movement. Gary McGee wrote,

> Since Pentecostalism is historically a renewal movement of the Holy Spirit, we must be sensitive and responsive to where He is working. Obviously, the AG alone cannot evangelize the world. It requires the energy of every born-again Christian, with particular denominational labels being of secondary value. Our input in the Dialogue, therefore, has the marvelous potential of aiding the renewing work of the Spirit among Catholics. We have much to share with them, but we can also learn some things from their journey in missions.[35]

The acknowledgement that the evangelistic task is too large for any one body or any one movement to accomplish without the help of others, the recognition that those who are known simply as "born-again" Christians must be accepted as co-workers in the ministry of evangelization, and the realization that Pentecostals must learn to give and take in the field of missions are only accomplished when Pentecostals take a position marked by attributes such as humility, gentleness, patience, and love, keys to maintaining "the unity of the Spirit in the bond of peace" (Eph 4:1–6).

McGee's Contribution to Subsequent Discussions

From the outset of this fourth round of dialogue, it was clear that Catholics and Pentecostals both understand that Jesus Christ has commanded His

---

34. Ibid., 2.
35. Ibid.

followers to engage in mission and evangelization. It was clear that both traditions take evangelization and mission very seriously. It was also clear that both groups saw the person and work of Jesus Christ to be at the center of the Gospel that is to be proclaimed. The teams also observed that both Father Karl Müller and Dr. Gary McGee called for a greater emphasis upon a holistic approach to evangelization. At the same time, they recognized that significant differences exist in the ways that Pentecostals and Catholics tend to view culture. Pentecostals are less optimistic than are Catholics regarding the virtues of culture, and this raised questions regarding the possibility of syncretism in later discussion.

Continuing discussion also opened up a number of places that required additional work. McGee's use of the term "nominal" when describing the lives of many Catholics led to intense debate that continued not only throughout the fourth round of discussions, but also, well into the fifth round. While the fourth round, which was ultimately extended to eight years, produced a remarkable document that ultimately addressed the differences between evangelization and proselytism, the question of what it meant to members of both teams for someone to move from entry into the Church, whether by a confession of faith or by baptism, into full participation in that Church would become the subject of another eight years of discussion in round five. Similarly, the fact that McGee placed such a strong emphasis upon the proclamation of the Gospel and the use of personal testimonies by ordinary people in this proclamation challenged the Catholic team to think more seriously about how to encourage and empower lay Catholics to do the same.

Although Gary McGee was unable to participate in all the subsequent discussions that followed the 1990 presentation of his paper at the International Roman Catholic-Pentecostal Dialogue, one can find his fingerprints throughout the fourth and fifth reports of the Dialogue. In light of this short exposition of one meeting, his contribution remains an important one to continuing developments between the Catholic Church and Pentecostals around the world.

Bibliography

Ad Gentes, Decree On the Church's Mission Activity, 1965. In *The Documents of Vatican II*, edited by Walter M. Abbot and Joseph Gallagher, translated by Joseph Gallagher, 584–630. New York: Guild, 1966.

Attanasi, Katherine, and Amos Yong, eds. *Pentecostalism and Prosperity: The Socio-Economics of the Global Charismatic Movement*. New York: Palgrave Macmillan, 2012.

"Bylaws of the General Council of the Assemblies of God, Article IX.B, List of Doctrines and Practices Disapproved, Section 11 The Ecumenical Movement." *Minutes of the 50th Session of The General Council of the Assemblies of God, with Revised Constitution and Bylaws 50th General Council, Washington, D.C. July 31–August 3, 2003*, 131–32. Springfield, MO: General Secretary's Office, 2003.

"Bylaws of the General Council of the Assemblies of God, Article IX.B, List of Doctrines and Practices Disapproved, Section 11 The Ecumenical Movement." *Minutes of the 51st Session of The General Council of the Assemblies of God, with Revised Constitution and Bylaws 51st General Council, Denver, Colorado, August 2–5, 2005*, 125. Springfield, MO: General Secretary's Office, 2005.

Cleary, Edward L. *The Rise of Charismatic Catholicism in Latin America*. Gainesville: University of Florida Press, 2011.

Dempster, Murray W., Byron D. Klaus, and Douglas Petersen, eds. *Called and Empowered: Global Mission in Pentecostal Perspective*. Peabody, MA: Hendrickson, 1991.

"Evangelization, Proselytism and Common Witness: The Report from the Fourth Phase of the International Dialogue 1990–1997 between the Roman Catholic Church and Some Classical Pentecostal Churches and Leaders." *Asian Journal of Pentecostal Studies* 2, no. 1 (1999) 105–51.

"Final Report: International Roman Catholic—Pentecostal Dialogue, 1972–1976." *Pneuma* 12, no. 2 (1990) 85–96.

"Final Report: International Roman Catholic—Pentecostal Dialogue, 1977–1982." *Pneuma* 12, no. 2 (1990) 97–116.

Green, Matthew D., ed. *Understanding the Fivefold Ministry*. Lake Mary, FL: Charisma House, 2005.

Gros, Jeffrey, Harding Meyer, and William G. Rusch, eds. *Growth in Agreement II, Reports and Agreed Statements of Ecumenical Conversations on a World Level, 1982–1998*. Geneva: WCC, 2000.

Gusmer, Charles W. "A Review/Appreciation of 'Perspectives on *Koinonia*.'" *Information Service* 4 (1990) 192–96.

Hodges, Melvin L. *The Indigenous Church*. Springfield, MO: Gospel, 1953.

McGee, Gary B. "Apostolic Power for End Times Evangelism: A Historical Review of Pentecostal Mission Theology." Unpublished paper in the private collection of Cecil M. Robeck, Jr.

———. Personal Correspondence to Loren Triplett, 3 pages, September 5, 1990, private collection of Cecil M. Robeck, Jr.

Müller, Father Karl. "A Catholic Perspective on Evangelization." Unpublished manuscript in the private collection of Cecil M. Robeck, Jr.

"On Becoming a Christian: Insights from Scripture and the Patristic Writings with Some Contemporary Reflections: The Report from the Fifth Phase of the International Dialogue between Some Classical Pentecostal Churches and Leaders and the Catholic Church (1998–2006)." *Information Service* 129, no. 3 (2008) 162–215. http://www.pctii.org/cyberj/cyberj18/2007RC_Pent_Dialogue.pdf. Accessed September 30, 2016.

Paul VI. *Evangelii Nuntiandi*, Apostolic Exhortation on Evangelization in the Modern World. 1975. http://w2.vatican.va/content/paul-vi/en/apost_exhortations/documents/hf_p-vi_exh_19751208_evangelii-nuntiandi.html. Accessed September 30, 2016.

Pearlman, Myer. *Knowing the Doctrines of the Bible.* Springfield, MO: Gospel, 1937.
"Perspectives on Koinonia: International Roman Catholic—Pentecostal Dialogue, 1989." *Pneuma* 12, no. 2 (1990) 117–42.
Robeck, Cecil M. Jr. "Roman Catholic-Pentecostal Dialogue: Challenges and Lessons for Living Together." In *Expressions, Faith and Politics of Latin American Pentecostalism,* edited by Calvin Smith, 249–76. Global Pentecostal and Charismatic Studies 6. Leiden: Brill, 2010.
Robeck, Cecil M., Jr., ed. "Catholic-Pentecostal Dialogues, 1972–1989." *Pneuma* 12, no. 2 (1990) 77–183.
Rusch, William G., and Jeffrey Gros, eds. *Deepening Communion: International Ecumenical Documents with Roman Catholic Participation.* Washington, DC: United States Catholic Conference, 1998.
Sandidge, Jerry L. *Roman Catholic/Pentecostal Dialogue (1977–1982): A Study in Developing Ecumenism.* 2 vols. Studies in the Intercultural History of Christianity 44. Frankfurt am Main: Lang, 1987.
Vondey, Wolfgang. *Pentecostalism and Christian Unity: Ecumenical Documents and Critical Assessments.* Eugene, OR: Pickwick, 2010.
Wagner, C. Peter. *Apostles Today.* Ventura, CA: Regal, 2006.
Ziefle, Joshua R. *David du Plessis and the Assemblies of God: The Struggle for the Soul of a Movement.* Global Pentecostal and Charismatic Studies 13. Leiden: Brill, 2013.

The persons in the photo include—left to right and back to front (with positions at time of the photo—1990)

Back Row

Fr. John Redford (Professor at Marymount, England)

Fr. John Haughey, SJ (Priest assigned to the banking community in Charleston, NC - later Professor at Loyola University, Chicago)

Francois Moller (Apostolic Faith Mission (AFM), South Africa, Professor at the AFM College)

Fourth Row

Coleman Phillips (International Church of the Foursquare Gospel)

Gary McGee (Professor, Assemblies of God Theological Seminary (AGTS), Springfield, MO)

Miroslav Volf (Yugoslavian Pentecostal Church, Professor, Fuller Theological Seminary)

Third Row

Howard Ervin (American Baptist, Professor at Oral Roberts University, Tulsa, OK)

Del Tarr (President of AGTS)

Fr. Herve Legrand, OP (Dean of the Institut Catholique, Paris, France)

Rev. Dr. Ronald A. N. Kydd (Pentecostal Assemblies of Canada)

Second Row

Fr. Karl Müller, SVD (Director of the Divine Word Missological Research Institute, St. Augustin, Germany)

Japie Lapoorta (AFM of South Africa, Executive over Social Ministries for the AFM)

Helen Rolfson, OFM (Professor at St. John's University, Collegeville, MN)

Jerry L. Sandidge (Pentecostal Co-Secretary, Pastor of Evangel Temple Christian Center, Springfield, MO)

Front Row

Monsignor Heinz-Albert Raem (Catholic Staff, German Diocesan Priest assigned to the Pontifical Council for Promoting Christian Unity, Rome)

Monsignor John Radano (Catholic Co-Secretary, NJ Diocesan Priest assigned to the Pontifical Council for Promoting Christian Unity, Rome)

Fr. Raniero Cantalamessa, OFMCap [standing in front of the 2nd row but behind the shoulders of Monsignor Radano and Justus du Plesis] (Former Head of the Patristics Dept. at the University of Milan, Charismatic, Pastor to the Papal Household, Vatican City)

Justus du Plessis (Pentecostal Co-Chair through 1985–1991, AFM of South Africa)

Fr. Kilian McDonnell, OSB (Professor at St. John's University, Collegeville, MN)

Cecil M. Robeck Jr. (Assemblies of God minister, Associate Dean of the School of Theology, and Associate Professor of Church History, Fuller Theological Seminary)

3

The Significance of the Classical Pentecostal-Catholic International Dialogue

A Catholic Perspective

JOHN A. RADANO

THE ROMAN CATHOLIC CHURCH today is celebrating the fiftieth anniversary of the Second Vatican Council (1962–1965). This great event renewed the Catholic Church in many ways and also fostered the ecumenical movement. It promoted the Catholic Church's participation in international bilateral dialogues as instruments to overcome misunderstanding and promote reconciliation between separated churches. The Classical Pentecostal-Catholic International Dialogue is one of these.

The purpose of this essay is to explore, from a Catholic perspective, the significance of the Classical Pentecostal-Catholic International Dialogue in which Professor Gary B. McGee took part and to which contributed in significant ways.

Vatican II and the Holy Spirit

More than 2,800 Catholic bishops and many others led by Pope John XXIII, then Paul VI, participated in Vatican II with a clear sense of being under the guidance of, and witnessing to, the Holy Spirit. Shortly after its beginning, the Council Fathers on October 20, 1962, issued a "Message to Humanity" stating that "under the guidance of the Holy Spirit we wish to inquire how we ought to renew ourselves so that we may be increasingly faithful to the gospel of Christ."[1] Further, "[t]he Spirit too has been bestowed on us by the Father, that living the life of God, we might love God and the brethren,

---

1. "Message to Humanity," 3.

who are all of us one in Christ."[2] Concluding, they stated "we lodge our trust in the power of God's Spirit, who was promised to the Church by the Lord Jesus Christ."[3] Furthermore, at every meeting (in Latin) of preparatory commissions and conciliar commissions of Vatican II, the Council Fathers prayed to the Holy Spirit with a special prayer for guidance. It reads in part:

> We are here before you, O Holy Spirit.... come and abide with us. Deign to penetrate our hearts. Be the guide of our actions, indicate the path we should take. May you be our only inspiration and the overseer of our intentions ... Unite our hearts to you alone, and do it strongly, so that with the gift of your grace, we may be one with you and may in nothing depart from the truth.[4]

The teaching of Vatican II is deeply Trinitarian. Thus, its Constitution on the Church, *Lumen Gentium* (*LG*) describes the many attributes of the mission of the Holy Spirit. He "forever sanctifies the Church," "is the Spirit of life", "gives life to men who are dead from sin," "dwells in the Church and in the hearts of the faithful as in a temple," "in them he prays and bears witness," "guides the church into the fullness of truth," "gives her a unity of fellowship and service," "furnishes and directs her with various gifts both hierarchical and charismatic, and adorns her with the fruits of his grace," and "perpetually renews her and leads her to perfect union with her spouse" (*LG* 4). The Holy Spirit arouses and sustains the sense of faith, by which God's people accepts the very Word of God, "penetrates it more deeply by accurate insights, and applies it more thoroughly to life" (*LG* 12).[5] Furthermore, "In all of Christ's disciples the Spirit arouses the desire to be peacefully united, in the manner determined by Christ as one flock under one shepherd ...." (*LG* 15).

The Holy Spirit and Ecumenism

One of the Council's four goals was "to nurture whatever can contribute to the unity of all who believe in Christ."[6] According to Vatican II, and many

---

2. Ibid., 4.
3. Ibid., 6.
4. "Prayer of the Council Fathers," xxii.
5. There are many more expressions of the work of the Holy Spirit in the documents of Vatican II; cf. Kloppenburg, *The Ecclesiology of Vatican II*, 30–32.
6. Vatican II's *Sacrosanctum Concilium,* Constitution on the Sacred Liturgy, no. 1, and *Unitatis Redintegratio,* Decree on Ecumenism, no. 1 (hereafter *UR*).

other Christians, the ecumenical movement itself is a movement fostered by the grace of the Holy Spirit (*UR* 1, 4). Vatican II teaches Catholics that though divided from other Christians (including Pentecostals), they are already linked to them in the Holy Spirit, since they possess "even very many of the most significant endowments . . . which give life to the church . . . (*UR* 3). It follows that "the Spirit of Christ has not refrained from using them (other separated Churches and Communities) as means of salvation which derive their efficacy from the very fullness of grace and truth entrusted to the Catholic Church" *(UR* 3*)*. Catholics are reminded that "whatever is wrought by the grace of the Holy Spirit in the hearts of our separated brethren can contribute to our own edification" (*UR* 4).

It is good to recall these teachings of Vatican II as we consider the Pentecostal-Catholic dialogue. This dialogue's beginning can be traced to that Council. The Council's teaching illustrates some of the theological convictions which the Catholic Church brings to this dialogue.

Experiencing the Holy Spirit.

Both partners in this Pentecostal-Catholic dialogue claim to have experienced outpourings of the Holy Spirit in the twentieth century, even if in different ways. The report of the fifth phase of Pentecostal-Catholic dialogue[7] illustrates parallels and convergences of ways in which Pentecostals and Catholics, for over a century, have experienced life in the Holy Spirit (*OBC* nos. 271–274). Central events are the Azusa Street experience in 1906, which Pentecostals describe as "an outpouring of the Holy Spirit," and the Second Vatican Council, "which Catholics believe was inspired by the Holy Spirit" (*OBC* no. 272).

The experience of the Holy Spirit at Azusa Street has had continuing worldwide impact. The work of the Holy Spirit through Vatican II has also had continuing worldwide impact. The vastness of Vatican II's achievements, after a unique and intense four year experience, is found in many aspects of renewal of church life: liturgical, biblical, catechetical, theological, renewed incorporation of patristic insights into its life, new challenges in the Catholic Church's relationships with other Christian churches and communions, with Judaism, with other world religions. Vatican II fostered ecumenical reconciliation and healing between divided churches. In light of the Council, Catholics can describe these great and positive changes as resulting from the inspiration of the Holy Spirit.[8]

7. *On Becoming a Christian*, no. 129 (hereafter *OBC*).

8. A number of Protestant authors of the World Council of Churches's sponsored

Again, according to the fifth report, "In acknowledging the work of the Holy Spirit in each of our traditions, we have been better able to learn from each other. Therefore we are grateful that the renewal and outpouring of the Holy Spirit in the twentieth century has opened our hearts and minds to one another" (*OBC* no. 274).

The Classical Pentecostal-Catholic International Dialogue

Vatican II led to a significant range of international dialogues involving the Catholic Church with various churches and Christian World Communions from which it has long been separated.[9] These dialogues, and many others involving other churches, have produced fine reports promoting important advances in mutual understanding, mutual reconciliation, and healing of memory.[10] Recent studies have begun to analyze the achievements of international dialogues.[11]

---

history of the ecumenical movement speak of the reconciliation and healing resulting from the impact of Vatican II. It "marks a turning point in the history of the ecumenical movement," and has helped open the way "to an era of trust and cooperation in many fields," D'Espino, "Introduction," xvi.

A result of bilateral dialogues that emerged in the 1960s after Vatican II and the Catholic Church's entrance into the ecumenical movement is that "their agreements and convergences have contributed to improved understanding, to growing communion and in a number of cases full communion between churches." They have healed deep differences and initiated new relationships. "A foremost example (of the latter) is the dialogue between Pentecostals and Roman Catholics," which is described briefly. May, "The Unity We Share, the Unity We Seek," 94–95. They do not offer here, of course, a theological interpretation for these positive changes.

9. These dialogues, and the year each began were: with the Lutheran World Federation (1967), the World Methodist Council (1967), The Anglican Communion (1970), The World Alliance of Reformed Churches (1970), the Pentecostals (1972), Coptic Orthodox Church (1976), Evangelical leaders (1977), Disciples of Christ (1977), Eastern Orthodox Church (1980), Baptist World Alliance (1984), Malankara Orthodox Churches (1990), World Evangelical Fellowship/Alliance (1993), Assyrian Church of the East (1996) Mennonite World Conference (1998), Oriental Orthodox Family of Churches (2003), Union of Utrecht Old Catholic Churches (2003); many of these dialogues have had multiple phases and continue today.

10. See Meyer and Vischer, *Growth in Agreement*; Gros, Meyer, and Rusch, *Growth in Agreement II*; and Gros, Best, and Fuchs, *Growth in Agreement III*.

11. Kasper, *Harvesting the Fruits*; and Radano, *Celebrating a Century of Ecumenism*.

What then can be said of the Pentecostal-Catholic International Dialogue?

Some Differences from other Dialogues

First, some differences between this and other dialogues. This dialogue takes place "between one of the most ecclesially focused traditions, and one of the least." Catholicism and Pentecostalism "represent the oldest and youngest expressions of Christian faith."[12] The partners in this dialogue represent the two largest Christian families: the Catholic Church with 1.2 billion members, and the Pentecostals with more than 600,000,000 adherents. Such factors make the dialogue all the more interesting, challenging and urgent.

The origin of this dialogue is very different from others. Most dialogues involving the Catholic Church began after Vatican II, resulting from good contacts made during that Council by official observer-delegates of various Churches and communions with the Pontifical Council for Promoting Christian Unity (PCPCU). The desire to continue good relations afterwards led to the official dialogues.

Classical Pentecostals were not represented by observer-delegates at the Council. But David Du Plessis, who had been defrocked by the Assemblies of God (USA) for his years of ecumenical activities and as such had no denominational backing, had been a "guest" of the PCPCU during Vatican II's third session in 1964. Out of his personal interest, Du Plessis later "took it upon himself to correspond with Cardinal Bea (President of the PCPCU) about the possibility of opening such a conversation. Thus it was through an individual contact with the PCPCU" and Du Plessis's friendship with Catholic ecumenist, Father Kilian McDonnell, OSB, "that the dialogue came into being."[13] It was McDonnell "who first coined the term 'Classical Pentecostalism' distinguishing that which was present in the Pentecostal churches founded since 1900 from charismatic renewal in the historic churches."[14] The dialogue began in 1972, co-chaired by Du Plessis and McDonnell.

Second, related to this beginning is another major difference from other dialogues. Pentecostal participants have not had the official institutional support of the Pentecostal world family as Catholic participants have had through the PCPCU. When the dialogue's fourth report, "Evangelism, Proselytism and Common Witness," (1990–1997) was published, Pentecostal co-chairman Cecil "Mel" Robeck described difficulties encountered by

---

12. Del Colle, "Pentecostal-Catholic International Dialogue: A Catholic Perspective," 195 and 196, respectively.

13. Robeck, 'The Achievements of the Pentecostal-Catholic," 170.

14. Robeck, "McDonnell, Kilian," 567.

Pentecostal participants. In the eight years of enormous effort that produced that report, twenty-nine Pentecostals from eleven different Pentecostal denominations on four continents had participated. But "very few of them . . . did so with institutional support. They came, sometimes, against great odds . . . . Sometimes they were called upon to endure deep public and personal criticism. They paid a price for their desire to build bridges with others that claim the name of Jesus Christ. But they persevered . . ."[15]

One significant difference this also made for Pentecostal-Catholic relations was that having institutional support often resulted in other forms of mutual contact, such as exchanges of visits of church leaders sponsoring the dialogue, or invitations to each other's events. These often grew out of the dialogue and/or supported the dialogue, and deepened the relationship. Not having institutional support hampered these other valuable contacts from taking place.

Third, related too, is the problem of reception. Press releases and reports of this dialogue would be published in the PCPCU *Information Service* and in other Catholic journals, but up to that time, in Pentecostal circles the dialogue did "not receive any public acknowledgement." Dialogue reports "have traditionally been 'locked out' of coverage or discussion within the larger Pentecostal press. The dissemination of information about the dialogue has been extremely difficult because of fear and mistrust by pastors and leaders alike. The lack of knowledge regarding the process and the outcomes resulting from this dialogue only further serve to exacerbate the situation."[16]

These conditions are changing. More than a decade later the same author could write that the Pentecostal-Catholic dialogue has now been progressively welcomed within the Global Pentecostal Community, first by the Pentecostal academic community, as reflected in the Society of Pentecostal Studies, and afterwards by a "small but growing list of Pentecostal denominations." Six denominations recognize the dialogue "as an official extension of their own ecumenical ministry."[17] Pentecostal scholars who are entrusted with the training of pastoral candidates for Pentecostal ministry throughout the world now take the subject of ecumenism seriously, as demonstrated in their scholarly meetings and publications. Furthermore, "this dialogue and the broader subject of ecumenism are now on the minds of Pentecostal

---

15. Robeck, "When Being a 'Martyr' Is Not Enough," 7.
16. Ibid., 10.
17. Robeck, "The Achievements of the Pentecostal-Catholic," 170–71.

leadership in ways . . . not possible just a few years ago. Ways of speaking about ecumenism within Pentecostal circles have begun to change."[18]

The difficulties experienced earlier (and there was a certain amount of resistance to the dialogue among Catholics as well) clearly show the great commitment of the Pentecostal participants in this dialogue from its beginning. They continued, often under extremely difficult and frustrating circumstances. For this, the Catholic partners are extremely grateful.

Some Important Achievements of this Dialogue

Since its beginning in 1972, the Dialogue has published five reports.[19] The achievements of this dialogue have already been well described elsewhere.[20] Here I wish, first, to lift up briefly several theological results of the Dialogue which are particularly important, and then point to what I believe is the major contribution of this dialogue thus far.

First, the focus on *koinonia* in the third round "Perspectives on Koinonia" (1990). In its lengthy study of *koinonia*, which was undertaken for various reasons, including the Dialogue's wish to continue to explore further the notion of the "communion of saints," the Dialogue makes its own contribution to the study of this issue which has become central in the exploration of the church in many dialogues, and on which much convergence/consensus is found in the modern ecumenical movement. But also in doing so, the two partners were able to clarify the theological bases on which they can speak of sharing *koinonia* (communion) with each other. For Catholics, unity is rooted in baptism, which implies a common faith in the Lord Jesus Christ. The "recognition by Roman Catholics of Pentecostal baptism means . . . that Roman Catholics believe that they share with Pentecostals a certain, though imperfect *koinonia*" (*PK* no. 54). For Pentecostals, the foundation of unity is a common faith and experience of Jesus Christ as Lord and Savior through the Holy Spirit. "This implies that to the extent that Pentecostals recognize that Roman Catholics have this common faith in and experience of Jesus as Lord, they share a real though imperfect *koinonia* with them" (*PK* no. 55).

Second, the unique extensive treatment was given to the theme of "Baptism in the Holy Spirit" including biblical, patristic, and contemporary

---

18. Ibid., 172, and 172n27.

19. "Final Report, Dialogue . . . 1972–1976," 713–20; "Final Report: Dialogue . . . 1977–1982," 721–34; "Perspectives on Koinonia," 735–52 (hereafter *PK*); "Evangelization, Proselytism and Common Witness," 753–59 (hereafter *EPC*); and "On Becoming a Christian," 162–215 (hereafter *OBC*).

20. Robeck, "The Achievements of the Pentecostal-Catholic," 163–94.

perspectives in both the Catholic Church and among Pentecostals, the convergences on their positions, as well as the great diversity between them and within both of them (*OBC*, nos. 192–262). It is a rich treatment. Catholics who are not members of the charismatic renewal might especially appreciate the overview of the debates on this subject, which need to continue within both communities.

Third, in the same report, the extensive use of patristics along with biblical materials, in seeking an understanding of five themes basic to being a Christian: conversion, faith, Christian formation and discipleship, experience, and Baptism in the Holy Spirit. This was the first extensive use of patristic materials by Pentecostals in a dialogue. In addition, it has a further importance: "this study of early post-biblical Christian writings, many of which were written in those early centuries which some call the Constantinian era, can be an initial step in dialogue between us on historical questions which are at the root of the Pentecostal views of Restorationism." This dialogue on history awaits another phase of international dialogue (*OBC*, nos. 270, 280).

The Primary Achievement

But in my view, this dialogue's primary achievement up to now is the concise theological basis it has developed for handling "conflicts in mission" between churches still divided, first of all conflicts between Pentecostals and Catholics. Conflicts in mission will continue to happen while Christians are still divided, and have different understandings of the church (cf. *EPC* 69) and other important aspects of faith. These conflicts have shown themselves in various ways. One side charges the other with proselytism. The other, in turn, charges the first with violating its religious freedom. Despite decades of the ecumenical movement, these conflicts continue to be a major problem, not only between Catholics and Pentecostals, but between various churches. But in this present period, where Christians, though still divided are on an ecumenical journey together, it is necessary to handle conflicts among us in matters relating to mission in a proper way.

Mission is a priority for both partners in this dialogue. The origin of the Pentecostal movement came in a fresh sense of the outpouring of the Holy Spirit empowering people for mission, and this continues. The Catholic Church has a long history of promoting mission, and in recent times has re-emphasized it in a number of ways.[21] There are many areas of Pentecostal-Catholic agreement on mission/evangelization.[22]

Helping to resolve Conflicts in Mission

The Pentecostal–Catholic Dialogue has reflected intensely on such conflicts, and treated this question with its fourth and fifth reports: "Evangelization, Proselytism and Common Witness" (1997) and "On Becoming a Christian: Insights from Scripture and the Patristic Writings with Some Contemporary Reflections" (2006). Together the two reports provide the most extensive treatment by any dialogue of the key issues that must be considered when challenging these conflicts.

EPC treats extensively four major interrelated subjects relating to mission, giving substantial, lengthy descriptions of the meaning of (1) evangelization (nos.11–67) covering mission and evangelization, the biblical and systematic foundation of evangelization, evangelization and culture, evangelization and social justice; (2) Proselytism (nos. 68–97), (3) religious freedom (nos. 98–104), and after these three, reflections on "Resolving conflicts in the quest for unity" (nos.105–109), and "Affirming principles for mutual understanding" (nos. 110–116); and finally (4) common witness (nos. 117–130). Some of these four have been taken up in other dialogues (see below).

But *OBC* adds an extensive treatment of a fifth question which has not been taken up at length elsewhere, namely: (5) factors involved *in becoming a Christian* (nos. 1–285). Participants in EPC had concluded that "some members of our churches do not always recognize one another as Christians," thus leading to conflicts between Pentecostals and Catholics. "By exploring *together* how one becomes a Christian, how one is initiated into the Christian community, how one is taught to follow Jesus and is formed by the community, and by reviewing the importance of religious experience in one's life, we believe that we might be able to assist our communities to

---

21 Vatican II's *Ad Gentes*, "Decree on the Church's Missionary Activity," stressed that "the church on earth is by its very nature missionary since, according to the plan of the Father, it has its origin in the mission of the Son and the Holy Spirit" (no. 2). After the Council Pope Paul VI's "Evangelization in the Modern World," *Evangelii Nuntiandi* (1974), John Paul II's encyclical, *Redemptoris Missio*, "The Mission of the Redeemer" (1991), and just recently Pope Francis's Apostolic Exhortation, *Evangelii Gaudium*, "On the Proclamation of the Gospel in Today's World" (2013), all offer further impetus to mission in our time. John Paul II and Benedict XVI have called for a "new evangelization."

22. *EPC*, nos. 11, 14, 16, 20, 22, 24.

recognize more easily that we are sisters and brothers in Christ" (emphasis original) (*OBC,* no. 6). This study explores five issues involved in becoming a Christian: faith, conversion, formation and discipleship, experience, and Baptism in the Holy Spirit, approaching each with biblical, patristic and contemporary analysis. There is nothing like it in other dialogues.

Other dialogues have published important and useful studies which have also dealt with some of these issues. These include multilateral studies,[23] and other bilateral studies.[24] All of these studies are important and serve well the two or more churches sponsoring the dialogue, and also the wider ecumenical movement.[25]

---

23. In 1971 the Joint Working Group (JWG) between the Catholic Church and the World Council of Churches published "Common Witness and Proselytism: A Study Document," and in 1982 "Common Witness." The first includes brief treatments of proselytism (nos. 8, 25-27, 28) and religious freedom (nos. 7, 20), and a more extensive treatment of common witness (nos. 6, 9-19, 21-24, 26, 28), but no analysis of evangelization. The second, as its title indicates, focuses on common witness. A third JWG study, the 1995 "The Challenge of Proselytism and the Calling to Common Witness," addresses common witness (nos. 3-4, 7-14), religious freedom (nos. 15-17), and proselytism (nos. 18-20), including steps toward resolving conflicts (nos. 31-33, 35), but no analysis of evangelization, although it treats problems in evangelization that can lead to conflicts (nos. 22-30).

24. "The Evangelical-Roman Catholic Dialogue on Mission (ERCDOM)," 1985, has lengthy sections on evangelization and mission (not numbered, 400, 409-12, 428-30), a lengthy section on common witness (430-35), a relatively brief section on "unworthy witness/proselytism" (435-36, but no direct treatment of religious freedom).

The Baptist-Catholic "Summons to Witness to Christ in Today's World: A Report on Conversations 1984-1988," addresses evangelism/evangelization (nos. 24-28), proselytism (nos. 31-36), religious freedom (nos. 37-44), and, briefly, common witness (nos. 30, 58). "Church, Evangelization and the Bonds of Koinonia" (hereafter: CEK) treats evangelization/mission (nos. 49-54), proselytism (nos. 61-69), religious freedom (nos. 74-78), and common witness (nos. 79-80).

25. CEK, for example, makes a fine contribution in Part II B, "Old Tensions in a new Context of *Koinonia*," by placing the issues of evangelization, proselytism, religious freedom, and common witness within an explicit spiritual framework of three interrelated components of *repentance, conversion,* and *commitment. Repentance,* discussed in light of the question "From what are we turning?" leads to a substantial treatment of proselytism (nos. 61-70) and a commitment to seek "newness of attitudes" toward each other's intensions" (no. 70). *Conversion* is developed (nos. 71-78) in response to the question "To what are we turning?" where religious liberty is discussed (nos. 74-78). Though previously in conflict over religious liberty, Evangelicals and Catholics now say together that "we grow in *koinonia* when we support one another and acknowledge one another's freedom" and "have been called to work together to promote freedom of conscience for all persons" (no. 74). *Commitment* involves turning to one another in common witness (nos. 79-81), convinced that "the possibility of Evangelicals and Catholics giving common witness lies in the fact that despite their disagreements, they share much of the Christian faith" (no. 79). "To the extent conscience and the clear recognition of agreement and disagreement allows, we commit ourselves to common

But the Pentecostal Catholic Dialogue with EPC and OBC combined, presents the most expansive treatment of five key issues that need to be addressed in the hope of helping divided churches avoid conflicts regarding mission. Gary B. McGee contributed to both of these studies, by participating in the drafting and editing of both reports.

Towards the Future:

The Pentecostal-Catholic Dialogue and The Global Christian Forum

As the Pentecostal-Catholic Dialogue continues, there are many doctrinal issues such as ecclesiology, ministry, and others which it still needs to face. But it has also contributed to a relatively new development with potentially great significance for the future: the Global Christian Forum (GCF).

The Global Christian Forum is an initiative which was suggested when the World Council of Churches undertook a self-study in the 1990s, but also had to acknowledge that millions of Christians, e.g., Pentecostals and Evangelicals, generally have not been part of the WCC, or the modern ecumenical movement. WCC General Secretary, Konrad Raiser, therefore suggested the creation of some type of "forum" in which they (non-participants), as well as the WCC, the Roman Catholic Church, and other mainline churches, might come together as equal partners. It would involve no structures except those created together by these equal partners. It would be new and independent. It would not replace the structures of the modern ecumenical movement, but would seek to be a neutral place where Christians who generally had not been in conversation with each other before, could come together. An independent "GCF Committee" guides the process.

The GCF is the most far reaching effort so far to bring Pentecostals/Evangelicals, on the one hand, and historic mainline churches on the other hand, into constructive contact with each other, to break down barriers between them and foster new relations. The process began with a series of small (50–60 persons) regional consultations from 2002–2007 in the USA, Asia, Africa, Europe, and Latin America. The method used was to bring together each time equal numbers of leaders of (1) Pentecostals/Evangelicals, and also of (2) "mainline" Christians (Orthodox, Protestant, Anglican, Catholics) to speak to each other face-to-face, to describe to each other their Christian commitment, the joys and difficulties of their journey of faith, in

---

witness" (80).
Cf. Radano, "International Dialogue between Catholics and Evangelicals," 181–84.

order to build mutual trust and begin to see one another as Christian brothers and sisters. There was no formal theological dialogue involved since there was the need to know each other before dialogue could take place. This regional process culminated in an international meeting at Limuru (Nairobi), Kenya, in November, 2007 with 230 persons from some 70 countries, and virtually every Christian tradition participating, with basically equal numbers from the Pentecostal/Evangelical communities and from the mainline traditions.[26] A second international meeting took place in 2011 in Menado, Indonesia. An Activity Plan for 2012–2015 was developed, and a Theological Working Group was established to assist the process in articulating theologically the history, experience, and significance of GCF as it continues to live out and witness to unity in Jesus Christ.[27]

Contributions of the Pentecostal-Catholic Dialogue to the GCF

The Pentecostal-Catholic dialogue has already been helpful to this GCF process in one way, and can be helpful in another. First, the Pentecostal-Catholic dialogue "has opened the way for other important dialogues" involving Pentecostals,[28] thereby increasing the numbers of "mainline churches" and Pentecostals in close contact with each other. They represent parts of the two major groups of GCF. Other international dialogues "with a direct line of influence from the international Pentecostal-Catholic dialogue" include the Pentecostal dialogue with the World Alliance of Reformed Churches which began in 1996, the Pentecostal conversation with members of the Lutheran World Federation aimed at an official dialogue, the establishment of the Joint Consultative Group between representatives of WCC member churches and Pentecostals; and beginning in 2010, preliminary discussions between the Ecumenical Patriarchate and Pentecostals. The Salvation Army and the Baptist World Alliance have inquired about Pentecostal interest in opening up international dialogue with them. And "Pentecostals have been participating regularly in the Global Christian Forum."[29] The dialogue

---

26. Detailed information about the Limuru event, a narrative history of the process leading to it, and evaluations of the process are found in van Beek, *Revisioning Christian Unity*. For information about the 2011 meeting in Indonesia one can consult the GCF website.

27. http.//www.globalchristianforum.org for this and further information.

28. Robeck, "The Achievements of the Pentecostal-Catholic," 172, and 172n26.

29. Ibid. The dialogues between the Catholic Church and Evangelicals have also helped contribute in this way to the GCF.

has already constructively engaged parts of the two constituencies now participating in GCF. Furthermore, persons with long involvement in the Pentecostal-Catholic Dialogue, even in leadership positions,[30] have served from the beginning, along with many others, on the GCF Committee which guides the process.

A second way the Pentecostal-Catholic Dialogue can be helpful to GCF concerns dialogue. Since 1972, this Dialogue has provided the experience and the theological reports from its five intense phases. The primary purpose and practices of GCF concern extending and deepening relationships rather than theological dialogue to produce agreed upon texts.[31] As GCF develops, and there is enough trust built up, another step that could (I think should) come at the right time is to begin more formal theological dialogue, to deal with issues that separate the constituencies represented in GCF. To those who may hesitate, dialogue reports now available from the Pentecostal-Catholic Dialogue (and others) illustrate what has already been achieved in a Pentecostal-"mainline-church" dialogue, and show the richness and importance of dialogue, and give them something to build upon.

A Concluding Comment

The Pentecostal-Catholic Dialogue is an important instrument of reconciliation between Pentecostals and Catholics, and has achieved a great deal. Serving on this dialogue with Gary McGee, I learned a great deal from him through conversation, from his writings, and from our mutual efforts in drafting for the reports. I was pleased to serve with him on this dialogue and on a personal note I am very happy to contribute to this volume in his honor.

Bibliography

Abbot, Walter M., ed. *The Documents of Vatican II*, translated and edited by Joseph Gallagher. New York: Guild, 1966.

Ad Gentes, Decree On the Church's Mission Activity (1965). In *The Documents of Vatican II*, edited by Walter M. Abbot and Joseph Gallagher, translated by Joseph Gallagher, 584–630. New York: Guild, 1966.

---

30. Cecil M. Robeck Jr. (Pentecostal participant 1985-and continuing, Pentecostal co-chair 1992-continuing) and John A. Radano (Catholic participant 1985–2008, Catholic co-chair 2001–2008). Huibert van Beek, who participated in the WCC-Pentecostal Joint Consultative group, served the GCF as Secretary of the GCF Committee 1998–2011.

31. Global Christian Forum, "Our Unfolding Journey with Jesus Christ."

The Baptist-Catholic International Dialogue. "Summons to Witness to Christ in Today's World: A Report on Conversations, 1984–1988." In *Growth in Agreement II, Reports and Agreed Statements of Ecumenical Conversations on a World Level, 1982–1998*, edited by Jeffrey Gros, Harding Meyer, and William G. Rusch, 373–85. Geneva: WCC, 2000.

"Church, Evangelization and the Bonds of Koinonia: A Report of the International Consultation between the Catholic Church and the World Evangelical Alliance (1993–2002)." In *Growth in Agreement III: International Dialogue Texts and Agreed Statements, 1998–2005*, edited by Jeffrey Gros, Thomas Best, and Lorelei F. Fuchs, 268–94. Geneva: WCC, 2007.

D'Espine, Henri. "Introduction." *A History of the Ecumenical Movement*, vol. 2, *1948–1968: The Ecumenical Advance*, edited by Harold E. Fey, xv–xvii. Philadelphia: Westminster, 1970.

Del Colle, Ralph. "Pentecostal-Catholic International Dialogue: A Catholic Perspective." In *Celebrating a Century of Ecumenism: Exploring the Achievements of International Dialogue*, edited by John A. Radano, 195–217. Grand Rapids: Eerdmans, 2012.

"The Evangelical-Roman Catholic Dialogue on Mission 1977–1984." In *Growth in Agreement II, Reports and Agreed Statements of Ecumenical Conversations on a World Level, 1982–1998*, edited by Jeffrey Gros, Harding Meyer, William G. Rusch, 399–437. Geneva: WCC: Eerdmans, 2000.

"Evangelization, Proselytism and Common Witness, 1990–1997." In *Growth in Agreement II, Reports and Agreed Statements of Ecumenical Conversations on a World Level, 1982–1998*, edited by Jeffrey Gros, Harding Meyer, and William G. Rusch, 753–59. Geneva: WCC: Eerdmans, 2000.

"Final Report, Dialogue Between the Secretariat for Promoting Christian Unity and leaders in Some Pentecostal Churches and Participants in the Charismatic Movement Within Protestant and Anglican Churches 1972–1976." In *Growth in Agreement II, Reports and Agreed Statements of Ecumenical Conversations on a World Level, 1982–1998*, edited by Jeffrey Gros, Harding Meyer, and William G. Rusch, 713–20. Geneva: WCC: Eerdmans, 2000.

"Final Report: Dialogue Between the Secretariat for Promoting Christian Unity and Some Classical Pentecostals 1977–1982." In *Growth in Agreement II, Reports and Agreed Statements of Ecumenical Conversations on a World Level, 1982–1998*, edited by Jeffrey Gros, Harding Meyer, and William G. Rusch, 721–34. Geneva: WCC: Eerdmans, 2000.

Francis, Pope. *Evangelii Gaudium*, Apostolic Exhortation on the Proclamation of the Gospel in Today's World (2013). http://w2.vatican.va/content/francesco/en/apost_exhortations/documents/papa-francesco_esortazione-ap_20131124_evangelii-gaudium.html. Accessed September 30, 2016.

Global Christian Forum. "Our Unfolding Journey with Jesus Christ: Reflections on the Global Christian Forum Experience." September 2013. http://www.globalchristianforum.org/LiteratureRetrieve.aspx?ID=152888. Accessed September 30, 2016.

Gros, Jeffrey, Harding Meyer, and William G. Rusch, eds. *Growth in Agreement II, Reports and Agreed Statements of Ecumenical Conversations on a World Level, 1982–1998*. Geneva: WCC: Eerdmans, 2000.

Gros, Jeffrey, Thomas Best, and Lorelei F. Fuchs, eds. *Growth in Agreement III: International Dialogue Texts and Agreed Statements, 1998–2005*. Geneva: WCC: Eerdmans, 2007.

John Paul II, Pope. *Redemptoris Missio*, Encyclical on the Permanent Validity of the Church's Missionary Mandate (1990). http://w2.vatican.va/content/john-paul-ii/en/encyclicals/documents/hf_jp-ii_enc_07121990_redemptoris-missio.html. Accessed September 30, 2016.

The Joint Working Group between the Catholic Church and the World Council of Churches. "Common Witness and Proselytism: A Study Document." 1971. http://www.prounione.urbe.it/dia-int/jwg/i_jwg-info.html. Accessed September 30, 2016.

The Joint Working Group between the Catholic Church and the World Council of Churches. "Common Witness." 1982. http://www.prounione.urbe.it/dia-int/jwg/i_jwg-info.html.

The Joint Working Group between the Catholic Church and the World Council of Churches. "The Challenge of Proselytism and the Calling to Common Witness." 1995. http://www.prounione.urbe.it/dia-int/jwg/i_jwg-info.html. Accessed September 30, 2016.

Kasper, Cardinal Walter. *Harvesting the Fruits: Basic Aspects of Christian Faith in Ecumenical Dialogue*. New York and London: Continuum, 2009.

Kloppenburg, Bonaventure. *The Ecclesiology of Vatican II*. Chicago: Franciscan Herald, 1974.

Lumen Gentium, Dogmatic Constitution On the Church (1964). In *The Documents of Vatican II*, edited by Walter M. Abbot and Joseph Gallagher, translated by Joseph Gallagher, 14–101. New York: Guild, 1966.

May, Melanie A. "The Unity We Share, the Unity We Seek." In *A History of the Ecumenical Movement: Volume 3, 1968–2000*, edited by John Briggs, Mercy Amba Oduyoye, and George Tsetsis, 83–102. Geneva: World Council of Churches, 2004.

"Message to Humanity (Opening Message)." In *Documents of Vatican II*, edited by Walter M. Abbot and Joseph Gallagher, translated by Joseph Gallagher. 3–8. New York: Guild, 1966.

Meyer, Harding, and Lukas Vischer, eds. *Growth in Agreement: Reports and Agreed Statements of Ecumenical Conversations on a World Level*. New York, Paulist, 1984.

Paul VI, Pope. *Evangelii Nuntiandi*, Apostolic Exhortation on Evangelization in the Modern World (1975). http://w2.vatican.va/content/paul-vi/en/apost_exhortations/documents/hf_p-vi_exh_19751208_evangelii-nuntiandi.html. Accessed September 30, 2016.

"Perspectives on Koinonia: Report of the Third Quinquennium of the Dialogue between the Pontifical Council for Promoting Christian Unity and Some Classical Pentecostal Churches and Leaders 1985–1989." In *Growth in Agreement II, Reports and Agreed Statements of Ecumenical Conversations on a World Level, 1982–1998*, edited by Jeffrey Gros, Harding Meyer, and William G. Rusch, 735–52. Geneva: WCC: Eerdmans, 2000.

"Prayer of the Council Fathers." In *The Documents of Vatican II*, edited by Walter M. Abbot and Joseph Gallagher, translated by Joseph Gallagher, xxii. New York: Guild, 1966.

"On Becoming a Christian: Insights From Scripture and the Patristic Writings with Some Contemporary Reflections: Report on the Fifth Phase of the International

Dialogue between some Classical Pentecostal Churches and Leaders and the Catholic Church (1998–2006)." *Information Service* (129) 162–215. http://www.vatican.va/roman_curia/pontifical_councils/chrstuni/eccl-comm-docs/rc_pc_chrstuni_doc_20060101_becoming-a-christian_en.html. Accessed September 30, 2016.

Radano, John A. "International Dialogue between Catholics and Evangelicals Since the Second Vatican Council." In *That the World May Believe: Essays on Mission and Unity in Honor of George Vandervelde,* edited by Michael W. Goheen and Margaret O'Gara, 173–85. Lanham, MD: University Press of America, 2006.

Radano, John A., ed. *Celebrating a Century of Ecumenism: Exploring the Achievements of International Dialogue.* Grand Rapids: Eerdmans, 2012.

Robeck, Cecil M., Jr. "The Achievements of the Pentecostal-Catholic International Dialogue." In *Celebrating a Century of Ecumenism: Exploring the Achievements of International Dialogue,* edited by John A. Radano, 163–94. Grand Rapids: Eerdmans, 2012.

———. "McDonnell, Kilian." *Dictionary of Pentecostal and Charismatic Movements,* edited by Stanley M. Burgess, Gary B. McGee, and Patrick H. Alexander, 566–67. Grand Rapids: Zondervan, 1988.

———. "When Being a 'Martyr' Is Not Enough: Catholics and Pentecostals." *Pneuma* 21, no. 1 (1999) 3–10.

Sacrosanctum Concilium, Constitution on the Sacred Liturgy (1963). In *The Documents of Vatican II,* edited by Walter M. Abbot and Joseph Gallagher, translated by Joseph Gallagher, 137–78. New York: Guild, 1966.

Unitatis Redintegratio, Decree on Ecumenism (1964). In *The Documents of Vatican II,* edited by Walter M. Abbot and Joseph Gallagher, translated by Joseph Gallagher, 341–66. New York: Guild, 1966.

van Beek, Huibert, ed. *Revisioning Christian Unity. The Global Christian Forum.* Oxford: Regnum, 2009.

4

Revival and Renewal Revisited

PETER HOCKEN

I HAVE TWICE PRESENTED papers to Pentecostal audiences on this theme, the first to the Society for Pentecostal Studies (1980)[1] and the second to a meeting at the Elim Pentecostal College, then in Nantwich, Cheshire, England in 1997.[2] My concern in both papers was to affirm the spiritual affinity between the Pentecostal and the charismatic movements. The concepts of revival and renewal express major differences of emphasis between the Evangelical-Pentecostal world and that of the historic churches without being mutually opposed or incompatible. Revival represents the core Evangelical focus on personal conversion through confessed faith in Jesus Christ, allied to the priority of evangelism, and to prayer for outpourings of the Holy Spirit impacting people on a mass scale. Renewal insists on the need for all Christian life, corporate and personal, to be continually brought afresh under the lordship of Jesus, so that the whole life of the church is continually receiving new life. Revival implies crisis moments of spiritual catharsis, whereas renewal lends itself more to a process of transformation over time.

How does this thesis look today? During the last fifteen years, the scenery has shifted, both in the world and in the church. The pace has intensified. Things have moved from an Evangelical-Pentecostal and Catholic complementarity appearing as a rather utopian dream to its emergence as a real possibility among the options facing church leaders. In this article I want to reflect on the changes that have been taking place since these earlier articles, particularly on those changes that show a coming together of revival and renewal, both conceptually in theological studies and existentially

---

1. Hocken, "The Pentecostal-Charismatic Movement as Revival and Renewal," 31–47.

2. Hocken, "Revival and Renewal," 49–63.

in pastoral practice. I will look first at the Catholic Church in communion with Rome,[3] and then turn to the Pentecostal and charismatic worlds.

Initially, we note that because the term renewal has a wider reference and is of more recent origin, it can easily acquire or be given new meanings. Two instances have arisen in the last twenty years: first, the adoption of the term "renewalist" by the editors of the *World Christian Encyclopaedia* to cover Pentecostals, Charismatics, and Independent Charismatics.[4] This usage pays insufficient attention to the social and cultural dimensions of church renewal. What these groupings have in common is not a shared vision for renewal, but the conviction that all new life comes from the Holy Spirit. Second, the Toronto current, or Father's blessing, that issued from the Toronto Airport Church from 1994 has been described as "the renewal," largely because the Toronto current was refreshing the already Spirit-baptized rather than converting the lost. This usage narrows the meaning of renewal.

The Catholic World

I write this contribution in honor of Gary B. McGee early into the exhilarating pontificate of Pope Francis, the first bishop of Rome from Latin America and the first from the Society of Jesus (the Jesuits). It is already clear that Francis seeks to promote a deeper and more thorough renewal and reform of the Catholic Church. He has made it clear that a change of attitudes or change of heart, has to precede reform in the structures. But he is aiming for both. We seem then to be at a key moment in the implementation of the renewal, for which Pope John XXIII called the Second Vatican Council. It was at Vatican II that the term "renewal" entered regular Catholic terminology—in general the Catholic world of the 18th, 19th, and early 20th centuries was not accustomed to the idea that the church might need renewal, as the focus combined a conservative defensiveness with an undoubted triumphalism.

To what extent has this renewal of the Catholic Church already been achieved? We can say that the foundations have been laid with the program indicated in the documents of Vatican II. Particularly through the leadership of John Paul II and Benedict XVI, there has been a new articulation of Christian faith as understood within the Catholic tradition: a formulation

---

3. I avoid speaking of the Roman Catholic Church, as the Eastern churches in communion with Rome do not consider themselves to be Roman Catholics, a term they restrict to Latin and Western Catholicism.

4. See Bellofatto and Johnson, "Key Findings of Christianity," 158.

that is strongly Christocentric, Trinitarian, and ecclesial. It is ecclesial in a way that is incipiently ecumenical and not sectarian. Fifty years of a renewed liturgy and greater exposure to the Scriptures have begun to produce a more dynamic and faith-filled life, particularly in the new ecclesial movements, among which the Catholic charismatic renewal is numbered.[5]

To what extent has the renewal of the Catholic Church been blessed by gifts from other Christian traditions, and in particular from the Evangelical and Pentecostal worlds? Where can convergence with these revivalistic worlds be observed? At Vatican II, comments from the observers from other churches produced significant improvements to some documents, for example, from the Orthodox on the role of the Holy Spirit, and from some Protestants on the role of the Word of God. The coming together of revival and renewal concerns is probably clearest in the emergence of the theme of evangelization. While evangelization was not a focus of the Council, several emphases of the bishops favored the emergence of this theme: the renewal of the liturgy as the living worship of the Catholic people, the teaching on the dignity and role of all the baptized, and the restoration of the catechumenate as the communal liturgical preparation of candidates for baptism. Evangelization was chosen as the theme of the 1974 Synod of Bishops in Rome, and Paul VI issued a letter *Evangelii Nuntiandi* on Evangelization in 1975, a document that remains an important source document for Catholic evangelism. Two short extracts can illustrate its affinity with Evangelical-Pentecostal convictions: "the Holy Spirit is the principal agent of evangelization."[6] "Evangelizing is in fact the grace and vocation proper to the Church, her deepest identity. She exists in order to evangelize."[7]

This evangelical note became stronger with John Paul II's call for a "New Evangelization," launched in 1983. It is called New Evangelization for two reasons: the first, the recognition that the nations formerly seen as Christian have become alienated from the church and Christian values, and need to be evangelized afresh; the second, that the renewal of the church calls all to a new centeredness on the person and mission of Jesus Christ. For John Paul II, evangelization cannot be new in its content since there is only one gospel given in Jesus Christ; evangelization needs to be new in its ardor, its methods, and its expression.[8] Benedict XVI gave a new institutional

---

5. Charismatic Catholics have often insisted that charismatic renewal is different from other new movements, in that it has no one human founder, and it is a current that did not originate in the Catholic Church.

6. Paul VI, *Evangelii Nuntiandi*, 75.

7. Ibid., 14.

8. See Dulles, "John Paul II and the New Evangelization," 2–16.

expression and impulse to this call in 2010 by the formation of a Pontifical Council for Promoting the New Evangelization.

As this initiative has developed in the Catholic world, the popes have been insisting that every Catholic needs to have a personal relationship with Jesus Christ and to experience a personal conversion. This is presented as the heart of authentic renewal. This evangelical note has been constant in recent papal statements, and is being continued by Pope Francis. However, this insistence has not yet become normal in the preaching of bishops and priests, but it is clearly spreading, aided by the New Evangelization. A sign of this changing climate is the warm welcome now being given to the Alpha course of Anglican origin by many bishops and Vatican officials, though the Latin Americans have been more receptive than their English-language peers.[9]

What role has the Catholic charismatic renewal (CCR) played in the awakening of the Catholic Church to the primacy of evangelization? This is hard to estimate. On the one hand, CCR has become an officially recognized movement with millions of adherents, who manifest a high level of commitment to the Lord within the church (the numbers are highest in the developing world of Africa, Asia, and Latin America). Although direct charismatic influence is hard to detect, CCR has clearly played a major role in awakening a love for the Bible, and an attention to Bible-reading and study at a popular level in the Catholic world. This cluster of Catholic pastoral concerns has nonetheless a different shape from Evangelical and Pentecostal patterns. The social, ecclesial, and cultural context is strongly present in Catholic thinking, so the new proclamation of Jesus is an ecclesial task, leading to a stronger experience of lived *koinonia*, which can help to form anew a Christian culture.

The well-known American Catholic commentator, George Weigel, published his book *Evangelical Catholicism* just as Pope Benedict XVI resigned and Francis was elected.[10] Its contents are highly relevant to my theme. Weigel uses the term "reform" where I have been using "renewal," but they are referring to the same process. Weigel's thesis is that the renewal of the Catholic Church, as shaped by John Paul II and Benedict XVI, is producing an Evangelical Catholicism. His prologue is entitled, "An Invitation to Evangelical Catholicism and Deep Catholic Reform."[11]

---

9. In January 2012 I heard Nicky Gumbel, the director of the Alpha course, say that the fastest growth of Alpha in the world is now in the Catholic Church.

10. Weigel, *Evangelical Catholicism*.

11. Ibid., 1.

Weigel identifies ten characteristics of Evangelical Catholicism, of which four connect more obviously with Evangelical and Pentecostal concerns than the other six: "1. Evangelical Catholicism is friendship with the Lord Jesus Christ."[12] "4. Evangelical Catholicism is a call to constant conversion of life, which involves both the rejection of evil, and active participation in the works of service and charity."[13] "6. Evangelical Catholicism is a biblically centered form of Catholic life that reads the Bible as the Word of God for the salvation of souls."[14] "10. Evangelical Catholicism awaits with eager anticipation the coming of the Lord Jesus in glory, and until that time, Evangelical Catholicism is ordered to mission—to the proclamation of the Gospel for the world's salvation."[15] Weigel refers to "the Great Commission," an Evangelical terminology not much used by Catholics.[16]

In chapter 4 on "True Reform in the Church," Weigel spells out the difference between the Evangelical Catholicism, espoused by John Paul II and Benedict XVI, and two major competitors for the hearts and minds of Catholics: what he calls "Catholic Antiquarianism," an appropriate label for traditionalist milieu, and the more serious danger he calls "Catholic Presentitis," the lust for relevance according to "post-modern cultural and intellectual canons."[17]

While Weigel accurately delineates the emergence of Evangelical emphases and concerns within the modern Catholic Church, he seems to see this Catholic renewal taking place without any significant interaction with or learning from other Christian traditions. There is not even an entry for ecumenism in the index. Indeed, Weigel explicitly states: "Evangelical Catholicism is not a way of being Catholic that adapts certain catechetical practices and modes of worship from evangelical, fundamentalist, and Pentecostalist Protestantism."[18] But at the end, he somewhat mitigates this exclusiveness: "the Pontifical Council for Promoting Christian Unity could reexamine its long-standing commitment to various bilateral dialogues with liberal Protestant bodies that seemed to be achieving very little, while opening new lines of conversation with the evangelical, fundamentalist, and Pentecostal Protestants who were manifestly the growing Protestant communities of the

---

12. Ibid., 56.
13. Ibid., 66.
14. Ibid., 74.
15. Ibid., 85.
16. Ibid., 88. It appears in several other places and has an entry in the index.
17. Ibid., 102.
18. Ibid., 3.

twenty-first century and beyond."[19] Part II on "The Reforms of Evangelical Catholicism" illustrates the need for reform/renewal in all aspects of the life of the church: the episcopate, the priesthood, the liturgy, the consecrated life, the lay vocation, the church's intellectual life, the church's public policy advocacy, and lastly the papacy.

Changes in the Pentecostal World

As the Pentecostal movement celebrated its first centenary, the question of how to preserve the distinctive Pentecostal heritage without losing its fire and dynamism becomes a more urgent question. We can already see a greater dynamism in the newer Pentecostal churches of Asia, Africa, and Latin America than those entering their fourth or fifth generation in North America and Europe. But as the Pentecostal movement acquires a longer history, what Catholics call renewal enters the Pentecostal agenda: how do you revivify the faith of congregations, of the institutions that the movement has birthed (denominational structures, patterns of worship and formation, missionary organizations, schools, colleges, and even universities)? With this development comes a recognition that classical revival patterns, while they are to be desired and prayed for, are not sufficient on their own without a process of renewal.

Where do we see a renewal focus in the Pentecostal movement of the last twenty years? The entrepreneurial leadership appears to be more focused on revival, which seeks a perpetuation of what has galvanized the movement from the beginning. This focus is evident in the Empowered 21 initiative, whose goal is that "every person on Earth would have an authentic, life transforming, encounter with the Power and Presence of the Living God . . . by 2033."[20]

It is in the theological world that Pentecostals are seeking to combine the experience and power of the Holy Spirit (revival emphasis) with the formation and reshaping of church and society (renewal emphasis). An important dimension of the flowering of Pentecostal scholarship is the formation of a truly Pentecostal theology of the church (ecclesiology). A Pentecostal ecclesiology requires a vision for renewal as well as the quest for revival. I give three examples: (1) Frank Macchia's study *Baptized in the Spirit*, particularly chapter 5 entitled "Toward a Spirit-Baptized Ecclesiology."[21] (2) Amos Yong's *The Spirit Poured Out on All Flesh*, particularly in chapter 3 sub-titled

19. Ibid., 255–56.
20. See Empowered 21, "E21 Vision."
21. Macchia, *Baptized in the Spirit*, 155–256.

"Toward a Pneumatological Ecclesiology."[22] (3) Wolfgang Vondey's *Beyond Pentecostalism*, whose sub-title includes "the renewal of the theological agenda."[23] Macchia speaks of "a critical dialectic" between two inseparable elements of the church as "both a pneumatological/eschatological reality and a fallen/historical reality."[24] The formation of a Pentecostal ecclesiology seeks to ground constant renewal through the Holy Spirit as a permanent dimension of church life.

Dale Coulter argues that a renewal dynamic was present from the Pentecostal origins.[25] For Coulter, early Pentecostalism was not simply a restorationist movement that regarded most of Christian history as irrelevant, but had at its core a "Catholic spirituality" that "enabled its global expansion and renewal of other Christian traditions."[26] In a subsequent article, Coulter has extended this argument to the whole Evangelical heritage.[27] He grounds his argument for a renewal element through instancing similarities between Catholic mystics and spiritual teachers on the one hand and Holiness advocates among Pentecostals, on the other hand. In a response to Coulter, Thomas Rausch argues that "modern Evangelical Christianity" moved the notion of evangelical "away from its [medieval] efforts to recover the apostolic life and towards a more individualistic doctrine of salvation."[28]

It can be argued more convincingly that the Pentecostal movement from the beginning contained a potential for renewal as well as revival, but that the renewal potential remained undeveloped until the emergence of a distinctively Pentecostal theology. This potential can be realized as Pentecostals live by a "Spirit-baptized" (Macchia) or a "pneumatological" (Yong) ecclesiology. This renewal potential is grounded in the Pentecostal distinctive of baptism in the Spirit that is more a transforming experience than a doctrine. An earlier renewal potential in the Evangelical movement was linked to its penetration of older Protestant traditions (e.g., the Clapham "sect" within the Church of England), but the mixture of independence and new denominations ensured that the beginnings of the Pentecostal movement were marked by the individualistic mentality noted by Rausch.

---

22. Yong, *The Spirit Poured Out*, 121–66.
23. Vondey, *Beyond Pentecostalism*.
24. Macchia, *Baptized in the Spirit*, 197.
25. Coulter, "The Spirit and the Bride Revisited," 298–319.
26. Ibid., 318.
27. Coulter, "Primitivism and Progressivism," 1–5.
28. Rausch, "The Evangelical Heritage," 6.

Changes in the Charismatic World

The charismatic world is sub-divided into charismatic renewal within existing churches and denominations, and new independent charismatic groupings and networks. However, the Catholic charismatic renewal apart, the former is in process of becoming an obsolete category, as various processes of integration or assimilation take place. In many Protestant denominations, the term "charismatic renewal" has been long since abandoned, often through the adoption of a more generic "spiritual renewal"[29] or simply "renewal,"[30] through the winding up of a denominational service organization,[31] or through the charismatic sector in a denomination amalgamating with other groupings affirming Evangelical values and basic Christian orthodoxy.[32] The Alpha course has contributed to this absorption of the charismatic through its low key introduction of speaking in tongues and spiritual gifts as elements in an Evangelical Christian initiation open to the Holy Spirit. The dissolution of charismatic renewal into wider streams of Christian renewal, whether seen as advance (deeper penetration of church milieu) or as regress (a loss of spiritual focus and vigor), still accentuates the importance of church renewal.

The new or independent charismatic groupings and networks are still largely in a pre-theological stage of development. They are generally entrepreneurial in character, focused on creativity, impact, and growth, with initial patterns of formation being typically "on the job" with mentoring from the pioneer figures. However, there are now signs of the formation of Bible schools or colleges. In this world, charismatic renewal is frequently seen as one phase or wave in the past preparing for greater waves and revelations of the Holy Spirit. In the early days of the House Church (independent charismatic) movement in Britain, it was common to regard renewal as at best a half-way house to restoration. Renewal as a goal was inherently a compromise that might initiate Christians into the things of the Spirit, but then tied them into "old wineskins" that could not hold the "new wine." As one early proponent of restoration wrote:

> The charismatic renewal moved in faith and obedience to possess its inheritance in the baptism and gifts of the Holy Spirit.

29. For example, by Episcopal Renewal and Presbyterian-Reformed Ministries International in the USA, and by the Lutheran Renewal in Germany.

30. For example, the Aldersgate Renewal Fellowship (United Methodist) in the USA.

31. For example, with the closure of Anglican Renewal Ministries in England.

32. For example, the Baptist group Mainstream, renamed Fresh Streams in 2011, and GEAR in the United Reformed Church, both in Great Britain.

Then came the challenge to shaky structures that were not adequate to contain and utilize the gifts that God was giving. It was a challenge to radical reformation and recovery, a casting out of what did not belong and a building of walls that had been broken down. Important as was the recovery of spiritual gifts, it was only one step towards the restoration of the church to New Testament Christianity.[33]

This new pattern of the "restored church" of the New Testament was perceived as the restoration of the Ephesians 4:11 ministries of apostle, prophet, evangelist, pastor and teacher, often referred to as the "fivefold ministries." Many have seen the restoration of these ministries, particularly of apostles and prophets, as the heart of their vision for the church. C. Peter Wagner coined the label "New Apostolic Reformation," claiming that this restoration is the beginning of a transformation at least as significant for Christian history as the Protestant Reformation.[34] Ron Myer places fivefold ministry within the framework of God's gifts as "gifts of Christ," a third category following gifts of the Father and gifts of the Spirit, again without any overall restoration framework.[35] Although Rick Joyner believes in a restoration of apostolic and prophetic ministries, he rebukes restorationists who look down on the charismatic renewal: "The Charismatic Renewal resulted in more salvations, more churches being renewed, more ministries and missionaries being released, than any other renewal, revival, or movement in history."[36] Joyner has read more history than most charismatic leaders[37]; for him, revival remains a major category, looking for new waves of revival as the future moves of the Spirit.[38] Bill Hamon sees a succession of restorations taking place, which has included the charismatic movement, followed by the restoration of apostles and prophets, but with further stages of restoration remaining to be unfolded. Hamon's book *The Eternal Church* presents a series of past and future restorations based on restoration of different facets of the "doctrine of Christ."[39] In this survey, the purpose of the Latter Rain and charismatic movements was "to restore the experiential reality of the biblical practice of 'laying on of hands,' thereby restoring to the Church

---

33. Wallis, *The Radical Christian*, 135.
34. Wagner, *Churchquake*.
35. Myer, *Fivefold Ministry made Practical*.
36. Joyner, *The Harvest*, 212.
37. See Joyner, *The World Aflame*; and *Shadows of Things to Come*.
38. Joyner, *A Prophetic Vision for the 21st Century*, chaps. 13–14.
39. Hamon, *The Eternal Church*.

the fourth doctrine of Christ."[40] For Hamon, there remain two doctrines of Christ still to be restored: the resurrection of the dead (5th) and the Eternal Judgment (6th), so his restorationism includes at least some stages of eschatological fulfilment.[41]

Revival, Renewal and Restoration

This short survey demonstrates that there is no coherent theology of restoration among the new or independent charismatics, even within the new apostolic networks. Pentecostals all believe in an element of restoration, shown in such designations as the Apostolic Faith (restoration of apostolic power as much as apostolic teaching), Latter Rain, and speaking of baptism in the Spirit as a personal Pentecost. Although the charismatic movement within the historic churches has not used the language of restoration, elements are clearly present, most notably a restoration of the spiritual gifts (*charismata*) as a necessary element in the equipment of the church to fulfil her mission. The rise of the Messianic Jewish movement which is largely charismatic is foundationally restorationist, with its faith in the restoration of Israel, centered on Israel's acceptance of Jesus (*Yeshua*) as Messiah, and the restoration of a distinctively Jewish witness to Jesus Christ.

The widespread view of church history as long decline followed by a series of restorations in preparation for the eschatological fulfilment has not generally won the approval of church historians. Any picture of total darkness between the time of Constantine and the Protestant Reformation is shockingly ignorant of the real ups and downs of church history. We have seen how a Pentecostal like Dale Coulter claims a continuity between Catholic renewal movements of the medieval period and Pentecostalism.

But there is much to be said for a series of restorations as part of an ecumenical vision for the renewal of the church, but in a framework that is historically well-informed and eschatologically-oriented. It has been assumed that the strongest objections to a decline and restoration view of Christian history would come from Orthodox and Catholics, who emphasize apostolic succession and continuity. However, the Catholic embrace at the Second Vatican Council of a vision of renewal for the whole church does contain some elements of genuine newness and of restoration. The newness can be seen in the acceptance of the ecumenical movement (the restoration of unity other than by return), the acceptance of the election of the Jewish

---

40. Ibid., 260.
41. See Hamon's charts, 1st–4th restorations: ibid., 154; 311 (5th); 337 (6th).

people, and the affirmation of religious liberty.[42] The whole liturgical renewal can be interpreted as a restoration: a restoration of the worship of the whole people, a restoration of a communion-centred vision of the church. Now Pope Francis is refusing the remaining accoutrements of the papal court, which represents a further distancing from an imperial model of the church and a restoration of evangelical simplicity. Interestingly, Francis's desire of "a church of the poor for the poor" reconnects with the medieval meaning of the apostolic life: living as itinerant preachers, receiving food and alms from those who received them. It is an aspect of apostolic restoration that has not featured in the New Apostolic Reformation!

I am suggesting then that an adequate Christian understanding of restoration in God's reviving and renewing purpose requires a much broader study of what the Holy Spirit is doing across the whole *oikoumene* than what is offered by the new charismatic networks. Such a broader study of the Holy Spirit's work of restoration would need to include first the concept of a return to Paradise (Eden), found in the Greek Fathers, which connects with the biblical vision of the deliverance of all creation from its "bondage to decay" (Rom 8:21).[43] It must address the theme of the restoration of Israel (see the question of the apostles in Acts 1:6) in a framework freed from all ideas that the church has replaced Israel. Here the theme of "rebuilding the ruins" a concept that is hard for Catholics, can become important, but which excludes the marginalization of the ruins![44] Then it can begin to integrate all the other elements of restoration (charisms, ministries, every-member participation, priesthood of all believers, synodality-communion, and evangelical simplicity of life). One key element is the restoration of the church of Jew and Gentile together, united not assimilated.[45]

In this fuller historical perspective, I would maintain the necessary complementarity of what is represented by revival and renewal. Each focus is weaker without the other. Renewal without revival tends to be weak on the transforming irruptions of the Holy Spirit and weak on eschatology (the second coming of the Lord is necessarily divine intervention). Revival without renewal tends to lack an adequate ecclesiology, is too individualistic,

---

42. It is no accident that these three elements are fiercely rejected by the traditionalist Society of St Pius X, who regard themselves as the authentic Catholic Church.

43. See Ladner, *The Idea of Reform*. "The mystical reform ideas of the Greek and eastern Fathers . . . centered around the key concepts of the return to Paradise, of divine resemblance and assimilation, and of the kingdom of God," 82. On the return to Eden theme, see Isa 51:3; Ezek 36:35.

44. See, for example, Jer 33:12–13; Ezek 36:10; Amos 9:14.

45. See Hocken, "Toward Jerusalem Council Two," 3–17.

and promotes short-term excitement with less long-term fruit. Both revival and renewal are needed until the end of this age.

The concept of restoration adds an important component to the understanding of God's work of redemption and transformation. But, as noted, restoration cannot be creation *ex nihilo*. What the new charismatic restorationist networks do contribute is a greater concern for the body of Christ and desire for the church than has characterized most of the Pentecostal movement. They draw attention to aspects of the sickness and ineffectiveness of the church. Their creativity raises the possibility of their being seen as an experimental laboratory from which all the churches can learn. Nonetheless, restoration does not replace or transcend revival and renewal, but belongs to them as a necessary element. This is because everything needs constant renewal. Any ecclesiology that does justice to both the continuity and discontinuity in God's dealings with humankind, with the glories and the shame in the history of Israel and the church, has to recognize that the church is *semper reformanda*, always in need of reform and renewal. This Protestant "slogan" was received by the Catholic Church at Vatican II: "Christ summons the church, as she goes her pilgrim way, to that continual reformation of which she always has need, insofar as she is a human institution here on earth."[46] The emphases of Pope Francis on evangelical simplicity of life, freeing the church from worldly patterns of privilege and status, are in fact a profound form of restoration that bring hope to the whole Christian world.

Bibliography

Bellofatto, Gina A., and Todd M. Johnson. "Key Findings of Christianity in its Global Context, 1970–2020." *International Bulletin of Missionary Research* 37, no. 3 (2013) 157–64.

Coulter, Dale M. "Primitivism and Progressivism: Two Claims About a Common Evangelical Heritage." *Ecumenical Trends* 42, no. 7 (2013) 1–5.

———. "The Spirit and the Bride Revisited: Pentecostalism, Renewal, and the Sense of History." *Pneuma* 21, no. 2 (2012) 298–319.

Dulles, Avery. "John Paul II and the New Evangelization: What Does It Mean?" In *John Paul II and the New Evangelization*, edited by Ralph Martin and Peter Williamson, 2–16. Cincinnati: Servant, 2006.

Empowered 21. "E21 Vision." www.empowered21.com. Accessed September 30, 2016.

Hamon, Bill. *The Eternal Church*. Rev. ed. Shippensburg, PA: Destiny Image, 2003.

Hocken, Peter. "The Pentecostal-Charismatic Movement as Revival and Renewal." *Pneuma* 3, no. 1 (1981) 31–47.

---

46. Decree on Ecumenism, *Unitatis Redintegratio*, 6.

———. "Revival and Renewal." *Journal of the European Pentecostal Theological Association* 18 (1998) 49–63.

———. "Toward Jerusalem Council Two." *Journal of Pentecostal Theology* 17, no. 1 (2007) 3–17.

Joyner, Rick. *The Harvest*. Vol. 2. Charlotte, NC: Morning Star, 1994.

———. *A Prophetic Vision for the 21st Century*. Nashville: Nelson, 1999.

———. *Shadows of Things to Come*. Nashville: Nelson, 2001.

———. *The World Aflame: The Welsh Revival and Its Lessons for Our Time*. Charlotte, NC: Morning Star, 1993.

Ladner, Gerhard B. *The Idea of Reform: Its Impact on Christian Thought and Action in the Age of the Fathers*. Cambridge, MA: Harvard University Press, 1959.

Macchia, Frank. *Baptized in the Spirit: A Global Pentecostal Theology*. Grand Rapids: Zondervan, 2006.

Myer, Ron. *Fivefold Ministry Made Practical*. Lititz, PA: House to House, 2006.

Paul VI, Pope. *Evangelii Nuntiandi*, Apostolic Exhortation on Evangelization in the Modern World (1975). http://w2.vatican.va/content/paul-vi/en/apost_exhortations/documents/hf_p-vi_exh_19751208_evangelii-nuntiandi.html. Accessed September 30, 2016.

Rausch, Thomas P. "The Evangelical Heritage: Primitive and Progressive. A Response to Dale Coulter." *Ecumenical Trends* 42, no. 7 (July/August 2013) 6.

Unitatis Redintegratio, Decree on Ecumenism (1964). In *The Documents of Vatican II*, edited by Walter M. Abbot and Joseph Gallagher, translated by Joseph Gallagher, 341–66. New York: Guild, 1966.

Vondey, Wolfgang. *Beyond Pentecostalism: The Crisis of Global Christianity and the Renewal of the Theological Agenda*. Grand Rapids: Eerdmans, 2010.

Wagner, C. Peter. *Churchquake*. Ventura, CA: Regal, 1999.

Wallis, Arthur. *The Radical Christian*. Eastbourne, UK: Kingsway, 1981.

Weigel, George. *Evangelical Catholicism: Deep Reform in the 21st-Century Church*. New York: Basic, 2013.

Yong, Amos. *The Spirit Poured Out on All Flesh: Pentecostalism and the Possibility of Global Theology*. Grand Rapids: Baker Academic, 2005.

5

A Radical Reorientation

Missiology Following the Second Vatican Council

MARY M. MOTTE, FMM

Introduction

POPE JOHN XXIII'S REMARKS about *opening windows* when he announced the Second Vatican Council have been quoted often. Images of "fresh air" blowing through open windows, and the imagined signs of the Holy Spirit capturing the best of those molecules of fresh air have, in one way or another, challenged the minds of many. This movement of fresh air and the spiritual awareness of the presence of God's Spirit always at work among us, include the gradual appearance of insights which contribute to a new vision of mission. The shift in vision for Roman Catholics began in earnest with the development of thinking about the current characteristics which nourish and express our faith rooted in the Word of God, especially after the Decree of Vatican II, *Dei Verbum*, on Divine Revelation.[1] Further, the Sixteen Documents of Vatican II[2] initiated a profound search to under-

---

1. Cf. Benedict XVI, *Address of His Holiness*.

2. 1. *Sacrosanctum concilium*, Constitution on the Sacred Liturgy, 1963; 2. *Inter Mirifica*, Decree On the Means of Social Communication, 1963; 3. *Lumen Gentium*, Dogmatic Constitution On the Church, 1964; 4. *Orientalium Ecclesiarum*, Decree On the Catholic Churches of the Eastern Rite, 1964; 5. *Unitatis Redintegratio*, Decree on Ecumenism, 1964; 6. *Christus Dominus*, Decree Concerning the Pastoral Office of Bishops In the Church, 1965; 7. *Perfectae Caritatis*, Decree On Renewal of Religious Life, 1965; 8. *Optatam Totius*, Decree On Priestly Training, 1965; 9. *Gravissimum Educationis*, Declaration On Christian Education, 1965; 10. *Nostra Aetate*, Ddeclaration On the Relation Of the

stand the mission of the Church in its insertion into the modern world.³ This essay, assumes the continued development of understandings that have emerged from Vatican II, already well documented, and which continue to be updated.⁴ The emphasis here will be to consider the continued emerging Vatican II Church from the perspective of the organic relation between mission and ecumenism.

The Organic Relation between Ecumenism and Mission

Consideration of the Council in light of the *New* Pentecost of which John XXIII spoke when he convoked the Council, as well as the subsequent reference of John Paul II to the *New Pentecost,* leads Thomas Hughson to recognize that mission interweaves a relation among all the council documents.⁵ Pope John XXIII, truly inspired by the Holy Spirit, convoked an ecumenical council that would reach far beyond Christian Churches to all those of good will.⁶ As for many Christians, the Roman Catholic understanding of mission as the transmission of the Gospel to those who had not heard the Good News, has been often accompanied by popular images. It also, became at

---

Church to Non-Christian Religions, 1965; 11. *Dei Verbum*, Dogmatic Constitution On Divine Revelation, 1965; 12. *Apostolicam Actuositatem*, Decree On the Apostolate of the Laity, 1965; 13. *Dignitatis Humanae*, Declaration On Religious Freedom, 1965; 14. *Ad Gentes*, Decree On the Mission Activity of the Church, 1965; 15. *Presbyterorum Ordinis*, Decree On the Ministry and Life of Priests, 1965; 16. *Gaudium et Spes*, Pastoral Constitution On the Church In the Modern World, 1965.

3. SEDOS is an organization of religious orders in Rome that the Superiors General of the Men missionary orders founded during Vatican II. Shortly after the Council ended, women's missionary congregations were allowed to join SEDOS. Now international congregations of men and women religious are members of SEDOS. The search for the meaning of mission became very evident among SEDOS members after Vatican II concluded. Already in 1969 SEDOS convened a seminar to study the motivation for mission. Following the Synod of 1974 and the subsequent publication of *Evangelii Nuntiandi,* the question was no longer why mission, but that sought the new dimensions and priorities of mission. Then in 1981 SEDOS held a major seminar on the future of mission, the results of which are published in Motte and Lang, *Mission in Dialogue.* The SEDOS Bulletin at www.sedosmission.org offers an overview of developing concepts of mission up to the present time. "A Century of Ecumenical Missiology," special issue, *International Review of Mission* 100, no. 2 (2011), offers overviews of different specific developments in understanding mission, especially from Protestant perspectives.

4. Cf. Gaillardetz and Clifford, *Keys to the Council*; and O'Malley, *What Happened at Vatican II.*

5. Hughson, "Interpreting Vatican II," 1.

6. Cf. McBrien, "Pope John XXIII's Opening Address."

times, somewhat tainted by historical events, such as the conception of European cultural supremacy as a formative, cultural experience for so many missionaries and sending organizations.

This radical reorientation of mission that begins in Vatican II, has been accompanied by a growing ecumenical collaboration.[7] A limited but far-reaching, ecumenical path opened fifty years before with the Edinburgh Mission Conference in 1910, which is also the beginning of the modern ecumenical movement. Catholics were not invited to the 1910 meeting, but the path of ecumenical collaboration among Protestant Christians of various traditions that began in 1910 eventually opened to Roman Catholic participation in 1963 after the beginning of Vatican II.[8] It is important to recall here that this growing awareness of the need for greater ecumenical collaboration among Protestants was rooted in the experience of missionaries gathered in Edinburgh. *Ad Gentes,* the Vatican II document on mission, "declares The Church is missionary by its very nature."[9] While these two events were not related to one another, they both offer significant, although separate, examples of the organic relation between ecumenism and mission. *Lumen Gentium,* the Council's Constitution on the Church, recognizes the relationship among all Christians and all those who seek truth. It also states clearly the responsibility for mission is included in Baptism.[10] In 1982 the International Faith and Order Commission, which includes Roman Catholic participation, reached agreement around Baptism, and recognized it as the foundation for Christian mission.[11]

Well before the Council, there was growing awareness of a profound relation between prayer and Christian unity. This understanding imbued the orientations of two catholic priests: Father Paul Wattson, SA (1863–1940), founder of the Week of Prayer for Christian Unity in the United States; and Abbé Paul Couturier (1881–1953), who was associated with the *Groupe de Dombes* (France), and who became an important promoter of prayer for unity especially in Europe. In fact, there he is often referred to as the "Father of Ecumenism." Couturier notably expressed the urgency of the work of common prayer. The missiological paradigm we appropriate today owes much to the energized convictions about the need of prayer for unity among Christians. This passion for unity continues to be expressed through many Bible Studies, Prayer Services, and Reflections in the various ecumenical

---

7. Cf. Scherer, and Bevans, *New Directions in Mission and Evangelization I, II.*
8. "Vatican II after Fifty Years."
9. *Ad Gentes,* 2.
10. *Lumen Gentium,* 32.
11. *Baptism Eucharist and Ministry.*

prayer gatherings, meetings and dialogues throughout the world. A true spiritual ecumenism has emerged which gives a new basis to relationships and the search together for common witness. Every prayer offered in common, "each act of common witness, indeed every act of spiritual communion is a gift of the Holy Spirit, who binds us together, and enables us to give visible expression to our Lord's desire for unity."[12]

Greater Ecumenical Participation among Roman Catholics

Vatican II gave a new and official orientation to Roman Catholics which led to greater ecumenical collaboration, beginning with the establishment of the Secretariat for Promoting Christian Unity in 1960.[13] At the time of planning the Council, Protestant Observers were formally invited to be present for all four sessions from 1962 to 1965. Tom Ryan has recently published comments made by some Council Observers which illustrate their far-reaching inspiration. These insights have been verified over time, and have helped to lead ecumenical partners into new spaces of vision. Douglas Horton, from the Reformed Church, noted the Council's orientation "toward unity and peace," working "toward the good of all." William Baker from the Disciples of Christ, Great Britain, characterized the Council as primarily "bearing a peculiarly spiritual quality of friendship, a quality which made it part of the fulfillment of the purpose of God: friendship in Christ." Another observer, Basil Holt, Disciples of Christ, expressed something shared by many Protestants and Catholics, when he wrote, "Imagine, in a Papal decree promulgated under the dome of St. Peter's, coming upon such sentiments as these: 'In all his activity a man is bound to follow his conscience, in order that he may come to God' . . . [14] Another observer, Edmund Schlink, Lutheran Church, Germany, recognized the "breakthrough of a dynamic" in the conciliar event that was both "more wide-spread and progressive" than the council's decisions.[15] He was deeply convinced that "Vatican II had been an ecumenical event" which changed the "theological status quo" of both Catholic and non-Catholic churches. He saw the tensions within the

---

12. Kasper, *A Handbook of Spiritual Ecumenism*, 9.

13. It is now the Pontifical Council for Promoting Christian Unity following the changes brought about in the organization of the Vatican offices in 1988 by John Paul II.

14. See Tom Ryan (website), http://www.tomryancsp.org/news/ProtestantObservers.htm.

15. Faggioli, *Vatican II*, 43.

Council as a kind of stirring or awakening oriented toward the coming into being of the *new*.[16]

The first official Roman Catholic missiological and ecumenical consultative participation occurred in the Conference of Mexico City in 1963 and has continued through all the Commission of World Mission and Evangelism (CWME) conferences.[17] There has also been official participation of Roman Catholic consultants in the Plenary Gatherings, as well as in other working groups of the World Council of Churches, including the most recent assembly in Busan, Korea.[18] In 1984 the first permanent Roman Catholic Consultant was appointed by the Vatican to the CWME Office in the World Council of Churches.[19] In addition to the work of the World Council of Churches in its many aspects, participation, either through membership or consultative status, is ongoing in various other international, national and local ecumenical commissions and teams. The many bi-lateral dialogues between the Roman Catholic Church and different Christian traditions, including the Pentecostal Churches, illustrate expanding realization of the importance of finding the path of genuine dialogue among the Christian traditions.[20] These dialogues at the international level, are generally organized by the Pontifical Council for Promoting Christian Unity together with the respective Churches or entities. They are also organized at national levels, organized by the respective ecumenical offices of the Catholic Bishops conferences and the different Churches, traditions, or entities. A list of some of these international dialogues was prepared for the Jubilee Year, 2000 and illustrate how far reaching is the common search for greater mutual understanding and the healing of past wounds. I include this list since it shows the beginning dates of the dialogues.[21]

- With the Anglican Communion (1966);
- With the World Lutheran Federation (1967);
- With the World Reformed Alliance (1970);
- With the World Methodist Council (1967);
- With international Pentecostal movements (1972);
- With the Coptic-Orthodox Church (1973);

16. Ibid., 44.
17. Matthey, "From 1910 to 2010," 258–75.
18. SEDOS, "Catholic Delegates Observes."
19. Rausch and Gros, *Deepening Communion*, 524.
20. Nnyombi, "A Catholic Missiological and Ecumenical Appreciation."
21. Fortino, "Dialogue of charity in the perspective of the Holy Year."

- With the Disciples of Christ (1977);
- With the Evangelicals (1977);
- With all the Orthodox Churches together (1980);
- With the World Baptist Alliance (1984);
- With the Sira Church of India (1989).

Parallel to these dialogues in which the Catholic Church is taking part there is another network of dialogues among Christians; some of these are:

- The Anglican-Orthodox dialogue (1966);
- The Anglican-Ancient Churches of the Orient dialogue (1990);
- The Baptist-Lutheran dialogue (1966);
- The Baptist-Reformed Churches dialogue (1973);
- The Lutheran-Orthodox dialogue (1978);
- The Methodist-Reformed dialogue (1985);
- The Old Catholics and Orthodox dialogue (1975);
- The Orthodox and Precalcedonese dialogue (1989);
- The Orthodox and Reformed dialogue (1979).

While this is not a complete list, it gives an idea of efforts being undertaken by Christians in their desire for Christian Unity. This list also clearly illustrates the widespread desire for unity among Christians.

The International Association of Mission Studies, as well as country-based societies of missiology (for example the American Society of Missiology and the American Professors of Mission) witness to the quality of consciousness achieved through ecumenical friendship solidly based on genuine and respectful cooperation to gain deeper insights into the presently unfolding meaning of mission. In these two organizations Conciliar Protestants, Evangelical Protestants, Roman Catholics, and Orthodox explore new issues emerging in mission. Together they search for appropriate ways of transmitting the Good News in the circumstances of today's world. They do so from the perspective of common worship, academic studies, and sharing of practical experiences, which offer views from different understandings, and mutual challenges towards new ways of seeing.[22] Also in the years following Vatican II, the themes of Peace, Social Justice, Care for Creation, and Just Economies have brought together many persons, Chris-

---

22. Bevans and Schroeder, *Constants in Context*, 275; Anderson et al., *Witness to World Christianity*; and American Society of Missiology.

tians and others. There are innumerable collaborative ecumenical efforts focusing on the concerns of all peoples around such issues as water, food, immigration, interracial and interreligious relations. These constitute new directions emerging in mission; they are pursued ecumenically and feature on many agendas of mission meetings, as well as in articles in a number of mission reviews. On three occasions the National Council of Churches USA and the United States Catholic Mission Association worked together to elaborate an ecumenical mission consultation. These conferences were held in Madison, Connecticut (1987), Simpsonwood, Georgia (1994), and in Minneapolis, Minnesota (1997).[23] There was significant participation in all three conferences by scholars and practitioners, seeking how to be together in mission.

The Ongoing Influence of Vatican II in the Years Following the Council

Hughson notes that the work undertaken by the bishops during the Council entailed a "micro-rupture from the preceding Constantinian, Gregorian, and Counter Reformation" organizational views that had prevented the Roman Catholic tradition from a full reception of the Gospel in contemporary situations.[24] Vatican II explored the idea that the Pope, "in his work as Universal Shepherd of the Church, could exercise his union with the Bishops, Members of the same episcopal order as the Bishop of Rome, in a more obvious and efficient way."[25] Based on this conviction, Paul VI created the Synod of Bishops for the whole Church on September 15, 1965. These Synods have been held every three years. Continental synodal meetings were held in the Vatican during the time of John Paul II. While there are a number of facets to these meetings given the variety incorporated with Bishops from all over the world, attention has always been given to some aspect of the full reception of the Gospel, which is basically a missiological question. The Synod in Rome held in 1971, which dealt with the ministerial priesthood and justice in the world, offered the profound insight that "Action on behalf of justice is a constitutive dimension of preaching the Gospel."[26] This insight in turn spurred new ways of thinking about the various situations missionaries were encountering throughout the world. Analyses led to greater emphasis on correcting past mistakes, and moving toward exploring in theory and

23. Continuing Committee on Common Witness.
24. Hughson, "Interpreting Vatican II."
25. *Christus Dominis,* the decree on the Pastoral Office of Bishops, 1965, nos. 2–5.
26. Synod of Bishops, *Justice in the World,* 6.

practice the profound implications of respecting just relationships with all of God's creation. Connecting the practice of justice with preaching the Gospel is foundational to the meaning of just relationships, namely that one cannot preach the Gospel and foster situations of injustice.

The following Synod in 1974 explored the theme of *Evangelization in the Modern World*. Following this Synod, Paul VI issued *Evangelii Nuntiandi* in 1975. Elements of a new missiology, new ways of understanding the significance and practice of proclaiming and witnessing the Gospel appear throughout the document. Evangelizing activity as described in this Apostolic Exhortation continues to find actualization today:

> For the Church, evangelizing means bringing the Good News into all the strata of humanity, and through its influence transforming humanity from within and making it new: "Now I am making the whole of creation new."[27]

Recognizing that it is the Gospel which transforms situations and brings about the new has gradually led missionaries to a more dynamic conviction that God is already present among all peoples in the Love God has for each one. The missionary's task is to discover how God is present and then collaborate with the people to bring about a fuller and deeper realization of God's presence and action in their midst. As Sivalon notes this requires a growth in a quality of contemplation that he describes using the example of an African herder and a Montanan angler:

> Both the herder and the angler are very much in the world living their lives, but they find a significant moment of solitude in pastures and streams, where they become aware of a mystery that is at once greater than themselves and yet an intimate part of themselves.[28]

The Church in Latin America (*Consejo Episcopal Latinoamericano* or CELAM) held a meeting in Medellin, Colombia in 1968. They chose a fundamental option for the poor and lay out a theological orientation that began from the life of the people on the continent, especially the poor. Liberation Theology, rooted in the theology of the Incarnation, offers a new approach in theological reflection, inductive in its methodology. Basic Christian Communities, an expression of liberation theology, which began in Brazil, soon spread throughout the continent, as well as in other places. These were very often communities of the poor. The people studied the Word of God together with their faith leaders, and grew positively in understanding the

27. Paul VI, *Evangelii Nuntiandi*, no. 46
28. Sivalon, *God's Mission and Postmodern Culture*, 73.

dignity within them as children of God, forming small Christian Communities (BCC). There were also Christian missionaries—Catholic and Protestant—who found their starting point in faith, recognizing the love of God for every person. Protestants and Catholics often worked together with the poor for change. This movement often took place in very unjust political contexts, and the people's awareness of their innate dignity and worth led to clashes when they no longer simply submitted to injustice often perpetrated by governments. Violence arose at times. Every struggle fails to offer complete clarity to those outside. However, as Christians, one has to consider those who died for their faith in the concrete struggles for justice. Among them, Bishop Oscar Romero in El Salvador, as well as so many, many struggling people who gave their lives for the sake of faith and justice.[29]

Ideas about how life and salvation are rooted in the lives of a people loved by God and called to participate in the fullness of God, have also been finding new expressions in the churches of Africa, Asia, Oceania, and North America. Multiple discoveries of how God is acting continue to motivate innovative ways of perceiving the action of God among the people within their cultural circumstances.

A New Mission Paradigm Leading with *the Freshness and Fragrance of the Gospel*

Faggioli suggests that "a key passage in the history of the reception of Vatican II is the translation of Catholic theology marked by its Greek, European, and Western cultural roots into a global culture."[30] The journey towards a global culture is accompanied increasingly by the developing theology of the Incarnation in the peoples of the world with its rich variety of insight and practice indicating movement towards a deeply unifying, but not uniform, expression of faith.

While this process of reception of Vatican II within the Roman Catholic Church, is only at the beginning, it is indisputable that the Council opened the way for a truly World Church, with a new missiological communication of the Gospel in the richness of all cultures. While many things apparently hindered reception of Vatican II over the past fifty years, there have been moments of tremendous insight confirming that God is indeed *making all things new*, even in the midst of limited understandings. John Paul II says that God's Spirit ". . . with a marvelous providence directs the unfolding of

---

29. Ellacuría and Sobrino, *Mysterium Liberationies*. References to the experiences of Liberation Theology and Practice in Latin America can be found in this book.

30. Faggioli, *Vatican II*, 59.

time and renews the face of the earth."[31] Unfolding time and renewing earth stir up thoughts of newness. Both images call to mind current scientific discoveries that creation is still incomplete. They also reflect emerging theological insights into the Mystery of God, Creator of an unfolding universe. Ilia Delio remarks that theology, if it is to be faithful to its basic defined task, namely that it is *faith seeking understanding,* must, from its perspective of faith, engage the consensus currently held by many scientists, a perspective that is directed toward a radically changed worldview.[32] More and more Christian theologians and missiologists are contemplating the mystery of the Trinitarian Creator God in the context of an evolutionary, unfolding universe.[33] In this process they are discovering a more profound experience of contemplation.

Divine Mystery will always be beyond the best human understanding, yet, scientific discoveries now provide facts about the universe that call for a deeper discernment and a more profound contemplation of the Mystery of God's Love and Presence in Creation. Earlier I noted how growing awareness of the relation between ecumenism and mission is leading to a radical reorientation of missiology in this time since the closing of the Council in 1965.

In a more intensive consideration of the role of the Holy Spirit, Hughson's study demonstrates the significance of the image of a New Pentecost in Vatican II from the initial action of John XXIII in convoking the council through to the writings of John Paul II in the years following the council. His analysis is rooted in the initial experience of Pentecost. Recalling Kasper's understanding that "the obvious distance between present divisions and a future unity also measures the gap between Vatican II and fulfillment of 'a New Pentecost,'" he concludes with a quote from Kasper, in which he queries whether "we find ourselves, similar to Mary and the disciples after the Ascension of Jesus in the pre-Pentecostal situation of the call '*Veni Sancte*'...."[34]

Today, Catholic missiologists and theologians, among those of other traditions, are probing more deeply into the significance of the Holy Spirit's presence and action in communicating God's Love and Word today. It is interesting to note that Gary B. McGee attributes the source of increasing attention to the Holy Spirit to the beginning of the 20th century when Pope

---

31. John Paul II, *Dominum et Vivificantem,* no. 26; see also John Paul II, *Redemptoris Missio,* chapter 3, *The Holy Spirit the Principal Agent of Mission,* 1990.

32. Delio, "Godhead or God Ahead?," 3–22.

33. Bevans, "God Inside Out," 102, 103; see also Bevans, and Schroeder, *Constants in Context,* 286–304; and Edwards, *Breath of Life,* 117–29; cf. also McDonnell, *The Other Hand of God.*

34. Hughson, "Interpreting Vatican II," 15.

Leo XIII solemnly intoned the hymn, *Veni Creator Spiritus* in the Basilica of St. Peter in Rome.[35] The image is powerful and recalls the continuing affirmation in history that God's action is not to be contained in specific space and time. Stephen Bevans offers a way of Spirit-inspired *seeing* scripturally and missiologically, in his consideration of texts referring to the *work* of the Holy Spirit in creation: *Life-giving Spirit* (Genesis 2:7), Mary conceives by the Spirit (Luke 1:35), and the Spirit is poured out on Jesus (Matthew 3:16). In Luke 4:18–19, the Spirit guides Jesus as he begins his public ministry; and in John 14:26 this same Spirit is promised to the disciples to enable them to understand God's purposes.[36] Bevans speaks of the Spirit's activity as "transcending immanence - immanence because God is totally and thoroughly involved and interwoven within cosmic and human history, transcendence because God's presence and activity is beyond the capacity of human beings to predict, control, grasp, or express."[37] The image of God thoroughly *involved and interwoven* within cosmic and human history challenges our way of believing and acting in the present time; it challenges our way of mission. In other words, this image of God caught up in the *everydayness* of life, requires greater attentiveness to the Word of God, allowing it to penetrate our patterns of thought and action.

Contemplation of the mystery of the Trinitarian Creator God in the context of an evolutionary, unfolding universe continues to deepen. Denis Edwards holds up the biblical image of the Breath of God breathing life into the universe in all its stages: its law, the initial conditions at its origin, and its evolution.[38] In sum, the Spirit makes possible the emergence of the *new* at every stage. Movement towards the new begins at the beginning of creation and is explained by the theory of emergence, namely that the new is dependent upon its pre-existing components, but it is not reducible to them.[39] Emergence theory understands that God empowers from within the entire process of ongoing creation. God gives creation the capacity to transcend itself and become more than it was. Theology is moving towards a more profound understanding of creation, nourished by the Word of God, together with the fruits of scientific discovery.

Central to Christian theology is the belief that God holds all things in existence over the abyss of nothingness. While recognizing that this

35. McGee, *Miracles, Missions, &American Pentecostalism*, 88.
36. Bevans, *God Inside Out*, 102–3.
37. Ibid., 103.
38. Edwards. *Breath of Life*, 43.
39. Edwards notes that among contemporary scholars, Nancey Murphy, George Ellis, Philip Clayton, Paul Davies, and Arthur Peacocke defend the concept of an emergent universe. Ibid., 45.

belief is essential, Edwards points out that it is in need of significant development. He notes how Karl Rahner's theory of active self-transcendence emphasizes God as the Absolute Future not only of human beings, but also of all creation. Rahner's evolutionary Christology presents Jesus in his humanity as a product of the evolutionary universe. Jesus is understood as self-transcendence of the universe to God and the self-communication of God to the universe.[40] Seeing ourselves as part of an evolving world requires a new understanding of reality, a new way of seeing, which in turn requires a transformed metaphysics and theology. Delio comments how we have moved from thinking about the universe launched by the Creator as it is, to a dynamic vision of the cosmos in which creation continues, always grounded in its Source, God-Trinity.[41] This shift holds the tension between science, influencing culture, and a church that is cautiously and very slowly abandoning a pre-modern awareness.[42] Theology facing the challenges of science, is moving towards, what William Stoeger calls, "a consistent integrated model of divine action."[43]

The source of Divine Action is the Trinitarian God who reaches out to the world in Love through creation, through the dynamic presence of the Holy Spirit. The action of the Spirit witnessed in Israel and in the life of Jesus is characterized as *creative, prophetic, life-giving,* and *death-negating.* These same qualities are expressed in the women and men who continue Jesus's mission in the world and in the midst of God's people.[44] Since Vatican II, there have been numerous challenges to mission paradigms which, in turn, have generated intensive studies and research.[45] These efforts continue to bring about new ways of seeing. A gospel focus and orientation lead to the discovery of how Jesus, the Face of God, taught about God's Kingdom. The mission of the Church, like the Mission of God, arises out of the passion for all that is and can be; it is a passion of relationship. Attitudes, behaviors, and actions, truly aligned with the action of the Creator Spirit, are shaped by commitment to justice, solidarity, and resistance to what is unjust. This radical missionary vision found in Jesus of Nazareth urges missionary disciples to discern where and how God is leading them in the world of today.[46] For over a quarter of a century women and men committed to mission have

40. Ibid., 88.
41. Delio, *Christ in Evolution*, 21.
42. Ibid., 22.
43. Stoeger, Foreword, x.
44. Ibid., 103.
45. Cf. Bosch, *Transforming Mission*.
46. Bevens, "God Inside Out," 105.

ecumenically been discovering the gospel significance of relationships that emerge in a dialogue of life especially among the poor, followers of different religious faiths, and different cultural groups.

Scholars have been exploring new ways of grasping the theological and missiological significance of scientific contributions of emergence theory, relationship, and the meaning of the new.[47] Amos Yong recently examined the historical path between Pentecostal theology and science. He develops a pneumatological theology of emergence and carries his analysis forward through his insight that God's actions in the life and resurrection of Jesus anticipate the redemption and point toward the communion which all things will experience with the Triune God: Father, Son, and Spirit.[48]

Conclusion

A new paradigm is emerging in mission as theology in general encounters and is questioned by developments in science. A new paradigm is likewise required by the changing reality of the universe and life today. According to Hughson, John Paul II, referring to the church's mission, took a daring position in asserting that " . . . of course Jesus entrusts this work to human beings: to the apostles of the Church. Nevertheless, in and through them the Holy Spirit remains the transcendent and principal agent for the accomplishment of this work in the human spirit and in the history of the world. The Holy Spirit is indeed the principal agent of the whole of the Church's mission."[49] Hughson goes on to remark that the image of a *new Pentecost* enables recognition that the mission of Christ is decisive in its continuity with the Pentecostal mission of the Spirit. The Second Vatican Council revived this realization among us:

> In this way 'a new Pentecost' also accents a diffused, underlying finality inherent in Vatican II toward mission, a finality *Lumen Gentium* and *Ad gentes* on the missionary activity of the church locate in the Trinitarian *Missio Dei* and the nature of the church, as well as in Christ's mandate. A renaissance of the church's missionary nature is an essential dimension of the event and documents of Vatican II associated with "a new Pentecost."[50]

---

47. Smith, "The Holy Spirit and Mission."
48. Yong, *The Spirit of Creation*.
49. John Paul II, *Redemptoris Missio*, 21.
50. Hughson, "Interpreting Vatican II," 34.

On March 13, 2013 the Roman Catholic Church began a new moment in the living of the Gospel in the modern world with the election of Jorge Mario Bergoglio as Bishop of Rome, 266th successor of St. Peter, who chose the name Francis, after Francis of Assisi. He began by bowing and asking the people to pray for him. A first desire he expressed was, "How I would love to have a poor church for the poor."[51] He has already set the direction by how he dresses and where he lives. His simple, conversational reflections on the Gospel each day uncover a deep well of relationship with Jesus. What is most reassuring in trying to understand how God is leading us, is the experience of life Pope Francis has learned in the streets and favellas of Buenos Aires. In his first Apostolic Exhortation, *The Joy of the Gospel*, he makes the images very concrete.

> God's word is unpredictable in its power. The Gospel speaks of a seed which, once sown, grows by itself, even as the farmer sleeps (Mk 4:26–29). The Church has to accept this unruly freedom of the word, which accomplishes what it wills in ways that surpass our calculations and ways of thinking.[52]

The event of Vatican II has provoked a radical reorientation in mission together with growing ecumenical commitment. The dynamism of this time is that we as Roman Catholics, together with our sisters and brothers of many Christian traditions, pray to "accept this unruly freedom of the word, which accomplishes what it wills in ways that surpass our calculations and ways of thinking."[53] Pope Francis reminds us that "the Gospel Joy which enlivens the community of disciples is a missionary joy."[54] Many missionaries, proceeding from various Christian traditions, live the organic relationship of ecumenism and mission in a developing way that opens to the newness of God in our midst.

Bibliography

Ad Gentes, Decree On the Church's Mission Activity, 1965. In *The Documents of Vatican II*, edited by Walter M. Abbot and Joseph Gallagher, translated by Joseph Gallagher, 584–630. New York: Guild, 1966.
American Society of Missiology. www.asmweb.org. Accessed September 30, 2016.
Anderson, Gerald H., et al. *Witness to World Christianity: The International Association for Mission Studies, 1972–2012*. New Haven, CT: OMSC, 2012.

---

51. Francis, "How I Would Love."
52. Francis, *Evangelii Gaudium*, 22
53. Ibid.
54. Ibid., 21

Apostolicam Actuositatem, Decree On the Apostolate of the Laity (1965). In *The Documents of Vatican II*, edited by Walter M. Abbot and Joseph Gallagher, translated by Joseph Gallagher, 489–521. New York: Guild, 1966.

Baptism Eucharist and Ministry, Faith and order paper no. 111. World council of churches, Geneva, 1982. http://www.oikoumene.org/en/resources/documents/commissions/faith-and-order/i-unity-the-church-and-its-mission/baptism-eucharist-and-ministry-faith-and-order-paper-no-111-the-lima-text. Accessed September 30, 2016.

Benedict XVI, Pope. *Address of His Holiness, Benedict XVI to the Participants of the International Congress organized to commemorate the 40th Anniversary of the Dogmatic Constitution on Divine Revelation "Dei Verbum."* 16 September 2005. http://w2.vatican.va/content/benedict-xvi/en/speeches/2005/september/documents/hf_ben-xvi_spe_20050916_40-dei-verbum.html. Accessed September 30, 2016.

Bevans, Stephen B. "God Inside Out: Toward a Missionary Theology of the Holy Spirit." *International Bulletin of Missionary Research* 22, no. 3 (1998) 102–5.

Bevans, Stephen B., and Roger P. Schroeder. *Constants in Context: A Theology of Mission for Today*. Maryknoll, NY: Orbis, 2004.

Bosch, David. *Transforming Mission: Paradigm Shifts in the Theology of Mission*. Maryknoll, NY: Orbis, 1991.

Christus Dominus, Decree on the Bishops's Pastoral Office in the Church (1965). In *The Documents of Vatican II*, edited by Walter M. Abbot and Joseph Gallagher, translated by Joseph Gallagher, 396–429. New York: Guild, 1966.

Continuing Committee on Common Witness, 1987. www.uscatholicmission.org/cccw.aspx. Accessed September 30, 2016.

Dei Verbum, Dogmatic Constitution On Divine Revelation, 1965. In *The Documents of Vatican II*, edited by Walter M. Abbot and Joseph Gallagher, translated by Joseph Gallagher, 111–28. New York: Guild, 1966.

Delio, Ilia. *Christ in Evolution*. Maryknoll, NY: Orbis, 2008.

———. "Godhead or God Ahead? Rethinking the Trinity in Light of Emergence." In *God, Grace and Creation*, edited by Philip J. Rossi, 3–22. Maryknoll, NY: Orbis, 2010.

Dignitatis Humanae, Declaration On Religious Freedom (1965). In *The Documents of Vatican II*, edited by Walter M. Abbot and Joseph Gallagher, translated by Joseph Gallagher, 675–96. New York: Guild, 1966.

Edwards, Denis. *Breath of Life: A Theology of the Creator Spirit*. Maryknoll, NY: Orbis, 2004.

Ellacuría, Ignacio, and Jon Sobrino, eds. *Mysterium Liberationies: Fundamental Concept of Liberation Theology*. Maryknoll, NY: Orbis, 2004.

Faggioli, Massimo. *Vatican II: The Battle for Meaning*. Mahwah, NJ: Paulist, 2012.

Fortino, Eleuterio F. "Dialogue of Charity in the Perspective of the Holy Year." www.vatican.va/jubilee_2000/magazine/documents/ju_mag_01071997_p-56_en.html. Accessed September 30, 2016.

Francis, Pope. *Evangelii Gaudium*, Apostolic Exhortation on the Proclamation of the Gospel in Today's World (2013). http://w2.vatican.va/content/francesco/en/apost_exhortations/documents/papa-francesco_esortazione-ap_20131124_evangelii-gaudium.html. Accessed September 30, 2016.

Francis, Pope. "How I Would Love to Have a Poor Church for the Poor." http://ncronline.org/blogs/francis-chronicles/pope-francis-i-would-love-church-poor. Accessed September 30, 2016.

Gaillardetz, Richard R., and Catherine E. Clifford. *Keys to the Council: Unlocking the Teaching of Vatican II*. Collegeville, MN: Order of St. Benedict, 2012.

Gaudium et Spes, Pastoral Constitution On the Church In the Modern World (1965). In *The Documents of Vatican II*, Edited by Walter M. Abbot and Joseph Gallagher, translated by Joseph Gallagher, 199–308. New York: Guild, 1966.

Gravissimum Educationis, Declaration On Christian Education (1965). In *The Documents of Vatican II*, Edited by Walter M. Abbot and Joseph Gallagher, translated by Joseph Gallagher, 637–51. New York: Guild, 1966.

Hughson, Thomas. "Interpreting Vatican II: 'A New Pentecost.'" *Theological Studies* 69, no. 1 (2008) 3–37.

Inter Mirifica, Decree On the Instruments of Social Communication (1963). In *The Documents of Vatican II*, edited by Walter M. Abbot and Joseph Gallagher, translated by Joseph Gallagher, 319–31. New York: Guild, 1966.

John Paul II, Pope. *Dominum et Vivificantem*, Encyclical on the Holy Spirit in the Life of the Church and the World (1986). http://w2.vatican.va/content/john-paul-ii/en/encyclicals/documents/hf_jp-ii_enc_18051986_dominum-et-vivificantem.html. Accessed September 30, 2016.

———. *Redemptoris Missio*, Encyclical on the Permanent Validity of the Church's Missionary Mandate (1990). http://w2.vatican.va/content/john-paul-ii/en/encyclicals/documents/hf_jp-ii_enc_07121990_redemptoris-missio.html. Accessed September 30, 2016.

Kasper, Cardinal Walter. *A Handbook of Spiritual Ecumenism*. Hyde Park, NY: New City, 2007.

Lumen Gentium, Dogmatic Constitution On the Church (1964). In *The Documents of Vatican II*, Edited by Walter M. Abbot and Joseph Gallagher, translated by Joseph Gallagher, 14–101. New York: Guild, 1966.

Matthey, Jacques. "From 1910 to 2010: A Post Edinburgh 2010 Reflection." *International Review of Mission* 99, no. 391 (2010) 258–75.

McBrien, Richard. "Pope John XXIII's Opening Address to the Second Vatican Council." *National Catholic Reporter*, November 5, 2012. http://ncronline.org/blogs/essays-theology/pope-john-xxiiis-opening-address-second-vatican-council. Accessed September 30, 2016.

McDonnell, Kilian. *The Other Hand of God: The Holy Spirit as Universal Touch and Goal*. Michael Glazer Book. Collegeville, MN: Liturgical, 2003.

McGee, Gary B. *Miracles, Missions, & American Pentecostalism*. American Society of Missiology Series 45. Maryknoll, NY: Orbis, 2010.

Motte, Mary, and Joseph R. Lang, eds. *Mission in Dialogue: the SEDOS Research Seminar on the Future of Mission, March 8–19, 1981, Rome, Italy*. New York: Orbis, 1982.

Nnyombi, Richard. "A Catholic Missiological and Ecumenical Appreciation of Together towards Life." *International Review of Mission* 102, no. 397 (2013) 185–90.

Nostra Aetate, Declaration On the Relationship of the Church to Non-Christian Religions (1965). In *The Documents of Vatican II*, edited by Walter M. Abbot and Joseph Gallagher, translated by Joseph Gallagher, 660–68. New York: Guild, 1966.

O'Malley, John. *What Happened at Vatican II?* Cambridge, MA: Belknap, 2008.

Optatam Totius, Decree On Priestly Formation (1965). In *The Documents of Vatican II*, edited by Walter M. Abbot and Joseph Gallagher, translated by Joseph Gallagher, 437–57. New York: Guild, 1966.

Orientalium Ecclesiarum, Decree On the Catholic Churches of the Eastern Rite (1964). In *The Documents of Vatican II*, edited by Walter M. Abbot and Joseph Gallagher, translated by Joseph Gallagher, 373–86. New York: Guild, 1966.

Paul VI, Pope. *Evangelii Nuntiandi*, Apostolic Exhortation on Evangelization in the Modern World (1975). http://w2.vatican.va/content/paul-vi/en/apost_exhortations/documents/hf_p-vi_exh_19751208_evangelii-nuntiandi.html. Accessed September 30, 2016.

Perfectae Caritatis, Decree On the Appropriate Renewal of the Religious Life (1965). In *The Documents of Vatican II*, edited by Walter M. Abbot and Joseph Gallagher, translated by Joseph Gallagher, 466–82. New York: Guild, 1966.

Presbyterorum Ordinis, Decree On the Ministry and Life of Priests (1965). In *The Documents of Vatican II*, edited by Walter M. Abbot and Joseph Gallagher, translated by Joseph Gallagher, 532–76. New York: Guild, 1966.

Rausch, William G., and Jeffrey Gros, eds. *Deepening Communion: International Ecumenical Documents with Roman Catholic Participation*. Washington, DC: United States Catholic Conference, 1998.

Ryan, Tom (website). http://www.tomryancsp.org/news/ProtestantObservers.htm. Accessed September 30, 2016.

Sacrosanctum concilium, Constitution on the Sacred Liturgy (1963). In *The Documents of Vatican II*, edited by Walter M. Abbot and Joseph Gallagher, translated by Joseph Gallagher, 137–78. New York: Guild, 1966.

Scherer, James A., and Stephen Bevans, eds. *New Directions in Mission and Evangelization*. 2 vols. Maryknoll, NY: Orbis, 1992, 1994.

SEDOS. "Catholic Delegated Observers went to prepare the Tenth Assembly in BUSA, Republic of Korea." http://www.sedosmission.org/web/en/component/content/article/25-english/news/46-geneva-catholic-delegated-observers-went-to-prepare-the-tenth-assembly-in-busa-republic-of-korea. Accessed September 30, 2016.

Sivalon, John C. *God's Mission and Postmodern Culture: The Gift of Uncertainty*. Maryknoll, NY: Orbis, 2012.

Smith, Susan. "The Holy Spirit and Mission in Some Contemporary Theologies of Mission." *SEDOS Bulletin* 18, no. 2 (2001) 87–114.

Stoeger, William R. Foreword to *How God Acts: Creation, Redemption, and Special Divine Action*, ix–x. Theology and the Sciences. Minneapolis: Fortress, 2010.

Synod of Bishops. *Justice in the World* (1971). § 6. *Ministerial Priesthood; Justice in the World*. Washington, DC: National Conference of Catholic Bishops, 1972. http://www.shc.edu/theolibrary/resources/synodjw.htm. Accessed September 30, 2016.

Unitatis Redintegratio, Decree on Ecumenism (1964). In *The Documents of Vatican II*, edited by Walter M. Abbot and Joseph Gallagher, translated by Joseph Gallagher, 341–66. New York: Guild, 1966.

"Vatican II after Fifty Years: Dialogue and Catholic Identity." http://www.georgetown.edu/vatican-II-dialogue.html. Accessed September 30, 2016.

World Council of Churches, JWG [Joint Working Group] with Roman Catholic Church. http://www.oikoumene.org/en/what-we-do/jwg-with-roman-catholic-church. Accessed September 30, 2016.

Yong, Amos. *The Spirit of Creation: Modern Science and Divine Action in the Pentecostal-Charismatic Imagination*. Pentecostal Manifestos. Grand Rapids: Eerdmans, 2011.

Missions, Missiology, and Missions History

6

An Overlooked Pillar
The Great Commission in Romans

BENNY C. AKER

FOR SOME TIME NOW I have needed to explore and place in the marketplace what I perceive to be some form of the great commission in Paul's letter to the Romans in 1:1–7. The invitation to contribute to such a worthy cause was an opportunity to develop this text. I count it a great privilege to contribute in some small way to honor and remember such an outstanding lifelong colleague and friend, Dr. Gary B. McGee. This choice of topic is further driven by his academic pursuit of mission history and by an event he experienced with Professor Martin Scharlemann—we were in the same class and the lesson that day dealt with Romans. It was an event that we both talked and laughed about for years.

This essay proposes to identify components of the great commission, especially with the commission in Matthew 28, in Romans 1:4–5 and explore some ramifications for exegesis and missions theology. If what I propose is even close to being right, it should offer some information about Paul and his theology of missions.

Present State of Research: The "Great Commission" in Paul and his Letter to Romans?

It is important to note that scholars, even if they know, certainly have not written about the presence of a commission in Romans 1:1–7 or anywhere in Paul's other letters, let alone any major connection to it, as far as I can discover.[1] Robert L. Plummer notes that "Gustav Warneck, 'the father of

---

1. To mention a few: Barrett, *Romans*; Black, *Romans*; Boring, "The Language of

modern missiology," attempted to found Paul's missionary vision on Jesus's Great Commission (Matt 28:18–20). Evangelical scholars up to the present time have followed in his footsteps." Yet he notes, "[t]he assertion that Paul or the Pauline churches were motivated to missionize by the Great Commission, however, lacks convincing evidence in the Pauline epistles."[2] Against Plummer it is in part correct to say that Paul grounded his missionary vision on the Great Commission, but no explicit connection or elaboration has been forthcoming.

Moreover, Paul Bowers, in an article attempting to address Paul and his mission first notes the "common" expectation:

> Did Paul intend that each new mission congregation should assume a responsibility in its own territory for completing the work which Paul had initiated there, so that, even as the apostle hastened onward in his missionary advance, the mission itself would continue in each region towards the larger goal of granting everyone there a hearing of the gospel and an opportunity to believe (cf. Rom 10.14–15)?[3]

And he notes further in light of this:

> How exactly does Paul view his communities in relation to the spread of the gospel? What is the relation, in Paul's thought, of church and mission? Here we are faced with a peculiar situation. For the Paul who at every turn is himself so preoccupied with active mission to the Gentiles fails nevertheless ever to indicate clearly an independent responsibility in such a mission for his churches. There are hints and debatable allusions, but there is no expression of a clarity comparable, for example, to the missionary commissions handed down in the post-resurrection traditions of the Gospels.[4]

Universal Salvation in Paul"; Cranfield, *Romans*; Dunn, *Romans*; Fitzmyer, *Romans*; Hubbard, *The Matthean Redaction of a Primitive Apostolic Commissioning*, 1–8; Jewett, *Romans: A Commentary*; Jeremias, *Jesus's Promise to the Nations*; Käsemann, *Commentary on Romans*; Lawless, "'To All the Nations': The Great Commission Passages in the Gospels and Acts"; Morosco, "Matthew's Formation of a Commissioning Type-Scene"; Moo, *Romans*; Müller, *Prophetie und Predigt im Neuen Testament*; Murray, *The Epistle to the Romans*; Plummer, "The Great Commission in the New Testament"; Plummer, "A Theological Basis for Church's Mission in Paul"; and Pohill, *Acts*. One would think that such an important issue as this would show up, at least in the major commentaries here listed.

2. Plummer, "A Theological Basis for the Church's Mission in Paul," 254n3: Warneck, *Evangelische Missionslehre*, 1: 91, 183–85. See also Plummer's PhD dissertation, "The Church's Missionary Nature." Noted in Schreiner, *Paul Apostle*, 68n29; Plummer emphasized the power of the spoken word.

3. Bowers, "Church and Mission in Paul," 89.

4. Ibid.

He continues to state that "The peculiarity of the situation merits a closer review of the evidence."[5] However, his research causes him to reject this "common" view.

So did Paul work with a sense of a personal Gentile mission without passing this responsibility on to others, namely to the congregations he founded, or did he somehow just leave that charge, picked up in rather scattered or in other ways, in the hands of those congregations?[6] As noted above, a variety of views exist. In studies on the Great Commission, scholars have explored well its presence in a number of places, usually in the Gospels and Acts. Paul is commonly left out, with allusions to his mission here and there.[7] Even a dictionary article fails to make the connection and certainly no direct connection is made with Romans 1:1-7.[8]

Romans itself has been the focus of a host of Pauline scholars, usually about Paul and justification.[9] Because of Paul's mention of the contents of the gospel in 1:3-4, its Christology has been much discussed, even from the early centuries of the church. In the greetings, both opening and closing, most if not all commentators have mentioned to some degree or another Paul's evangelism or mission techniques. They have also focused on its genre, and it remains an open question even yet.[10] A few have hinted at such a presence of the great commission in Romans. Everett F. Harrison, for

---

5. Ibid., 90.

6. Studies have focused on the dynamic nature of the gospel. Cf. Plummer, "A Theological Basis," 255; Plummer writes: "Possibly the most promising theological basis for the mission of the church (in Paul's letters) can be found in the apostle's references to the gospel. A few scholars have recently noted the importance of the nature of the gospel in Paul's thought—suggesting that the dynamic nature of the gospel is key to understanding what motivated the church to engage in mission. In speaking of the apostle's understanding of 'the dynamic nature of the gospel,' I mean that Paul viewed the gospel (or 'the word of God') as an 'effective force' which inevitably goes forth and accomplishes God's will. The same 'word' that indwells apostles also indwells ordinary Christians in the church." So, Bornkamm, *Paul*, 54: just by preaching it, it will spread automatically, noted in Plummer, "A Theological Basis."

7. Arias and Johnson, *The Great Commission*. In addition, see note 1 above.

8. See Luter, "Great, Commission," 2: 1090-91. He connects the commission more with Colossians. Understandably, the commission is not even listed in Hawthorne, *Dictionary of Paul and His Letters*.

9. Soderlund and Wright, the editors of Gordon Fee's Festschrift, *Romans and the People of God*, write: "Of late, a great deal of scholarly energy has been dedicated to the Interpretation of Paul's letter to the Romans" (ix). Most if not all commentators mention justification in some sense; an example is Boers, *The Justification of the Gentiles*. This is not to forget about the much ink that has been used on the new perspective in Paul issue. See also such discussions: Friedrich, "Muß ὑπακοὴν πίστεως *Röm*1:5," 118-23; and Elliot, "The Language art Style," 124-30.

10. I believe that Jewett comes closer to an appropriate suggestion than others: Jewett, "Romans as an Ambassadorial Letter," 5-20; and Jewett, *Romans*. Cf. Fitzmyer, *Romans*, 68-79, especially 79. See also Donfried, *The Romans Debate*.

one, writes: "He [Paul] is simply doing his duty, fulfilling the commission God in his grace has granted him as a minister of Christ (vv. 15, 16)."[11] At another place he notes: "If Paul were ever to reach Spain, he would no doubt feel that he had realized in his own ministry a measure of fulfillment of the Lord's Great Commission that bade his followers go the ends of the earth (Acts 1:8)."[12] He does write, though, that

> The command of the eternal God points to the Great Commission, which includes all the nations as embraced in the divine purpose (Matt 28:19). This emphasis recalls the language Paul used in speaking of his own commission ([Romans] 1:1, 5; cf. Titus 1:3). Colossians 1:25–27 is in the same vein. Paul had a special concern to reach the Gentiles (11:13).[13]

Craig Keener likewise notes in parentheses about Matt 28:19 ff. that "perhaps Rom 1:5; 16:26 indirectly reflect the tradition Matthew preserves here."[14]

Moreover and pertinent to this lacuna in modern research of the great commission in Paul—is the question—was he a universalist? Some think so, drawing attention to Paul's contradicting statements wherein the apostle at some places wrote that all are lost and in other places all will be saved. M. Eugene Boring, for example, argued that Paul wrote of both positions but that this was a result of his rabbinic-like reasoning (synchronic thinking). He disagreed with the methodology of scholars like U. B. Müller who argued that Paul's thinking developed over time (diachronic) and thus contradictions occurred as his theology changed.[15] However, according to Boring and Müller, Paul was a universalist.[16]

On the other hand, both liberal and conservative scholars think that Paul was particularistic—that Paul believed that some were outside and needed to be brought into the covenant or, to use the language of E.P. Sanders, "needed to convert, to transfer from the old reality to the new by an

---

11. Harrison, "Romans," see especially 14–16; 154–71. This quote comes from 155 where he comments on 15:14–16.

12. Ibid., 158.

13. Ibid., 171; comments on 16:26.

14. Keener, *Gospel of Matthew*, 720.

15. For other views and methodical approaches see Boring, "The Language of Universal Salvation," 269–74. He takes E. P. Sanders as his "principle dialogue partner" in developing his own view, and summarily writes: "My central thesis is that the range of Paul's soteriological language—that is, how inclusive it is—is not determined by propositional systematic consistency [Best, Rissi, and a host of others], nor by his developments in his theology [Dodd, Müller] nor by the tension between depth and surface structures [Beker and Patte], but by the demands of the central encompassing images within which his language functions, images that necessarily involve him in conflicting language games" (274–75).

16. Boring, "The Language of Universal Salvation," 271; Müller, *Prophetie*, 227–30.

act of belief and commitment."[17] Some, like Rudolf Bultmann, believed that Paul used conflicting language, but in the end, by subordinating universalist language, thought that Paul came down on the particularist side. Evangelical scholars, like Thomas R. Schreiner, cogently argue for a straightforward particularistic view, believing that Paul taught that all were sinners and that those who were saved from sin have escaped God's wrath through grace and faith. In particular, Schreiner argues against the universalistic position of Boring's (noted above).[18]

Exploring the "Great" Commission in Romans 1:1–7

While some have developed a *gattung* of a commissioning scene and explored Old Testament and gospel accounts of such in regards to Matthew, especially, such formal elements cannot be applied to Romans 1:1–7. Furthermore, if we find connections between Paul and the Gospels, this would be the earliest extant written evidence of a commission, albeit from a different perspective—as has been often pointed out—each Gospel has a commission in different forms and in slightly different places in the scheme of the gospel story, functioning in differing ways, though all commissions are placed strategically at the climax of the gospels.[19]

Structural Display of Romans 1:1–7[20]

It is helpful to place up front of our exploration a structural display of the opening greeting of Romans, the larger framework for the commission in Paul. I lay out here what I perceive to be an analytical, structural outline.[21]

---

17. Boring's words about Sanders, "The Language of Universal Salvation," 274.

18. Schreiner, *Paul Apostle*, 49–150; and "An Excursus on Universalism in Paul," in ibid., 182–88.

19. Arias, "Church in the World," 410, "It also may come as a surprise to realize that there are at least four different versions of the last commission, one in each gospel. Each version appears in a different context and with a different emphasis (Mark 16:15–18; Luke 24:44–47; John 20:21; cf. 17:18).

20. "In recent years, more has been written about this than about any other New Testament text," Hengel, *The Son of God*, 59, quoted in Hurtado, "Jesus's Divine Sonship," 223.

21. I will provide this in English translation. Byrskog, "Epistolography, Rhetoric and Letter," 28–29, has provided a syntactical analysis for Rom 1:1–7 for the readers benefit.

1. Sender

Paul, v. 1

> *a servant of Christ Jesus, called to be an apostle,* (both nouns [servant and apostle] are in simple apposition and serving as descriptors of the sender[22])

> *set apart for the gospel of God,* (a participle modifying Paul; though syntactically somewhat parallel to the other two it climaxes the identity of Paul; it also and especially points forward, introduces, and directs the next verses)

2. The Gospel in a nutshell (patterned after a pool of Jesus material that, eventually, some of which came to be written in the gospel accounts; they proceed with Jesus: from OT Scripture to his death and resurrection)(these verses modify "gospel of God in v. 1 and define gospel[23])

vv. 2–4

Old Testament promise v. 2

> *² which He promised beforehand through His prophets in the holy Scriptures,*

Life, death, and resurrection of Jesus vv. 3–4 (emphasis upon his Davidic messianic ministry and human state/status leading up to his death; climax of the gospel; emphasis upon Son of God—exalted, glorified state/status, work finished)

> *³ the gospel concerning his Son, who was descended[24] from David according to the flesh*

> *⁴ and was declared to be Son of God with power according to the spirit of holiness by resurrection from the dead, Jesus Christ our Lord,*[25]

---

22. Wallace, *Greek Grammar*, 48–49.

23. Whitsett, "Son of God, Seed of David," 674–75, notes correctly that "concerning his son" modifies "holy writings," not God's gospel. This demonstrates Paul's exegetical technique: "it [concerning his son] is the organizing principle of Paul's exegesis." He argues, correctly, that 2 Sam 7 is behind Rom 1:3 but 2 Sam 7 is rather significant for a number of NT writers. Whitsett looks to Paul's personal exegetical methods. Others place emphasis upon rather fragmented "traditions." See especially ibid., 661, in this regard. The view I espouse is that Paul was aware of larger chunks of material. (The chapter number "2" in his title should be "1.")

24. The birth of Jesus is suggested here, as some have noted, and connection to David certainly echoes Matt 1.

25. It is largely agreed by scholars that Paul used earlier traditions in Rom 1:3–4. I go beyond this view, emphasizing that Paul had in mind a larger amount of material

3. **The Great Commission Applied** (Paul appeals to the Great Commission as has been preserved and transmitted in and through the primitive church and applies it to Roman Christians)

    vv. 5–6

Common call v. 5a (God gives enabling grace and call through Christ Jesus)

⁵ through whom we have received grace and apostleship

Goal of the call v. 5b (equal to the command to disciple all nations—to obey what Jesus commands, cf. Matt 28:19)

to bring about the obedience of faith among all the Gentiles,

Authority v. 5c (Matt 28:18–19—"all authority given me from heaven" and "I am with you always")

for the sake of his name,

Congregational responsibility v. 6 (Gentiles of 5c points to the peoples among whom the Jesus congregations live (6) and sets forth their responsibility to evangelize them)

⁶ including[26] yourselves who are called to belong to Jesus Christ,

4. **Recepients v. 7**

⁷ To all God's beloved in Rome, who are called to be saints: Grace to you and peace from God our Father and the Lord Jesus Christ.[27]

---

about the Jesus traditions than normally thought. Hurtado, "Jesus's Divine Sonship," 220, following Hengel and offering a correction to scholars's reference to Paul's use of "traditions," rightly notes: "[I]f one can find in a writer such as Paul what appear to be remnants of an earlier tradition, these remnants should be subtracted from the data to be used for portraying the religious emphases of the writer whose text(s) one is studying. That is, whatever is judged to be 'tradition' cannot be used to characterize the author's own thought. But surely to identify this procedure is immediately to communicate its absurdity. If a writer incorporates into his/her text without refutation or criticism elements of a tradition, this is surely because the author accepts these elements and indeed regards them as expressive as his/her own thoughts. Consequently, in drawing up the data to be used for characterizing Paul's Christological thought, it is irrelevant whether a given phrase is Paul's own coinage or is appropriated from the wider Christian tradition."

26. This translation is not the best: "among whom" reflects the better sense.

27. NRSV.

So, the commission in Romans 1:5–6, as in the Gospel traditions, occurs immediately after the resurrection of the exalted Jesus as it appears in the climax of each gospel—all that Jesus has done and all that has happened to him up to this point flows significantly into the Great Commission. It is argued cogently that if one wants to know all about the Great Commission, read the Gospel. If one wants to know what the Gospel (or gospel) is about, look at the Great Commission.[28] In like manner, Paul notes the significance of the culmination of the gospel (i.e., Jesus's resurrection) and brings forth the application of this commission after his summary of gospel tradition, connecting this commission with the gospel, explaining the purpose of the gospel, and defining what it is about.[29]

Discussion of the Structural Elements of Romans 1:1–7

Paul, the Sender of the letter v. 1

Παῦλος δοῦλος Χριστοῦ Ἰησοῦ, κλητὸς ἀπόστολος ἀφωρισμένος εἰς εὐαγγέλιον θεοῦ

Paul begins his greeting with three terms which describe him; at least most scholars think that three exist: slave, apostle and having been separated—Samuel Byrskog is typical of many commentators. I argue for the three modifying syntactical units (the last is a participle), but with the third serving as a climax of Paul's identity and clarifying "apostle."[30] This participle serving as

---

28. Arias notes also: "So, if we are serious about understanding Matthew's version of the commission, read it in the context of that gospel. Viewed in context, the 'great commission' is the climax of Matthew's Gospel, 'the summary,' and 'the key to the understanding of the whole Gospel'. In other words, to understand the Gospel of Matthew we must decipher this 'last commission', and, conversely, to understand the 'last commission' we must comprehend the totality of Matthew" (410). Also in others, e.g., LaGrand, "The Earliest Christian Mission," 297, concurs by referring to Michel, "The Conclusion of Matthew's Gospel," 297: "[T]he whole Gospel was written under this theological premise of Matt 28:18–20 . . . is the key to understanding of the whole book." And Brooks, "Matthew 28:16–20," 298: "[F]ollowing different lines of analysis, similarly declares that 'the concluding pericope (xxviii 16–20) has controlled the entire design of the Gospel of Matthew . . . The chiasmic order of this concluding summary is fundamental.'"

29. This is where I go beyond the traditional view of these verses. Dunn, *The Theology of Paul*, 174–75, 186, 187–95; commenting on Rom 1: 2–4, points in this direction by observing that Paul summarized the life and ministry of Jesus (cf. Peter also in Acts 10:34–43). On page 175: "[F]irst churches would inevitably develop such summaries in the preaching, catechesis, and worship." Interestingly, Dunn has little to write about Paul and his mission/evangelizing, though he is excellent in other matters.

30. In this greeting, two head nouns—slave and apostle—that modify "Paul" are

an adjectival clause modifying Paul, however, is important in a special way. Paul quickly moves to the gospel after introducing himself and his association with it. By the way Paul structures his greeting, he does two things. One, he defines himself in terms of his relationship with Christ Jesus—"slave of Christ Jesus"—and his ministry—"called apostle." More so, he wants to be clear about what "called" apostle means. "Called" is a verbal adjective specifying the meaning of "apostle" and denoting a divine setting Paul apart as a special servant who proclaims the gospel message and establishes communities who follow Jesus.[31] As such, his ministry is an itinerant one.

Two, in climax of his self-identity and in anticipation of the definition of the gospel in the next verses, Paul sets forth in clear language that "apostle" is one who has been "marked off." The Greek word here is ἀφωρισμένος[32] ("set apart" or "marked off" is better and carries a stronger sense) and it is a perfect, passive participle functioning as an adjectival clause particularizing "apostle" though modifying Paul.[33] As such it is adjectival restricting (ascriptive) "apostle" to this certain ministry—as opposed to any other— "having been set apart." "Called" in front of the noun (apostle) strengthens this view. It is appropriate to see this passive participle a divine passive— i.e., it is Christ Jesus who has set Paul apart and Paul is thus a servant of the gospel—a gospel distinguished by prophetic and divine means. Paul's use of this word rhetorically connects his setting apart with the "declaring/ marking off" of Jesus and his redemptive mission in 1:4 (ὁρισθέντος). This opening identification is crucial, not only for the greeting contents but for the entire letter. The "gospel of God" in this clause becomes the heart of the entire letter about which we will have more to say. The lengthy opening

---

followed by a participle. Though a participle can function as a noun it is best to take this participle as adjectival modifying the noun "Paul." Wallace, *Greek Grammar*, 48n41, writes: "An apposition [what we have here], strictly speaking, is *substantival*, [sic] not adjectival. Thus, adjectives or participles in second attributive position are not generally appositives, but usually have an adjectival force." Editors of Greek texts also consider that this participial clause modifies "apostle," also by placing no comma after "apostle," as no comma is placed after "slave" and before "Christ Jesus." See for instance: UBS 4th edition and Nestle's 25th edition of *Novum Testamentum*. Thus Cranfield, *Romans*, 1:53, who takes all three as being in apposition to Paul.

31. Most translators/commentators lose the significance of this verbal adjective by translating κλητὸς as "called to be," e.g., NRSV.

32. ἀφωρισμένος in Gal 1:15 is parallel with "called" and associated with Paul's call to evangelize. See Acts 13:2 where the Holy Spirit separates Paul and Barnabas unto the work (i.e., evangelization) for which he *had called* them.

33. It could be argued that this is a perfect participle functioning as a noun and in parallel with the other two that are nouns. However, these three elements together describe the person, Paul. It is for this reason I think of it as a perfect participle functioning as an adjective describing an ongoing status.

greeting, as has so often and still is believed, is necessary to introduce Paul since he has never been to Rome. However, this is not necessarily entirely the case. The lengthy greeting sets forth the gospel of God: 1) what it is, 2) what its theological and practical implications are, and especially, 3) the responsibility of believers to its call.

The Gospel in a Nutshell vv. 2–4

Old Testament announcements v. 2

ὃ προεπηγγείλατο διὰ τῶν προφητῶν αὐτοῦ ἐν γραφαῖς ἁγίαις

While all the Gospels connect Jesus to the Old Testament, Matthew's Gospel is useful with which to illustrate. Matt chapters 1–2 in midrashic form (like Paul in Romans 1) connect the early life and events of Jesus with Old Testament texts to explain Jesus's life and importance for Israel and the world.[34] Likewise, Paul in highly summary fashion follows what was known among Jesus congregations (along with his exegesis) and written later in the Gospels by connecting Jesus to OT texts. Paul in v. 2 defines the gospel by connecting it[35] (Christ Jesus) with the OT via an adjectival, relative pronoun clause modifying "gospel of God" in v. 1.

The Gospel: The life, death, and resurrection of Jesus the Messiah, God's Son vv. 3–4

περὶ τοῦ υἱοῦ αὐτοῦ τοῦ γενομένου ἐκ σπέρματος Δαυὶδ κατὰ σάρκα, τοῦ ὁρισθέντος υἱοῦ θεοῦ ἐν δυνάμει κατὰ πνεῦμα ἁγιωσύνης ἐξ ἀναστάσεως νεκρῶν, Ἰησοῦ Χριστοῦ τοῦ κυρίου ἡμῶν,

The gospel is Jesus—his life and ministry—as summed up in this verse with emphasis upon David's lineage according to the flesh. That this encompasses Jesus's death as the Messiah, connecting Jesus with David, is suggested strongly by the closely followed resurrection statement.[36] By including

---

34. It should go without saying, perhaps, that each Gospel connects Jesus to the Old Testament.

35. The relative pronoun is singular, neuter—thus "it" is appropriate, though Jesus is its intended focus. Of course its antecedent noun is neuter, so it too is neuter. But as we will see, gospel (*euaggelion*) is much more involved—it pertains to a comprehensive community life under God affected by his Son, Jesus.

36. This is intended by the co-text in which Jesus and God are connected—see Hurtado, "Jesus's Divine Sonship."

David, the long awaited king's son, Paul intends to connect Jesus with the messianic work of redemption.[37] Though Abraham is not mentioned here, he and David are important in the theology of Romans (cf. chap. 4). They are also important in the Gospels as well, especially Matthew and Luke.[38] This insight strengthens the high probability that Paul had embraced the teachings of Jesus from others in the primitive community and had worked them out through exegesis of the scriptures. He was now bringing them to bear on the Roman situation.

The Great Commission Applied vv 5-6

δι' οὗ ἐλάβομεν χάριν καὶ ἀποστολὴν εἰς ὑπακοὴν πίστεως ἐν πᾶσιν τοῖς ἔθνεσιν ὑπὲρ τοῦ ὀνόματος αὐτοῦ, ἐν οἷς ἐστε καὶ ὑμεῖς κλητοὶ Ἰησοῦ Χριστοῦ, πᾶσιν τοῖς οὖσιν ἐν Ῥώμῃ ἀγαπητοῖς θεοῦ, κλητοῖς ἁγίοις, χάρις ὑμῖν καὶ εἰρήνη ἀπὸ θεοῦ πατρὸς ἡμῶν καὶ κυρίου Ἰησοῦ Χριστοῦ

What is striking about these verses is language (1:5-6) that has the semantic ring about it similar to Matthew's Great Commission in 28:19-20a. *"Through whom we have received grace and apostleship to bring about the obedience of faith among all the Gentiles"* echoes strongly *"Go therefore and make disciples of all nations, baptizing them in the name of the Father and of the Son and of the Holy Spirit, and teaching them to obey everything that I have commanded you."*

It is clear that key ideas and terms appear in each text: "obedience," "making disciples/teaching them/obedience of faith," "behalf of his name," and "Gentiles." It is also clear that Paul is including himself in Romans as "having received" (ἐλάβομεν [39]) this "call through Jesus Christ." So, the per-

---

37. I am aware of the tremendous amount of scholarly work and views on the Christology of this section, which I think detracts from the point in this study. And space does not allow me to proceed in discussing them. Jipp, "Ancient, Modern, and Future Interpretations," 242-42. Hurtado makes the point well. I refer the reader to his "Jesus's Divine Sonship," 221-28, where he cogently and summarily says that the divinity of Jesus is clearly in mind in Rom1:3-4. He gives three major points, the third is most important for us here: "[D]ivine rhetoric is also used to link the salvation of the elect with the status of Jesus," 223.

38. LaGrand, "'The Earliest Christian Mission," 212; LaGrand stresses this point; also see Schreiner, *Paul Apostle*, in contrast to some scholars, believes that the Pauline letters assumed that Jesus played a prominent role as David's promised heir: "[T]he natural answer is that Paul argued extensively that Jesus was the promised Messiah when he evangelized the churches" 76-77. Schreiner, *New Testament Theology*, 318-20.

39. ἐλάβομεν is translated as a perfective aorist. The results of the reception are still in effect and have not been altered.

spective is different, coming from the view of a receiver rather than that of the Giver. The more formal categorical elements I have provided above.[40]

Paul's introduction, "through whom,"[41] modifies "*Jesus Christ Lord*" and echoes the risen Lord giving his commission—"all power is given unto me" in Matthew 28:18 and manifests the Christology of the hymn of Philippians 2:6–11. That hymn concludes celebrating the resurrection with "Every tongue may confess that *Jesus Christ is Lord* to the glory of the Father." Though one cannot help but see in Paul references to his conversion that are recorded in Acts, here in Rom 1:5–6 he appeals to the commission that derives from the pre-ascension Lord himself. (It has been noted that these conversion experiences are as much or more so a "call to mission" as a "conversion.") He does that to make sure all believers are united in the same call from the Lord to evangelize all people groups.

This is further substantiated with the inclusive "we" in "we have received." The problem is how to take "we." Many scholars understand "we" as a literary plural (referring only to Paul), noting the special call that Paul had received. What I argue suggests otherwise.

Let us first note the various theories about the interpretation of "we."[42] Byrskog lists four uses of "we" in letters: 1) *pluralis sociativus*— when it includes the addressees, 2) when it refers to a special group within the larger

---

40. Lawless, "'To All the Nations,'" 17, after analyzing the various commissions in the Gospels, not noting Romans, gives three formal characteristics of them: authority of Christ, 1) command to make disciples, 2) primacy of proclamation, and 3) empowerment of disciples.

41. Though with the passive, it is likely that Paul intends Jesus and God to be involved—this is the way Paul connects Jesus Christ and God in the context. See Hurtado, "Jesus's Divine Sonship"; translations usually leave out this aspect of the participle. This verb is passive in only two places in the NT, here and in 2 Cor 6:17 where the passive is brought out. This is certainly the case as the διa (*dia*) with the genitive case in v. 5 brings out: Jesus is the mediating Person; it is God the Father who is the Originator of the call. This fact echoes John 5:21–30, where the Father and the Son work together to bring life.

42. Byrskog, "Co-Senders, Co-Authors," 232–33. For his discussion of the history of investigation see 230–36. For additional views, see Jewett, *Romans*, 108–9. See similarly Harrison, "Romans," 15. Bowers, "Church and Mission in Paul," 93, argues "Paul, it must be remembered, traces back his own involvement in Gentile mission not to something commonly implicit in the believer's experience of Christ, but to a quite personal summons. He does not account for his vocation by explaining it as something natural to Christian experience but by explaining it as something quite particular to his own experience (e.g. 1 Thess 2.4; Gal 1.15, 16; 2.7–9; Rom 1.5, 6; 15.15, 16; Col 1.23). When, therefore, one comes upon passages where Paul appears to represent his own missionary activity as something appropriate to all who are Christ's, one must proceed cautiously." See also his entire article; many points are made but we cannot go into them all here. "However vital to Paul's own mission the founding of churches was, nowhere in Paul do we get even a hint that his churches were to participate in founding additional churches" (95). He investigates Romans very little.

group being addressed, 3) when workers with Paul are included, and 4) when the writer uses the literary plural. The most prominent and abiding view is the last one. Paul is addressing all the church here so it cannot be #2, nor can it be #3.[43] However in light of this being the Great Commission, he is including all of the believers in Rome in the Great Commission. (It is not unusual for there to be only one sender in letters at large.) It does not, therefore, need to be #4. Scholars from various traditions argue from an ecclesiastical position saying that the apostle was unique and the only office to evangelize, leaving out "laypersons."

Others note, in addition, that the obedience to evangelize did not arrive out of a common religious experience—that is, it did not come because Paul and other believers had the same kind of faith experience—Paul's unique standing as an apostle who was dedicated to the gospel came in a special way. What this view propounds, then, is that the responsibility to evangelize does not lie in the conversion experience common to all, but rather it lies in a special office or experience that only some have. We note in this Romans opening greeting, however, that Paul roots his call to evangelize in the same experience and calling as that of other believers—"through whom" of v. 5 has as its antecedent "Jesus Christ our Lord" of v. 4 (i.e., as above, Paul appeals more to the Great Commission given by Jesus than to his own conversion/call recorded in Acts). The "our" just mentioned is commensurate with the "we" of "through whom we have received" in v. 5.

In particular, the main phrase that is approximate to the commission in Matthew (et al.) is Rom 1:5: "to bring about the obedience of faith among all the Gentiles." "Obedience of faith" is roughly equal to Matthew's "make disciples of all nations and teach them to obey." "Obedience of faith" has been much discussed.[44] Its locus of meaning can be found especially in Rom 6 and 8. Faith in Jesus and identification with Jesus in all aspects of his suffering, death, burial, and resurrection produces the kind of life that Rom 1:16–17 describe. By identifying with Jesus in all these aspects, the believer

---

43. Against Jewett, *Romans*.
44. See MacLeod, "Eternal Son, Davidic Son," 76–94, esp. 92n80, who says:

> Seven interpretations have been suggested for the expression "obedience of faith" (ὑπακοὴν πίστεως). (1) "Obedience to the faith," that is, obedience in the sense of accepting the faith as the body of doctrine. However, the phrase does not have the article "the" before the word "faith." (2) "Obedience to the authority of faith." (3) "Obedience to God's faithfulness as tested in the gospel." (4) "The obedience which faith works." (5) "Obedience which faith demands," or "the obedience required by faith," as opposed to the obedience demanded or required by the Law (Black, *Romans*, 38). (6) "Believing obedience," that is, "obedience which is the product of faith." (Garlington, "The Obedience of Faith," 201–24; and Schreiner, *Romans*, 35). (7) "The faith which consists of obedience."

is free to present himself/herself as priestly servants to serve God in the community of faith and in society at large (6:13–14, 12:1–8). What Paul does is to combine faith with obedience to illustrate the successful transformation that glorifies God and not law works that glorify human nature. Paul and Matthew are similar in their understanding of discipleship.

Another phrase that is important to explore is "grace and apostleship" in 1:5. I submit that this is a hendiadys: grace and apostleship (χάριν καὶ ἀποστολὴν). The two nouns are connected with a simple "and"—both nouns are anarthrous (without the article). The meaning would be: apostolic grace. "Apostolic" pertains to the kind of enabling "grace." It is God's gracious call and enablement of believers to bring about obedience of faith among all the nations. The responsibility to mature believers in this Christian life lies also with each believer, perhaps more emphasis upon the community of believers. "Apostleship" (*apostolēn*) occurs four times in the NT: Acts 1:25; Rom 1:5; 1 Cor 9:2; Gal 2:8 (Gal most closely resembles Rom). In each case it refers to the office or work of evangelism among people groups. This work includes what the Gospels call "making disciples." This enabling for missions echoes the commission and context in Acts 1:8.

The meaning of "nations" (*ethnē*) here needs some clarification. Both in Matthew 28:19 and Romans 1:5 it is best to understand it to refer to people groups rather than "nations" as in a national sense.[45] Scholars, generally, now take *ethnē* in the sense of people groups.[46] If this is so, then the theory that Romans was written to primarily a Gentile audience does not necessarily hold.

"Among whom you are also the called of Jesus Christ" in v. 6 is part of the commission to the Roman Christians and Paul subtly reminds them that they are in the middle of "missions" territory (*ethnē*).[47] Robert Jewett appropriately concludes that Paul uses ambassadorial language in Romans in his appeal to solicit assistance in his mission to the West.[48] The language of an ambassador here does fit an ingratiating manner of appeal. With the addition of this clause, and with the inclusion of "our" and "we" above, this establishes a mutual responsibility contained in the commission.

Other vocabulary in the greeting also points to a partnership between Paul and the Roman Christians. "Called" (*klētos/oi*) describes Paul (v. 1)

---

45. Later in Romans, Paul uses several people groups that are included under this term (*ethnē*) as well as ethnic distinction: Jew/Gentile (non-Jew).

46. See LaGrand, "The Earliest Christian Mission," 46–57, for the discussion of problems with what "nations" means.

47. Contra Cranfield, *Romans*, 1:67–68.

48. See Jewett, "Romans as an Ambassadorial Letter," 5–20; and Jewett, *Romans*, 44–46.

and the Roman Christians (vv. 6, 7). Note the presence and placement of "also" (*kai*) in the clause, placing the Roman believers alongside of Paul (v. 6). God and the Lord Jesus Christ (v. 7) are associated with both Paul and the Christians ("our" v. 7).

This observation points in the direction of Paul's mission strategy based on the Great Commission. As scholars have noted, Paul had a unique call to be an apostle, i.e., as a missionary to people groups. His was an itinerant ministry. But this called for assistance in the commission task. He would plant churches and mature them to be evangelists to the area around them, and then he would move on to the next unreached area. So, they all were involved in the carrying out of the commission but in different yet complimentary ways.

There is one thing in Romans 1:5–6 that does not occur, unlike in Matthew's Great Commission, and that is "baptizing." However, this is commensurate with Pauline mission strategy—his goal was not to baptize (cf. 1 Cor 1:13–17).[49] Yet, baptism does play a role in Romans 6 where it becomes a "theological" symbol for interpreting the death and resurrection of Jesus: by faith the believer must identify with Jesus's dying, burial, coming to life, and the process of living in sacred service. This is understood if Paul wrote this letter as a mission maturing document and a basis for Christian life.

One other thing in the commissions, especially Matthew's, that does not occur in Romans is a Trinitarian formula in baptism. The binitarian language of Romans's opening greeting has been noted (the unusual term in 1:4 "spirit of holiness," notwithstanding). However, Paul in Romans places a great deal of emphasis on the Spirit in chapter 8 (Spirit chapter of the Bible), and that chapter is connected with chapter 6. The theological activities driven by faith in chapter 6 must be thought of and experienced along with the presentation of the Spirit in chapter 8. Note that in Rom 8:9 it is the *Spirit of Christ* that dwells in the believer. The Spirit is "the Spirit of life that is in Jesus" (8:2). The role of the Spirit is most vitally connected with the new covenant—without the Spirit there is no new covenant, and without Jesus and his work there is no activity of the Spirit, and quite likely the new covenant is in view throughout chapters 6–8.[50] The baptismal formula situation in Romans may reflect the early one in Acts 2 where new believers were baptized in "Jesus's name."

---

49. See Dunn, *The Theology of Paul*, 453.

50. This is suggested by Wright, *The Climax of the Covenant*, 195, and others as opposed to Dunn.

The Gospel

It is now appropriate to discuss what the "gospel" (*euangelion*) means. The noun "gospel" is especially a Pauline term and (proportionally or not) occurs more times in Romans (9 times in 432 verses) than in any other letter or gospel. It occurs 3 times in chapter one alone. It occurs in 1:1 as: "gospel of God." There is no article, which suggests that the term takes on a breadth of significant meaning. That is, Paul is entirely devoted to it and the way he connects everything to it from that verse on covers much territory. Even when we extend our focus beyond the first seven verses to the full *exordium* (or for some, the *narratio*, see below) (vv. 1–15) as we do, it is worth noting that the *exordium* should state in condensed form the central matters of the entire speech.[51] The gospel of God directs the whole of Romans and is God's plan for the ages, centering on his Son—his person, status, function, and goal. The verb form occurs three times in Romans: 1:15, 10:15, and 15:20. Many scholars emphasize that "gospel" is proclamation. When we look more closely, however, "gospel" (both verb and noun forms) takes on a different cast. It becomes the term in appropriate contexts for the comprehensive plan of God centered in the person of his Son: from the "foundation of the world" to its *telos*, the consummation of time. Already, some have pointed in this direction: Joseph Fitzmyer has also expanded it, as has Schreiner.[52] Bowers captures the sense of "gospel" well for Paul and for our assessment in Romans in particular:

> Assuredly proclamation had a primal status in Paul's sense of mission, as his characteristic terminology suggests. And yet from the larger body of evidence it is equally apparent that Paul's evangelic mission embraced for him very much more than mere oral activity stage by stage throughout the world. That the gospel had been heard was not by any means enough for the apostle. He expected more before the parousia, and he attempted more.[53]

In the next part of the letter, the *narratio*,[54] Paul expresses more fully his intentions in the gospel. His service to God in the gospel of his Son is to pray that at last he may come to them. He has planned for some time

---

51. Byrskog, "Epistolography, Rhetoric and Letter Prescript," 40.

52. Fitzmyer, "The Gospel in the Theology of Paul," *Interpretation*, 339–50, later appearing in *To Advance the Gospel*, 149–61. Schreiner, *Paul Apostle*, 66–69, in regards to other Pauline epistles. Dunn, *The Theology of Paul the Apostle*, 634–35.

53. Bowers, "Fulfilling the Gospel," *Interpretation*, 186. The entire article speaks to this fact.

54. This word comes from the field of rhetoric and it includes the part of the epistle that contains his case or cause.

to come so that he may strengthen them, that both they and he may be mutually strengthened in faith. "Thus," he concludes at v. 15, "I may evangelize" "you" who are in Rome. Why does he want to "preach the gospel" to them if they are believers (cf. 1:1–7)? How does this relate to his desire to strengthen them and to build their faith? And how does this strengthen his faith? In his longing to be with them, he wants to impart[55] some spiritual gift which accomplishes this. Paul's statement here is vague (to us?) and stated generally. Scholars have not quite known what to make of it.

Our suggestion about the great commission and the meaning of "gospel" (*euaggelion*) here in Romans makes sense of this interpretation in light of this *narratio*. Paul wants to nurture them through teaching (discipleship) so that they would be stable and mature in the faith and able to evangelize the peoples around them—and to help him and others in their mission itinerary ventures. It should be noted at this point that, if this is the case, the great commission should be at the heart of every congregation's identity and mission statement. Romans is a highly integrated, interpretative theological reflection and assessment of Jesus and his work with roots in the earliest foundational teachings and traditions of and about Jesus. The letter itself should then be perceived as a "discipleship" and mission training document providing a theological foundation and an explanation of Jesus (as well as soliciting support for his trip to the West). In case Paul did not get to Rome—this document served the purpose—and served as "some spiritual gift."[56] To put it another way—Paul was moving to the West where no apostle had been, and he wanted the congregations in the West to have the same foundational and primitive teachings (i.e., from Palestinian sources) in theological/interpretative form. This is certainly his desire—the unity of the faith, as noted in the letter to the Ephesians—but first in Rome.

Great Commission in other Places in Romans

We have waited until now to discuss other places where elements of the commission occur in Romans. We have noted that it appears first in the opening greeting, an intentionally long one, unusual among letters. It is

---

55. "Impart" may not be a good word to use here because some renewalists (and some Evangelicals) from the Charismatic and Pentecostal traditions take this word in the sense of laying on of hands and "giving" people something.

56. See Longenecker, "The Focus of Romans," 49–50. He refers to Fee, *God's Empowering Presence*, 486–89, which I reference above. Of note, Longenecker, "The Focus of Romans," 50, believes that the central thrust of the letter is not to be found in 1:17—4:25 but in the reference in his title. Longenecker, as with many others, have overlooked the import of the text of the thesis of this work.

no secret that Paul has included a number of changes in the letter form in Romans, most of which can be noted that they "catch" the ear of the listener and the eye of the reader.[57] Studies involving oral and written rhetoric with letter forms have increased, clarifying possibilities, especially, regarding the study of Romans. Letters in antiquity functioned in a number of ways, which makes it difficult to determine the exact purpose and form of Romans in particular. But the reality of persuasion via written rhetoric has pointed in helpful directions. And the Pauline uniqueness resulting from these changes adds to the suggestion that this letter encompassed a commission to evangelize (in the sense of the word above) and to stabilize believers, and for them to be able to do so from the heart.

The rhetorical development of the letter reveals that what has appeared in the *exordium* (1:1–7 or 1:1–15) has been emphasized by appearing again in the *peroratio* in an expanded form.[58] Byrskog, arguing against Wilhelm Wueller and J. K. Elliot has restricted himself to Romans and the first seven verses of the greeting.[59] In so doing, he has shortened the focus of the study of the *exordium*, which covers vv. 1–15 (or 17) to 1:1–7. We have focused on 1:1–7, too, but, by necessity of the contents of vv. 8–15, we have extended the discussion to include them. This extension was necessary because Paul pursued in more detail what he began in the presentation of the gospel and the commission of 1–7:

But the *peroratio* in the rhetorical letter form of Romans summarizes, repeats, and expands what was in the *exordium* (1:1–15) especially. The *peroratio* begins at 15:14 where Paul mentions that he wrote earlier about his missionary responsibilities and ventures. It is in this way that we find an even more condensed form of the commission, at which Keener hinted and noted in the beginning of this chapter. It is in 16:25–27.[60] The appropriate clause is in v. 26: ". . . having been made known [my gospel and preaching] for (*eis*) obedience of faith unto (*eis*) all the people groups (*ethnē*)." Other

---

57. Byrskog, "Epistolography, Rhetoric and Letter Prescript," 40, notes that "[t]he rhetorically trained hearers/readers of Romans knew apparently what was at stake when coming across such an extended letter opening as in other *exordia* of some length, the author/speaker needed to argue his case strongly and was, accordingly, concerned to win the audience's favour already from the start."

58. Ibid., 43: "The *peroratio* could, of course, take many different forms. But it should always be clearly connected with the *exordium*."

59. Ibid., 27–28. Wuellner, "Paul's Rhetoric of Argumentation," 128–46; and Elliott, *The Rhetoric of Romans*, 70–86.

60. I am aware of the many difficulties and proposed solutions involved in the text of the *peroratio*. Many scholars now give credence to the unity of Romans. The presence of the commission elements in these last verses supports this claim. They provide a sort of inclusion of Romans.

words that belong to the commission, especially as it occurs in the *exordium* are (v. 25) "strengthen," "prophetic scriptures," and "commandment of the eternal God." A shorter phrase occurring earlier in the *peroratio* and equivalent to the fuller one in 16:26 and 1:5 is (εἰς ὑπακοὴν ἐθνῶν) "unto obedience of the people groups." The occurrence of this phrase and its closely associated terms occur only in Romans and in its commission contexts. ("Unto obedience" is in 6:16; "obedience" is a key term in chapter 6.)

Several items need brief discussion. One of these is an elaboration of the word "gospel," previously discussed. "My *gospel* and the *preaching* of Jesus Christ" in 16:25 and its carrying forward in v. 26 emphasizes "proclamation." But we have to take this into consideration in light of Paul's statement in v. 25, which also occurs in the section following 1:1–7 at 1:11. He states that he has wanted to see them, to impart some spiritual gift *to strengthen* them. In 16:25 he is praising God who is able *to strengthen* them according to what he has delivered to them. "Strengthen" is part of the work of the gospel and Paul's work as an apostle—he has given them this letter and wants to come to them, but as yet they are not yet strengthened (i.e., discipled) or grounded in the faith with the commission at the congregations's center (Apparently, the congregations still lack unity, for one thing, cf. chps. 12–15).

A second item is this. What is meant by his statement in 15:19–20—that "from Jerusalem all the way around to Illyricum the gospel has been fulfilled." Scholars are not yet settled as to the meaning of this statement.[61] In particular, what does "fulfill" mean? Frederick William Danker is influential with his definition of "fulfill": "*bring* (the preaching of) *the gospel to completion* [sic] by proclaiming it in the most remote areas Ro 15:19."[62] I suggest that what Paul meant with this statement is that he had planted churches and had trained/matured them so as to be able to continue on as self-sufficient communities and to do the work of church planting in their surrounding areas, thus finishing their part of the Great Commission. 15:20 rounds out the meaning of evangel/gospel with a construction metaphor. He goes where the gospel has not been preached—and proclaims it, i.e., lays a foundation and then builds on it. Now, in Rome, he wants to do the same.

---

61. Note just a few translations regarding this. ESV has "have fulfilled the ministry of the gospel of Christ"; NAS, "have fully preached the gospel of Christ"; NIV, "have fully proclaimed the gospel of Christ"; and NRS "have fully proclaimed the good news of Christ." The ESV has captured best the sense of the clause πεπληρωκέναι τὸ εὐαγγέλιον τοῦ Χριστοῦ, containing τὸ εὐαγγέλιον (*euaggelion*/gospel). "Ministry" is still somewhat vague but it captures Paul's sense of "some spiritual gift." The others emphasize "proclamation."

62. Bauer, "*plērow*," 828; italics and bold in original.

Conclusion

Much more could be written but we come now to conclude with these remarks. If what we have proposed is correct, some interpretive and theological issues about Romans and the early church have been resolved. And the implications can be great for the church. Paul was not a universalist, and, having a great concern for spreading the gospel, he laid it out in his "chief" letter. He set out what he perceives to be the way to maturity in the gospel. The entire epistle should be read in this light. This makes sense, for example, just in looking at the first major part of the letter. He spends much time and rhetoric, even, to establish universal and total depravity. This is the building block of missions. Unless one knows and believes that every human is lost and why they are lost, it is not likely that, that person will be concerned with either proclaiming or living out the gospel. For sure, this explains the grounds and necessity for the coming of Jesus, God's gospel. Furthermore, its place in the canon may give evidence of this being a "chief" letter.[63] Romans stands first in front of all the NT letters. If this reasoning is correct, the primitive and early Church noted the implications of what I have argued here.

Bibliography

Arias, Mortimer. "Church in the World: Rethinking the Great Commission." *Theology Today* 7, no. 4 (1991) 410–18.

Arias, Mortimer, and Alan Johnson. *The Great Commission: Biblical Models for Evangelism*. Nashville: Abingdon, 1992.

Barrett, C. K. *The Epistle to the Romans*. Harper's New Testament Commentaries. New York: Harper & Row, 1957.

Bauer, Walter, et al. "*plērow*." In *A Greek-English Lexicon of the New Testament and other Early Christian Literature*, revised and edited by Frederick William Danker, 827–29. 3rd ed. Chicago: University of Chicago Press, 2000.

Black, Matthew. *Romans*. New Century Bible. 1973. Reprint, Greenwood, SC: Attic, 1977.

Boers, Hendrickus. *The Justification of the Gentiles: Paul's Letters to Galatians and Romans*. Peabody, MA: Hendrickson, 1994.

Boring, M. Eugene. "The Language of Universal Salvation in Paul." *Journal of Biblical Literature* 105, no. 2 (1986) 269–92.

Bornkamm, Günther. *Paul*. Translated by D. M. G. Stalker. Minneapolis: Fortress, 1995.

Bowers, Paul. "Church and Mission in Paul." *Journal for the Study of the New Testament* 44 (1991) 89–111.

———. "Fulfilling the Gospel: The Scope of the Pauline Mission." *Journal of the Evangelical Theological Society* 30, no. 2 (1987) 185–98.

---

63. See Goswell, "Two Testaments in Parallel," 459–74.

Brooks, O. S., Sr. "Matthew 28:16–20 and the Design of the First Gospel." *Journal for the Study of the New Testament* 10 (1981) 2–18.

Byrskog, Samuel. "Co-Senders, Co-Authors and Paul's Use of the First Person Plural." *Zeitschrift für Die Neutestamentliche Wissenschaft* 87, nos. 3–4 (1996) 230–50.

———. "Epistolography, Rhetoric and Letter Prescript: Romans 1:1–7 as a Test Case." *Journal for the Study of the New Testament* 65 (1997) 27–46.

Cranfield, C. E. B. *A Critical and Exegetical Commentary on the Epistle to the Romans*, Vol. 1. International Critical Commentary. Edinburgh: T. & T. Clark, 1975.

Donfried, Karl P., ed. *The Romans Debate*. 2nd ed. Peabody, MA: Hendrickson, 2001.

Dunn, J. D. G. *The Theology of Paul the Apostle*. Grand Rapids: Eerdmans, 1998.

———. *Romans 1–8* and *Romans 9–16*. Word Biblical Commentary 38A–38B. Waco, TX: Word, 1988.

Elliot, J. K. "The Language art Style of the Concluding Doxology to the Epistle to the Romans." *Zeitschrift für Die Neutestamentliche Wissenschaft* 72 (1981) 124–30.

———. *The Rhetoric of Romans: Argumentative Constraint and Strategy and Paul's Dialogue with Judaism*. Journal for the Study of the New Testament Supplement 45. Sheffield, UK: JSOT, 1990.

Fee, Gordon D. *God's Empowering Presence: The Holy Spirit in the Letters of Paul*. Peabody, MA: Hendrickson, 1994.

Fitzmyer, Joseph A. *Romans*. Anchor Bible. NY: Doubleday, 1993.

———. "The Gospel in the Theology of Paul." In *To Advance the Gospel: New Testament Studies*, 149–61. New York: Crossroad, 1981.

———. "The Gospel in the Theology of Paul." *Interpretation* 33, no. 4 (1992) 339–50.

———. *Romans*. Anchor Bible. NY: Doubleday, 1993.

Friedrich, Gerhard. "Muß ὑπακοὴν πίστεως Röm1:5 'Glaubensgehoram' übersetzt werden?" *Zeitschrift für Die Neutestamentliche Wissenschaft* 72, nos. 1–2 (1981) 118–23.

Garlington, Don B. "The Obedience of Faith in the Letter to the Romans." *Westminster Theological Journal* 52, no. 2 (1990) 201–24.

Goswell, Gregory. "Two Testaments in Parallel: The Influence of the Old Testament on the Structuring of the New Testament Canon." *Journal of the Evangelical Theological Society* 56, no. 3 (2013) 459–74

Harrison, Everett F. "Romans." In *The Expositor's Bible Commentary: Vol. 10 Romans through Galatians*, 1–171. Grand Rapids: Zondervan, 1976.

Hawthorne, Gerald F., et al., eds. *Dictionary of Paul and His Letters*. Downers Grove, IL: InterVarsity, 1993.

Hengel, Martin. *The Son of God: The Origin of Christology and the History of Jewish-Hellenistic Religion*. Translated by John Bowden. Rev. ed. Philadelphia: Fortress, 1977.

Hubbard, Benjamin J. *The Matthean Redaction of a Primitive Apostolic Commissioning: An Exegesis of Matthew 28:16–20*. Society of Biblical Literature Dissertation Series 19. Missoula, MT: Scholars, 1974.

Hurtado, L. W. "Jesus's Divine Sonship in Paul's Epistle to the Romans." In *Romans & the People of God*, edited by Sven K. Soderlund and N. T. Wright, 217–33. Grand Rapids: Eerdmans, 1999.

Jeremias, Joachim. *Jesus's Promise to the Nations*. Translated by S. H. Hooke. London: SCM, 1958.

Jewett, Robert. *Romans: A Commentary*. Minneapolis: Fortress, 2007.

———. "Romans as an Ambassadorial Letter." *Interpretation* 36, no. 1 (1982) 5–20.

Jipp, Joshua W. "Ancient, Modern, and Future Interpretations of Romans 1:3–4: Reception History and Biblical Interpretation." *Journal of Theological Interpretation* 3, no. 2 (2009) 241–59.

Käsemann, Ernst. *Commentary on Romans*. Grand Rapids: Eerdmans, 1980.

Keener, Craig S. *A Commentary on the Gospel of Matthew*. Grand Rapids: Eerdmans, 1999.

LaGrand, James. "The Earliest Christian Mission to 'All Nations's in Light of Matthew's Gospel." PhD diss., University of Basel, April 1989.

Lawless, Chuck. "'To All the Nations': The Great Commission Passages in the Gospels and Acts." *Southern Baptist Journal of Theology* 15, no. 2 (2011) 16–27.

Luter, A. Boyd, Jr. "Great, Commission, The." In *The Anchor Bible Dictionary*, 2: 1090–91. New York: Doubleday, 1992.

Longenecker, Richard N. "The Focus of Romans: The Central Role of 5:1—8:39 in the Argument of the Letter." In *Romans & the People of God*, edited by Sven K. Soderlund and N. T. Wright, 49–69. Grand Rapids: Eerdmans, 1999.

MacLeod, David J. "Eternal Son, Davidic Son, Messianic Son: An Exposition of Romans 1:1–7." *Bibliotheca Sacra* 162, no. 645 (2005) 76–94.

Michel, Otto. "The Conclusion of Matthew's Gospel: A Contribution to the History of the Easter Message." Translated by R. Morgan. In *The Interpretation of Matthew*, edited by Graham Stanton, 30–41. Philadelphia: Fortress, 1983.

Moo, Douglas J. *The Epistle to the Romans*. Grand Rapids: Eerdmans, 1996.

Morosco, Robert E. "Matthew's Formation of a Commissioning Type-Scene." *Journal of Biblical Literature* 103, no. 4 (1984) 539–56.

Müller, U. B. *Prophetie und Predigt im Neuen Testament*. Gütersloh: Ger. Mohn, 1975.

Murray, John. *The Epistle to the Romans*. New International Commentary of the New Testament. Grand Rapids: Eerdmans, 1968.

Plummer, Robert L. "The Church's Missionary Nature: The Apostle Paul and His Churches." PhD diss., Southern Baptist Theological Seminary, 2001.

———. "The Great Commission in the New Testament." *The Southern Baptist Journal of Theology* 9, no. 4 (2005) 3–11.

———. "A Theological Basis for Church's Mission in Paul." *Westminster Theological Journal* 64, no. 2 (2002) 253–71.

Pohill, John. *Acts*. New American Commentary. Nashville: Broadman, 1993.

———. *Paul Apostle of God's Glory in Christ: A Pauline Theology*. Downers Grove, IL: InterVarsity, 2001.

Schreiner, Thomas R. *New Testament Theology: Magnifying God in Christ*. Grand Rapids: Baker Academic, 2008.

———. *Romans*. Baker Exegetical Commentary on the New Testament. Grand Rapids: Baker Academic, 1998.

Soderlund, Sven K., and N. T. Wright, eds. In *Romans & the People of God*. Grand Rapids: Eerdmans, 1999.

Wallace, Daniel B. *Greek Grammar beyond the Basics*. Grand Rapids: Zondervan, 1996.

Warneck, Gustav. *Evangelische Missionslehre: Ein missionstheoretischer Versuch*. 3 vols. 2nd ed. Gotha: Ger. Perthes, 1892–1903.

Whitsett, Christopher G. "Son of God, Seed of David: Paul's Messianic Exegesis in Romans 2 [sic]:3–4." *Journal of Biblical Literature* 119, no. 4 (2000) 661–81.

Willitts, J. "The Friendship of Matthew and Paul: A Response to the Recent Trend in the Interpretation of Matthew's Gospel." *HTS Teologiese Studies/Theological Studies* 65, no. 1 (2009) Art. #151, 8 pages. DOI: 10.4102/hts.v65i1.151.

Wright, N. T. *The Climax of the Covenant: Christ and Law in Pauline Theology*. Minneapolis: Fortress, 1993.

Wuellner, Wilhelm. "Paul's Rhetoric of Argumentation in Romans: An Alternative to the Donfried-Karris Debate over Romans." In *The Romans Debate*, edited by Karl P. Donfred, 128–46. 2nd ed. Peabody, MA: Hendrickson, 2001.

7

Conversion and its Consequences
Nineteenth-Century Missionary Understanding

JONATHAN J. BONK

IT IS AN HONOR to contribute to this volume in honor of my esteemed friend and peer, the late Gary B. McGee. Our friendship goes back a long way, since we were approximately the same age, involved in many of the same academic societies, and we were both candidates for the position I have occupied these past sixteen years at the Overseas Ministry Study Center. He was a regular contributor to the *International Bulletin of Missionary Research*, a constant and reliable source of encouragement, and a soft-spoken but profoundly insightful scholar and pastor. The grace with which he lived through the affliction that would eventually send him home to his Father was exemplary and inspiring. My regret is that this essay—presented as the "Day Associates Lecture" at the annual meeting of the Yale-Edinburgh History Group on the History of the Missionary Movement and Non-Western Christianity, convened at Yale Divinity School, July 3–5, 2003 around the theme "Conversion and Converts"—could not be more worthy of the man who flourished and grew in the Spirit, and whose multi-faceted life yielded a bountiful harvest of the fruits of that Spirit.[1]

---

1. A version of this essay was published as pamphlet No. 17 in the Yale Divinity School Library's *Occasional Publication* series, Bonk, "Not the Bloom, but the Root..."

Christianity is not the bloom, but the root; culture is not the root, but the bloom, of Christianity.²

—Gustav Warneck (1834–1910)

The days of supernatural signs have not passed away. God's Word does not return to Him void. Instead of the thorn comes up the fir-tree; instead of the brier comes up the myrtle tree; and this displacement, in the soil of society, of noxious and offensive growths of sin, by useful and fragrant trees of righteousness, is the unanswerable proof and sign of God's Husbandry—the planting of the Lord, that He might be glorified. Such individual, social, spiritual transformation shall be to the Lord for a name, for an everlasting sign that shall not be cut off. The Church of Christ has only to go forth and preach everywhere. The Lord will work with and confirm the word with signs following. Amen.³

—Arthur T. Pierson (1837–1911)

It may not be in harmony with the current naturalistic theories of social evolution, yet it is the open secret of missionary experience that the humble work of missions is a factor in the social progress of the world which it would be intellectual dishonesty to ignore and philosophic treason to deny.⁴

—James S. Dennis (1842–1914)

---

2. Warneck, *Modern Missions and Culture*, 245. "We plant and promote civilization when we present the Gospel, and we make the nature-peoples human by making them Christians. Christianity is not the bloom but the root; culture is not the root but a bloom of Christianity." Warneck is here arguing against an alternative view held by "even so sound a theologian as priest Gerland" that argued that "[t]he nature-peoples must first be made human, then Christian. They are slowly trained to and through culture, whose highest bloom is Christianity" (242). Gustav Warneck (1834–1910) (see Gensichen, "Warneck, Gustav") was professor of mission at Halle from 1897–1908, the first chair of its kind in Germany. Although he never served as a missionary himself, he pioneered missiology as an academic discipline encompassing both Protestant and Catholic mission through his monthly journal *Allgemeine Missions-Zeitschrift* (1874). His wide-ranging publications cover the gamut of mission subjects, from history to theology and praxis.

3. Pierson, Introduction, v.

4. Dennis, *Christian Missions and Social Progress*, x.

Introduction

The venerable William Carey's *Enquiry*[5] sparked the remarkable phenomenon known as "the William Carey Era" in Christian mission. *The Leicester Herald* for Saturday, May 12, 1792, drew attention to Carey's slim volume with this advertisement:

> This day is published, Price 1S. 6d.
> An Enquiry into the Obligations of Christians
> to use means for the
> Conversion of the Heathens
> in which the religious state of the world, the
> success of former undertakings and the
> practicability of further undertakings
> for that Purpose are considered
> By William Carey
>
> Leicester: Printed and sold by A. Ireland,
> And the other booksellers: sold also by
> J. Johnson in St. Paul's Churchyard; Dilly
> In the Poultry; Knott, Lombard Street,
> London, and Smith, Sheffield.[6]

Rightly anticipating objections to the pre-emptive world-wide evangelical missionary thrust that he was proposing, Carey asked, rhetorically:

> Can we as men, or as Christians, hear that a great part of our fellow creatures, whose souls are as immortal as ours, and who are as capable as ourselves, of adorning the gospel, and contributing by their preaching, writings, or practices to the glory of our Redeemer's name, and the good of his church, are enveloped in ignorance and barbarism? Can we hear that they are without the gospel, without government, without laws, and without arts, and sciences; and not exert ourselves to introduce amongst them the sentiments of men, and of Christians? Would not the spread of the gospel be the most effectual means of their civilization?[7]

---

5. Carey, *An Enquiry*.
6. Payne's "Introduction" to the 1961 new facsimile edition, v.
7. Carey, *An Enquiry*, 69–70.

Among those who responded negatively to Carey's queries was Canon Sidney Smith (1771–1845) who took the "nest of consecrated cobblers and their perilous heap of trash" severely to task in a series of articles appearing in the *Edinburgh Review* (which he co-founded and edited) in 1808. "It is scarcely possible to reduce the drunken declamations of Methodism to a point, to grasp the wriggling lubricity of these cunning animals, and to fix them in one position," he complained. Not only would their efforts to convert the heathen, especially Hindus, fail to elevate them to civilization, he predicted, but their meddling would have catastrophic effects on British interests abroad. Missionary efforts to convert "a few degraded wretches," Smith was convinced, ". . . would infallibly produce the massacre of every European in India; the loss of [British] settlements, and consequently of the chance of that slow, solid and temperate introduction of Christianity, which the superiority of European character may ultimately effect in the Eastern world."[8]

Well before the end of the century, however, close observers of the mission enterprise—admittedly not disinterested—published a growing volume of documentation vindicating William Carey's hypothesis that "the spread of the gospel [*was*] the most effectual means of [human] civilization." It is to the work of four representative mission apologists that we now turn our attention.

William Warren (1806–1879)[9]

First chronologically among the books being considered is William Warren's *These for Those. Our Indebtedness to Foreign Missions: or, What we Get for What we Give.*[10] Warren was an ordained Congregational minister who served variously in Windham, Maine and Upton, Massachusetts from 1840 until 1856. In 1856 he served briefly as an agent for the American Colonization Society,[11] before being appointed by the American Board of Commis-

---

8. Smith, "Indian Missions," 40, 42, 50. Smith had entered the debate over whether East India Company regulations limiting missionary activity on the Indian subcontinent should be relaxed in the February 1808 issue of the *Edinburgh Review*, but in the end, neither his wit nor his wisdom prevailed. In 1813—the year of the founding of the Methodist Missionary Society—the charter of the East India Company was revised by Parliament, granting legal recognition to missionary work in India.

9. "Warren, William."

10. Warren, *These for Those*.

11. The American Colonization Society promulgated a solution to the problem of slavery—other than general abolition—that could unite both Northern and Southern moderates. Originating with slaveholders in reaction to an attempted slave insurrection,

sioners for Foreign Missions (ABCFM) as district secretary for northern New England—a post he held until his death in January 1879.[12]

Warren launches his defense of the missionary enterprise by reminding his fellow Anglo-Saxon readers of "The Idolatry of our Ancestors."[13] "The ancient Britons," he notes, ". . . were a fierce race of savages. . . . [converted] by missionaries sent to them early in the second century." They would not survive long enough to reap the long-term benefits of their conversion, however, for with the arrival of the Anglo-Saxons, ". . . the taper light of education and of Christianity were extinguished . . . the work of Christian civilization stopped, [and] Britain was paganized once more."[14]

The virtual obliteration from the island of both Britons and Christianity at the hands of Anglo-Saxon invaders required that England be re-evangelized, this time by missionaries from Ireland and Rome. And scarcely had people stood in greater need of conversion. "The Anglo-Saxons were a savage people, passionately fond of warfare," Warren noted, "[with] Cruelty . . . their one characteristic. Their ruling passion was for revenge and blood."[15] Faint vestiges of Britain's pagan heritage remained embedded in the names for the days of the week, he reminded his readers. In "Wednesday"—once *Wodens-daeg*—resounded echoes of the mighty god Woden, sire of all gods, inspirer of courage and giver of success in battle; to the memory and honor of Woden's consort, Frea—fecund goddess of love and sensual pleasure, from whose womb sprang all gods—was devoted the sixth day of the week, *Freas-daeg*, or Friday; Thor, bravest and most powerful of the sons of Woden and Frea, was likewise memorialized in *Thors-daeg*, or Thursday.[16] "At their feasts in honor of the gods, intoxicating liquors were drank, and their gods were toasted," Warren observed, "for they were bacchanalian in character. Scenes of fearful crime [including human sacrifices] accompanied them."[17]

---

it organized in 1817 with the purpose of establishing a colony in Africa for "free people of color and those who afterwards might become free." It was instrumental in establishing a colony of on the West coast of Africa that, in 1847, became recognized as the Republic of Liberia. For an early account of the Society, see Goodell, *Slavery and Anti-Slavery*, 341–52. Following the general emancipation in the wake of the Civil War (1861–1865), the Society assisted in populating and otherwise assisting the new newly founded republic. The Society also had a missionary impulse, for, in the words of Latourette, "The hope was cherished that through the colony the conversion and progress of the people of Africa would be furthered." *Christianity in a Revolutionary Age*, 205.

12. "Warren, William."
13. This is the chapter heading, Warren, *These for Those*, 17.
14. Ibid., 25.
15. Ibid., 33.
16. Ibid., 33–37.
17. Ibid., 38.

Warren questioned whether the Anglo-Saxon race could have survived its profound degradation without the "diffusion" of Christianity among them. "Many a people as powerful as our ancestors, are now no more," he noted. "No trace of them can be found upon the earth. They have been extinguished. It might have been thus with the Anglo-Saxon race. They that take the sword shall perish by the sword."[18] Even had the race survived to carry on "its career of conquest and of barbarism," its ultimate doom would have been no less certain, Warren argued, since "idolatry never heals itself. Heathenism has no element or principle of self-recuperation. It goes on from worse to worse."[19] Christianity alone regenerates humankind, but since it never "springs up spontaneously,"[20] it must be "propagated and diffused among the people, in order to save the world."[21]

This was Warren's apologia for Christian missions: cultural vitality and racial survival alike hinged upon Christian—preferably Protestant—conversion. But since Christian faith was not intuited but learned, and since his readers were the beneficiaries of missionaries who at great personal risk had brought the gospel to their ancestors, it followed that these redeemed societies should likewise send missionaries into all the world to proclaim the gospel.

Thomas Laurie (1821–1897)[22]

We turn next to Thomas Laurie, Scotland-born but American-trained Congregational (ABCFM) missionary to southeastern Turkey's Nestorians, but better known for his book *The Ely Volume; or, The Contributions of our Foreign Missions to Science and Human Well-Being*.[23] Some 532 pages in length, including appendices and index, the book is comprised of 22 chap-

18. Ibid., 41–42.
19. Ibid., 42.
20. Ibid., 43.
21. Ibid., 20.
22. Smalley, "Laurie, Thomas."
23. Laurie, *The Ely Volume*. The book's peculiar title derives from the wishes of the book's patron, "The Hon. Alfred B. Ely, Newton, Mass., who made provision for the publication of this volume" in memory of his father, the Rev. Alfred Ely, D.D., Monson, Mass. In the Introduction to his book, Laurie explains that the book's patron, "the late Hon. Alfred B. Ely inherited his father's love for the missionary work. He felt that the amount of scientific information given by it to the world during the past fifty years was greatly underestimated, and, therefore, made provision for the preparation and publication of this volume, to show what the missionaries of the American Board had done, especially for geography, philology, and archæology, not overlooking any contribution they had made to the advancement of human well-being." vii.

ters, encompassing all spheres of human thought and endeavor: geography, geology, meteorology, natural science, archaeology, philology, ethnography, literature, music, theology, education, medicine, commerce, and philanthropy.[24] Thirty-two pages are devoted to the missionary role in "national regeneration," providing "an account of some of the instances in which . . . missionaries have regenerated communities and lifted them from the mire of the pit."[25]

A sampling of African and Asian peoples thus regenerated are included in Laurie's survey, with the most astounding success story, by his own account, coming from the Sandwich Islands. "At the Sandwich Islands the property of an entire community was less than that of our average citizen," he began. "Books they had none. The knowledge of their wisest men was exceeded by that of our little children. They spent their time in sleeping and swimming, clapping their hands and tattooing their skins, roasting breadfruit, climbing for cocoanuts, and catching fish. The women, with long patience, beat out the cloth from the bark of trees, played in the surf, and painted with turmeric." But with the conversion of the islands to Christianity, bloody wars, nudity, and tyranny had been transcended by gentleness, clothes, and a constitution declaring that "no law shall be enacted at variance with the Word of the Lord Jehovah, or with the general spirit of his Word." In 1870, a correspondent from the *Boston Journal*, reporting from Honolulu, had observed: "Fifty years ago [Sandwich Islanders] were a horde of naked savages, offering human sacrifices and sunk in the grossest sensuality. Today they hold a place among Christian nations. A constitutional government administers equitable laws. They have the appliances of advanced civilization. Churches dot the islands, and the proportion of readers is larger than in Boston."[26]

While not all of the virtues accruing to Christian conversion were quantifiable, the transformation of Sandwich Islanders from indolence to industry had proven to be deeply gratifying from a pecuniary point of view. ". . . we have the startling fact," noted Laurie, "that a group of islands of no commercial importance whatever when the Gospel was carried there . . .

---

24. Peculiarly, given the title and argument of the book, Laurie (ibid.) includes a chapter on "Wines of the Bible," 430–41, in which the author responds to "[s]ome good men, [who] intensely moved by the evils of intemperance, and distressed by the impiety of those who wrest certain Scriptures to their own destruction, have been led to affirm that two kinds of wine were spoken of in Scripture: one good and commendable, the other poisonous and pernicious; and have made the process of fermentation the dividing line between the two." 430.

25. Ibid., 442.

26. Ibid., 443.

now pay in one year at a single American port more money by $367,343 than the entire cost of their Christianization during these sixty years."[27]

Laurie here echoes earlier conclusions drawn from the careful calculations of a Yale graduate (M.D. 1824) Rev. T. S. Williamson (1800–1879), who had served as a missionary with the ABCFM until 1872, and thereafter with the Presbyterian mission board, among the Dakota Indians in what is now Minnesota.[28] Quoted extensively by William Warren in *These for Those*[29] a full decade earlier, Rev. Williamson had calculated that it "cost more to fight than to feed those [Sioux] Indians."[30] Lamenting "the millions that it costs to subdue and govern the Indians," and pointing out that American "consumers" (*sic!*) ultimately foot the bill for the "insensible but omnipresent taxation" requisite to underwriting the country's Indian affairs, Warren had invoked Williamson's ledger: He calculated that it cost government agencies on the Missouri "one hundred and twenty dollars a year to feed, clothe, and thus restrain each [of some 15,000 heathen Sioux or Dakotas]."[31]

In contrast, twenty years of missionary work among the Sioux and Wahpeton elsewhere resulted not only in substantial fifteen-fold per capita savings to the government, but in the saving of settlers's lives as well. For during "the Indian war of 1862 . . . . the Christian Indians, without exception . . . befriended the whites; and through their assistance, the missionaries and employees of Government, who otherwise would probably have been murdered, made their escape. . . . In the spring of 1863 those Dakota men who had been most active in befriending us in the war, interposed as a shield between the frontiers of Minnesota and Iowa, and the hostile Dakotas who had made war and committed the massacres. . . . From the spring of 1863 . . . to the present time, very few of the hostile Sioux have ever reached the settlements of Minnesota and Iowa. Less than a dozen persons in these two States have been murdered by them."[32]

Laurie was not blind to the hypocrisy of the United States in its chronic failure to live up to its own treaties and constitution. "The history of combined Turkish and Kurdish oppression, as recorded by our missionaries, is full of sadness," he agreed, "but it rouses the indignation of every good man to read the missionary record of American oppression on our own territory. . . . Americans [with honorable exceptions] have contradicted every precept

27. Ibid., 425.
28. Smalley, "Williamson, Thomas Smith"
29. Warren, *These for Those*, 219–31.
30. Ibid., 225.
31. Ibid., 219–27.
32. Ibid., 226–27.

of the Gospel in their treatment of our Indian tribes. . . . in the face of energetic protests of good men, who did their utmost to resist, though they could not prevent them. . . . the crimes have not yet all become things of the past, as the wrongs endured by the Poncas at this moment testify; but the expulsion of the Cherokees is selected as a specimen of all these wrongs, both because it is so marked, and because both the missionaries and officers of the American Board had so much to do with efforts to avert it."[33] Tracing the sorry tale of U.S. betrayal of the Cherokees, Laurie is scathing in his denunciation. This "frightful compound of perfidy and wrong; a breach of faith unparalleled in history . . .", he warned, cannot go unpunished in a moral universe. Given the divine verity that greater light meant greater guilt, God's vengeance was sure. "Had Thomas Jefferson lived to see this new triumph of might over right," Laurie concluded, "he had found additional cause for saying, 'I tremble for my country when I remember that God is just.'"[34]

John Liggins (1829–1912)[35]

Rev. John Liggins, an Episcopalian, was the first Protestant missionary to Japan. It is to his book that we now turn. He emigrated as a twelve-year-old with his family from Warwickshire, England to Philadelphia in 1841. Following graduation from Virginia Theological Seminary in Alexandria in 1855, he was immediately assigned to China as an Episcopal missionary. Injured by a mob two years later, and sent to Nagasaki, Japan to recuperate, he was there when Japan opened up its borders to missionaries in 1859, becoming the first Protestant missionary to be appointed to Japan. Bedeviled by ill health, he returned to the United States in 1860, where he actively promoted foreign missions for the rest of his life through his speaking and writing.

Probably best known among his several publications is the book, *The Great Value and Success of Foreign Missions. Proved by Distinguished Witnesses: Being the Testimony of Diplomatic Ministers, Consuls, Naval Officers, and Scientific and Other Travelers in Heathen and Mohammedan Countries; together with that of English Viceroys, Governors, and Military Officers in*

---

33. Ibid., 361.

34. Ibid., 362, 371. Laurie's indignation was evidently not shared by all Christian devotees. Colonel John Chivington, former Methodist missionary and still an elder in his church, personally directed the Sand Creek (Colorado) massacre of some six hundred Cheyenne women and children in November of 1864. His announced policy was to "kill and scalp all, little and big," for, as he was fond of saying, "Nits make lice." There was not a single survivor. Stannard tells the gruesome details in his book, *American Holocaust*, 129–34. In the same vein, see Wright, *Stolen Continents*.

35. Long, "Liggins, John."

India and in the British Colonies: Also Leading Facts and Late Statistics of the Missions. The title comprising so thorough a synopsis, the reader might well wonder whether the book itself is necessary. "This most timely book," wrote Arthur T. Pierson in his introduction, "fits the need of the day, as a ball fits socket, or tenon fits mortise.... [and] the high character and grand influence of Christian missions are established beyond a doubt."[36]

Hounded by the censure of distinguished and highly publicized critics, missionaries and their advocates found in Liggins a trove of evidence sufficient to reassure believers, regenerate agnostics, and neutralize skeptics. Was there an explorer doubtful of the intentions, methods or outcomes of missionary endeavor? The approbation of numerous, even more distinguished explorers was mustered. Had travelers been critical of the effects of Christian conversion on native life and society? Their voices were drowned in the laudations of peripatetics more famous still. Had highly placed intellectuals scoffed at missions? The opinions of the still better informed and highly placed were invoked.

In a twenty-seven-chapter, region-by-region tour of the world, the reader hears from explorers, travelers, admirals, generals, consuls, clergymen, physicians, scientists, and government officials, each attesting to the extraordinary efficacy of missionary work generally and Christian conversion in particular. Dyak headhunters had become church members in Borneo; dawn was now visible across much of the Dark Continent; the growth of the church, with its concomitant transformation of tribal societies, was astounding; missionary churches, schools, and hospitals springing up here and there across China were doing immense good; even Fiji, "formerly the darkest place on earth.... [had] been so transformed by the Divine blessing upon missionary labors, that [it was now] one of the most Christian of countries."[37] In India, the misdeeds of the East India Company had been exposed and to some extent rectified, and the "monstrous evils" of suttee, infanticide, human sacrifice, leper immolation, and self-flagellation had been outlawed; all of this, thanks largely to missionary efforts.[38]

"I assure you," Sir Bartle Frere told a London audience in 1872, "that, whatever you may be told to the contrary, the teaching of Christianity among 160 millions of civilized, industrious Hindoos and Mohammedans in India is effecting changes, moral, social, and political, which for extent

---

36. Liggins, *The Great Value*, iii, iv.
37. Ibid., 70–71.
38. Ibid., 79–111.

and rapidity of effect are far more extraordinary than anything you or your fathers have witnessed in modern Europe."[39]

Wherever one turned in the world, Christian conversion led to palpable good. In Japan, "Gently, but resistlessly, Christianity [was] leavening the nation."[40] By the agency of the gospel, the populace of Madagascar was being "raised and purified," and "the abolition of cruel customs and laws belonging to the heathen state [had] been largely effected by the kindly and merciful spirit of Christianity."[41] Conversions to Christianity in Java, New Guinea, New Zealand, Persia, Polynesia, Siam, Siberia, the Ottoman Empire, and among North American Indians produced similar results, setting persons and societies on a trajectory not unlike that of the ancient Anglo-Saxons, whose social institutions, economic vitality, and military power served as harbingers of what Christianized societies could anticipate as a result of their conversion.

"The large amount of testimony given in this book," Liggins concludes, "is mainly from non-missionary sources, and it would seem as if every candid reader of it must agree that Archdeacon Farrar was right when he said that 'to talk of the failure of Foreign Missions is to talk at once like an ignorant and like a faithless man.'"[42]

---

39. Ibid., 93. The quotation is from a lecture on "Christianity suited to all forms of Civilization" delivered at a Christian Evidence Society meeting in London, July 9, 1872. Sir Bartle Edward Frere (1815–1884), former Governor of Bombay, qualified his remarks by saying: "I speak simply as to matters of experience and observation, and not of opinion; just as a Roman prefect might have reported to Trajan or the Antonines." It was the Rt. Honorable Sir Bartle Edward Frere—member of the Indian Council and President of the Royal Geographical Society—who would later make the case for missionaries in East Africa to the Archbishop of Canterbury in a series of letters published as Frere, *Eastern Africa as a Field for Missionary Labour*. Frere (1815–84) was a famous British colonial administrator, and nephew of John Hookham Frere. He served (1850–59) as chief commissioner of Sind, distinguishing himself during the Indian Mutiny, and was (1862–67) governor of Bombay. In 1872 he negotiated a treaty with the sultan of Zanzibar for the suppression of the slave trade. Appointed (1877) governor of Cape Colony and high commissioner of British South Africa, Frere had to cope with Boer discontent in the newly annexed Transvaal and with Zulu unrest. Intent on breaking the military power of the Zulus, he precipitated (1878) the Zulu War. His action was disapproved in London, and although he was popular in the Cape he was recalled to England in 1880. He was created Baron Frere in 1876.

40. Liggins, *The Great Value*, 114.

41. Ibid., 129, 130.

42. Ibid., 232.

James Dennis (1842–1914)[43]

We turn, finally, to James Dennis, for it is in his prodigious output that this genre of missionary apology reaches its apogee. Dennis was born and raised in Newark, New Jersey. Following graduation from Princeton Theological Seminary and ordination by the Presbyterian Church, U.S.A. (PCUSA), between 1868 and 1871 Dennis served with the ABCFM in Syria. Following a brief furlough and marriage to Mary Elizabeth Pinneo, he returned to Syria under the auspices of the PCUSA to serve as principal and professor of theology at Beirut Theological Seminary. Returning to the United States in 1891, Dennis began to indulge his passion for world missionary statistics, lecturing and publishing widely on missiological themes.[44]

Dennis inaugurated the newly established Students's Lectureship on Missions at Princeton Theological Seminary by giving six lectures in the spring of 1893, published in the fall of that year in a 368-page volume, *Foreign Missions after a Century*.[45]

Still in its infancy as a discipline, sociology was regarded as being largely the domain of skeptics and atheists. In assaying to apply the methods of science to an understanding of the development, structure, and functioning of human society, however, sociology was viewed by Dennis as a natural complement to missionary endeavor. A joint invitation by Princeton's Sociological Institute and Missionary Society brought Dennis back to Princeton in 1896 to lecture on "The Sociological Aspects of Foreign Missions."[46] His intention, he said, was to demonstrate that while "Christianity as yet touches the age-encrusted and unyielding surfaces of heathen society only in spots.... It is sufficiently apparent... that a new force of transcendent energy has entered the gateway of the nations and has planted itself with a quiet persistency and staying power in the very centres of the social life of the people."[47] "It may not be in harmony with the current naturalistic theories of social evolution," he admitted, "yet it is the open secret of missionary experience that the humble work of missions is a factor in the social progress of the world which it would be intellectual dishonesty to ignore and philosophic treason to deny."[48]

43. Goodpasture, "Dennis, James."

44. "The very smell of a statistic," Walls writes, "can send Dennis into an orgy of calculation." *The Cross-Cultural Process in Christian History*, 52.

45. Dennis, *Foreign Missions*.

46. Dennis, *Christian Missions and Social Progress*, 1:vii.

47. Ibid., ix.

48. Ibid., x. Dennis made a distinction between Christian sociology and Christian socialism, making clear that his book was an illustration of the former, not the latter.

Among those in attendance was Malbone Graham, who preserved his recollection of the lectures in an unpublished manuscript entitled "Origin of a Great Missionary Book."[49] The "book"—four large volumes published between 1897 and 1906, comprising a total of 2034 pages replete with illustrations, 307 in all, illustrating the tangible challenges, means and results of missionary endeavor[50]—was by any measure an outstanding accomplishment, easily rivaling the prodigies of our own twentieth-century, computer-assisted missiometrician, David Barrett.[51]

The table of contents alone—totaling some 40 pages—makes illuminating if daunting reading. Dennis makes no apology for this, although he does anticipate reader fatigue. "If any reader is inclined to think that the author has trespassed upon his patience," he writes in his Preface to the third volume, ". . . it would be well for him to recall that very large and significant claims on behalf of missions which have been advanced in the previous lectures ought to be made good by ample and sufficing evidence."[52]

See his chapter, "The Sociological Scope of Christian Missions," in ibid., 1:21–59.

49. The manuscript, by Malbone Watson Graham of Berkeley, California, had been evidently sent to Delavan L. Pierson, editor of *The Missionary Review of the World* (*MRW*). The manuscript, accompanied by a letter from Pierson, dated April 18, 1916, was sent to Charles H. Fahs of New York (who, with Harlan Beach, would co-edit the 1925 *World Missionary Atlas*) indicating that, while the *MRW* could not make use of it, perhaps it might be of interest to James Dennis himself. The manuscript and the letter are found in folder 55, Box I, of the James Dennis Papers in the Union Theological Seminary (New York) archives.

50. Dennis, *Christian Missions and Social Progress*; Dennis, *Centennial Survey of Foreign Missions*. So popular were his 1896 (February 9–14) Princeton lectures that Dennis delivered them as The Morgan Lectureship at Auburn Theological Seminary in New York a week later (February 19–27), as Lane Theological Seminary's "Lectures on Missions" in Cincinnati two weeks later (March 4–10), and as The Elliott Lectureship at Western Theological Seminary in Cincinnati a week after that (March 12–18)! Although I was not able to locate Dennis's letters requesting photographs from missionaries all over the world, the James Sheppard Dennis Papers in the archives of the Union Theological Seminary in New York do contain fifty-one personal letters from all over the world, all dated in 1905, from his respondents. In all instances, they are responding to his request for photographs to include in the third volume of *Christian Missions and Social Progress*. This gives some intimation of the prodigious correspondence that Dennis must have carried on with missionary correspondents around the world. I am assuming that most of his papers are held in the Speer Library at Princeton Theological Seminary.

51. Barrett is editor of the 1010-page *World Christian Encyclopedia*. The second edition of his encyclopedia, co-edited by George T. Kurian and Todd M. Johnson, was published in 2001. Two volumes were published by Oxford University Press, while a third companion volume, *World Christian Trends AD 30–AD 2200*, was published by William Carey Library. The total number of pages in the three volumes is 2633.

52. Dennis, *Christian Missions and Social Progress*, 3:v.

One reviewer, acknowledging the commonly held view that "Christian missions in foreign lands and sociological theories have nothing in common," echoed Dennis's argument that in the "Christian scheme" not only does society play a direct role in the extent to which an individual might actualize his full divinely given human potential, but that remarkable individuals exert a significant influence on the health and transformation of society. This being the case, the reviewer went on, Christian missions and sociology shared considerable common ground.[53] As Benjamin Kidd acknowledged, religion—especially the Christian religion—was an elemental force in human social evolution. ". . . In the eyes of the evolutionist," he explained, ". . . the Christian religion has tended to raise the peoples affected by it to the commanding place they have come to occupy in the world."[54]

"Christian missions are a social force," Dennis argued, "because if they change the religious and moral character of the man, they put him immediately into a new attitude toward the domestic, civil, economic, and ethical aspects of society. They introduce also new institutions into social life; not only new ecclesiastical organizations, but new educational and philanthropic movements. Plant germs of new political and industrial ideals, open a new realm of intellectual and religious thought, stir a new conception of liberty and a nobler, purer social life."[55]

Dennis devotes more than half of the first volume to his second lecture, "The Social Evils of the Non-Christian World."[56] The table of contents for Lecture II constitutes a dense, five-page, tiered synopsis of social evils. Individuals in the non-Christian world were particularly prone to intemperance, drug addiction, gambling, immorality, self-torture, suicide, idleness, improvidence, excessive pride, and dishonesty; evils affecting families included the degradation of women, polygamy and concubinage, adultery and divorce, child marriage and widowhood, defective family training, and infanticide; tribal groups to various degrees suffered from the traffic in human flesh, slavery, cannibalism, human sacrifice, cruel ordeals, punishments and torture, brutality in war, blood feuds, and lawlessness; social relationships among non-Christians were distorted by ignorance, quackery, witchcraft, neglect of the poor and sick, cruel customs, insanitary conditions, lack of public spirit, mutual suspicion, poverty, tyrannical customs, and caste; nationally, the shortcomings included civil tyranny, oppressive taxation, subversion of legal rights, corruption and bribery, and massacre

53. Newton, "The Contribution of Christian Missions," 239–45.
54. Kidd, *Social Evolution*, 165–66.
55. Dennis, *Christian Missions and Social Progress*, 1:43.
56. Ibid., 71–352.

and pillage; commercially, a lack of business confidence, together with deceit, fraud, financial irregularities, and primitive methodologies frustrated advance; and as for religion, the well-spring of everything else, the non-Christian world suffered from degrading conceptions of nature, idolatry, superstition, religious tyranny and persecution, and scandalously immoral leaders. Attempts at reform had proven to be consistently ineffectual and would continue to fail (Lecture III). The nations required a supernatural remedy, and Christianity—as a moral force that provided a philosophy of progress, a solution for sin, a true estimation of humankind, and a stimulus to philanthropy—was the only social hope of the nations (Lecture IV).[57] "Christian missions enter this socially disorganized environment with its varying aspects of degeneracy," Dennis observed, "from the higher civilization of the Orient to that of barbarous races, and in most cases without the aid of legal enactments, engage in a moral struggle with old traditions and immemorial customs which have long held sway in society. They deal with a religious consciousness almost painfully immature in spiritual things, so that the splendid task of Christian missions is to take by the hand this childhood of heart and mind, put it to school, and lead it by the shortest path into the largeness of vision and ripeness of culture which have come to us all too slowly and painfully.... And yet, slowly and surely change comes. It comes through the secret and majestic power of moral guidance and social transformation which seems to inhere in that gospel which Christian missions teach."[58]

It is in Dennis's contribution to one of the greatest of all missionary gatherings, the New York 1900 Ecumenical Missionary Conference,[59] that we find the most succinct summary of his apologia. The list of delegates to the New York Ecumenical Missionary Conference of 1900 suggests that Christian missions had reached a level of public acceptance never before, or since, achieved. Representing approximately 15,000 Protestant missionaries serving with 400 societies all over the world, some 2500 delegates—including internationally acclaimed Christian leaders and missionary heroes—mingled with dignitaries, politicians, and national celebrities. On opening night (Saturday, April 21, 1900), a wave of emotion swept through the 2500 attendees as, directed by Ira D. Sankey himself, they rose to sing "Jesus Shall Reign."[60] Theodore Roosevelt, John G. Paton, Bishop Thoburn, Hudson Taylor, and Robert Laws were among the luminaries seated in the front row on

57. Ibid., 10–16.
58. Ibid., 45.
59. *Ecumenical Missionary Conference New York, 1900.*
60. See Askew, "The New York 1900 Ecumenical Missionary Conference," 146–54.

the platform. In his capacity as honorary chairman, former President of the United States Benjamin Harrison gave the opening address.

He was followed by the then current President of the United States, William McKinley, who—greeted with an outburst of cheering as he made his way to the podium on the arm of Morris K. Jessup, chair of the New York Chamber of Commerce—welcomed the delegates on behalf of his nation. Pointing to the convergence of Christian conversion and the ideals of Western civilization, McKinley said:

> I am glad of the opportunity to offer without stint my tribute of praise and respect to the missionary effort which has wrought such wonderful triumphs for civilization. The story of Christian missions is one of thrilling interest and marvelous results. . . .
>
> Wielding the sword of the Spirit, they have conquered ignorance and prejudice. They have been among the pioneers of civilization. . . .
>
> Who can estimate their value to the progress of nations? Their contribution to the onward and upward march of humanity is beyond all calculation. They have inculcated industry and taught the various trades. They have promoted concord and amity, and brought nations and races closer together. They have made men better. They have increased the regard for home; have strengthened the sacred ties of family; have made the community well ordered, and their work has been a potent influence in the development of law and the establishing of government.[61]

Dennis played a key role, serving as Chairman of the Committee on Statistics "appointed to present a paper" at the conference.[62] Having already published two volumes of his three-volume *Christian Mission and Social Progress*, Dennis had amassed data for a volume that was to serve as a statistical complement.[63] The distillation of this 400+ page volume was printed and distributed to conference attendees, subsequently appearing as an appendix in the official two-volume report of the conference.[64]

---

61. *Ecumenical Missionary Conference New York, 1900*, 1:38–40.

62. Dennis, *Centennial Statistics*, vii.

63. This data was published in 1902 in his book, Dennis, *Centennial Survey of Foreign Missions*. The volume, including table of contents and tables of abbreviation and maps, runs to 430 pages.

64. Dennis, "Statistical Summary of Foreign Missions," 419–34. In compiling the statistics, Dennis benefited from an incredible 90-percent response to his questionnaire, with most of the missing 10 percent accounted for by the Boer War in South Africa.

The nine categories beneath which the data were arranged provide insight into what missionaries regarded as the natural concomitants of Christian conversion. Foremost and lengthiest of the categories was "Evangelistic," providing detailed statistics on the "income, staff, and evangelistic returns of missionary societies."[65] This was followed with statistical information on educational, literary, medical, philanthropic and reformatory, and cultural expressions of missionary endeavor and accomplishment.

Education statistics (section II of the summary) included information on 93 universities and colleges, 358 theological and training schools, 858 boarding and high schools and seminaries, 167 industrial training institutions, 63 medical schools, 127 kindergartens, and 18,742 elementary or village day schools. Over one million students were enrolled—nearly one third of these women—in 20,407 institutions.[66]

Section III of the summary, under the heading "Literary," provided statistics on 427 Bible translations and more than ten million pieces of general literature published by 148 mission publishing houses on every continent; some 366 periodicals with a combined circulation of nearly 300,000 reinforced missionary evangelistic and educational efforts.[67]

Medical statistics (section IV of the summary) tabulated 355 hospitals—including 10 in Palestine, 40 in Africa, 106 in India, and 124 in China—and 753 dispensaries, having treated some 2.5 million patients the previous year.[68] The Philanthropic and Reformatory section of the report provided "statistics of institutions and societies for relief and rescue" including 213 orphanages, 90 leper hospitals and asylums, and 30 schools and homes for the blind and the deaf. This section also included mention of the work of some 280 temperance societies, " rescue work" through the aegis of 154 homes for converts, widows, homeless women, and rescued slaves, and 126 societies established "for the promotion of purity, prison reform, abolishment of foot-binding, and work for soldiers, sailors, and prisoners."[69]

The sixth section of the summary, labeled "Cultural," included "the reproduction abroad of many well-known agencies at home."[70] Dennis's

---

65. Askew, *"New York 1900,"* 2:424. Interestingly, the U.S. dollar–British pound/sterling exchange rate was calculated at $4.90 to the pound.

66. *Ecumenical Missionary Conference New York, 1900*, 2:428–29.

67. Ibid., 430–31.

68. Ibid., 432.

69. Ibid., 433.

70. Ibid., 434. Included in this list of well-known agencies are: the United Society of Christian Endeavor, the Methodist Church (North), the Methodist Church (South), the Brotherhood of St. Andrew, the Order of the Daughters of the King, YMCA, YWCA, World's Student Christian Federation, Student Volunteer Movement in Mission Lands,

summary concluded with statistics on fifty-four "Native organizations for extension of knowledge and the furtherance of national, social, moral, and religious reform" (Section VII), eighty seven "missionary training institutions and agencies in Christian lands" (Section VIII), and sixty seven "Mission steamers and ships used in evangelistic, medical, and other departments of mission service in the foreign field" (Section IX).[71]

Edinburgh 1910 World Missionary Conference

At the Edinburgh 1910 World Missionary Conference ten years later, the venerable Dennis rendered service as one of eighteen vice-chairmen of the commission (chaired by John R. Mott) responsible for producing the *Statistical Atlas of Christian Missions*.[72] The categories are familiar, and information is impressive for both its quantity and its organization. Twenty maps, in color, locate all known mission stations—19 maps for Protestant missions, and 1 map for Roman Catholic, and Greek Catholic missions.[73] The Committee estimated the "total fruitage of modern Christian missions [Protestant, Roman Catholic, and Russian Orthodox] of the past century, represented by living converts Christianized from non-Christian peoples, as approaching 21,000,000."[74] Educational summary tables tallied 81 universities, 489 theological schools, 1594 boarding schools, 284 industrial training schools, 28,901 elementary schools, and 113 kindergartens.[75] 550 hospitals, 1024 dispensaries, and 111 medical schools represented missionary medical activities, to which benevolences could be added 265 orphanages, 88 leper hospitals, 25 institutions for the blind, and 21 rescue homes.[76]

The Edinburgh Commission on Carrying the Gospel to all the Non-Christian World, chaired by John R. Mott and including [among others] James Dennis, Harlan Beach, Samuel Zwemer, and Eugene Stock, emphasized "the opportunity and the urgency of carrying the gospel to all the non-Christian world," the title of the first chapter in their report.[77] "One of the most significant and hopeful facts with reference to world evangelisation," the Commission noted, "is that the vast majority of the people of

---

Children's Scripture Unions, Boys Brigades, Gleaners Unions, and Sowers's Bands.

71. Ibid., 434.
72. *Statistical Atlas of Christian Missions.*
73. These maps were the work of Professor Harlan P. Beach of Yale University.
74. *Statistical Atlas of Christian Missions*, 61.
75. Ibid., 63.
76. Ibid., 64.
77. World Missionary Conference, *Report of Commission I*, 5–49.

the non-Christian nations and races are under the sway, either of Christian governments or of those not antagonistic to Christian missions."[78]

Missionaries were not the exclusive beneficiaries of improved government, transportation, and communication systems, however. Islam may have been "Christianity's most formidable enemy,"[79] but a more sinister threat was posed by "the deadly gift" of western civilization itself, with its "habits of luxury and self-indulgence,"[80] and its myriad corrupting influences. It was important that missionary activity pre-empt the building of African and Asian railways, for example, since "the advent of railways [would] bring a large influx of ungodly men, who [would] make the task of evangelisation much more difficult. [For it had] always been true that while men slept the enemy came and sowed tares."[81] "There are but a few primitive races or peoples left in the world, and the opportunity afforded the Christian Church to reach them under most favorable conditions can last but a brief season," the Commission warned. "The present opportunity will pass away. Every year will bring new and powerful counter attractions within easy reach of the natives. The wise and experienced missionary workers show convincingly that it is much easier to bring the Gospel to bear on the heathen in his natural state than it is upon the man who has become familiar with the worst side of so-called civilisation."[82]

Missionaries, while not uncritical of Western civilization, were nevertheless animated by the belief that its core principles were traceable directly to Christianity. In a required textbook written by their Professor, students at the Disciples of Christ Bible College of Missouri read that "It is in its social message that Christianity outruns the other missionary religions in its permanent power to uplift. . . . It becomes a civilizer through its implanting of humane social principles and social ideals in the hearts of its converts, and

78. Ibid., 6.
79. Ibid., 20.
80. Ibid., 22.
81. Ibid., 23.

82. Ibid., 22-24. The themes and concerns identified in the Edinburgh 1910 conference continued to be promoted through the aegis of its Continuation Committee and its scholarly quarterly, the *International Review of Missions*. The disbanding of the Continuation Committee at the conclusion of the Great War did not mean that mission organizations had abandoned their interests in global mission. With the formal establishment in 1921 of the permanent, international, co-operative agency known as the International Missionary Council, the nation building and development agendas of Christian mission continued to absorb the attention of conciliar Protestants as evidenced in the three great ecumenical assemblies convened in Jerusalem (1928), Oxford (1937), and Tambaram (1938-39). All three conferences dealt hopefully and extensively with nation building.

they leaven the whole of the life about them. . . . It is . . . our implanting of the life of Christ, with all it means to our civilization in higher ideals, purer thinking, better homes, greater equality, more value on life as such, a higher standard of living, and more of the spirit of service, that brings the world to him."[83] Among the plates included in the book is one featuring a group of students posing in front of a large American flag. The caption beneath it reads: "Advanced Class in Urumia College, Persia. Moslems, Jews, and Christians are here drawn together, and ancient hates are lost under missionary instruction."[84]

The Great War 1914–1918

The assassination of Austrian Archduke Franz Ferdinand by teenage members of The Black Hand plunged "Christian" Europe and its colonies into the bloodiest and quite possibly the most meaningless conflagration in human history. It also marked the end of innocence for missionary apologists, who, until then, had held up their own societies as evidence of the vitality and virtue of Christian influence.

In his admirable book on the subject, Hew Strachan points out that this European war became known as the First World War because people from all over the world came to fight in the civilized nations's cause. Britain mobilized more than three million troops from her colonies (two million of these from Africa), while France mobilized half-a-million from hers. The war's ultimately pointless savagery sent a shudder through the terra firma on which confidence in the moral, social, and political superiority on which Western Christendom was based.[85] Missionaries who had confidently proclaimed European civilization to be the natural and inevitable result of a society permeated by Christian values were likewise shaken to their ideological foundations by the war and its aftermath.[86] Commenting on the decline of Chinese interest in mission school education, the Hocking Commission observed that while "By 1920 it had become 'almost the fashion to become a Christian'; since 1922 the tide [had] turned," due, understandably,

---

83. Taylor, *The Social Work of Christian Missions*, 15. Taylor was Professor of Social Service and Christian Mission in the Bible College of Missouri (Disciples of Christ). His textbook, published in 1911, was enjoying its third printing by 1914.

84. Taylor, *The Social Work of Christian Missions*, bottom plate facing, 172.

85. Niall Ferguson, Review of *The First World War*, by Strachan, 21–23. See also Webster, *Aftermath*.

86. Pfaff, *The Wrath of Nations*, "The Great War was the most important event of the twentieth century. It was a decisive historical event, a marker" 232–33.

to "... the disillusionment of the World War and the widespread impression it left that the West did not really believe the Christianity it taught."[87]

After the Great War, missionary advocacy of *civilization* through *Christian* conversion was gradually displaced by secular programs of *development* through *Western* education, finance, and political rearrangement. The *modus operandi* of missions continued to function much as before, since it was embedded in the very warp and woof of Christian missionary identity. But the confident, sometimes breathless, and often patronizing tone of nineteenth-century missionary apologists migrated into the language and agendas of contemporary non-religious organizations such as the United Nations, the World Bank, and the International Monetary Fund.

Conclusion

The sweeping range of nineteenth-century missionary activities, while staggering, is hardly surprising. Progeny of evangelical nonconformists were better remembered for their social work than for their theology,[88] missionaries were acutely aware that "faith without works is dead" (James 2:26), and that faith was much more than simply mental assent to a series of theologically correct propositions about God and related matters. Love of God without love of neighbor was heresy. And the way to love neighbor was to do for your neighbor what you would want your neighbor to do for you. What this meant was, understandably, defined in largely Western terms. The lost needed evangelizing; the ignorant needed educating; the illiterate needed illuminating; the destitute needed nurturing; society needed transforming.

Christendom and Christian Mission

It has not been the intention of this paper to trace the metamorphosis of the word "conversion" from patristic to later Christian understandings, but it is helpful to recall that the social contexts in which Christians employed the term profoundly impacted their understanding of its formal, functional, and motivational dimensions. From its Jewish and Gentile genesis as related in Acts of the Apostles, the church engaged in spontaneous and aggressive proclamation, with a view to convert men and women to belief in its risen Lord, and to a new way of life described by Luke in Acts 2:42–47. In its

---

87. Hocking, *Re-thinking Missions*, 154–55.

88. See Briggs and Sellers, *Victorian Nonconformity*; Heasman, *Evangelicals in Action*; and Magnuson, *Salvation in the Slums*.

earliest days as a Jerusalem-based Jewish sect, the church offered converts teaching, fellowship, prayer, miracles, and a common life, and—in the words of St. Luke—"the Lord added to their number daily those who were being saved" (Acts 2:47 KJV).

Yale's Ramsay MacMullen estimates that from the end of the first century the church grew by half a million in each generation so that by the time of Constantine's conversion in AD 312, Christians constituted a demographically significant proportion of the imperial population.[89] In the words of MacMullen, "No other new cult anywhere nearly approached the same success. It can only be called extraordinary.... [The Christian credo] was presented in sharply yes-or-no, black-and-white, friend-or-foe terms; and those were unique.... Belief in no other God but Yahweh entailed an obligation to speak in his praise and win over other worshipers to his service.... Urgency, evangelism, and the demand that the new believer deny the title of god to all but one, made up the force that alternative beliefs could not match."[90]

Significantly, this growth occurred in the face of often formidable disincentives. Alan Kreider—mindful of the sporadic, sometimes lethal persecution that awaited converts to the Christian faith—observes that "if one wanted a soft life, or to get ahead in respectable circles, one did not become a Christian."[91] Conversion to Christianity was the sure road to marginality.[92]

With the conversion of Constantine, Christianity quickly mutated into Christendom—the grandsire of what is today known as "The West"—a civilization in which Christian religious dominance was guaranteed by both social and legal compulsions.[93] Between the Edict of Milan in AD 313 and Justinian's edict of AD 529, Christianity's status in the Empire evolved from being one among several equally legitimate religious options, to being the only legal public cult in AD 392. Pagan worship was increasingly marginalized, stigmatized, and finally illegitimized. Having moved from the margins of society to its center, the "other way" became the *only* way.[94]

---

89. MacMullen, *Christianizing the Roman Empire*, 86, 109–10.
90. Ibid., 110.
91. Kreider, *Worship and Evangelism in Pre-Christendom*, 6.
92. Hoornaert, *The Memory of the Christian People*, 81.
93. Herrin, *The Formation of Christendom*, 8, 47.
94. Kreider, *The Origins of Christendom in the West*, 22–24. See also Wilkin, *Seeking the Face of God*. Wilkin observes that the early Christian Fathers lived in a pagan world in which they represented a marginalized minority of the population around the Mediterranean. After Constantine, however, they made their pronouncements as secure spokesmen for a state-supported religion.

It is to Christendom that the missionary movement from the West must trace the still prevalent assumption that Christian mission is "out there somewhere"—anywhere but in Europe or in its cultural-political progeny, the United States and Canada.[95] This notion—despite deeply regrettable and frequently noted flaws, lapses, and sometimes outright evils evident in Western lands—is implicit and explicit both in the apologetic literature surveyed in this paper, and in the *modus operandi* of contemporary Western-based missions. Without Christianity, the social, cultural, political, and economic institutions of their societies could not be accounted for.

That economic, political, and military domination should generate self-confidence, assertiveness, and illusions of superior virtue on the part of those who most directly benefit from it is a truism. As John Kenneth Galbraith wryly observed, "nothing so gives the illusion of intelligence as association with large sums of money."[96] Nor are similar sentiments uncommonly associated with overwhelming economic and military power. When James Dennis wrote his books, Europe dominated all of Africa, the entire Middle East except for Turkey, and most of the Asian subcontinent. The 35 percent of the earth's surface controlled by Europeans when Carey sailed for Serampore had grown to 84 percent by 1914. The British Empire, encompassing 20 million subjects spread over 1.5 million square miles in 1800, engulfed 390 million people inhabiting 11 million square miles one century later.[97] In missionary thinking, this domination was both inevitable and providential.

Christian Conversion, Social Regeneration, and the Still-Missionary West

Enjoying the considerable advantage of those who debate the deceased, a later critical generation might convincingly distance itself from the views and practices of its forebears. If the agendas and outspoken confidence of nineteenth century missionaries grates on the sensibilities of the twenty-first century ear, there is much to suggest that our newfound modesty may be largely cosmetic, a façade fashioned from sheer forgetfulness, selective memory, and self-delusion—the materials preferred by those charged with fabricating the flattering wardrobes of national mythologies.

---

95. Kreider, *The Origins of Christendom in the West*, x.

96. Galbraith, "The 1929 Parallel," 62.

97. Huntington, *The Clash of Civilizations* 51. Huntington cites Fieldhouse, *Economics and Empire*, 3; and Hearnshaw, *Sea Power and Empire*, 179.

Many of the impulses that motivated nineteenth century missionaries continue to animate secularized Western societies. The West, it seems, is intrinsically missionary, absolutizing its way of life and institutions to drive globalization and proclaim the good news of a Western way of life to the uttermost parts of the earth—especially those parts with commodities and markets requisite to the steadily escalating, consumption-driven entitlements of its aging populations. The conflict between Islamic fundamentalism and the West, Samuel Huntington rightly observes, is rooted in irreconcilable values at the very heart of two civilizations. "The problem for Islam," he says, "is not the CIA or the U.S. Department of Defense. It is the West, a different civilization whose people are convinced of the universality of their culture and believe that their superior, if declining, power imposes on them the obligation to extend that culture throughout the world."[98]

Can it be that the *civilizing mission* of the nineteenth century has metamorphosed into the *development agendas* of our day, with quantifiable data enabling statisticians to arrange all countries and people somewhere on the continuum between *underdeveloped* and *developed*? Development, as popularly understood in the contemporary West, has nothing to do with *religion* but much to do with *democracy* and the *free market*—the terms invoked so fondly by Americans advocating their peculiar plutocracy and its global hegemonic impulses. The development agendas, trajectories and *modus operandi* of the World Bank, the IMF, and the United Nations bear uncanny resemblance to the civilizing mission of a bygone era. World Bank indicators of "World Development" include the familiar fields relating to education, health, and poverty.[99] Nineteenth century descriptive parlance—"groping through long ages in the darkness," "native minds steeped in superstition," and "degrading customs"—has been displaced by functional, if not lexical, equivalents such as "underdevelopment," "dehumanization," and "sub-human conditions"—all variations on the same theme.[100]

---

98. Huntington, *The Clash of Civilizations*, 217–18.

99. See World Bank, *2000 World Development Indicators*.

100. If there is a difference between missionary thinking 100 years ago and contemporary discourse concerning the "other," it is in the remarkable extent to which the West reveals its implicit assumptions about its own superiority by taking the blame for everything that happens in the world, whether it be starvation, genocide, or underdevelopment. If missionaries of a bygone era operated on the assumption that people of the world were steeped in darkness but that missionaries held the key to helping them turn on the lights, their secular counterparts today as often as not take the blame for the sad condition of people who still sit in the darkness of underdevelopment, but with at least the faint illumination afforded them by the flickering images of ABC or NBC. If we do not have the answer to the world's problems, at least we can take the blame for them.

Missing, however, is any sense that religion—Christian or otherwise—might have a direct bearing on either the viability or ultimate outcomes of development efforts. The missionary's insistence on religion as the foundation of human development in all of its social and material manifestations is no longer admissible, and the missionary voice today is scarcely audible.

But if nineteenth-century missionaries—along with such luminaries as Benjamin Kidd, Arnold Toynbee, or Christopher Dawson—were right; if religion *is* the central defining characteristic of any civilization; and if *Christianity* is the defining DNA of all that we know as Western; if, in Warneck's words, "culture is not the *root* but the *bloom*, of Christianity,"[101] then "development" efforts—insofar as they intend to replicate elsewhere "the good life" of the West—will not get very far. A train without an engine either stands still, or, if it is on an incline, it goes forward or backward until stopped by its own intrinsic inertia.[102] And this may be a good thing, given the doubtful possibility of generating globally the prodigious levels of consumption that must be indulged in order to merit the official stamp, "developed." The fact that a majority of the world's vital Christian populations today remain "underdeveloped" suggests that the world Church, detached from its Western roots, may more closely resemble the "underdeveloped" but spiritually dynamic churches of the first century than the "developed" but now becalmed Western churches of the twenty-first.

Andrew Walls's observation that the expansion of Christianity tends to be serial rather than progressive, and that the old heartlands of Christianity are the new mission fields of the twenty-first century is borne out in the recently drafted text of the Preamble of the European Convention's Treaty establishing the Constitution which, in its studied attempt to avoid explicit mention of its Christian cultural heritage, has elicited shock and outrage on the part of Catholic and Orthodox Churches. Nowhere explicitly alluded to, in place of the Great Code one finds simply a bland reference to "the cultural, religious and humanist inheritance of Europe."[103]

Critics of Christian missionary activity are disingenuous and, at times, highly patronizing in their seeming presumption that persons other than themselves should not be permitted to make significant religious choices, presumably on the grounds that when confronted with religious

---

101. Warneck, *Modern Missions and Culture*, 245.

102. Anthropologist Dichter, in his book *Despite Good Intentions*, makes the case that macro development efforts over the past fifty years have failed, and that the poor would possibly be better off had there been no development at all.

103. The full text of the Draft may be found on the web at: European Union Constitution, 2003, http://www.unizar.es/euroconstitucion/Treaties/Treaty_Const.htm (accessed September 30, 2016).

alternatives, people who are not like us must inevitably choose to their own disadvantage! The historically unprecedented scale of Christian conversion throughout the past two centuries has not been coerced, but voluntary. The great movements into Christian faith have not been the byproduct of bombs, threats, sanctions, or political arm-twisting, but the voluntary responses of men and women and families and communities for whom the Christian message is an attractive and compelling alternative to the status quo. Indeed, many have responded at great inconvenience, and even peril, to themselves and to their families. The simple fact is that Christianity today is no longer a religion to which the West can even pretend to hold proprietary rights; it is a *world* religion.[104]

In *The Gifts of the Jews*,[105] Thomas Cahill argued that the greatest gifts of the Jews were their linear theory of history (vs. the cyclical theory of other ancients), with its implication that life can get better and avoid decline, and the idea of the equality and dignity of each individual that culminated in the declaration that "All men are created equal." To the extent that much, perhaps most, of humankind now agrees that this is so, Christian missionaries must be credited with sharing this gift with most of the rest of the world. And I, for one, welcome the opportunity to pay them and their tribe tribute.

Bibliography

Askew, Thomas. "The New York 1900 Ecumenical Missionary Conference: A Centennial Reflection." *International Bulletin of Missionary Research* 24, no. 4 (2000) 146–54.

Barrett, David B. *World Christian Encyclopedia: A Comprehensive Survey of Churches and Religions in the Modern World, A.D. 1900–2000.* Oxford: Oxford University Press, 1982.

Bonk, Jonathan J. "Not the Bloom, but the Root . . .": *Conversion and Its Consequences in Nineteenth-Century Protestant Missionary Discourse.* New Haven, CT: Yale Divinity School Library, 2003.

Briggs, John, and Ian Sellers. *Victorian Nonconformity.* London: Arnold, 1973.

Cahill, Thomas. *The Gifts of the Jews: How a Tribe of Desert Nomads Changed the Way Everyone Thinks and Feels.* Hinges of History 2. New York: Doubleday, 1997.

Carey, William. *An Enquiry into the Obligations of Christians, to Use Means for the Conversion of the Heathens. In which the Religious State of the Different Nations of the World, the Success of Former Undertakings, and the Practicability of Further Undertaking, are Considered.* Leicester, UK: Ann Ireland, 1792.

Dennis, James S. *Centennial Statistics: Paper Prepared for the Ecumenical Conference on Foreign Missions. New York City, April 21–May 1, 1900.* New York: Committee on Statistics, 1900.

---

104. See Jenkins, *The Next Christendom*.
105. Cahill, *The Gifts of the Jews*.

———. *Centennial Survey of Foreign Missions: A Statistical Supplement to "Christian Missions and Social Progress," Being a Conspectus of the Achievements and Results of Evangelical Missions in All Lands at the Close of the Nineteenth Century*. New York: Revell, 1902.

———. *Christian Missions and Social Progress: A Sociological Study of Foreign Missions*. 3 vols. New York: Revell, 1897–1906.

———. *Foreign Missions A Century*. New York: Revell, 1893.

———. "Statistical Summary of Foreign Missions Throughout the World." In *Ecumenical Missionary Conference New York*, 2:419–34. 1900. Reprint, Ithaca, NY: Cornell University Press, 2009.

Dichter, Thomas W. *Despite Good Intentions: Why Development Assistance to the Third World Has Failed*. Boston: University of Massachusetts Press, 2003.

Ecumenical Missionary Conference New York, 1900. Report of the Ecumenical Conference on Foreign Missions, Held in Carnegie Hall and Neighboring Churches, April 21 to May 1. 2 vols. London: Religious Tract Society, 1900.

Ferguson, Niall. Review of *The First World War*, Vol. I, *To Arms*, by Hew Strachan. London: Oxford University Press, 2002. *New York Review of Books*, February 13, 2003, p. 21–23.

Fieldhouse, D. K. *Economics and Empire, 1830–1914*. London: Macmillan, 1984.

Frere, Rt. Honorable Sir Bartle Edward. *Eastern Africa as a Field for Missionary Labour. Four Letters to His Grace the Archbishop of Canterbury*. London: Murray, 1874.

Galbraith, John Kenneth. "The 1929 Parallel." *Atlantic Monthly* 259, no. 1 (1987) 62–66.

Gensichen, Hans-Werner. "Warneck, Gustav." In *Biographical Dictionary of Christian Missions*, edited by Gerald H. Anderson, 718. New York: Macmillan, 1998

Goodell, William. *Slavery and Anti-Slavery: A History of the Great Struggle in Both Hemispheres with a View of the Slavery Question in the United States*. New York: Goodell, 1853.

Goodpasture, H. McKennie. "Dennis, James." In *Biographical Dictionary of Christian Missions*, edited by Gerald H. Anderson, 176. New York: Macmillan, 1998.

Hearnshaw, F. J. C. *Sea Power and Empire*. London: Harrap, 1940.

Heasman, Kathleen. *Evangelicals in Action: An Appraisal of their Social Work*. Letchworth, UK: Bles, 1962.

Herrin, Judith. *The Formation of Christendom*. Princeton: Princeton University Press, 1987.

Hocking, William Ernest. *Re-thinking Missions: A Laymen's Inquiry After One Hundred Years*. New York: Harper & Bros., 1932.

Hoornaert, Eduardo. *The Memory of the Christian People*. Translated by R. R. Barr. Maryknoll, NY: Orbis, 1988.

Huntington, Samuel P. *The Clash of Civilizations and the Remaking of World Order*. New York: Simon & Schuster, 1996.

Jenkins, Philip. *The Next Christendom: The Coming of Global Christianity*. New York: Oxford University Press, 2002.

Kidd, Benjamin. *Social Evolution*. London: Macmillan, 1895.

Kreider, Alan. *Worship and Evangelism in Pre-Christendom*. Joint Liturgical Studies. Cambridge, UK: Grove. 1995.

Kreider, Alan, ed. *The Origins of Christendom in the West*. Edinburgh: T. & T. Clark, 2001.

Kurian, George T., and Todd M. Johnson. *World Christian Encyclopedia: A Comprehensive Survey of Churches and Religions in the Modern World, A.D. 1900–2000.* 2 vols. 2nd ed. Oxford: Oxford University Press, 2001.

———. *World Christian Trends AD 30–AD 2200: Interpreting the Annual Christian Megacensus.* Pasadena, CA: William Carey Library, 2001.

Latourette, Kenneth Scott. *Christianity in a Revolutionary Age: A History of Christianity in the Nineteenth and Twentieth Centuries.* Vol. 3, *The Nineteenth Century Outside Europe: The Americas, the Pacific, Asia, and Africa.* New York: Harper & Row, 1961.

Laurie, Thomas. *The Ely Volume; or, The Contributions of our Foreign Missions to Science and Human Well-Being.* Boston: American Board of Commissioners for Foreign Missions, Congregational House, 1881.

Liggins, John. *The Great Value and Success of Foreign Missions. Proved by Distinguished Witnesses: Being the Testimony of Diplomatic Ministers, Consuls, Naval Officers, and Scientific and Other Travelers in Heathen and Mohammedan Countries; Together with That of English Viceroys, Governors, and Military Officers in India and in the British Colonies: Also Leading Facts and Late Statistics of the Missions.* London: Nisbet, 1889.

Long, Charles Henry. "Liggins, John." In *Biographical Dictionary of Christian Missions*, edited by Gerald H. Anderson, 401–2. New York: Macmillan, 1998.

MacMullen, Ramsay. *Christianizing the Roman Empire (A.D. 100–400).* New Haven, CT: Yale University Press, 1984.

Magnuson, Norris. *Salvation in the Slums: Evangelical Social Work 1865–1920.* Grand Rapids: Baker, 1977.

Newton, J. C. Calhoun. "The Contribution of Christian Missions to Sociology." *Methodist Review* 47 (1898) 239–45.

"On Carrying the Gospel to All the Non-Christian World." *Statistical Atlas of Christian Missions: Containing a Directory of Mission Societies, A Classified Summary of Statistics, an Index of Mission Stations, and a Series of Specially Prepared Maps of Mission Fields.* Edinburgh: World Missionary Conference. 1910.

Payne, Ernest A. "Introduction" to the 1961 new facsimile edition of William Carey, *An Enquiry into the Obligations of Christians, to Use Means for the Conversion of the Heathens. In Which the Religious State of the Different Nations of the World, the Success of Former Undertakings, and the Practicability of Further Undertaking, Are Considered.* London: Kingsgate, 1961.

Pfaff, William. *The Wrath of Nations: Civilization and the Furies of Nationalism.* New York: Simon & Schuster, 1993.

Pierson, Arthur T. Introduction to *The Great Value and Success of Foreign Missions. Proved by Distinguished Witnesses: Being the Testimony of Diplomatic Ministers, Consuls, Naval Officers, and Scientific and Other Travelers in Heathen and Mohammedan Countries; together with that of English Viceroys, Governors, and Military Officers in India and in the British Colonies: Also Leading Facts and Late Statistics of the Missions*, by John Liggins. New York: Baker and Taylor, 1888.

Smalley, Martha Lund. "Laurie, Thomas." In *Biographical Dictionary of Christian Missions*, edited by Gerald H. Anderson, 386. New York: Macmillan, 1998.

———. "Williamson, Thomas Smith." In *Biographical Dictionary of Christian Missions*, edited by Gerald H. Anderson, 738. New York: Macmillan, 1998.

Smith, Sydney. "Indian Missions." *Edinburgh Review* (1809) 40, 42, 50.

Stannard, David E. *American Holocaust: Columbus and the Conquest of the New World.* New York: Oxford University Press, 1992.

Statistical Atlas of Christian Missions. Containing a Directory of Mission Societies, A Classified Summary of Statistics, an Index of Mission Stations, and a Series of Specially Prepared Maps of Mission Fields. As an Integral Part of Its Report to the World Missionary Conference, Edinburgh, June 14–23, 1910. Edinburgh: World Missionary Conference, 1910.

Strachan, Hew. *The First World War.* Vol. 1, *To Arms.* London: Oxford University Press, 2002.

Taylor, Alva W. *The Social Work of Christian Missions.* Cincinnati: Foreign Christian Missionary Society, 1914.

Walls, Andrew. *The Cross-Cultural Process in Christian History.* Maryknoll, NY: Orbis, 2002.

Warneck, Gustav. *Modern Missions and Culture: Their Mutual Relations.* Edinburgh: Gemmell, 1883.

Warren, William. *These for Those. Our Indebtedness to Foreign Missions: or, What we Get for What we Give.* Portland, ME: Hout, Fogg and Breed, 1870.

"Warren, William." In *Appleton's Cyclopaedia of American Biography,* edited by James Grant Wilson and John Fiske. 6:368. Rev. ed. New York: Appleton, 1999.

Webster, Donovan. *Aftermath: The Remnants of War.* New York: Random House, 1996.

Wilkin, Robert Lewis. *Seeking the Face of God.* New Haven, CT: Yale University Press, 2003.

World Bank. *2000 World Development Indicators.* Washington, DC: World Bank, Development Data Center, 2000.

World Missionary Conference. *Report of Commission I: Carrying the Gospel to All the Non-Christian World.* Edinburgh: Oliphant, Anderson & Ferrier, 1910.

Wright, Ronald. *Stolen Continents: The Americas through Indian Eyes since 1492.* Boston: Houghton Mifflin, 1992.

8

The Holy Spirit and Christian Mission Today

Stephen B. Bevans, SVD

Introduction

From the very beginnings of the Pentecostal Movement in which Gary B. McGee rooted his life of faith and in which he served so admirably, Mission was at its center.[1] What I intend to present in this paper, as a tribute to Gary, is what might be called a phenomenological and missiological perspective on the continuing connection between the Holy Spirit and Mission as it is manifest today in all parts of the world. Although my perspective is definitely ecumenical, it is unabashedly Roman Catholic (as I think Gary would want me to be). And to such a phenomenological and missiological approach, I will add a deeply-grounded theological perspective as well.

The reason for this theological perspective is twofold. First, my academic training is not really in missiology, but in theology. I always say that I came to missiology "through the back door," as it were.[2] A number of circumstances coalesced to shape the way I do theology, and these circumstances—being a member of a missionary society, having been a missionary, being at the right place at the right time and so having been invited to do editorial work in missiology, writing a book on theological method that has been claimed as missiological—have made me a missiologist. Second, however—and this more importantly—I am convinced on the one hand that all theology needs to be missiological, that mission is indeed, as Martin Kähler

---

1. See McGee, *Miracles, Missions, and American Pentecostalism*; Klaus, "Pentecostalism and Mission"; and Robeck Jr., "Pentecostalism and Mission."
2. See Bevans, "Missiology through the Back Door," 367–77.

said a century ago and as David Bosch has reminded us, the "mother of theology."³ On the other hand, my conviction is that missiology needs to be thoroughly theological as well, even though it is a discipline that dialogues with many disciplines, such as anthropology, history, and communication theory. Nevertheless, missiology is a *theological* discipline in the fullest sense, and so can never be confined merely to "Practical Theology" as theologians like Schleiermacher suggested.⁴

Two Theological Statements

Accordingly, this paper will be rooted in two theological statements about the Holy Spirit and her role in God's mission that is shared by the church. The first is the famous statement written first by Pope Paul VI in his Apostolic Exhortation *Evangelii Nuntiandi*, and then repeated by Pope John Paul II in the Encyclical *Redemptoris Missio*: that the Holy Spirit is the "principal agent" of evangelization/mission.⁵ The second statement comes from Rowan Williams, the former Archbishop of Canterbury: Mission is "finding out where the Holy Spirit is at work and joining in."⁶ Such a perspective is anchored in the idea that mission is first and foremost about the *missio Dei*, but it is further nuanced in the idea that mission gets its impetus from the *missio Spiritus*—that God's mission is carried out by the Spirit, sent from the first moment of creation by the Father,⁷ concretized in the mission of the Son, Jesus of Nazareth, in the "fullness of time" (Gal 4:4), and "entrusted to us" (2 Cor 5:19).

Two Interpretations of the Spirit's Work

There seem to be two ways in particular that the Holy Spirit can be characterized as "the principle agent of mission," and these two ways will be significant as we point out ways that the Spirit is active throughout the world today. We can speak, on the one hand, of the "Spirit *of* Mission," and, on the other hand, as the "Spirit *in* Mission."

---

3. Kähler, *Schriften zur Christologie und Mission*, 190; and Bosch, *Transforming Mission*, 16.

4. Schleiermacher, *Brief Outline on the Study of Theology*, 102.

5. Paul VI, *Evangelii Nuntiandi*, § 75; John Paul II, *Redemptoris Missio*, §§ 21 and 30.

6. Quoted on the "Fresh Expression." (Anglican Church), quoted in Kim, *Joining in with the Spirit*, 1.

7. See John Paul II, *Dominum et Vivificantem*, § 53.

In the first characterization of the Spirit's work, the Spirit "comes" or "falls" upon a person, transforming him or her to participate in God's work. We see this already, at least in sign, in the Old Testament as God's spirit falls upon a prophet and calls upon him or her to prophesy. Perhaps the clearest example is in Isaiah 61:1–3: "The spirit of the Lord God is upon me, because the Lord has anointed me; he has sent me to bring glad tidings to the lowly, to heal the brokenhearted, to proclaim liberty to captives . . . ." This, of course, is the passage Jesus reads in the synagogue at Nazareth in Luke 4:18–19, a passage Luke renders as adding ". . . recovery of sight to the blind, to let the oppressed go free . . . ." At Jesus's baptism, the Spirit descends upon him as a dove, and anoints him, as it were, for his mission (Luke 3:22; Mark 1:10; Matt 3:16). In Chapter 2 of the Acts of the Apostles that same Spirit descends upon the disciples and strengthens them for proclaiming the good news of the Resurrection, and in the rest of Acts the Spirit works so forcefully within the community that Acts is now commonly known as "the gospel of the Holy Spirit."[8] That the Spirit is the "principle agent of evangelization," Paul VI explains, is because the Spirit "impels each individual to proclaim the gospel," whispers to people "in the depth of their consciences," urging them to faith, and "stirs up the new creation," the ultimate "goal of evangelization."[9] This is the Holy Spirit as experienced in movements like El Shaddai in the Philippines, or in the African Independent Churches, or in McGee's own Assemblies of God.

Paul VI's dictum, however, can also be understood in the light of that of Rowan Williams, and this presents a second characterization of the way the Spirit acts in the world. The Spirit is already at work in the world, Williams says, and Christian mission is about discerning that work and "joining in." The Book of Acts can also be interpreted as the story of the Spirit leading the community to a new understanding of Jesus's mission. The Spirit goes ahead of the community, as it were, and the disciples simply follow. "It is the decision of the Holy Spirit and of us . . . ." (Acts 15:28). John Paul II speaks about the Spirit being "present and active in every time and place," who "sows the 'seeds of the Word,'" who is present in peoples's customs and cultures, and in the prayers of people of every religion.[10] The Spirit is present before the arrival of any missionary, and rather than "bringing Christ," the missionary merely points to what has long been present yet hidden in the lives, the cultures, and the religions of all peoples, and fulfilled in Christ. A document written by Asian theologians for the Federation of Asian Bishops's Confer-

8. See, e.g., González, *Acts*.
9. Paul VI, *Evangelii Nuntiandi*, § 75.
10. John Paul II, *Redemptoris Missio*, §§ 28–29.

ences speaks of the development of a "pneumatology from below," woven together "from prayerful and systematic reflection in the light of revelation on events, encounters and movements in Asia."[11] "The church can never be sure," writes Orthodox theologian Michael Oleska, "where the Spirit is not."[12] This is the Holy Spirit of Indian theologians, of Australian Aboriginal Christians committed to the integrity of creation, and of Latin Americans struggling for justice and liberation.

A Third Theological Statement

This paper is founded on yet a third theological statement, one that is also *missiological*, and one that will serve as a basis for the paper's organization. The statement is by John Paul II and is found in *Redemptoris Missio*, although it appears in earlier documents as well. Writing about the various "paths of mission," John Paul II speaks about mission as "a single but complex reality."[13] In my own writing, along with my colleagues Eleanor Doidge and Roger Schroeder, I have interpreted the multifaceted meaning of mission in terms of six basic elements. In this understanding, mission cannot be reduced to any one of them, and yet each is constitutive of mission itself. These elements are: (1) Witness and Proclamation; (2) Liturgy, Prayer, and Contemplation; (3) Justice, Peace, and the Integrity of Creation; (4) Interreligious and Secular Dialogue; (5) Inculturation; and (6) Reconciliation.[14]

It seems to me that if I am to offer a phenomenological and missiological reflection on the way mission is lived out and done today in the light of the action and presence of the Holy Spirit, these six elements might provide a good framework around which to organize my ideas. God's mission through the Spirit's mysterious yet dynamic presence, concretized in Jesus, and shared by the church, takes place through these six elements. What follows in this paper, therefore, are reflections in how the Holy Spirit is working and manifest in each of these elements, and how this action is being experienced and responded to in various parts of our world today.

---

11. Office of Theological Concerns, "The Spirit at Work in Asia Today," 306–7.
12. Oleska, The Holy Spirit's Action in Human Society," 331.
13. John Paul II, *Redemptoris Missio*, § 41.
14. See, for example, Bevans and Schroeder, *Constants in Context*, 348–95.

Witness and Proclamation

U. S. American journalist and Vatican correspondent John L. Allen Jr. writes that "when future histories of Christianity are written, the late twentieth century will probably come to be known as the era of the 'Pentecostal Explosion.'"[15] As is well known, Pentecostalism is the fastest growing religious movement in the world today. It grew, Allen says, from less than six percent in the 1970s of global Christianity to about twenty percent in the first decade of the twenty-first century.[16] According to the 1997 document on the Holy Spirit written by Asian theologians, the charismatic movement in the Philippines involves some thirty percent of Filipinos, and this was some fifteen years ago. Malaysian-American Pentecostal Amos Yong writes of how Pentecostalism is flourishing in Guatemala, Chile, Korea, India, Zimbabwe, and South Africa.[17]

What is the secret of such phenomenal growth? Allen gives a number of plausible sociological reasons, but says that any Pentecostal or Charismatic would undoubtedly say that the Holy Spirit is the answer.[18] My own sense is that many factors are at play in such growth, but if the Holy Spirit is at work in this movement, the resultant vitality of the Pentecostal and Charismatic communities is certainly a major factor. These communities are *witnesses* to what faith in Christ can be: they are joyful, they provide good pastoral care, they read and study the Bible together, there is a sense of empowerment of laity, there is a growing role for women in the church.[19] A survey in India about why people are attracted to Pentecostal churches included the reasons that they wanted to be involved in a warm and welcoming community, and that they wanted more personal pastoral care to support their spiritual life.[20] The Spirit works to make the church community a witness to the power of the gospel. Very often it is this attractive witness that persuades Catholics to join Pentecostal churches, something that the 2007 Aparecida Conference has noted.[21] Catholics might do well to join in the Holy Spirit's work and ensure that their own communities are as vital as those of Pentecostalism. This may be a true agenda item for mission in the light of the work of the Holy Spirit.

15. Allen, *The Future Church*, 378.
16. Ibid.
17. Yong, *The Spirit Poured Out on All Flesh*, 31–80.
18. Allen, *The Future Church*, 389.
19. Allen, *The Future Church*, 406–7; Office of Theological Concerns, "The Spirit at Work in Asia Today," 317; and Yong, *The Spirit Poured Out on All Flesh*, 39–42.
20. Office of Theological Concerns, "The Spirit at Work in Asia Today," 317.
21. "Concluding Document," §§ 85, 226.

Allen begins his report on Pentecostalism with a portrait of Oscar Osorio, a Honduran Catholic Charismatic lay preacher and televangelist. Osorio was born Seventh Day Adventist, but his marriage to a Catholic woman and subsequent conversion at a Catholic Charismatic retreat changed his life. Now he is a man on fire to preach the gospel. Preaching is "something that we laity must do . . . We can't sit back and wait to be led. We have to want it, to feel it, to burn to evangelize."[22]

Such passionate commitment to preaching the gospel is a rare thing outside of Pentecostal or Evangelical circles, but it is certainly called for by Paul VI, John Paul II, and by Benedict XVI, particularly in Benedict's establishment of the Pontifical Council for Promoting the New Evangelization, all of whom appeal to the power of the Spirit as the One who empowers Christians to proclaim the gospel.[23] The Aparecida Conference also spoke of how, when one is touched by the Spirit, one is moved to the proclamation of one's faith to others: "Life in the Spirit," it says, "does not enclose us in cozy intimacy, but makes us generous and creative persons, happy in proclamation and missionary service."[24]

But proclamation must always today be a fruit of respectful dialogue with women and men of particular places, cultures, and religious roots. The various elements of mission are distinct, but they overlap with each other, and in this case proclamation overlaps with the conviction that the Holy Spirit is present and active within peoples's ordinary experiences, cultural values, and religious convictions. Any proclamation of the gospel has to honor and discern the Spirit present in the deepest joys and struggles of women and men. As American theologian Elizabeth Johnson expresses so eloquently: "Wherever we encounter the world and ourselves as held by, open to, gifted by, mourning the absence of, or yearning for something ineffably more than immediately appears, whether that 'more' be mediated by beauty and joy or in contrast to powers that crush, there the experience of the Spirit transpires."[25] Any kind of proclamation needs to dovetail with these experiences, respectful of the Spirit who is there, raising the questions. In a similar way, and we will reflect on this more under the elements of inculturation and dialogue, proclamation has to respect the Spirit already present in culture and religion. Proclamation in the Spirit needs to be bold

---

22. Quoted in Allen, *The Future Church*, 377.

23. Paul VI, *Evangelii Nuntiandi*, § 75; John Paul II, *Redemptoris Missio*, § 27, 44–45; and Benedict XVI, *Ubicumque et Semper*, §1.

24. "Concluding Document," § 285.

25. Johnson, *She Who Is*, 124–25.

and confident, but it has to connect with that deep presence where the Spirit is at work.

Liturgy, Prayer, and Contemplation

Liturgy, Prayer, and Contemplation are not spontaneously seen as elements of *mission*. They are certainly seen as important, but are more actions for the sake of the church, not the church's outreach. But missiological thought in the last several years has seen in them valuable contributions to missionary action as such, and reflection on them, I am convinced, is at the cutting edge of missiological thinking.[26] Liturgy, prayer, and contemplation are missionary acts, and are ways of joining in the work of the Spirit.

The Pentecostal and Charismatic movements carry over into the area of liturgy, prayer, and contemplation. Several years ago a missionary from Papua New Guinea shared with me the fact that it is almost impossible to be an effective missionary in that country without in some way being charismatic, and in many ways this is true as well in many parts of Asia (e.g. the Philippines, Korea), Latin America, and Africa. Recently I led a retreat for my SVD (*Societas Verbi Divini* or Society of the Divine Word) brothers working in the Caribbean, and their testimony was very much the same. People in these areas want vibrant, beautiful, joyful, Spirit-filled, energetic, and prayerful liturgies. They want fewer formal and set prayers and more spontaneous ones. Perhaps the Holy Spirit is telling us something here: that we need to be more alive when we celebrate liturgy, that our music has to be more appropriate to local cultures and has to be more biblically based, that our prayers have to be more heartfelt and free.

The Asian theologians of the Federation of Asian Bishop's Conferences (FABC) list several "signs of the presence of the Spirit" in the basic Christian communities of the Asian church today, and several of them reflect the importance of liturgy, prayer, and contemplation. First is "a kind of a thirst for prayer, both personal and communitarian," and they have a sense of contemplation that leads them "to concrete acts of service to humanity." Second, there is "a real hunger for the word of God." Asian people want to hear the word of God, reflect on it personally and communally, and "apply it to their lives." Asian Christians, third, have a love for the Eucharist that calls for full participation of all the members of the community. And, "as the Eucharistic bread is shared they feel strengthened in their solidarity, mutual concern and care."[27]

---

26. See Bevans and Schroeder, *Constants in Context*, 361–68.
27. See Office of Theological Concerns, "The Spirit at Work in Asia Today," 313–14.

Paul speaks about the Holy Spirit being the source of our prayer, through whom we cry out in our hearts "Abba" (Rom 8:15). Christians need to allow the Spirit to lead them to pray for the world. Prayer is not just about oneself, but also, and perhaps chiefly, about the needs of others in our world. We pray for various peoples in the world, for the church throughout the world, for the world's peace, for an end to poverty and discrimination, for reconciliation, for a spirit of dialogue among peoples, for persecuted Christians. We pray also as the Spirit moves us for particular situations in the world: for earthquake victims in Haiti and Japan, for political freedom for the peoples of the Middle East, for refugees in Italy and the rest of Europe. Prayer in the Spirit is a missionary act.

Biblical scholar James D. G. Dunn points out, as noted by British theologian Kirsteen Kim, that "if mission is understood as *missio Dei*, then mission amounts to participating in the mission of God carried out by the Spirit (Rom 8:14–17). If this is so, then the first act of mission is discernment, to discover the way in which the Spirit is moving in the world, in order to join in."[28] The condition for such discernment is a sense of contemplation, the ability to be attentive, open, and perceptive. It is only by cultivating such an attitude that one is able to recognize the working of the Spirit in one's life, and in the world. Contemplation, then, like prayer, is a missionary act.

Justice, Peace, and the Integrity of Creation

Liberation theologian José Comblin speaks eloquently of the Holy Spirit as the *Dios Liberador*, who is present in the fabric of history and calls people to work for liberation and justice. He quotes the document from the 1979 meeting of the Latin American Bishops at Puebla de los Angeles, Mexico, to the effect that "the renovation of human beings, and subsequently of society, will depend first of all on the action of the Holy Spirit."[29] The Spirit is the force and energy that is present within ordinary people, within the hearts of charismatic leaders who organize women and men for justice, within communities who nurture and inspire people to move toward liberation. "Latin American Christians," he writes, "recognize the God of liberation and feel the presence of such a God in their very midst, acting in their own actions and commitments." This is the Holy Spirit, Comblin says, "whether known

---

28. See Dunn, *The Christ and the Spirit*, 72; and Kim, *The Holy Spirit in the World*, 165.

29. Comblin, "The Holy Spirit," 462, quoting the Final Document of the Puebla Conference, no. 199.

by name or not."[30] Asian theologians, similarly, speak of the Spirit as the "Power of the Powerless." The presence of the Spirit in the Asian churches, they write, "will be seen in that we become truly Churches of the poor, breathing into the struggling masses hope for greater humanity and fuller forms of life."[31] Working for justice is inspired and guided by the Spirit. It is indeed a matter of discerning where the Spirit is at work, and joining in.

Feminist theologian Elizabeth Johnson argues persuasively that both the marginalization of women in church and society and the exploitation of the earth are "intrinsically related to forgetting the Creator Spirit who pervades the world in the dance of life."[32] Both the mistreatment of women and the mistreatment of the earth are based on an understanding of God that is basically monarchical—outside of and dominating human beings and the world. A recognition of the creative power of the Holy Spirit, however, points to a different kind of power at work in the world. The Spirit is the power of God immanent in the processes of history, constantly working with God's power in Christ in the creation of the world, and calling humanity, especially, to participate in that creation. As Australian theologian Denis Edwards writes, however, the Spirit not only breathes in the hearts of human beings, but is "the love that surrounds and sustains the uncounted insects, animals, and trees that share the exuberant life of a rain forest, the love that is at work in the mysterious and counterintuitive nature of quantum reality and in the nuclear furnaces of the twinkling stars."[33] Creation is the first act of God in mission—in the Spirit and through the Word—and so humanity's partnership in creation is partnership in mission. Working especially to protect God's creation, and to restore it and reconcile it through commitment to ecology and ecojustice is therefore a special partnership with the Spirit in the Spirit's mission in the continuing act of creation.

Interreligious and Secular Dialogue

Church teaching is consistent in emphasizing that the Spirit "sows the 'seeds of the Word'" in the cultures of the world, and all human "efforts to attain truth, goodness and God himself."[34] In the various religions of the world there can be discerned rays of the Truth that is fully revealed in Christ, and acknowledges that anyone who sincerely follows the dictates of conscience

30. Comblin, "The Holy Spirit," 464.
31. Office of Theological Concerns, "The Spirit at Work in Asia Today," 322.
32. Johnson, *Women, Earth, and Creator Spirit*, 2.
33. Edwards, *Breath of Life*, 177.
34. John Paul II, *Redemptoris Missio*, § 28.

can attain salvation.³⁵ Indeed, "the Holy Spirit in a manner known only to God offers to every person the possibility of being associated with the paschal mystery."³⁶

It is in recognition of the Spirit's activity in the world's religions, and even among sincere unbelievers, that impels Christians to cooperate with the Spirit in the various forms of dialogue: of life, of action, of theological exchange, of spiritual experiences.³⁷ Such dialogue is part of the church's evangelizing mission.³⁸

The Asian theologians of the FABC have an extensive reflection on the presence of the Spirit in the various Asian religions, including primal religions,³⁹ and they speak of dialogue as "the work of the Spirit."⁴⁰ We recognize an overlap with the importance in contemplation when these Asian theologians tell us that "it is the Spirit who leads [participants in dialogue] to discern the face of God and to contemplate His splendour in the other."⁴¹ Working with the Spirit demands openness, humility, patience, but also the courage to proclaim their Christian faith when the opportunity arises.

The bishops of Latin America and the Caribbean strongly endorse the importance of ecumenical and interreligious dialogue in the final document from the Aparecida Conference.⁴² God's grace, the bishops write, comes into the world by the breath of the Holy Spirit, and "explaining and promoting this salvation already at work in the world is one of the tasks of the church with regard to the Lord's words: "be my witnesses . . . to the ends of the earth" (Acts 1:8)."⁴³ The *Instrumentum Laboris* of the Synod for Africa in 1993 speaks of the presence of the Spirit among the religions of all peoples and connects the search for that presence in other religions as an integral part of the church's mission. "The Church," it points out, "as 'the universal sacrament of salvation,' has been entrusted with the ministry of unity and has the duty of continuing the 'dialogue of salvation' with all men. She is called to continue discovering and acknowledging the signs of Christ's

---

35. See *Nostra Aetate*, § 2, and *Lumen Gentium*, § 16.

36. *Gaudium et Spes*, § 22.

37. "Dialogue and Proclamation," § 42.

38. John Paul II, *Redemptoris Missio*, § 55. This text only acknowledges interreligious dialogue, but it seems logical to include secular dialogue as well.

39. Office of Theological Concerns, "The Spirit at Work in Asia Today," 238–66.

40. Ibid., 307.

41. Ibid.

42. "Concluding Document," §§ 227–39.

43. Ibid., § 236.

presence and of the working of the Spirit in history, and to cooperate with all men and women of good will for the salvation and welfare of all."[44]

Inculturation

As the Asian theologians have said, "the Spirit binds us in a marvelous way with all those who have left the indelible imprint of their spirit, heart and mind in innumerable forms on our cultures and on our traditions."[45] It is this bond with culture and tradition, the Latin American bishops say at Aparecida, that makes inculturation possible, especially as such inculturation is revealed in Latin American popular religiosity. We need to "value positively what the Holy Spirit has already sown,"[46] and so when we speak of inculturation purifying and perfecting faith in a particular context or culture, we acknowledge that we do not start from the *absence* of the Spirit, but from her constant presence in history and culture. Australian Aboriginal theology affirms this presence, as does the Korean theology of Tong-Shik Ryu.[47] It is in the discernment of the Spirit in local cultures and contexts that one finds the "stuff" out of which a true inculturation of the gospel can be fashioned.

The Spirit is never the Spirit of uniformity, but always works for unity within plurality. Plurality is not simply something that is provisional, a stage on the way to *true* unity with one "universal" theology. Plurality itself is the work of the Spirit, and needs to be recognized as such and celebrated by the church in mission. The Asian bishops have called for a "receptive pluralism," meaning that "the many ways of responding to the prompting of the Holy Spirit must be continually in conversation with one another."[48] Dialogue, then, is not just something that is done with other religions, but also with the various cultures and contexts in Asian nations and within Asia itself. In this way, there can emerge various particular theologies and a distinctly Asian theology as well.

Not only does the Spirit provide the *basis* for inculturation, however. She also guides the process. There is no doubt that the inculturation process is one of risk. There is always the danger of "selling out" the faith, or falling into an inappropriate syncretism. This is why the need to discern the

44. *Instrumentum Laboris*, 18.
45. Office of Theological Concerns, "The Spirit at Work in Asia Today," 237.
46. "Concluding Document," § 262.
47. See Kim, *The Holy Spirit in the World*, 134; and Rainbow Spirit Elders, *Rainbow Spirit Theology*, 29–41.
48. See Office of Theological Concerns, "The Spirit at Work in Asia Today," 321.

working of the Spirit is so important for those working in the inculturation process. Of the five criteria presented by Robert Schreiter for the genuineness of an expression of local theology, it seems that the last two—an openness to correction from other local theologies, and the strength of such a local expression to do the same for others—are particularly relevant here. Both point to the rich pluralism that the Spirit provides among the world's cultures and situations. The pluralism that the Spirit creates becomes a criterion of a theology's authenticity.[49]

Reconciliation

In his many writings on mission as reconciliation, Robert Schreiter insists particularly on two elements of the reconciliation process. First and foremost, he says, reconciliation is possible only because it is *God* who takes the initiative, who offers the insight, courage, and grace to a particular victim or group of victims to forgive the violence that has been committed against them. Secondly, Schreiter points out that reconciliation does not restore things as they were before—to the *status quo ante*. Rather, reconciliation moves both victim and perpetrator to a new place, a place that is created by grace.[50] Schreiter speaks more generally of "God" performing this work of reconciliation, but we might more appropriately speak of this work as the work of the Holy Spirit, especially because healing, reconciliation, and surprising newness are always signs of her work: *Fons vivus, ignis, caritas, et spiritalis unction* (The living spring, the living fire, sweet unction and true love); *Emitte Spiritum tuum, et creabuntur, et renovabis faciem terrae* (Send forth Thy Spirit and they shall be created. And Thou shalt renew the face of the earth).

The work of the Spirit in the process of reconciliation was noted in particular at the Commission on Mission and Evangelization's 2005 meeting in Athens, which was entitled "Come, Holy Spirit, Heal and Reconcile," a meeting attended by women and men from all over the world, with special participation by Pentecostals and Orthodox. In a paper written after the conference on mission and reconciliation we read: "We look to the Holy Spirit, who in the Bible is related with communion (2 Cor 13:13) to lead us and all creation in integrity and wholeness towards reconciliation with God and one another."[51]

---

49. See Schrieter, *Constructing Local Theologies*, 119–21.
50. Schreiter, *Constructing Local Theologies*.
51. World Council of Churches, "Mission as Ministry of Reconciliation," 94.

In today's violent world, reconciliation is to be sought on various levels, and is clearly in the forefront of the church's evangelizing mission, for the word of the possibility of reconciliation is indeed good and often surprising news. The Spirit might work on the individual level reconciling abused spouses or children to abusive parents. She might also work at the political level, bringing reconciliation to victims of torture or genocide in places like South Africa, Argentina, and Rwanda; or between nations that have been torn apart—like Germany in the past or like the continuing rift between South and North Korea. Or the Spirit might work on the cultural level reconciling Native Americans in North America, or Aboriginals or Maori in Australia or New Zealand, respectively. Finally, mission might also encompass the work of the Spirit within the church itself, reconciling women who have been slighted in the past, or victims of sexual abuse in places like the United States, Belgium, and Ireland.[52]

Kirsteen Kim evokes the image of the Spirit at work in reconciliation as a "dove with color and strength."[53] Often the dove that represents the Spirit is a misleading image, resembling either the "fat turkey of consumerism" or the "eagle of empire,"[54] neither of which is a meaningful symbol for reconciliation. For the dove to be a true representation of the Spirit, she says, we must recognize that reconciliation "takes place under the wings of the dynamic and vigorous Spirit of God, who brooded over the waters to bring forth creation, and hovers still today."[55] The Spirit leads humanity in the real struggle for reconciliation, a struggle that takes strength and courage, and one that unifies humanity in all its colorful variety. It is participation in such work of the Spirit that-is the task of mission today.

Conclusion

The Holy Spirit is the "principle agent of mission." Mission is nothing else but "finding out where the Spirit is at work and joining in." These two statements by a bishop of Rome and an archbishop of Canterbury have been the two principles at work in this essay, in dialogue, as it were, with a third statement: mission is "a single, complex reality." They are statements with which, I am sure, McGee would agree enthusiastically, and statements that illumine in a particular way the wonderful scholarship to which he devoted

---

52. See Bevans and Schroeder, *Constants in Context*, 391–92.
53. Kim, *The Holy Spirit in the World*, 179.
54. Ibid., 180.
55. Ibid., 181.

such a large part of his life—scholarship that has touched this one Catholic's heart profoundly.

Bibliography

Allen, John L., Jr. *The Future Church: How Ten Trends Are Revolutionizing the Catholic Church.* New York: Doubleday, 2009.

Benedict XVI, Pope. Motu Proprio *Ubicumque et Semper.* 2010. http://www.vatican.va/holy_father/benedict_xvi/apost_letters/documents/hf_ben-xvi_apl_20100921_ubicumque-et-semper_en.html. Last Accessed June 1, 2011.

Bevans, Stephen. "Missiology through the Back Door: Reflections of an SVD Mission Theologian." *Verbum SVD* 52, no. 4 (2011) 367–77.

Bevans, Stephen B., and Roger P. Schroeder. *Constants in Context: A Theology of Mission for Today.* Maryknoll, NY: Orbis, 2004.

Bosch, David J. *Transforming Mission: Paradigm Shifts in Theology of Mission.* Maryknoll, NY: Orbis, 1991.

Comblin, José. "The Holy Spirit." In *Mysterium Liberationis: Fundamental Concepts of Liberation Theology,* edited by Ignacio Ellacuría and Jon Sobrino, 462–82. Maryknoll, NY: Orbis, 1993.

"Concluding Document." Fifth General Conference of the Bishops of Latin America and the Caribbean. Aparecida, Brazil. http://www.aecrc.org/documents/Aparecida-Concluding Document.pdf. Accessed June 1, 2007.

"Dialogue and Proclamation." Pontifical Council for Interreligious Dialogue and Congregation for the Evangelization of Peoples, 1991. http://www.vatican.va/roman_curia/pontifical_councils/interelg/documents/rc_pc_interelg_doc_19051991_dialogue-and-proclamatio_en.html. Last accessed June 22, 2011.

Dunn, James D. G. *The Christ and the Spirit: Collected Essays.* Vol. 2. Edinburgh: T. & T. Clark, 1998.

Edwards, Denis. *Breath of Life: A Theology of the Creator Spirit.* Maryknoll, NY: Orbis, 2004.

"Fresh Expressions." Website front page, September 2006. www.freshexpressions.org.uk.

González, Justo L. *Acts: The Gospel of the Holy Spirit.* Maryknoll, NY: Orbis, 2001.

Gaudium et Spes, Pastoral Constitution On the Church In the Modern World (1965). In *The Documents of Vatican II,* edited by Walter M. Abbot and Joseph Gallagher, translated by Joseph Gallagher, 199–308. New York: Guild, 1966.

Instrumentum Laboris for the Synod for Africa. 1991. http://www.afrikaworld.net/synod/inlaboris.htm. Last accessed June 22, 2011.

John Paul II. *Dominum et Vivificantem,* Encyclical on the Holy Spirit in the Life of the Church and the World (1986). http://w2.vatican.va/content/john-paul-ii/en/encyclicals/documents/hf_jp-ii_enc_18051986_dominum-et-vivificantem.html

———. *Redemptoris Missio,* Encyclical on the Permanent Validity of the Church's Missionary Mandate (1990). http://w2.vatican.va/content/john-paul-ii/en/encyclicals/documents/hf_jp-ii_enc_07121990_redemptoris-missio.html

Johnson, Elizabeth. *Women, Earth, and Creator Spirit.* Mahwah, NJ: Paulist, 1993.

———. *She Who Is: The Mystery of God in Feminist Theological Discourse.* New York: Crossroad, 1992.

Kähler, Martin. *Schriften zur Christologie und Mission.* 1908. Reprint, Munich: Kaiser Verlag, 1971.
Kim, Kirsteen. *The Holy Spirit in the World: A Global Conversation.* Maryknoll, NY: Orbis, 2007.
———. *Joining in with the Spirit: Connecting World Church and Local Mission.* London: Epworth, 2009.
Klaus, Byron D. 2007. "Pentecostalism and Mission." *Missiology: An International Review* 35, no. 1 (2007) 39–54.
Lumen Gentium, Dogmatic Constitution On the Church, 1964. In *The Documents of Vatican II*, edited by Walter M. Abbot and Joseph Gallagher, translated by Joseph Gallagher, 14–101. New York: Guild, 1966.
McGee, Gary B. *Miracles, Missions, & American Pentecostalism*, American Society of Missiology Series 45. Maryknoll, NY: Orbis, 2010.
Nostra Aetate, Declaration On the Relationship of the Church to Non-Christian Religions (1965). In *The Documents of Vatican II*, edited by Walter M. Abbot and Joseph Gallagher, translated by Joseph Gallagher, 660–68. New York: Guild, 1966.
Office of Theological Concerns. "The Spirit at Work in Asia Today, 1997." In *For All the Peoples of Asia: Federation of Asian Bishops's Conferences, Documents from 1997 to 2001*," edited by Franz-Josef Eilers, 237–327. Quezon City, Philippines: Claretian, 2002.
Oleska, Michael J. "The Holy Spirit's Action in Human Society: An Orthodox Perspective." *International Review of Mission* 79, no. 515 (1990) 311–37.
Paul VI, Pope. *Evangelii Nuntiandi*, Apostolic Exhortation on Evangelization in the Modern World (1975). http://w2.vatican.va/content/paul-vi/en/apost_exhortations/documents/hf_p-vi_exh_19751208_evangelii-nuntiandi.html. Accessed September 30, 2016.
Rainbow Spirit Elders. *Rainbow Spirit Theology: Towards an Australian Aboriginal Theology.* Hindmarsh, SA: ATF, 2007.
Robeck, Cecil M., Jr. "Pentecostalism and Mission: From Asusa Street to the Ends of the Earth." *Missiology: An International Review* 35, no. 1 (2007) 75–92.
Schleiermacher, Friederich. *Brief Outline on the Study of Theology.* Translated by Terrence N. Tice. 1830. Reprint, Atlanta: Knox, 1966.
Schreiter, Robert J. *Constructing Local Theologies.* Maryknoll, NY: Orbis, 1985.
———. "Globalization and Reconciliation: Challenges to Mission." In *Mission in the Third Millennium*, edited by Robert J. Schreiter, 121–43. Maryknoll, NY: Orbis, 2001.
World Council of Churches. "Mission as Ministry of Reconciliation." In *You Are the Light of the World: Statements on Mission by the World Council of Churches*, edited by Jacques Matthey, 90–126. Geneva: WCC, 2005.
Yong, Amos. *The Spirit Poured Out on All Flesh: Pentecostalism and the Possibility of Global Theology.* Grand Rapids: Baker Academic, 2005.

9

Essential Characteristics of Pentecostal Mission

Grant McClung

GARY B. MCGEE WAS known for his personal involvement in missional efforts beyond the borders of his denomination and Pentecostal family. Among other notable characteristics, McGee's teaching, scholarship, and publishing were creative initiatives that the current generation may take for granted: (1) A broadened and balanced Pentecostal mission with specific appreciation for the supernatural work of the Holy Spirit, (2) Publishing of a distinctive Pentecostal missiology (including a dream for a Pentecostal journal of missiology) in the broader evangelical and ecumenical mission circles, (3) Increased cooperation among Pentecostals with the evangelical Great Commission community, and (4) closer conversation on mission with the broader, historical Christian family.

McGee was among the first Pentecostal missions scholars[1] to trace the ecumenical cooperation abroad on the part of early Pentecostal missionaries and the eventual increase of collaborative associations and networks such as the Pentecostal World Conference. He took note of Pentecostal integration into such cooperative networks as the National Association of Evangelicals and other evangelical initiatives toward collaboration in mission. [2]

The Lausanne Movement for World Evangelization, that included Pentecostals from the outset, has typified the kind of cooperation in world evangelization that McGee celebrated in his teaching and scholarship. Although Pentecostal understandings and practices of mission are historically

---

1. See under sub-heading "Pentecostal Ecumenism," in McClung, *Azusa Street and Beyond: Pentecostal Missions*, 5; this volume is now revised as *Azusa Street and beyond: Missional Commentary on The Global Pentecostal/Charismatic Movement*.

2. McGee, "Missions, Overseas (North American)," 617.

deeper than the Lausanne movement, I have chosen the Lausanne story and missional statements because they parallel the general *ethos* and essence of Pentecostal mission.

The story of Lausanne begins with Billy Graham. Evangelist Billy Graham rose to prominence in the United States through the 1940s and 50s. As he began preaching internationally Graham developed a passion to unite all evangelicals in the common task of the total evangelization of the world. That converged in the 1966 World Congress on Evangelism in Berlin, Germany, co-sponsored by the Billy Graham Evangelistic Association and *Christianity Today* magazine (founded by Graham in 1956). The Berlin meeting brought together some 1,200 delegates from over 100 countries and inspired a number of follow-up conferences.

A few years later there was a perceived need by Graham and others for a larger, more diverse congress. A globally representative planning group was put in place in 1971 and a field office was opened in Lausanne, Switzerland. In July, 1974, some 2,700 participants from over 150 nations met in Lausanne for ten days of discussion, fellowship, worship, and prayer. The location of the congress in the city of Lausanne would ultimately provide the name *Lausanne* Congress and the title of *The Lausanne Covenant* (one of the crowning achievements of the congress). In addition, a continuation committee formed out of the gathering was eventually named as the Lausanne Committee for World Evangelization (LCWE).

Fifteen years after the original Lausanne Congress, the so-called "Lausanne II" convened in Manila in July 1989. The major affirmation document coming out of that gathering was *The Manila Manifesto*. In October, 2010, the third global Lausanne congress was convened in Cape Town, South Africa and gave rise to its concluding document, *The Cape Town Commitment*. These three major Lausanne publications can be read in their entirety, along with over sixty "Lausanne Occasional Papers" (LOPs).[3] This essay intersects with the first two, *The Lausanne Covenant* and *The Manila Manifesto* since they were more concurrent with the time frame of the mission and missiology of Gary B. McGee.

In examining the core of Pentecostal understandings and practices of mission, *eight essential characteristics* are noteworthy. For Pentecostals, mission is (1) Experiential, (2) Exegetical, (3) Expressive, (4) Eschatologically urgent, (5) Exposure and confrontation, (6) Ecologically active, (7) Egalitarian in recruitment and leadership, and (8) Ecumenically interdependent.

---

3. You can find these at the Lausanne website (www.lausanne.org) under "Documents."

1. Pentecostal mission is *Experiential*

We believe that one must know God personally through Jesus Christ and that our evangelistic witness flows out of that personal experience. *The Manila Manifesto* says it like this, "Our proclamation that Christ died to bring us to God appeals to people who are spiritually thirsty, but they will not believe us if we give no evidence of knowing the living God ourselves . . . ."[4] The full experience of the Holy Spirit, said Arthur Glasser, ". . . will not only move the Church closer to Jesus at its center, but at the same time, press the Church to move out into the world in mission."[5]

2. Pentecostal mission is *Exegetical*

Statements regarding biblical authority are central to *The Lausanne Covenant* and *The Manila Manifesto*.[6] Because of their own high regard for Scripture, Pentecostals have earned themselves the nickname "people of The Book." Anthropologist Eugene Nida called Latin American Pentecostals, "The Church of the Dirty Bibles." There, he observed, the Bible is used frequently in worship services, being read along by the poor with their soiled fingers as a reading guide.

Whenever and wherever there is rising deterrence from non-Christian religions and secularization, along with the alarming drift toward theological "slippage" in the Christian community, the ballast and balance of biblical exegesis and theological scholarship is needed in the task of evangelization. In fact, let it be asserted that, "Exegesis and evangelization need not, and cannot, be mutually exclusive."[7] Thus, for example, in the United States and Canada, Pentecostal missions professors have found a home as founding members of the Evangelical Missiological Society (EMS). [8]

---

4. Section 7. "The Integrity of The Witnesses," in *The Manila Manifesto*; Cf. Graham, "Are We Evangelists Acceptable to God," 73.

5. Glasser, Foreword, vii.

6. Not only are there entire paragraphs on biblical authority, such as Section 2, "The Authority and Power of The Bible," in *The Lausanne Covenant*, but both documents are supported heavily with a wide array of biblical references for each of their main sections.

7. McClung, "Pentecostal/Charismatic Perspectives on a Missiology for the Twenty-First Century," 14; see also McClung, "Pentecostal/Charismatic Perspectives on Missiological Education," 57–66.

8. More on the Evangelical Missiological Society is found at: www.emsweb.org and in their "Occasional Bulletin," published by EMS.

3. Pentecostal mission is *Expressive*

The truth of the gospel is meant to be verbally expressed with the expectation of a verdict on the part of the listener. Even a cursory reading of scripture shows the centrality of proclamation in the ministry of evangelization, starting with our Lord Jesus Christ as the primary case in point:

> The Spirit of the Lord is on me, because he has anointed me *to preach* good news to the poor. He has sent me *to proclaim* freedom for the prisoners and recovery of sight for the blind, to release the oppressed, *to proclaim* the year of the Lord's favor. (Luke 4:18–19, *italics* mine, KJV and Quotes hereafter)

George Peters asks the question:

> What if Jesus had silently walked the paths of Galilee or the streets of Jerusalem? If He had only demonstrated the love of God and the compassion of His own heart, but had never proclaimed and expounded the motive, meaning and purpose of His life, service, death, and resurrection? What if He had never informed us of the nature and mind of God? [9]

The straightforward introduction of Jesus by the gospel writers shows him launching his public ministry with the ministry of proclamation:

> Now after John was put in prison, Jesus came into Galilee, *preaching* the gospel of the kingdom of God (Mark 1:14, KJV, *italics* mine)[10]

> I must *preach* the good news of the kingdom of God to the other towns also, because that is why I was sent. And *he kept on preaching* in the synagogues of Judea" (Luke 4:43–44, KJV, *italics* mine)

Note the symbiotic and successive correlation between being filled and anointed with the Holy Spirit and the verbal expression of the gospel in Jesus's proclamation (and on into the public life of the early church).[11] "And Jesus returned to Galilee *in the power of the Spirit . . . He taught* in their synagogues . . . *his message had authority*" (Luke 4:14, 15, 32, KJV, *italics* mine).

The Lausanne Covenant illustrates the Pentecostal prioritization of proclamation by stating that, "Our Christian presence in the world is

---

9. Peters, *Saturation Evangelism*, 19.

10. Or "*proclaiming* the good news of God," NIV.

11. Note the pattern "filled with the Spirit and spoke boldly" in Acts 2:4; 4:31; 9:17, 20; 12:9, 10; 19:6, etc.

indispensable to evangelism, and so is that kind of dialogue whose purpose is to listen sensitively in order to understand. But evangelism itself is the proclamation of the historical, biblical Christ as Saviour and Lord, with a view to persuading people to come to him personally and so be reconciled to God."[12]

4. Pentecostal mission is *Eschatologically urgent*

The expectation of the return of Jesus Christ is highlighted in *The Lausanne Covenant* as a major motivational force in evangelization:

> We believe that Jesus Christ will return personally and visibly, in power and glory, to consummate his salvation and his judgment. This promise of his coming is a further spur to our evangelism, for we remember his words that the gospel must first be preached to all nations." [13]

"Proclaim Christ Until He Comes" was the congress theme at Lausanne II in Manila, reflected in the final lines of *The Manila Manifesto*: "Our manifesto at Manila is that the whole church is called to take the whole gospel to the whole world, proclaiming Christ until he comes, with all necessary urgency, unity and sacrifice."[14]

Eschatological urgency was at the very heart and soul of the missionary fervor in early Pentecostalism. When supernatural phenomena burst on the scene at the Azusa Street revival and other locations in 1906, Pentecostals were sure that they were living in and directly experiencing the end-time restoration of New Testament apostolic power. Signs and wonders were a portent of Christ's imminent return. Everything else was put aside for the urgent business of world evangelization.[15] Scores of Pentecostal missionaries, most of them ill-prepared in language/culture learning and without adequate financial support, took off for the far-flung corners of the

---

12. Section 4, "The Nature of Evangelism," in *The Lausanne Covenant*.
13. Section 15, "The Return of Christ," in *The Lausanne Covenant*.
14. "Conclusion: Proclaim Christ Until He Comes," in *The Manila Manifesto*.
15. McClung, "Try To Get People Saved: Azusa 'Street Missiology,'" 5; this chapter was first published as McClung, "'Try To Get People Saved:' Revisiting the Paradigm of an Urgent Pentecostal Missiology," 30–51; cf. McClung, "Salvation Shock Troops," 80–90; see also the following by McClung on the unique contribution of Pentecostal/Charismatic understandings of evangelization: McClung, "The Pentecostal/Charismatic Contribution to World Evangelization," 65–70; McClung, "Evangelism," 617–20; McClung, "Evangelists," 620–23; McClung, "Exorcism," 624–28; McClung, "'Waiting on the Gift,'" 64–65; McClung, "Pentecostals: The Sequel," 30–36; and McClung, "People of Persuasion."

globe, "... expecting to remain there until the rapture, which they believed was very near at hand."[16] Pentecostal historian Vinson Synan characterized these early evangelists as "missionaries of the one-way ticket."[17]

5. Pentecostal mission is *Exposure and confrontation*

Whether it was with John the Baptist, Jesus of Nazareth, or the early church throughout the Book of Acts, the work of evangelization ultimately exposed and confronted evil powers in spiritual warfare (note, for example, the confrontation of Paul and Elymas, the sorcerer, in Acts 13:6–12).

Both statements, from Lausanne and from Manila, addressed this reality:

> We believe that we are engaged in constant spiritual warfare with the principalities and powers of evil, who are seeking to overthrow the Church and frustrate its task of world evangelization. We know our need to equip ourselves with God's armour and to fight this battle with the spiritual weapons of truth and prayer....[18]

And

> We affirm that spiritual warfare demands spiritual weapons, and that we must both preach the word in the power of the Spirit, and pray constantly that we may enter into Christ's victory over the principalities and powers of evil.[19]

In the fifteen years between Lausanne (1974) and Lausanne II in Manila (1989), there had been a proliferation of discussion and publication on the topics of spiritual warfare, power encounter, and signs and wonders in world evangelization, much of it reflecting the realities and experiences from the burgeoning Pentecostal/Charismatic Movement in the Majority World.

This was reflected in Neuza Itioka's research in which she made the case for, "Recovering the Biblical Worldview for Effective Mission." Itioka, a

---

16. Cited in Gee, *The Pentecostal Movement*, 30.

17. Synan, *The Spirit Said "Grow,"* 39; cf. Anderson, "Spreading Fires," 8–14; and Faupel, *The Everlasting Gospel*.

18. The first lines of Section 12, "Spiritual Conflict," in *The Lausanne Covenant*.

19. Affirmation 11, *The Manila Manifesto*; cf. also Lausanne Occasional Paper (LOP) no. 29, "Spiritual Conflict in Today's Mission," and the report ("Gatherings") on "Deliver Us From Evil Consultation," Nairobi, Kenya (August 2000) on the Lausanne website www.lausanne.org.

Japanese-Brazilian missions leader, asserted that, "Certainly one of the most important issues worldwide missions must face . . . is how to confront the destructive supernatural forces that oppose the missionary enterprise." [20]

Consultations and literary discussions of power encounter, signs and wonders, and spiritual warfare had highlighted the decade of the 1980s. It is likely that these discussions and attention to these issues helped to produce the following statement in the 1989 *Manila Manifesto*:

> All evangelism involves spiritual warfare with the principalities and powers of evil, in which only spiritual weapons can prevail, especially the Word and the Spirit, with prayer. We therefore call on all Christian people to be diligent in their prayers both for the renewal of the church and for the evangelization of the world.
>
> Every true conversion involves a power encounter, in which the superior authority of Jesus Christ is demonstrated. There is no greater miracle than this, in which the believer is set free from the bondage of Satan and sin, fear and futility, darkness and death.[21]
>
> In the Pentecostal family of churches there have also been discussions of and active experience with the realities of evil that are displayed in economic and political systems. They resonate with the section of *The Lausanne Covenant* which calls upon leaders of nations to safeguard the protections set forth in The Universal Declaration of Human Rights.[22]

By 1989 at Lausanne II in Manila, the language had become more expressive and direct. For example, one of the opening twenty-one affirmations declared:

> We affirm that the proclamation of God's kingdom of justice and peace *demands the denunciation* of all injustice and oppression,

---

20. Itioka, "Recovering the Biblical Worldview for Effective Mission," 34–38. Some of the other publications that reflected the discussions of the 1980s included: Kraft, *Christianity With Power*; Reddin, *Power Encounter*; Springer, *Power Encounters among Christians in the Western World*; Wagner and Pennoyer, *Wrestling with Dark Angels*; White, *When the Spirit Comes in Power*; Williams, *Signs, Wonders, and the Kingdom of God*; and Wimber, *Power Evangelism*; cf. Kraft, "Spiritual Warfare: A NeoCharismatic Perspective," 1091–96.

21. Under Section 5. "God The Evangelist," in *The Manila Manifesto*.

22. Under Section 13. "Freedom and Persecution," in *The Lausanne Covenant*.

both personal and structural; we will not shrink from this prophetic witness.[23]

In the section called "Good News for Today," there is the language of struggle in the concern for "... *the majority of the world's population who are destitute, suffering or oppressed*," and the acknowledgement that scripture addresses, "... *God's concern for the materially poor and our consequent duty to defend and care for them*."[24] In addition, *The Manila Manifesto* section, "The Gospel and Social Responsibility" speaks of the Kingdom of God and "... *its demands of justice and peace*."[25]

6. Pentecostal mission is *Ecologically active*

Technically understood, *Ecology* is defined as that branch of biology that deals with relations and interactions between organisms and their environment, including other organisms. *Human ecology* is the branch of sociology that is concerned with studying the relationship between human groups and their physical and social environment.[26]

Biblical evangelization should be seen as ecologically active, that is, bringing the message and realities of the kingdom of God into the social affairs of human beings and into responsible stewardship of all creation. Pentecostal mission must practice an integrated paradigm of evangelization and social action with a continued focus

> ... upon the Word (*exegesis*) and the Spirit (*experience*). This internal soul of Pentecostalism then reaches outward in continual prioritized *evangelism*, and across in *ecumenical* cooperation with those who are the true Body of Christ within every Christian communion. It reaches up in a constant *eschatological* expectation of Christ's return while at the same time reaching down ["*Ecology*"] in prophetic social activism and change, and in the responsible care of earth's resources until the day of the new heavens and a new earth (Isaiah 65.17).[27]

---

23. Affirmation 9 (of "The Twenty-One Affirmations), in *The Manila Manifesto*;s italics mine.

24. In Section 2. "Good News For Today," in *The Manila Manifesto*; italics mine.

25. In Section 4. "The Gospel and Social Responsibility," in *The Manila Manifesto*; italics mine.

26. "Ecology."

27. McClung, "Try To Get People Saved: Azusa 'Street Missiology,'" 19; note also the diagram on page 18, "Figure 3. A Pentecostal Missiological Paradigm."

Integrated social activism and a *scripturally*-based "ecological ethic"[28] is commendable and is being pursued by the "Evangelical Environmental Network" and their *Creation Care* magazine (www.creationcare.org), an extension of "Evangelicals for Social Action" (www.esa-online.org). *The Manila Manifesto* specifically deplores " . . . all forms of exploitation of people and *of the earth.*" [29]

The primary documents used for this overview, *The Lausanne Covenant* and *The Manila Manifesto*, are explicit in their integration of evangelization and social justice. The Lausanne document asserts

> . . . that God is both the Creator and the Judge of all men. We therefore should share his concern for *justice and reconciliation throughout human society and for the liberation of men and women from every kind of oppression* . . . we express penitence both for our neglect and for *having sometimes regarded evangelism and social concern as mutually exclusive.* Although reconciliation with other people is not reconciliation with God, *nor is social action evangelism, nor is political liberation salvation,* nevertheless we affirm that evangelism and socio-political involvement are both part of our Christian duty.[30]

The Manila statement asserts that

> *Evangelism is primary* because our chief concern is with the gospel, that all people may have the opportunity to accept Jesus Christ as Lord and Saviour. Yet Jesus not only proclaimed the

---

28. The term "ecological ethic" is used by Cox in *Fire From Heaven*, 245. It is doubtful, however, that Evangelicals and Pentecostals (though keen on the need for biblical contextualization and indigenization) would buy into the value placed by Cox on generic "spirituality" and animistic-based "primal religion."

29. Section 4, "The Gospel and Social Responsibility," in *The Manila Manifesto*. A statement on creation is also included in the "Kingdom Manifesto on The Whole Gospel," as follows: "WHEN CHRIST RETURNS, the whole creation will be healed and restored. So we will value the material elements of creation now and seek to demonstrate the kingdom here on earth." *Word, Kingdom, & Spirit*, 4. The *Word, Kingdom & Spirit International Consultation* was "the third gathering in a process begun in 1988 to bring together Charismatic/Pentecostals and Evangelical Social Activists. The first gathering on *Words, Works and Wonders*, held in January 1988 at Pasadena, USA recognized that 'an emphasis upon the Kingdom of God has become central in the theology of both evangelical social activists and Pentecostals/Charismatics'. At the second gathering on *Spirit, Kingdom, Church and Creation*, held in London (1990), there was enthusiasm to develop a Kingdom Manifesto and an international process was initiated." Jayasooria, "Introduction," 1; cf. also "Conference findings report," "Pentecostal/Charismatic Renewal," and "The Gospel, the Spirit," all in *Transformation*.

30. Section 5, "Christian Social Responsibility," in *The Lausanne Covenant*; italics mine.

Kingdom of God, he also demonstrated its arrival by *works of mercy and power*. We are called today to a similar *integration of words and deeds*. In a spirit of humility we are to preach and teach, minister to the sick, feed the hungry, care for prisoners, help the disadvantaged and handicapped, and deliver the oppressed. While we acknowledge the diversity of spiritual gifts, callings and contexts, we also affirm that *good news and good works are inseparable*.[31]

As one seeks to find integration between evangelization and social justice, a three-word declaration is central for understanding Pentecostal theology and practice of mission. Both documents from Lausanne and Manila state matter-of-factly that evangelism is primary.[32] This is balanced with Christopher Sugden's observation that ". . . every evangelistic activity has a social dimension, and every social activity in the name of Christ has an evangelistic dimension."[33]

A number of years ago, I read (and have subsequently used in teaching) a very helpful clarification on this relationship between social action and evangelism. It was from African church leader, Gottfried Osei-Mensah (of Ghana), who was based in Kenya as the Executive Secretary of the Lausanne Committee for World Evangelization (LCWE). Osei-Mensah said that four words could demonstrate the different opinions held by Christians on this matter: *is, or, for, and,* stating them in these four options:

1. Social action *is* evangelism—anything and everything done as a social action could be called evangelism.

2. Social action *or* evangelism—a choice of one over against the other.

3. Social action *for* evangelism—using social action/benevolence as a method or channel towards opening up an opportunity for evangelistic witness.

---

31. Section 4, "The Gospel and Social Responsibility," in *The Manila Manifesto*; italics mine.

32. The reader is referred again to www.lausanne.org where documents and summaries of various congresses and consultations on evangelism and social responsibility can be found. Noteworthy among the Lausanne occasional papers (LOPS) are: no. 20. "Evangelical Commitment to Simple Life-Style: Exposition and Commentary," no. 21 "Evangelism and Social Responsibility: An Evangelical Commitment," no. 22 "Christian Witness to the Urban Poor," no. 33 "Holistic Mission," no. 51 "Reconciliation as The Mission of God: Faithful Christian Witness in a World of Destructive Conflicts and Division."

33. Sugden, "Evangelicals and Wholistic Evangelism," 40.

4. Social action *and* evangelism—acknowledging that scripture commands *both*. (Most evangelicals and pentecostals would emphasize at this point, the "prioritization of evangelization," or, to use the language of the Lausanne and Manila documents, "evangelism is primary."[34])

Over the years, after discussing Osei-Mensah's categories with seminary students, local pastors and laity, and church leaders in various cultural settings, I have suggested a *fifth* option:

5. Social action *in* evangelism—evangelism in and of itself as an action and process is social action.

John Stott, looking back to the 1982 Grand Rapids Consultation on "The Relationship Between Evangelism and Social Responsibility,"[35] said that ". . . social activity is a consequence of, a bridge to, and a partner with evangelism."[36]

Another way to express this is to turn it around and formulate it as "Evangelism *is* Social Action."[37] This is the conclusion of Evangelist Luis Palau and the title of his 1990 article in *World Vision* magazine:

> The people of this world create the problems of this world. If we can lead them to Christ, we will create a climate for other positive, practical changes to take place . . . Conversion leads to the greatest social action. As people's lives are changed, they are different in their families, in their jobs, and in society.[38]

Palau, an Argentine-born international evangelist whose well-recognized ministry has centered on the *kergymatic* side of the church's ministry stated

> I am proud to preach the gospel, which is the power of God, because nothing helps people more than introducing them to Jesus Christ. Evangelism saves people not only from dying without Christ, but also from living without him. As they live with him, and for him, they become salt and light in a world lost in sorrow, injustice, violence, hunger, and disease.[39]

---

34. Reference on Osei-Mensah model unknown. The source believed to be an article in *World Vision* magazine.

35. The Grand Rapids 1982 summary report is found as a Lausanne Occasional Paper (LOP) on www.lausanne.org.

36. Stott, "A Note about the Stuttgart Statement on Evangelism," 209.

37. Palau, "Evangelism *is* Social Action," 4–8.

38. Ibid., 4–5

39. Ibid., 8

According to Pentecostal social ethicist, Murray Dempster, "Walter Rauschenbusch held this same conviction when he stated unequivocally that the greatest contribution any person could make to the social order was the power of a regenerate personality."[40] Pentecostal/Charismatic evangelization is obviously focused on, *but not limited to*, the prioritization of evangelization, church planting, and so-called "Great Commission" missions. This balance is evident in the rapid evangelistic growth and transformational social activism of our churches in the massive urban centers of our world. Already in the late 1980s, David Barrett documented a Pentecostal/Charismatic presence in 80% of the world's 3,300 largest cities.[41]

One could dare to say that, from the beginning of the modern Pentecostal awakening, there has *always been* a social awareness and activism in our churches, especially given the fact of our humble beginnings among the poor in numerous global venues.[42] Observers visiting the Azusa Street Mission in 1906, a ministry led by an "African American son of former slaves from Louisiana" took notice that the attendees "included immigrants, prostitutes, and the poor."[43]

What has been overlooked, says William Menzies of the Assemblies of God, "is that Pentecostals have quietly gone about social renewal in unobtrusive ways, working with the poor of this world in unheralded corners."[44] Internal reflection and self-definition by Pentecostals and Charismatics on their mission and missiology has also taken note of the integration of proclamation and social action.[45] At the risk of sounding triumphalistic,[46] here is one Pentecostal assessment of social action from within Pentecostalism:

40. Cited in Dempster, "Evangelism, Social Concern, and The Kingdom of God," 26; the original Rauschenbusch quote is from Rauschenbusch, *Christianity and the Social Crisis*, 351.

41. Barrett, "The Twentieth-Century Pentecostal/Charismatic Renewal," 119–29; Cf. also the Barrett team's annual statistical update in Barrett, Johnson, and Crossing, "Missiometrics 2007," 25–32; and World Christian Database.

42. Cf. Anderson, "Spreading Fires," 8–14, among others on the origins of Pentecostalism simultaneously in various global venues.

43. McClung, "Pentecostals: The Sequel," 32.

44. Menzies, "Current Pentecostal Theology of the End Times," 9.

45. See the numerous publications by Pentecostal/Charismatic writers in the bibliography after 1985 as representative.

46. When called upon in 1990 to make an assessment of my own movement's missiology, I expressed concern over our potential "distraction" from our task and "surviving our own success" and brought in the observations of my Pentecostal colleague, Russell P. Spittler, "There are always the twin perils of triumphalism and elitism, says Russell Spittler, who relates the insights of Chicago church historian Martin Marty. Marty, says Spittler, "once observed that Pentecostals used to argue God's approval upon them because they numbered so few. But more recently, he said, the proof has shifted to the fact

> From the inception of the Pentecostal movement, our mission has always been missions. Indeed, Pentecostalism cannot be understood apart from its self-identity as a missionary movement raised up by God to evangelize the world in the last days.[47]

This internal self-examination asserts that the "broader mission" of the church has been part and parcel of the Pentecostal/Charismatic branch of the international Christian communion as a natural outgrowth of its *ethos* as a missionary movement.[48]

In the first decade of the 21st century, a widely celebrated and highly publicized report, "Spirit and Power: A 10-Country Survey of Pentecostals," found its place in the arena of "religion and public life." The report, unveiled at the October 2006 "Spirit in The World" symposium,[49] sponsored by the John Templeton Foundation, was made available at the website for *The Pew Forum on Religion & Public Life*.[50]

In what could be qualified as "the understatement of the year," the survey's results were summarized in five journalistic sound bytes for public consumption, indicating that "renewalists" (A *World Christian Database* umbrella term referring to Pentecostals *and* Charismatics):

1. Are prevalent
2. Have distinctive experiences
3. Are intense in their beliefs
4. Support political engagement

---

that there are so many," Castro, Bosch, and McClung, "Mission in the 1990s," 154–55 (McClung portion); original Spittler quotation is from, "Maintaining Distinctives,"122.

47. McClung, "Pentecostals: The Sequel," 30.

48. More on the "broader mission" and social involvement of the Pentecostal and Charismatic Movements found in such references (not an exhaustive listing) as: Cox, *Fire From Heaven*; Dempster, Klaus, Petersen, eds., *Called and Empowered*; Dempster, Klaus, Petersen, eds., *The Globalization of Pentecostalism*; Hadden and Shupe, *Prophetic Religions and Politics*; and Pousson, *Spreading The Flame*; and see essays by Hollenweger, "Social Justice and The Pentecostal/Charismatic Movement," 1076–79; and Palmer, "Ethics in The Classical Pentecostal Tradition,"605–10; and articles by Lowe, "No More Urban Slavery," 34–39; and Mundy, "Who Will Cry for Justice," 50–54; Mundy's article reports on the work of International Justice Mission.

49. "Spirit in the World," October 5–7, 2006.

50. "Spirit and Power," Pew Forum. The public opinion survey was conducted in the countries of the United States, Brazil, Chile, Guatemala, Kenya, Nigeria, South Africa, India, the Philippines, and South Korea. The methodology of the survey is found at the Pew Forum website in the Executive Summary under "About this Survey."

5. Are morally conservative[51]

On the social justice side of Pentecostal understandings of mission, one should note the fourth result of the *Pew Forum* opinion survey, that Pentecostals "Support political engagement." For many, that was one of the most surprising of the survey results.[52]

In his commentary on the Pew Forum report, Justin Evans stated that "[b]y their very nature, missionary movements are intrinsically political, insofar as political involvement includes advancing social and moral concerns. Consider the words of Isaiah: "Learn to do good; seek justice, correct oppression; vindicate the orphan, defend the widow," (Isaiah 1.17). It should be no surprise that a missions movement is at its core concerned with social matters."[53] This is the socio-political impact of the Pentecostal missions movement.

7. Pentecostal mission is *Egalitarian in recruitment and leadership*

As an adjective, the word "Egalitarian" is ". . . characterized by belief in the equality of all people, especially in political, economic, or social life."[54] Although there is much room for improvement, Pentecostal doctrine, experience, and evangelistic expression has been marked by the recognition of human equality and interdependence.

Pentecostals would agree with the lines of *The Manila Manifesto* that recognize the partnerships and equal involvement of women and men, laity and vocational clergy, youth and children, and all races and cultures:

> We affirm that we who affirm that the gifts of the Spirit are distributed to all God's people, women and men, and that their partnership in evangelization must be welcomed for the common good. [55]

Partnerships described in *The Manila Manifesto* extend to all the people of God regardless of age, race, and gender:

---

51. "Spirit and Power."
52. Ibid.
53. Evans, "Pentecostals: Missions Movement or Voting Bloc?"
54. "Egalitarian."
55. Affirmations 13 and 14, "The Twenty-One Affirmations of the Manila Manifesto," in *The Manila Manifesto*.

> We therefore, who have for centuries insisted on 'the priesthood of all believers's now also insist on the *ministry of all believers*.
>
> We gratefully recognize that *children and young people* enrich the church's worship and outreach by their enthusiasm and faith. We need to train them in discipleship and evangelism, so that they may reach their own generation for Christ.
>
> God created men and women as equal *bearers of his image*, accepts them equally in Christ and poured out his Spirit on *all flesh, sons and daughters* alike. In addition, because the Holy Spirit distributes his gifts to women as well as to men, they must be given opportunities to exercise their gifts. We celebrate their distinguished record in the history of missions and are convinced that *God calls women* to similar roles today . . . We determine in the future to encourage all Christ's followers to take their place, rightfully and naturally, as his witnesses. For true evangelism comes from the overflow of a heart in love with Christ. That is why it belongs to *all his people* without exception.[56]

A large part of the dynamic growth of the Pentecostal Movement, described by Vinson Synan as "An Equal Opportunity Movement,"[57] is due to its ability since its inception to mobilize and deploy women into evangelistic witness and church leadership.[58] In fact, seven of the twelve members of the interracial "Credential Committee" at the Azusa Street Mission in 1906 were women. This committee selected and proved candidates for ministerial licensing and supervised the deployment of evangelists across the nation and around the world.[59]

The empowerment experience on the Day of Pentecost broke the last barrier of separation between humanity, according to Pentecostal Ecumenist David J. du Plessis (1905–1987). On the Day of Pentecost, du Plessis stated in a 1983 interview, Jesus ". . . baptized the women exactly like the men, and I say for the exact same purpose as the men are baptized so the women are baptized."[60]

---

56. Section 6. "The Human Witness," in *The Manila Manifesto*; italics mine. Cf. also articles in the section, "Women's Meetings," by and about women in Douglas, *The Work of An Evangelist*, 271–316.

57. Synan, "An Equal Opportunity Movement," 43–50.

58. See the section, "Your Daughters Shall Prophesy," in McClung, "Spontaneous Strategy of the Spirit," 76–77; see Alexander, "The Role of Women in the Azusa Street Revival," 61–77; and Holmes, "The 'Place' of Women in Pentecostal/Charismatic Ministry," 297–315.

59. Corum, *Like as of Fire*, 6.

60. In Robeck, *Theology, News and Notes*, 6.

This biblical experiential equality was a great source of encouragement for Agnes Nevada Ozman, a young Bible college student in Topeka, Kansas. Vinson Synan noted that Ozman was the first recipient of the Baptism of the Holy Spirit (an *inclusive* gift, intended for "all people," Acts 2:17 [61]) in the twentieth century—five years prior to the Azusa Street Revival. With the backdrop of Scripture, Ozman recalled that *egalitarian experience* some years later:

> As first former outpouring of the Spirit, the Word says: 'Then returned they unto Jerusalem' the eleven are named, and it reads: 'These all continued with one accord in supplication with the women, and Mary the mother of Jesus's was present and among those who tarried for the promise of the Father, and received the Holy Spirit. That is a great encouragement to us women today. We know God who gave the woman the languages spoken in them also is giving today.[62]

Ozman's testimony provides a rearview mirror historical glance. From all observations and forecasts, equality in gender and race will also be a characteristic of global Christianity in the future. This is the prediction of Philip Jenkins for "the new churches," (characterized by Pentecostal/Charismatic beliefs and practices) in his widely celebrated book, *The Next Christendom: The Coming of Global Christianity.* [63]

From the outset at Azusa Street and for the past 100 years, media observers and researchers have noted the flattening demographic affect of Pentecostalism. Pentecostal adherents, especially in the Southern World, come not from the ranks of the privileged, but from the powerless. In our history, most of our outstanding pastors, evangelists, and missionaries were laymen from the ranks of the working classes, with little or no education.

Thus, the release and participation of the laity ("laity" meaning men *and* women, boys *and* girls) is one of the most oft-quoted marks of Pentecostal/Charismatic growth cited both by inside participants and outside observers. In *An Introduction to Pentecostalism: Global Charismatic Christianity*, Allan Anderson provides this observation on early Pentecostalism's appeal to the masses:

> Cerebral and clerical Christianity had in the minds of many people already failed them. What was needed was a demonstration of power by people to whom ordinary people could easily

61. McClung, "Waiting on the Gift," 65.
62. LaBerge, *What God Hath Wrought*, 31.
63. Jenkins, *The Next Christendom*, 75.

relate. This was the democratization of Christianity, for henceforth the mystery of the gospel would no longer be reserved for a select privileged and educated few, but would be revealed to whoever was willing to receive it and pass it on.[64]

8. Pentecostal mission is *Ecumenically interdependent*

The missional *heritage* and *horizon* for the "Pentecostalized evangelical family"[65] is that we "pass it on" together in cooperative interdependence with a global family of brothers and sisters who are responsive and faithful to the Lord Jesus Christ in all Christian communions in this new millennium.

Typically, Pentecostals have understood this interdependence to be a spiritual, not structural, ecumenism—a partnership of spirit among all who know and personally follow Jesus Christ. We understand that we must work together in evangelism with the global Great Commission family, especially as we are confronted with hostility, marginalization, and persecution. This was typified so aptly in David Shibley's observation that "world evangelization can never be accomplished by Charismatics [Pentecostals] alone. Neither can it be accomplished without us."[66]

Interdependence is expressed in the great theme of the Lausanne movement, "The Whole Church Taking the Whole Gospel to the Whole World." Two entire sections of *The Lausanne Covenant* are devoted to cooperation and lengthy statements on interdependence are found in *The*

---

64. Anderson, *An Introduction to Pentecostalism*, 217.

65. Although now a common phrase (cf. a word/phrase search at www.google.com or other search engines) Spittler may be one of the original writers to speak of "the pentecostalization of the church." See Spittler, "Implicit Values in Pentecostal Missions," 421; helpful also, in the same issue of *Missiology* is Dayton, "The Holy Spirit and Christian Expansion in the Twentieth Century," 397–407. Although it is beyond the scope of this paper (another discussion for another time!), Dayton is helpful in the following observation "I am suggesting that Pentecostalism ought to be studied as *Pentecostalism*, without the assumptions created by assuming it to be a part of a larger genus called 'evangelicalism' . . . Indeed, one of the greatest dangers that the Pentecostal traditions face is that they will assimilate into 'evangelicalism' in such a way as to lose the distinctive features that are their major gifts to the rest of the church . . . I would thus prefer to emphasize the distance of Pentecostalism and related movements from the traditional churches—so much so that I wonder about the appropriateness of speaking of them (as I admit I have done above) as a form of Protestantism. I prefer the language of the 'third force' and see the movement as a corrective to the classical traditions of Christian faith. For this reason I would advise you to abandon the category of 'evangelical' in your discussions to cover the range of such 'third-force' traditions." 402–403; also helpful is Dayton, *Theological Roots of Pentecostalism*.

66. Shibley, *A Force in the Earth*, 29.

Manila Manifesto. In 2012, the first major publication of the World Missions Commission of the Pentecostal World Fellowship was devoted to collaboration in mission. Twenty-five international essays were gathered by Arto Hamalainen and Grant McClung and published as *Together in One Mission: Pentecostal Cooperation in World Evangelization.*[67]

Looking forward to our future in world evangelization, Pentecostals will be challenged to live out a missional practice that is experiential, exegetical, expressive, eschatalogically urgent, exposing and confrontational [to evil powers], ecologically active, egalitarian in recruitment and leadership, and ecumenically interdependent with the global church.

Bibliography

Alexander, Estrelda. "The Role of Women in the Azusa Street Revival." In *The Azusa Street Revival and Its Legacy*, edited by Harold D. Hunter and Cecil M. Robeck Jr., 61–77. Cleveland, TN: Pathway, 2006.

Anderson, Allan. *An Introduction to Pentecostalism: Global Charismatic Christianity.* Cambridge, UK: Cambridge University Press, 2004.

———. "Spreading Fires: The Globalization of Pentecostalism in the Twentieth Century." *International Bulletin of Missionary Research* 31, no. 1 (2007) 8–14.

Barrett, David B. "The Twentieth-Century Pentecostal/Charismatic Renewal in The Holy Spirit, with Its Goal of World Evangelization." *International Bulletin of Missionary Research* 12, no. 3 (1988) 119–24, 126–29.

Barrett, David B., Todd M. Johnson, and Peter F. Crossing. "Missiometrics 2007: Creating Your Own Analysis of Global Data." *International Bulletin of Missionary Research* 31 (2007) 25–32.

Castro, Emilio, David J. Bosch, and Grant McClung. "Mission in the 1990s: Three Views." *International Bulletin of Missionary Research* 14, no. 4 (1990) 146–57.

"Conference Findings Report." *Transformation* 5, no. 4 (1988) 1–2.

Corum, Fred T., compiler. *Like as of Fire: A Reprint of the Old Azusa Street Papers.* N.p.: privately published, 1981.

Cox, Harvey. *Fire From Heaven: The Rise of Pentecostal Spirituality and the Reshaping of Religion in the Twenty-First Century.* Reading, MA: Addison-Wesley, 1995.

Dayton, Donald W. "The Holy Spirit and Christian Expansion in the Twentieth Century." *Missiology: An International Review* 16, no. 4 (1988) 397–407.

———. *Theological Roots of Pentecostalism.* Metuchen, NJ: Scarecrow, 1987.

Dempster, Murray W. "Evangelism, Social Concern, and The Kingdom of God." In *Called and Empowered: Global Mission in Pentecostal Perspective*, edited by Murray W. Dempster, Byron D. Klaus, and Douglas Petersen, 22–43. Peabody, MA: Hendrickson, 1991.

Dempster, Murray W., Byron D. Klaus, and Douglas Petersen, eds. *Called and Empowered: Global Mission in Pentecostal Perspective.* Peabody, MA: Hendrickson, 1991.

---

67. Hamalainen and McClung, *Together in One Mission*.

———. *The Globalization of Pentecostalism: A Religion Made to Travel.* Carlisle, UK: Regnum 1999.
Douglas, J. D., ed. *The Work of An Evangelist: International Congress for Itinerant Evangelists.* Minneapolis: World Wide, 1984.
"Ecology." http://dictionary.reference.com/browse/ecology. Accessed September 30, 2016.
"Egalitarian." http://dictionary.reference.com/browse/Egalitarian. Accessed September 30, 2016.
Evans, Justin. "Pentecostals: Missions Movement or Voting Bloc?" www.lausanneworldpulse.com/01-2007. Accessed September 30, 2016.
Faupel, D. William. *The Everlasting Gospel: The Significance of Eschatology in the Development of Pentecostal Thought.* Journal of Pentecostal Theology Supplemental Series 10. Sheffield, UK: Sheffield Academic, 1996.
Gee, Donald. *The Pentecostal Movement.* London: Elim, 1949.
Glasser, Arthur F. Foreword to *The Third Force in Missions*, by Paul A. Pomerville, vii-viii. Peabody, MA: Hendrickson, 1985.
"The Gospel, the Spirit, Justice and Hope." *Transformation* 7, no. 3 (1990) 1–32.
Graham, Billy. "Are We Evangelists Acceptable To God." In *The Work of An Evangelist: International Congress for Itinerant Evangelists Amsterdam, The Netherlands*, edited by J. D. Douglas, 73–78. Minneapolis: World Wide, 1983.
Hadden, Jeffrey, and Anson Shupe, eds. *Prophetic Religions and Politics: Religion and the Political Order.* Vol. 1. New York: Paragon House, 1986.
Hamalainen, Arto, and Grant McClung. *Together in One Mission: Pentecostal Cooperation in World Evangelization.* Foreword by Tetsunao Yamamori. Cleveland, TN: Pathway, 2012.
Hollenweger, Walter J. "Social Justice and The Pentecostal/Charismatic Movement." In *International Dictionary of Pentecostal and Charismatic Movements*, edited by Stanley M. Burgess and Eduard M. Van Der Maas, 1076–79. Grand Rapids: Zondervan, 2002.
Holmes, Pamela. "The 'Place' of Women in Pentecostal/Charismatic Ministry since the Azusa Street Revival." In *The Azusa Street Revival and Its Legacy*, edited by Harold D. Hunter and Cecil M. Robeck Jr., 297–315. Cleveland, TN: Pathway, 2006.
International Justice Mission, www.ijm.org. Accessed September 30, 2016.
Itioka, Neuza. "Recovering the Biblical Worldview for Effective Mission." In *Mission in the Nineteen 90s*, edited by Gerald H. Anderson, James M. Phillips, and Robert T. Coote, 34–38. International Bulletin of Missionary Research. Grand Rapids: Eerdmans, 1991.
Jayasooria, Denison. "Introduction." In *Word, Kingdom, & Spirit: An International Consultation to Discover and Celebrate God's Work in Evangelism, Social Responsibility and Renewal in the Holy Spirit*, 1–2. Kuala Lumpur, Malaysia: Centre for Community Studies, 1994.
Jenkins, Philip. *The Next Christendom: The Coming of Global Christianity.* Oxford: Oxford University Press, 2002.
Kraft, Charles H. *Christianity with Power: Your Worldview and Your Experience of the Supernatural.* Ann Arbor, MI: Vine, 1989.
———. "Spiritual Warfare: A NeoCharismatic Perspective." In *New International Dictionary of Pentecostal and Charismatic Movements*, edited by Stanley M. Burgess, 1091–96. Rev. and expanded ed. Grand Rapids: Zondervan, 2002.

LaBerge, (née Ozman), Agnes, *What God Hath Wrought*. N.p.: privately published, n.d.
The Lausanne Covenant. https://www.lausanne.org/content/covenant/lausanne-covenant. Accessed September 30, 2016.
Lowe, Valerie G. "No More Urban Slavery." *Charisma* 32, no. 7 (2007) 34–39.
The Manila Manifesto. https://www.lausanne.org/content/manifesto/the-manila-manifesto. Accessed September 30, 2016.
McClung, Grant. "Evangelism." In *International Dictionary of Pentecostal and Charismatic Movements*, edited by Stanley M. Burgess and Eduard M. Van Der Maas, 617–20. Grand Rapids: Zondervan, 2002.
———. "Evangelists." In *International Dictionary of Pentecostal and Charismatic Movements*, edited by Stanley M. Burgess and Eduard M. Van Der Maas, 620–23. Grand Rapids: Zondervan, 2002.
———. "Exorcism." In *International Dictionary of Pentecostal and Charismatic Movements*, edited by Stanley M. Burgess and Eduard M. Van Der Maas, 624–28. Grand Rapids: Zondervan, 2002.
———. "The Pentecostal/Charismatic Contribution to World Evangelization." In *Mission in the Nineteen 90s*, edited by Gerald H. Anderson, James M. Phillips, and Robert T. Coote, 65–70. Grand Rapids: Eerdmans, 1991.
———. "Pentecostal/Charismatic Perspectives on a Missiology for the Twenty-First Century." *Pneuma* 6, no. 1 (1994) 11–21.
———. "Pentecostal/Charismatic Perspectives on Missiological Education." In *Missiological Education for The Twenty-First Century*, edited by J. Dudley Woodberry, Charles Van Engen, and Edgar J. Elliston, 57–66. Maryknoll, NY: Orbis, 1996.
———. "Pentecostals: The Sequel." *Christianity Today* 50, no. 4 (2006) 30–36.
———. "People of Persuasion: Evangelism and the Pentecostal/Charismatic Revival." August 2006. www.lausanneworldpulse.com/08-2006. Accessed September 30, 2016.
———. "Salvation Shock Troops." In *Pentecostals From The Inside Out*, edited by Harold B. Smith, 81–90. Wheaton, IL: Victor, 1990.
———. "Spontaneous Strategy of the Spirit: Pentecostal Missionary Practices." In *Azusa Street and Beyond: Pentecostal Missions and Church Growth in the Twentieth Century*, edited by Grant McClung, 71–81. South Plainfield, NJ: Bridge-Logos, 1986.
———. "Try To Get People Saved: Azusa 'Street Missiology." In *Azusa Street and Beyond: Missional Commentary on The Global Pentecostal/Charismatic Movement*, edited by Grant McClung, 1–21. Gainesville, FL: Bridge-Logos, 2006.
———. "'Try To Get People Saved': Revisiting the Paradigm of an Urgent Pentecostal Missiology." In *The Globalization of Pentecostalism: A Religion Made To Travel*, edited by Murray W. Dempster, Byron D. Klaus, and Douglas Petersen, 30–51. Carlisle, UK: Regnum, 1999.
———. "'Waiting on the Gift': An Insider Looks Back on One Hundred Years of Pentecostal Witness." *International Bulletin of Missionary Research* 30, no. 2 (2006) 64–65.
McClung, Grant, ed. *Azusa Street and beyond: Missional Commentary on The Global Pentecostal/Charismatic Movement*. Newberry, FL: Bridge-Logos 2012.
———. *Azusa Street and beyond: Pentecostal Missions and Church Growth in the Twentieth Century*. South Plainfield, NJ: Bridge-Logos, 1986.

McGee, Gary B. "Missions, Overseas (North American)." In *Dictionary of Pentecostal and Charismatic Movements*, edited by Stanley M. Burgess, Gary B. McGee and Patrick H. Alexander, 610–25. Grand Rapids: Zondervan, 1988.

Menzies, William. "Current Pentecostal Theology of the End Times." *Pentecostal Minister* 8 (1988) 9.

Mundy, David Lee. "Who Will Cry for Justice." *Charisma* 32, no. 7 (2007) 50–54.

Palau, Luis. "Evangelism *is* Social Action." *World Vision* (1990) 4–8.

Palmer, Michael D. "Ethics in The Classical Pentecostal Tradition." In *New International Dictionary of Pentecostal and Charismatic Movements*, edited by Stanley M. Burgess and Eduard M. Van Der Maas, 605–10. Grand Rapids: Zondervan, 2002.

"Pentecostal/Charismatic Renewal and Evangelical Social Action." *Transformation* 5, no. 4 (1988) 1–31.

Peters, George. *Saturation Evangelism*. Grand Rapids: Zondervan, 1970.

Pousson, Edward K. *Spreading The Flame: Charismatic Churches and Missions Today*. Grand Rapids: Zondervan, 1992.

Rauschenbusch, Walter. *Christianity and the Social Crisis,* edited by Robert D. Cross. San Francisco: Harper & Row, 1964.

Reddin, Opal L., ed. *Power Encounter: A Pentecostal Perspective*. Springfield, MO: Central Bible College Press, 1989.

Robeck, Cecil M., Jr., compiler. *Theology, News and Notes*. Pasadena, CA: Fuller Theological Seminary, March 1983.

Shibley, David. *A Force in the Earth: The Move of the Holy Spirit in World Evangelization*. Orlando: Creation House, 1997.

"Spirit and Power: A 10-Country Survey of Pentecostals." Pew Forum on Religion and Public Life, October 2006. http://pewforum.org/surveys/pentecostal. Accessed September 30, 2016.

"Spirit in the World: An International Symposium on the Dynamics of Pentecostal Growth and Experience." October 5–7, 2006, hosted by the Center for Religion and Civic Culture at the University of Southern California.

Spittler, Russell P. "Implicit Values in Pentecostal Missions." *Missiology: An International Review* 16, no. 4 (1988) 409–24.

———. "Maintaining Distinctives: The Future of Pentecostalism." In *Pentecostals From The Inside Out*, edited by Harold B. Smith, 121–34. Wheaton, IL: Victor, 1990.

Springer, Kevin, ed. *Power Encounters Among Christians in the Western World*, introduction and afterword by John Wimber. San Francisco: Harper & Row, 1988.

Stott, John. "A Note about the Stuttgart Statement on Evangelism." In *Proclaiming Christ in Christ's Way*, edited by Vinay Samuel and Albrecht Hauser, 208–11. Oxford: Regnum 1989.

Sugden, Christopher. "Evangelicals and Wholistic Evangelism." In *Proclaiming Christ in Christ's Way*, edited by Vinay Samuel and Albrecht Hauser, 29–51. Oxford: Regnum, 1989.

Synan, Vinson. "An Equal Opportunity Movement." In *Pentecostals from The Inside Out*, edited by Harold B. Smith, 43–50. Wheaton, IL: Victor, 1990.

———. *The Spirit Said "Grow."* Monrovia, CA: MARC, 1992.

Wagner, C. Peter, and F. Douglas Pennoyer, ed. *Wrestling with Dark Angels*. Ventura, CA: Regal, 1990.

White, John. *When The Spirit Comes in Power: Signs and Wonders Among God's People*. Downers Grove, IL: InterVarsity, 1988.

Williams, Don. *Signs, Wonders, and the Kingdom of God: A Biblical Guide for the Reluctant Skeptic*. Ann Arbor, MI: Vine, 1989.

Wimber, John. *Power Evangelism*. Harper & Row, 1986.

Word, Kingdom, & Spirit: An International Consultation to Discover and Celebrate God's Work in Evangelism, Social Responsibility and Renewal in the Holy Spirit. Kuala Lumpur, Malaysia: Centre for Community Studies, 1994.

World Christian Database. http://worldchristiandatabase.org/wcd/. Accessed September 30, 2016.

10

Pentecostal Church Mission and Social Ethics

Love, Justice, and Just Peacemaking

MURRAY W. DEMPSTER

IN 1991 I GAVE the Presidential Address at the Twenty-First Annual Meeting of the Society for Pentecostal Studies (SPS) hosted by Southeastern University in Lakeland, Florida. When I finished my address Dr. Gary B. McGee was one of the first persons to head to the podium to express his personal appreciation to me for narrating the story of the expansion of social ministries in three of the largest Pentecostal denominations in the United States at that time—The Church of God in Christ (COGIC), The Church of God, Cleveland, Tennessee (CG), and The Assemblies of God (AG).[1] At the same time, Gary graciously encouraged me to develop further my view of eschatology that supported Pentecostal social concern.[2] Even though Gary expressed his view that my already / not yet "material" eschatology was a bit off the mark, I appreciated the fact that his critique was subtle and gentle, a mark of his gracious character.

---

1. Dempster, "Christian Social Concern in Pentecostal Perspective," SPS, 1–48. If I had prescience at that time I would have included the United Pentecostal Church International (UPCI) as one of the four largest Pentecostal denominations that today has expanded in its vibrant growth and social impact on the United States, its North American neighbor of Canada, and its global presence in one hundred and seventy other nations. See "United Pentecostal Church, International," 1 of 3. See also "United Pentecostal Church, District and Leadership."

2. The already / not yet "material" eschatology that I outlined in my presidential address—largely based on a composite of insights from George Eldon Ladd, Roger Stronstad, and Miroslav Volf—was later published and retitled, Dempster "Christian Social Concern in Pentecostal Perspective: Reformulating Pentecostal Eschatology," 53–66.

What an opportunity I have in writing this chapter in remembrance of, and in honor to, my Pentecostal colleague, Gary McGee. His works follow him, and they are empowering for a new generation of Pentecostal ministers, leaders and scholars who encounter his significant research on the particular social history of the Assemblies of God, the broader US history of the Pentecostal movement, as well as the global expansion of Pentecostalism. In his honor, this chapter on Pentecostal church mission and social ethics will advocate the adoption of a three-fold strategy of ministry for the Assemblies of God in achieving global evangelization and social transformation: 1) re-affirming the integration of evangelism and social concern in compassion ministries; 2) redressing the injustices of economic class disparity of rich and poor, racism, immigration reform, and human trafficking; and, 3) promoting just peacemaking as the new paradigm for advancing reconciliation, creating peace and preventing war.

Compassion Ministries Creating Social Transformation

In the 1960s through the 1980s one of the hot button issues of controversy among Pentecostal denominational leaders, their church ministers, their college academic faculties, and their constituents in the pew was the explicit promotion of the church's holistic mission in integrating the ministry of evangelism and the ministries of social concern, often referred to in the AG as "compassion ministries." The proliferation of social programs during these decades was aimed at expressing concern for the welfare of people, especially the poor and the marginalized. There should be no surprise with this development in the 60s through the 80s in light of the fact that Pentecostal social concern had created expressions of compassion ministries in the formative years of the movement.

Two of the most recognized expressions of Christian care and social concern in the early years of AG global missionary outreach were the New Hope Town leprosy mission in Liberia, West Africa, and the Assiout orphanage in Egypt. Of these two, the oldest is the Assiout orphanage which began in 1911 when missionary Lillian Trasher rented a home to care for "Baby Leah," a child left orphaned by an Egyptian mother while Lillian Trasher prayed for the mother and sought to comfort her in the hour of her death.[3] By the time of her own death in 1961, Lillian Trasher, known worldwide in Christian circles by that time as "The Nile Mother," had raised 8,000 chil-

---

3. Dalton, "Mama Lillian's Answer," 14. The information on Compassion Ministries in this section of my chapter is taken and updated from my Dempster, "Christian Social Concern in Pentecostal Perspective," 18–26.

dren, many of whom she had nursed back to life. Some of the graduates have established their own businesses or hold government positions; others have become school teachers, nurses, doctors, secretaries, and over fifty are in full-time ministry.[4] Inspired by Lillian Trasher's example, the AG noted in 1988 that orphanages were established to provide physical, educational, and spiritual care to homeless children in Italy, Japan, and several Latin American countries.[5] Scott Shemeth notes in *The New International Dictionary of Pentecostal and Charismatics Movements* that "'Mamma Lillian' was buried at the site of the orphanage, which today consists of 13 main buildings on 12 acres, housing about 650 children, widows, and blind women. Today it is known as the Lillian Trasher Memorial Orphanage."[6]

Despite this background in the early years of expressions of social concern within the AG and the later proliferation of compassion ministries through the 60s, 70s and 80s, there was still a contingent within the leadership of the Department of Foreign Missions (DFM) in 1989 who championed the view that evangelism was the priority mission of the church and that involvement in social ministries would get the church's priority mission of saving souls off track.[7] Since this view was explicitly advanced in the DFM's monthly magazine, *Mountain Movers*, J. Philip Hogan—as the Executive Director of the DFM at this time—responded in no uncertain terms over this controversy of evangelism and social concern. In light of Jesus's mission, life, and teaching, Hogan stated that the AG global church mission was committed to both evangelism and social concern. Moreover, Hogan declared that "DFM has . . . invested millions of dollars and devoted countless lives to feed starving people, clothe poor people, shelter homeless people, educate children, train disadvantaged adults, and provide medical care for the physically ill of all ages." Revealing his own commitment to social concern and social action, Hogan made clear that "in recent years, we have dramatically intensified our efforts in these areas, especially where they involve elementary education.[8] By his leadership, Hogan helped overcome the stereotype that identified social concern as an enterprise of theological liberals.

During the Hogan era there were several flagship social programs that were established and are still flourishing in bringing about social

---

4. Information compiled from Dalton, "Mama Lillian's Answer," 14–15; and Beatty, "Nile Mother," 1.

5. Division of Foreign Missions, *All about Missions*, 27.

6. Shemeth, "Trasher, Lillian Hunt," 1153.

7. "Sidetracked," 3.

8. Hogan, "Because Jesus Did," 10–11.

transformation in various areas of the globe: the Calcutta Mission of Mercy; Latin American ChildCare; Disaster Relief Program now partnered with Convoy of Hope; and Health Care Ministries.[9] The Calcutta Mission of Mercy was birthed by Mark and Hulda Buntain in 1953. They started the mission when Mark heard a person cry as he preached, "Don't give us food for our souls until you give us food for our stomachs."[10] The cry represented the intolerable fate of the poor, the sick, and the hungry of the city. The response was that the mission fed every day somewhere between 22,000 and 27,000 of Calcutta's most desperately poor of all ages.[11] The Buntains believed, however, that impoverished children needed more than food for each day. They also need hope for tomorrow which prompted the Buntains to start an education program that, in time, evolved into a center for high school and junior college students and twelve branch schools in and around Calcutta which today still educate about 6,000 students.[12] Also included in the ministry of the mission are a drug prevention program, a youth hostel for the destitute and six village clinics dispensing elemental medical treatment for the needy.[13]

By far the most ambitious project in the Mission of Mercy is the Calcutta Christian Mission Hospital, a 160-bed hospital that also houses a research center and provides intern experience for the mission's school of

---

9. In addition to the list of these global social ministries, the domestic AG social programs include: 1) Teen Challenge USA, a program of multiple centers throughout the US designed "[t]o provide youth, adults and families with an effective and comprehensive Christian faith-based solution to life-controlling drug and alcohol problems in order to become productive members of society," 1 of 4; 2) Compact Family Services in Hillcrest Children's Home, a private Christian residential care campus located in Hot Springs, AR designed to care and share God's redemptive love for children who have been abused, neglected, sexually exploited, abandoned, or who have experienced the divorce or death of their parents, 1 of 2; 3) Compact Family Services in Highlands Maternity Home is also located on the AG national campus in Hot Springs, AR and is dedicated to bringing hope and healing to young women facing an unplanned pregnancy by providing professional services, life-skill training based on Christian core values, unconditional love, accountability, and renewing hope for the future, 1 of 3. In conjunction with Hillcrest and Highlands, Compact Family Services also provide Ministries of COMPACT Adoptions, COMPACT Foster Care, and COMPACT Transitional Living Center, 1 of 1.

10. Shemeth, "Buntain, Daniel Mark," 449.

11. Ibid., 449, reports that the mission feeds twenty-two thousand daily, while the report "Funeral Services Held for Mark Buntain," 1, claims that the mission fed twenty-seven thousand people every day.

12. "Mark Buntain Honored by World Relief," 8; "Funeral Services Held for Mark Buntain," 1; and Shemeth, "Buntain, Daniel Mark," 449.

13. Shemeth, "Buntain, Daniel Mark," 449.

nursing.[14] The hospital annually cares for some 80,000 outpatients.[15] All the facilities of the mission serve the poor, and keeping with the AG principle of indigenous ministry, the mission is run by 1,000 Indian nationals.[16] When Mark Buntain passed away in 1989, Scott Shemeth calculated that due to his ministry "more than 250,000 have been saved from hunger, more than 100,000 have had the chance to go to school, and tens of thousands have been treated at the hospital."[17] At Mark's prior request, Huldah remained to carry on their ministry in Calcutta and she has vigorously done so.[18] The mission has changed names to Calcutta Mercy Ministries but the mission remains the same under Huldah's leadership: "Calcutta Mercy Ministries's mission is to be the hands, the feet, and hearts that serve the poor of Calcutta."[19]

Latin American ChildCare (LACC), although not as diversified in programs as Calcutta Mercy Ministries, has made a social impact over a much greater geographical area. The roots of LACC go back to the missionary experience of John and Lois Bueno in San Salvador, El Salvador. In addressing the grinding poverty that had such a pervasive debilitating effect on the entire way of life in the city, the Buenos started the Evangelistic Center, and in 1963, they realized their dream and built a small school for children who attended the church. Seeing the flicker of hope brought about in the lives of the children through the mix of daily school education, daily food lunches, and formation in Christian values, the Buenos were inspired to spearhead the building of more schools and churches in the slums and squatters villages of El Salvador, and eventually in other countries of Central America and broader Latin America.[20]

In 1978, John Bueno made a decision that would propel their children's program in San Salvador in a quantum leap forward. Bueno enlisted Doug and Myrna Petersen to internationalize the children's ministry of San Salvador into Latin American ChildCare (LACC), a program appealing

14. "Funeral Services Held for Mark Buntain," 1; and Shemeth, "Buntain, Daniel Mark," 449.

15. Ketcham and Warner, "When the Pentecostal Fire Fell in Calcutta," 6n2.

16. "Funeral Services Held for Mark Buntain," 1; and Shemeth, "Buntain, Daniel Mark," 449.

17. Shemeth, "Buntain, Daniel Mark," 449.

18. Information compiled from "Funeral Services Held for Mark Buntain," 1; and Shemeth, "Buntain, Daniel Mark," 449.

19. Ibid. For the name change to Calcutta Mercy Ministries that continues the various ministries of the Calcutta Mission of Mercy and keeps updated data on the various ministries, see Calcutta Mercy Ministries. "Who We Are: Our History," and Calcutta Mercy Ministries, "Who We Are: Our Mission."

20. Latin America ChildCare, "Is There Hope for Tomorrow's Child?," 30; and Bueno, "Lord, Let Me Hold Their Hands," 7.

financially to North American sponsorships primarily from AG churches to support a quality and practical educational schooling of Latin American needy children. Petersen designed the long-range vision, strategy, and commitment for the LACC program to grow from 81 to 50,000 children and to expand into sixteen Latin American countries. The heart and soul of the LACC mission—at that strategic time—was to build an alternative system of education that could help children break out of the cycle of poverty. LACC's ultimate aim was to change the conditions that perpetuated a life of poverty for children by establishing a new educational system within the infrastructure of the region which institutionalizes an alternative future for children in the slum areas.[21]

The LACC program typically begins by building a church and a school next to each other in a slum area of Latin America, and then seeks to find sponsors in the United States who will give long-term monthly pledges which provide a child with a solid education, including Bible study, from qualified Christian teachers. In addition, the sponsorships provide for a nutritious hot lunch every school day that supports learning—which for the poorest children may be the only food they will eat that day—a school uniform to enhance their sense of personal worth and dignity, as well as basic preventative medical and dental care, and training in practical life skills for a self-sufficient future.[22] Fund raising is also important to pay for the hundreds of indigenous national leaders and teachers who carry out the administration and provide a quality education.

LACC has become the largest integrated network of Evangelical Christian Schools in Latin America and the Caribbean: 300 schools in 21 countries transforming the lives of nearly 100,000 children each day. With its roots in 1963 in the establishment of a school in Centro Evangelistico in San Salvador, "more than a million children have attended an LACC school."[23] In November, 2013, LACC leaders, students, alumni, parents, supporters, and Latin AG ministers and churchgoers gathered to celebrate the 30th Anniversary of LACC in Costa Rica. LACC celebrated its integrated network that provided "30 years of comprehensive care to children, adolescents, and young people who live in areas with strong population rates of vulnerability and social risk."[24] From its organizational center in Costa Rica, LACC celebrated 30 years of opportunity "to touch thousands of Latin Americans with

21. Petersen, "The Kingdom of God and the Hermeneutical Circle," 44–58. Cf. John Bueno, "Lord, Let Me Hold Their Hands," 30.
   22. Latin America ChildCare, "Love Is to Care."
   23. Latin America ChildCare, "What We Do."
   24. Latin America ChildCare, "30th Anniversary."

the truth of the gospel . . . to equip them with the basic skills for competing in, and transforming, their society."[25] Bringing about social transformation was the outcome sought by the personal transformation of individuals responding to the good news of God's salvation. The testimony is joyful and authentic: "With 30 years of LACC at work in the nation of Costa Rica, our former students are making an impact in all walks of life! They've become teachers, medical professionals, bankers, pastors, moms, dads. . . ."[26]

Providing immediate relief to the victims of natural disasters also became a formalized ministry in the Hogan era. In his last report in the year of his retirement (1989), it was noted that the Division of Foreign Missions Overseas Relief program had provided hundreds and thousands of dollars to disaster victims in more than sixty nations. Food, seed for crops, water wells, medical supplies, distribution personnel, machinery and work animals were some of the forms of relief provided. Immediate help was given to the victims as a consequence of a famine in Ethiopia, a flood in Bangladesh, a hurricane in the West Indies, and disasters in other countries. Relief in money or supplies was channeled at times through World Relief, a leading evangelical relief organization at the time, or the missionaries on the field who can work with the national church, or Health Care Ministries, one of the most recent ministries established by the AG Division of Foreign Missions.[27]

Partnership with the Convoy of Hope and its Disaster Arm that began in 1998 as an "early responder" has made the AG Disaster Relief program more timely and effective in providing aid to the victims of a disaster whether in the United States or in other countries.[28] By the end of 2009 Convoy had responded to 168 unique disaster events, including,

> Tropical Storm Allison in 2001, the terrorist attacks on September 11, 2001 in New York and Washington, D.C., Hurricane Charley, Frances, Ivan and Jeanne that hit Florida in 2004, the catastrophic storms of Hurricane Katrina and Rita that pummeled the Gulf Coast in 2005, Hurricane Gustav and Ivan in the Gulf Coast in 2008. The following year we responded to disasters in the Philippines, the Samoan Islands, Indonesia as well as major flooding in the state of Georgia. 2010 began with devastating earthquakes in Haiti and Chile. We have also provided relief to victims of fires, tornadoes, ice storms, power outages,

25. Latin America ChildCare, "Who We Are."
26. Latin America ChildCare, "30th Anniversary."
27. Division of Foreign Missions, "All about Missions," 9, 35–36.
28. AG Disaster Relief Fund.

earthquakes, cyclones, tsunamis and floods in various parts of the country and around the world.²⁹

The Convoy of Hope with its partners and AG Disaster Relief with its constituents on the ground worked hand in glove when the recent typhoon hit the Philippines on November 8, 2013, which has been dubbed as one the worst tropical storms ever. Incredibly, Typhoon Haiyan was 300 miles wide with winds over 175 miles per hour creating a storm surge of 30 feet that crashed into the coastal areas with devastating results. An estimated seven million people have been directly affected by the disaster. Fortunately, prior to the storm, Convoy had already sent 600,000 meals to the Philippines in anticipation of the coming disaster that was broadcast through the media. In addition to meals on-hand, Convoy had nine shipping containers earmarked for the Philippines within the first week that would bring 3,000,000 meals for survivors over an extended period to address dehydration, waterborne illness and starvation. The logistic challenge was to mobilize distribution across several provinces of the Philippines with food and water but also with water filtration units, diarrhea kits, dehydration kits, shoes, and hygiene supplies as needed.³⁰

On December 20, 2013, Convoy gave a report that the distribution of food and supplies to the survivors continue, that there are many people exposed to the elements that challenge their health, and that there are still thousands of children hungry for food. At the same time the response of help has been remarkable: "Since Convoy of Hope began its relief effort in the Philippines, nearly 1 million meals have been distributed in eight provinces and 50-plus communities. In addition, response teams have delivered 260 water filtration units and enough Tarps and roofing supplies to provide up to 100 families with temporary shelter."³¹ In the past, Health Care Ministries has partnered with Convoy of Hope in providing professional medical intervention into disasters that deal with water-based diseases, advancing the nutritional needs for children and adults within a disaster, and intervening in death-dealing situations. Health Care Ministries committed to go to Oriental Mindoro, Philippines, Jan 24 to Feb 3, 2014, and another team of health professionals went to Cebu City, Philippines, April 25 to May 4, 2014.³²

29. Convoy of Hope, "Disaster Response."
30. The Hope Supply: Philippines Typhoon Response, 2, 9, 11, 14, 16 of 22.
31. Ibid., 2 of 22.
32. AG Health Care Ministries (HCM) was established in 1984 to demonstrate God's love through a ministry of compassion in various global areas where health care is needed and in which short-term teams of voluntary medical professionals can travel

This narrative of Pentecostal social concern that I have highlighted through the 1960s, 70s, 80s, and beyond to this current date has culminated in expanding the AG church's three-fold mission into a four-fold mission in the AG denomination's "Statement of Fundamental Truths." The adoption of a four-fold mission and ministry made it clear that compassion ministries are in the DNA of AG church mission and ministry and are here to stay. Here is the specific language:[33]

10. The Church and Its Mission

The Church is the body of Christ, the habitation of God through the Spirit, with divine appointments for the fulfillment of her Great Commission. Each believer, born of the Spirit, is an integral part of the general assembly and church of the first-born, which are written in heaven (Ephesians 1:22, 23; 2:22; Hebrews 12:23).

Since God's purpose concerning man is to seek and to save that which is lost, to be worshiped by man, to build a body of believers in the image of His son, and *to demonstrate His love and compassion for all the world*, the priority reason-for-being of the Assemblies of God as part of the Church is:

a. To be an agency of God for evangelizing the world (Acts 1:8; Matthew 28:19, 20; Mark 16:15, 16).

b. To be a corporate body in which man may worship God (1 Corinthians 12:13).

c. To be a channel of God's purpose to build a body of saints perfected in the image of His Son (Ephesians 4:11-16; I Corinthians 12:28; 14:12).

---

to provide health care education, especially for chronic diseases of hypertension, diabetes, and heart disease when no prescribed medications are available. In some countries medications are not allowed to be brought in by the medical teams of HCM, yet the medications can be purchased within the country. Since 1984 HCM has held 447 clinics in 89 different countries, with 443,438 patients receiving treatment and many receiving and accepting a one-on-one witness to Jesus Christ as Savior and Lord. (Statistics as of 10/2012). See AG Health Care Ministries expanding, 1–4 of 4. When AG Disaster Relief partnered with Convoy of Hope, AG Health Care Ministries was brought into the loop to carry out health care intervention from disasters when HCM was requested for its involvement by Convoy of Hope. In response, HCM responded to two "outreaches" "to the disasters in the Philippines."

33. Assemblies of God, The General Council of the Assemblies of God Statement of Fundamental Truths, Articles 10 and 11, Assemblies of God website, page 5 of 6; italics mine.

d. *To be a people who demonstrate God's love and compassion for all the world (Psalm 112:9; Galatians 2:10; 6:10; I Corinthians 12:28; 14:12).*

The Assemblies of God exists expressly to give continuing emphasis to the reason-for-being in the New Testament apostolic pattern by teaching and encouraging believers to be baptized in the Holy Spirit. This experience:

a. Enables them to evangelize in the power of the Spirit with the accompanying supernatural signs (Mark 16:15–29; Acts 4: 29–31; Hebrews 2:3, 4).

b. Adds a necessary dimension to a worshipful relationship with God (I Corinthians 2:10–16; I Corinthians 12–14).

c. *Enables them to respond to the full working of the Holy Spirit in expression of Fruit and gifts and ministries as in the New Testament times for edifying of the body of Christ and care for the poor and needy of the world.* (Galatians 5:22–26; Matthew 25:37–40; Galatians 6:10; 1 Corinthians 14:12; Ephesians 4:11, 12:1; I Corinthians 12:28; Colossians 1:29)

11. The Ministry

A divinely called and scripturally ordained ministry has been provided by our Lord for the fourfold purpose of leading the Church in (1) evangelization of the world (Mark 16:15–20), (2) worship of God (John 4:23,24), (3) building a Body of saints being perfected in the image of His son (Ephesians 4:11,16), and (4) meeting human need and ministries of love and compassion (Psalm 112:9; Galatians 2:10; 6:10; James 1:27).

Love and Justice Working Together for Social Transformation

The pursuit of justice has not been utilized in AG ethical reflection and discourse to the same degree that love and compassion have been used to characterize the Church's moral mission and ministry. In fact from a moral point of view, several of the compassion ministries could easily be viewed as ministries of redressing injustice and establishing equitable treatment for the poor and needy. For example, the ministry of LACC certainly was motivated by compassion which led to redress an injustice and break the cycle of poverty by social action, to build a church and a school to provide an education, food, medical care, and a uniform that will bring an outcome of justice for children in the slums receiving equitable treatment in regards to other children in families with financial means. From a theological perspective, the LACC children are God's image bearers and therefore deserve to be treated equitably on a fair playing field. The same moral logic of compassion leading to the outcome of social justice could be applied to Calcutta Mercy Ministries, AG Disaster Relief with Convoy of Hope, Health Care Ministries, as well as the domestic programs mentioned earlier in this chapter: Teen Challenge, Hillcrest Children's Highlands Maternity Home, and COMPACT Adoptions, Foster Care, and Transitional Living Center.[34]

Donald E. Miller and Tetsunao Yamamori in their groundbreaking research on Pentecostalism in Asia, Latin America, Africa, and Eastern Europe, including Russia, identified the global expressions of Pentecostal identity, experience, mission, and ministry in these continents and their countries by the label of "Progressive Pentecostalism." Progressive Pentecostalism is a term developed by Miller and Yamamori to underscore the point that Pentecostalism in these regions had largely moved beyond the view that the sole purpose of the church was world evangelization. The "progressive" modifier signified a commitment to a holistic approach of mission and ministry that integrated evangelism with programs of social concern aimed at addressing the well-being of people with their basic spiritual, physical, social, and economic needs.[35]

Pentecostalism within different global regions, according to Miller and Yamamori, is not monolithic when it comes to the relationship of Christian faith and social change. The authors identified at least three different roads that Pentecostals travel in addressing social transformation and through their research found there was a mixture of these three in all global regions: 1) withdrawing from society as a critique of the status quo that provides a social witness to the need for social change; 2) developing alternative organizational systems to the status quo that advances social change and opportunity; and 3) promoting human welfare through compassion ministries and changing social systems for human betterment through social action. Miller and Yamamori noted that Pentecostal believers and churches in this third way focused on human rights: "Everyone is made in God's image and

---

34. See note 9 for Domestic Social Programs.
35. Miller and Yamamori, *Global Pentecostalism*, 29–30.

all people have equal value in God's sight."[36] From the extensive breadth of their research, Miller and Tamamori note that Progressive Pentecostals had developed "a rather dizzying array of programs . . . in a continuum." They explain:

> At one end of the spectrum are programs that focus on relief, while at the other end are programs intended to effect systemic change. Crossing this spectrum is another polarity—namely programs that minister primarily to individuals versus those that seek to change conditions of an entire population of people with shared characteristics.[37]

Miller and Tamamori's research and interpretive framework make clear that love and justice do work together in the way I suggested earlier with the LACC. My view from the reading of Scripture is that God is a God of love and justice, and if we claim to be God's people then we ought to practice love and justice in our relationship with our fellow human sojourners and the creation.[38] This moral point of view of the integration of love and justice was confirmed to me when Doug Petersen asked me to present a paper at the Latin America Child Conference in San Salvador that would provide biblical support for the LACC workforce to catch a vision of Pentecostal social transformation through the LACC experience.

My presentation at the LACC conference was broken up into multiple plenary sessions with a Spanish-speaking interpreter. In my session on Amos I laid out the context for understanding his prophetic pronouncements of social justice in light of Jeroboam II who led Israel into a period of eighth century commercial expansionism. Prior to this time, Israel was primarily a rural culture; now under Jeroboam a class of entrepreneurial merchants became the power-brokers of the new urban class and economy. Further the merchants created a power structure—with the bankers, the courts, and even members of the priesthood—that created a shift in land ownership and

36. Ibid., 32–33.

37. Ibid., 42–43.

38. Maston in his study of biblical ethics claims that the concept of the *imitatio Dei* (imitation of God) "is the nearest thing we have in biblical ethics to one unifying theme or motif." In Scripture, ethics are theocentric in nature and therefore grounded in God's self-revelation. Every theological statement describing God's character and action is simultaneously an ethical imperative prescribing who God's people ought to be in character and what they ought to do in conduct. If God is love, then God's people ought to love. Maston, *Biblical Ethics*, 282. Birch and Rasmussen articulate the theological indicative-moral imperative structure of ethical thinking similarly to Maston except they ask this basic question explicitly for the Christian community: "Who are we as the people of God, and what character and conduct is in keeping with who we are as the people of God?" Birch and Rasmussen, *Bible and Ethics in the Christian Life*, 189–202.

exacerbated the class structure between rich and poor, with the rich getting richer and the poor getting poorer. As I narrated Amos's story, one table of LACC participants became a bit demonstrative in their own table talk, especially when Amos gave his prophetic critique of the inequitable system and declared: ". . . let justice roll down like waters. And righteousness like an ever-flowing stream" (Amos 5: 23-24). The discussion at their table became even more animated when I quoted Jack Nelson that Amos's prophetic criticism aimed not only at individuals but the social system which makes injustice self-perpetuating:

> Merchants formed alliance with bankers, members of the court took bribes, and the unjust prosperity of the urban classes spilled over into the coffers of the temple. The result was a mutually beneficial and cozy alliance, complete with economic rewards and religious ideology, which undermined the well-being of the poor.[39]

When I talked with Doug Petersen during the break I wanted to know if the chatter at the table signified that my remarks were offensive to their views. Doug told me that the LACC workers at that particular table were talking back and forth with animation because when they heard Amos identifying the reality of systemic injustice they discerned that Amos's prophetic analysis was exactly happening in their own country where thirteen rich families control the center of power and created an economic class structure that divided a minority of rich people from a majority of poor people. The "table chatter" embodied a symbol that gave me an interpretive reinforcement that programs of compassion ministries like LACC are motivated by the *love* of the teachers, staff, and pastors, and achieve an outcome of *justice* for the children.[40] Recently, the AG, as well as other Pentecostal denominations, have weighed in on justice issues of racial reconciliation, immigration, and human trafficking. While compassion still hooks and motivates Pentecostal leaders, ministers, and parishioners to act in dealing with these three areas, there is a clear recognition that these are social justice issues. It is somewhat surprising that racial discrimination took hold so quickly after the original surge of the outpouring of the Holy Spirit from 1906 to 1908 that occurred at the Azusa Street Mission in Los Angeles. This out-

---

39. Nelson, *Hunger for Justice*, 5.

40. Dempster, "The Old Testament Foundations of Christian Social Concern." A revision of the paper was substantially edited and translated into Spanish by Floyd Woodworth for distribution to missionaries and national church leaders in Latin America in three parts: "Fundamentos en el Antiguo Testamento de la Inquietud Social Christiana," *Conozca* 12 (1986) 10-11, 13; *Conozca* 12 (1986) 5, 14, 16; *Conozca* 12 (1986) 12-13. Later expanded and modified, Dempster, "Pentecostal Social Concern and the Biblical Mandate of Social Justice," 129-53.

pouring of the Spirit created a diversified interracial church at the Azusa Mission under the leadership of a black Elder, William J. Seymour. When C. H. Mason, who was a founder of the Church of God in Christ, heard of this Pentecostal outpouring he travelled to the Azusa Street Mission and received the baptism of the Holy Spirit. Mason carried this message back to his COGIC churches and reorganized the denomination as a Pentecostal church that could ordain Pentecostal ministers of all races.[41] Bishop Itheal Clemmons states that between 1909 and 1914 "there were as many white COGIC churches as there were black" within the COGIC denomination.[42]

December 20, 1913 was a day that presaged the color line that had been washed away in the blood of Jesus and the Azusa Mission was about to rejoin the mainstream USA culture of racial segregation that divided white Pentecostals from black Pentecostals.[43] Elders E. N. Bell and H. A. Goss sent out a call to "all pentecostal saints and Churches of God in Christ" to meet for a Full Gospel Organizational Meeting in Hot Springs, Arkansas, where Jim Crow laws were strongly applied. At that meeting, a consensus supported the establishment of the Assemblies of God. With that development, the Assemblies of God over time became known as a white Pentecostal denomination and the Church of God in Christ became—not of its own doing—a black Pentecostal denomination.[44]

The divide between white Pentecostals and black Pentecostals became further solidified in 1948 when the all-white Pentecostal Fellowship of North America (PFNA) was formed. Once again, no black churches, or their church leaders, were invited to join in the Pentecostal Fellowship. As a consequence, over nearly five decades the status quo of the white-PFNA reigned in representing Pentecostalism in the USA and Canada. Through a series of institutional leadership recognitions, however, Bishop Bernard E. Underwood of the International Pentecostal Holiness Church—a nonpartisan of AG and COGIC positions on race relations—was elected to head the PFNA in 1991. He vowed to himself that he would use his term of office to overcome the racial divide and bring about some form of racial reconciliation. Bishop Underwood with Bishop Ithiel Clemmons of COGIC created a step-ladder series of four meetings that would culminate in a

41. Clemmons, "Mason, Charles Harrison," 866; and Robeck Jr., "Azusa Street Revival," 347–48.

42. Clemmons, "Mason, Charles Harrison," 866.

43. For an interpretive analysis of the black roots of Pentecostalism that led the way to understand the racial divide between white Pentecostals and black Pentecostals given the context of a racially segregated USA, see MacRobert, *The Black Roots and White Racism*.

44. Clemmons, "Mason, Charles Harrison," 866.

"20/20 Meeting" in 1994. The 20/20 Meeting was designed for 20 whites and 20 blacks to develop a conference on October 17–19, 1994 that would pronounce the death of the PFNA and hopefully birth a new expression of racial reconciliation.[45]

Over a thousand Pentecostal pastors, bishops, leaders, denominational executives and scholars gathered in Memphis, Tennessee, for what turned out to be a historic conference, "Pentecostal Partners: A Reconciliation Strategy for Twenty-first Century Ministry." About three thousand attended the evening sessions at Cook Convention Center. The morning sessions were dedicated to presentations by a team of leading Pentecostal scholars.[46] Derrick Rosenoir, who attended from Vanguard University, believed that "[t]hese presentations precipitated the climatic moment of the conference, when white Pentecostal leaders repented for a history of prejudice and racism. . ." that "culminated in an onstage, spontaneous, and extemporaneous 'footwashing.'"[47]

Historian Vinson Synan summarizes the major breakthrough that took place in "the Miracle of Memphis." By October 19th, 1994,

> . . . the old all-white Pentecostal Fellowship of North America was disbanded in favor of a racially inclusive association named the "Pentecostal and Charismatic Churches of North America." In what was dubbed "the Miracle in Memphis," leaders of the mostly white movements repented of their historic racial shortcomings and signed a "Racial Reconciliation Manifesto" pledging to "oppose racism prophetically in all its manifestations." A new Board made up of six whites and six blacks was led by Bishop Ithiel Clemmons of the Church of God in Christ. The high point of the historic gathering was the session where a white Assemblies of God pastor washed the feet of Bishop Clemmons while begging forgiveness for sins of the past. After this, Bishop

---

45. Synan, "Memphis 1994: Miracle and Mandate," 1–2 of 4.

46. The presentations were in four parts: 1) Robeck, "The Past: Historical Roots of Racial Unity and Division in American Pentecostalism;" 2) Lovett, "The Present: The Problem Racism in the Contemporary Pentecostal Movement;" 3) Synan, "The Future: A Strategy for Reconciliation;" and 4) Turner, "The Ideal: The Biblical Pattern of Unity, Endeavoring to Keep the Spirit's Unity." See also Rosenoir, "The Rhetoric of Pentecostal Racial Reconciliation," 73–74.

47. Rosenior noted that "The first presentation by Dr. Robeck, focusing on the past, was by far the most extensive, both in length and depth." Robeck's paper captured "the collective memory" of Azusa Street for both black and white with a sense of "myth making" and "nostalgia," Rosenoir, "The Rhetoric of Pentecostal Racial Reconciliation," 75–82.

Charles Blake of Los Angeles washed the feet of Thomas Trask, General Superintendent of the Assemblies of God.[48]

Recently, Dr. George O. Wood, AG General Superintendent, has become more proactive in nurturing racial reconciliation. In the spirit of creating "Thoughts for Thanksgiving," 2013, Wood invited the executive leadership of the Church of God in Christ (COGIC) to the AG national office in Springfield, Missouri for a time of dialogue, fellowship, worship and unity-building in preparing for Thanksgiving Day. The COGIC leadership accepted the invitation. Since the 1994 "Memphis Miracle," this coming together was the first time the leadership of the two denominations met explicitly to bond together and express their face-to-face commitment to the Racial Reconciliation Manifesto. During the Tuesday chapel service, Wood emphasized that "the Assemblies of God and COGIC were children of the Azusa Street revival." He lamented that the American racial culture at that time shaped the church into racial division rather than being shaped by the Bible. But a new day had come, and Wood affirmed that this "coming together of COGIC and AG leadership in a historic-time dialogue represented another step in the healing of a rift that occurred long ago." COGIC Presiding Bishop Charles E. Blake, Sr., shared a chapel message of following Paul's example in the Acts to thank God both during and after the storms of life. Apparently, this meeting was desired by both AG and COGIC leadership for years, but now the leadership meeting had finally happened.[49]

An incredible development in racial reconciliation based on social justice has recently occurred in this Month of Black History in February, 2014. Two Pentecostal organizations—the General Council of the Assemblies of God (AG) and the United Pentecostal Council of the Assemblies of God (UPCAG)—have announced their cooperative affiliation. The story of Alexander Howard, an African-American Pentecostal believer, is numbing to the AG conscience of today but not surprising of the AG conscience in the racist American culture of 1914–1920 when this injustice occurred with its Jim Crow laws. Three years after the incorporation of the General Council of the AG in 1914, an African-American Pentecostal believer from Chicago, named Alexander Howard, requested to be sent as a missionary to

---

48. Synan, *The Holiness-Pentecostal Tradition*, 186. Synan footnotes the following articles that recorded various reactions to "the Memphis Miracle": *The Pentecostal Evangel*, Jan.1, 1995, 8–9; *Pentecostal Holiness Advocate*, Jan. 1995, 6–7; *Church of God Evangel*, Jan. 1995, 23; "Pentecostals Experience a 'Miracle in Memphis's *Memphis Commercial Appeal*; Reynolds, "Oregon Voters Can Learn from the Memphis Miracle"; Clemmons, "Racial and Spiritual Unity in the Body of Christ"; and West, "That His People May Be One."

49. Wood, "AG and COGIC Leaders Gather in Historic Meeting."

Liberia. The AG leaders refused to appoint Howard on the basis of his race. Fortunately, Howard was able to connect with a group of African-American churches in New England that became incorporated in 1920 as the United Pentecostal Council of the Assemblies of God (UPCAG). Howard had now created a new Pentecostal denomination—in response to the AG—in order to fulfill his calling as a missionary to Liberia.[50]

It is truly astonishing to see how a single decision in 1917 based on race resulted in two separate Pentecostal denominations. And, even more astonishing, the AG and UPCAG for nearly a century remained separate organizations. Enter Rev. Thomas Barclay, the UPCAG International Presiding Elder, who became stirred following the Racial Reconciliation in Memphis to connect the UPCAG and the AG, and mend the racial divide. Barclay's appeal to George Wood toward reconciliation was based on 1 Corinthians 1:10 (KJV), "I appeal to you, brothers, in the name of the Lord Jesus Christ, that all of you agree with one another so that there be no divisions among you and that you may be perfectly united in mind and thought." Barclay's declaration connected with Wood and the road to reconciliation to repair the relationship was underway. UPCAG delegates and the AG Executive Presbytery approved an agreement: any UPCAG church that so desired would be welcomed into local AG districts, as well as all national AG programs and missions, while maintaining their own credentialing practices and autonomy. This historic reconciliation during Black History Month was celebrated when the UPCAG leadership joined the AG leadership for a celebratory chapel on February 11, 2014. In his chapel sermon, Barclay expressed his belief that God had put the two organizations together and stated, "No longer will we be separated from you. We came to lock arms with you."[51]

In addition to racial reconciliation, the AG has also dealt with the justice issue of immigration, including the controversy over immigrant illegal status, and the justice issue of human trafficking. The AG's position on immigration reform goes back to the Immigration Resolution 2009, developed by the Board of Directors of the National Association of Evangelicals (NAE) in which the AG is a member and the AG General Superintendent is a member of the NAE Board of Directors.[52] The Executive Presbytery of the AG

---

50. Wood, "A Vital Step Forward."

51. Ibid., 3–4 of 4.

52. See National Association of Evangelicals. http://www.nae.net/government-relations/policy-resolutions/354-immigration-2009.

adopted the NAE resolution on Immigration 2009 and sent a copy of the resolution to the constituency in the *AG News* in August 2011.[53]

Drawing upon the NAE document "For the Health of the Nation: An Evangelical Call to Civic Responsibility"[54] that identified how the biblical narrative described the migration of people and the values of compassion and justice, the NAE called for the reform of the immigration system based on the following principles for immigrants who are already here and those who are yet to come:

- That immigrants be treated with respect and mercy by churches. Exemplary treatment of immigrants by Christians can serve as the moral basis to call for government attitudes and legislation to reflect the same virtues.
- That the government develop structures and mechanisms that safeguard and monitor the national borders with efficiency and respect for human dignity.
- That the government establish more functional legal mechanisms for the annual entry of a responsible number of immigrant workers and families.
- That the government recognize the central importance of the family in society by reconsidering the number and categories of visas available for family unification, by dedicating more resources to reducing the backlog of cases in process, and by reevaluating the impact of deportation on families.
- That the government establish a sound, equitable process toward earned legal status for currently undocumented immigrants, who desire to embrace the responsibilities and privileges that accompany citizenship.
- That the government legislate fair labor and civil laws for all residing within the United States that reflect the best of this country's heritage.
- That immigration enforcement be conducted in ways that recognize the importance of the process of law, the sanctity of the human person, and the incomparable value of family.[55]

---

53. "Assemblies of God endorses NAE immigration resolution."

54. See National Association of Evangelicals. http://www.nae.net/government-relations/for-the-health-of-the-nation/human-rights/immigration.

55. "A Letter to AG News Readers." 2–3 of 3.

The AG has also weighed in on the justice issue of human trafficking, a global phenomena of human slavery in shocking numbers of victimization. The U.S. Department of State Trafficking in Persons Report (TIP) 2010 estimates that in cities there are "12.3 million adults and children in forced labor, bonded labor, and forced prostitution around the world."[56] AG missionaries in different parts of the world frequently observe vulnerable family members and individuals who are enslaved and trafficked against their will, whether from the growing slums and brothels of Asia, or other regions experiencing economic deprivation and the lack of the basics of life. The United States has not been vaccinated from this epidemic. Shared Hope International in looking at the sexual trafficking of minors in the US—which is only one slice of human trafficking in the US and the globe—has discovered the following disturbing statistics:

- At least 100,000 children are used in prostitution every year in the United States.
- The average age of entry into prostitution is 13 years old.
- At least 75 percent of minors exploited through prostitution are controlled by a pimp.
- There are three primary manifestations of child sex trafficking in the US:
  - pimp-controlled prostitution,
  - familial prostitution (the selling of one's family member for sex in exchange for drugs, shelter or money), and/or
  - survival sex[57]

In confronting human trafficking, the AG document makes clear that the community of faith must ground its mission and ministry in biblical foundations in order to bring about social transformation and correct systemic injustices. These principles include, among others, that God is a God of justice; that God blesses those who pursue justice; that every person is created in God's image and is deserving of love, justice, and human respect as God's image-bearers; that God shows solidarity with the poor and the marginalized; that God, through the redemptive work of Jesus Christ, can

---

56. This "U.S. Department of State Trafficking in Persons," is cited in "Human Trafficking" (Approved by the General Presbytery in session July 30, 2011)." See the "Statement on Human Trafficking."

57. *The National Report on Domestic Minor Trafficking*, cited in "Human Trafficking."

confront the depth of victimization and bring about the transformation of the whole person as a new creation "in Christ."[58]

A number of key ministries within the AG address human trafficking globally and in the United States. Two Assemblies of God universities have created academic centers to address human trafficking: the Center for Biblical Justice at North Central University and the Global Center for Women and Justice at Vanguard University. AG US Missions organizations that are dedicated to the fight against trafficking are Teen Challenge International USA and F.R.E.E., an organization working to Find, Rescue, Embrace, and Empower victims of this modern day slavery. Mike and Denise Bartel worked on human trafficking in India for years before coming back to the USA to found F.R.E.E. Missionaries working overseas have created AG indigenous organizations and networks that seek to emancipate victims of trafficking, namely Global Teen Challenge; Nurture Hope Network; Breaking Chains Network—Belgium; and Global Network Against Human Trafficking—a network of AGWM ministries and missionaries addressing human trafficking that includes Sparrows Nest, Cambodia, and Project Rescue.[59]

Project Rescue is also in a broader network of Christian organizations, namely, Live 2 Free; Salvation Army US; Salvation Army World Service Organization; World Hope International; and World Relief, all of which create a significant network within the umbrella of Faith Alliance Against Slavery and Trafficking (FAAST). Two other independent Christian organizations are International Justice Mission and Love 146.[60] Project Rescue as a member of FAAST affirms "The mission of FAAST is to eliminate human trafficking through prevention, prosecution, victim protection, and sustainable restoration. Our target population includes all those victimized by human trafficking: children and adults, males and females." While Project Rescue and FAAST recognize the trafficking in persons (TIP) victimizes all people regardless of age or gender, there is a greater degree of danger for women, young or old, in the sex slave industry in light of the global epidemic of HIV/AIDS. The Statement from FAAST clarifies the danger:

> According to the U.S. State Department, an estimated 42 million people live with HIV/AIDS worldwide. While the global epidemic of HIV/AIDS affects various populations, women and children who are trafficked into prostitution and other sexual purposes are particularly impacted. Due to the violent nature of sex with trafficked victims, the lack of control over

---

58. "Human Trafficking," 1–2 of 11.
59. Ibid., 10 of 11.
60. Ibid.

the circumstances and number of "customers," the inability to insist on regular condom use, and the youth of many trafficked victims, victims of sex trafficking are severely at risk for contracting HIV.[61]

This fact of vulnerability is born out from a story told by Hillary Rodham Clinton in David and Beth Grant's book about young girls being victimized by HIV/AIDS: "I've seen the results of this horrific violation of human rights. I remember meeting a young girl who had been sold by her family and taken to a brothel where she was forced into prostitution. And when she escaped and returned home, she was sold again. When she contracted AIDS and was too sick to work, she was turned out of the brothel, made her way home, was turned away again and died in a house of refuge for girls like herself."[62]

Beth and David Grant, along with K. K. Devaraj, were the founders of Project Rescue in India in 1997.[63] Although David and Beth gained an understanding of the caste system of India by working previously with Mark and Huldah Buntain in the Calcutta Mission of Mercy, it was still a formidable task to establish a ministry dealing with the sex-slave industry given the culture of India and its neighboring countries. Starting from scratch in 1997, Project Rescue had achieved by 2013 a remarkable outcome in building the infrastructure that would facilitate an effective strategy of rescue and restoration of girl victims of sex trafficking. Project Rescue also looked for the local churches in the cities to partner in the cause to bring freedom and a new life in Christ to girls imprisoned in sexual slavery. Over the last sixteen years Project Rescue, using the Rescue/Restore/Prevent strategy, had developed fifteen ministry-affiliated sites in six countries: India, Nepal, Moldova, Tajikisten, Bangladesh, and Spain; sixteen aftercare homes for restoration of women/girls who have been in sexual slavery, or for their daughters/sons for prevention; four night-care centers for children of women in sexual slavery; six vocational training centers; ten red-light district outreaches; two red-light district churches; two HIV/AIDS clinics; six medical outreaches; six awareness and prevention programs; and approximately 24,450 exploited women and children ministered by a partnership with FAAST.[64]

In its coming of age, the AG has connected its evangelism and social concern to both compassion ministries and justice issues, and now awaits

---

61. Grant and Grant, *Beyond the Soiled Curtain*, Appendix II, "A Statement from FAAST," 201–4.

62. Cited in Grant and Grant, *Beyond the Soiled Curtain*, 56.

63. Ibid., 57.

64. Ibid., Appendix I, "Project Rescue at a Glance—1997 to 2013," 186.

for a new challenge that has come over the horizon to engage the mission and ministry of the church in the task of just peacemaking.

Just Peacemaking Working for Social Transformation

Just peacemaking has recently emerged to join the longstanding Christian traditions of just war theory and pacifism. Advocates of just peacemaking now claim that there are three paradigms that inform the Christian ethics of peace and war. Just war and pacifism focus on whether a specific war is justifiable and whether participating in war in the destruction of human life is ever warranted. In contrast, just peacemaking aims to prevent war and create peace. For example, in a world marked by the rise of terrorism and its operational strategy of the "random murder of innocent people" and by the threat of "weapons of mass destruction," there is a need for the development of a new paradigm of just peacemaking. Advocates of the new paradigm make a compelling argument:

> We need initiatives to correct injustices that cause terrorism; structures of justice that dry up the sources of recruitment of terrorists; we need international networks of cooperation against terrorism. Precisely such initiatives, structures of justice, and international cooperation that just peacemaking points to.[65]

Just peacemaking, however, points to a much broader agenda than dealing with terrorism alone; as crucially important as that is, the broader goal is developing transforming initiatives and putting into practice the initiatives that will help to make our world a more just and peaceful place for human habitation. Glen Stassen, Lewis B. Smedes Professor of Christian Ethics at Fuller Seminary, has been a prime mover in organizing a collaborative effort with a diversity of scholars who would work together in identifying the proactive practices aimed at creating peace and preventing war. A group of 23 scholars—some identified with just war, others identified with pacifism—across the spectrum of denominations collaborated annually for six years to develop 10 steps toward abolishing war and creating peace.[66] Four years later, a new edition on just peacemaking was published that engaged 30 scholars into the collaborative effort to update content and nuances in articulating the 10 proactive practices within the conceptual framework

---

65. Brubaker, "Introduction," 1–2.
66. Stassen, *Peacemaking*.

of three undergirding principles of initiating peacemaking, working for justice, and building community and love.[67]

PEACEMAKING INITIATIVES

1. Support Nonviolent Action
2. Take Independent Initiatives to Reduce Threat
3. Use Cooperative Conflict Resolution
4. Acknowledge Responsibility for Conflict and Injustice and Seek Repentance and Forgiveness

JUSTICE

5. Advance Democracy, Human Rights, and Interdependence
6. Foster Just and Sustainable Economic Development

LOVE AND COMMUNITY

7. Work with Emerging Cooperative Forces in the International System
8. Strengthen the United Nations and International Efforts for Cooperation and Human Rights
9. Reduce Offensive Weapons and Weapons Trade
10. Encourage Grassroots Peacemaking Groups and Voluntary Associations.

The concept of "transformative initiatives" in just peacemaking came out of Stassen's insightful interpretation of Jesus teaching in the Sermon on the Mount. Stassen noted that, unfortunately, many read the ethical teachings of Jesus found in the Sermon by a dyadic, or twofold, structure of interpretation that leads the reader astray from understanding "transformative initiatives." For example, the legal sayings—on the face of it—seem to have a twofold structure: "You have heard it said . . . but I say unto you." Below is the juxtaposition of Jesus teaching concerning the sixth commandment "You shall not kill" from the traditional dyadic or twofold structure:[68]

---

67. Stassen, *Just Peacemaking* (2008). The ten practical steps arranged within the framework of three principles is taken verbatim from the Table of Contents, iii–iv.

68. In contrast to the traditional dyadic or twofold interpretive structure, Stassen identified the triadic threefold interpretive structure of "Traditional Piety—Mechanism of Bondage—Transformative Initiative" in his 1992 study, *Just Peacemaking*. Later in his

Traditional Righteousness	Jesus's Teaching
Matthew 5:21: "You have heard that it was said to those of ancient times, 'You shall not kill; and whoever kills shall be liable to judgment.'" (Author's translations in this chapter to follow the Greek verb forms more closely.)	Matthew 5:22-26: "But I say unto you that every one being angry with his brother will be liable to judgment; whoever insults his brother will be liable to the council, and whoever says, 'You fool!'" will be liable to hell of fire. (Illustrations: So if you are offering your gift at the altar . . . make friends quickly with your accuser.)

So after Jesus had cited the commandment "You shall not kill" and the consequence of liability for breaking the law, Jesus gave his ethical teaching. According to the dyadic structure of interpretation, Jesus taught his disciples not to kill and to overcome anger, to stop making insults, to resist name-calling like "You fool"—all of which can lead to killing and being found liable before the Sanhedrin (Matt 5:22). These behaviors were taught as the moral rules to follow in order to keep the commandment, "You shall not kill." Jesus then gives illustrations on offering your gift at the altar as a peace symbol and making friends with your accuser. Stassen disagreed with this interpretation of the ethical teachings of Jesus.

First, Stassen noted that when the commandment of old, "You shall not kill," expanded Jesus ethical teaching not to be angry with a brother, not to insult a brother, or not to call someone "a fool," the additions made this interpretation incompatible with what Jesus said and did in other passages in the synoptic gospels. Let me give one example in the case of the "blessing of the children" narrative. The disciples scolded the parents who were bringing their children to Jesus for a blessing. Jesus became "indignant," or literally translated, he was boiling inside. What he said to his disciples, therefore, should not be heard as a polite reprimand, but expressive of his deep feelings of anger: "Let the children come to me and do not hinder them; for to such belongs the kingdom of God" (Mark 10:13-15).[69] Stassen notes that Jesus shows anger and was angry according to Mark 1:41, Mark 3:5, and Matthew 21:12-17. In Matthew 23, Jesus is angry to the point that he calls his opponents "fools" which would contradict Matthew 5:22 if that verse is read as a command.[70] Second, there are actually five moral impera-

---

co-authored book with Gushie, *Kingdom Ethics*, the middle header was modified in the threefold structure to "Traditional Piety—Vicious Cycle—Transformative Initiative." The three tables in this chapter are taken from *Kingdom Ethics*, 134–37.

69. Dempster, "Social Concern in the Context of Jesus's Kingdom Mission and Ministry," 52.

70. Stassen and Gushie, *Kingdom Ethics*, 134.

tives in this ethical teaching; however, the imperatives are tacked on as illustrations of the commandment in the twofold structure of interpretation. Third, the five moral imperatives that Jesus commands are "transforming initiatives" that identify the path of deliverance from anger and killing.[71] The moral imperatives in Jesus's ethical teachings are "transforming initiatives" because they are linked to the mission, ministry, and message of Jesus in his declaration that "The time is fulfilled, the Kingdom of God is near, repent and believe the good news" (Mark 1:15 = Matt 4:17). Jesus made clear the distinction between the law and the gospel: "The Law and the Prophets were proclaimed until John; since that time the gospel of the Kingdom has been preached, and everyone is forcing his way into it" (Luke 16:16 = Matt 11:12–13). Jesus claimed that through his ministry God's reign had been inaugurated in human history. When the followers of Jesus came under the reign of God they were empowered to break the vicious cycle of anger and initiate the transformation of the moral life from anger to peacemaking. Stassen provides the triad, or threefold, structure of interpretation of the ethical teaching of Jesus that highlights the climatic third part focusing on the moral imperatives.[72]

PEACEMAKING INITIATIVE

Traditional Righteousness	**Vicious Cycle**	**Transforming Initiative**
Matthew 5:21: You have heard that it was said to those of ancient times, "You shall not kill; and whoever kills shall be liable to judgment." (In the Greek, "shall not" and "shall be" are not imperatives, but futures; as translations of the Hebrew in the Ten Commandments, they do of course imply a command.)	Matthew 5:22: But I say to you that every one being angry with his brother will be liable to judgment; whoever insults his brother will be liable to the council, and whoever says, "You fool!" will be liable to the hell of fire. (No imperatives in the Greek.)	Matthew 5:23–26: So if you are offering your gift at the altar, and you remember that your brother or sister has something against you, *leave* your gift there . . . and *go*; first *be reconciled* to your brother, and then coming, *offer* your gift. *Make friends* quickly with your accuser. (Italics mark the Greek imperatives.)

Stassen notes there are three senses in this transforming initiative: "it transforms the person who was angry into an active peacemaker; it transforms

---

71. Ibid., 134–35.
72. Ibid., 19–31, 135.

the relationship from one of anger into a peacemaking process; and it hopes to transform an enemy into a friend."[73] This transforming initiative carries with it God's benediction of blessing: "Blessed are the peacemakers for they will be called children of God" (Matt 5:9). Stassen notes "peacemaker . . . is the right translation . . . for positive action, reconciliation is envisioned: the 'peacemakers's seek to bring peace."[74]

JUSTICE

Traditional Righteousness	Vicious Cycle	Transforming Initiative
Matthew 5:38: You have heard that it was said, "An eye for an eye and a tooth for a tooth."	Matthew 5: 39: But I say to you, do not retaliate revengefully by evil means. (Not an imperative in the Greek, but an infinitive—probably with implied imperatival meaning.)	Matthew 5:40–42: But if anyone strikes you on the right cheek, *turn* the other also; and if any one wants to sue you and take your coat, *give* your cloak as well; and if any one forces you to go one mile, *go* also the second mile. *Give* to one who begs from you, and do not refuse one who would borrow from you.

The *Lex talionis* governing retributive law is the rule of law that the punishment paid should match the crime made. Yet the vicious cycle and transforming initiative also focus on distributive justice and its ethical principle of the equitable distribution of goods and services. Stassen's translation of the vicious cycle is "do not retaliate revengefully by evil means," instead of the usual translation, "do not resist evil." There are four transforming initiatives with their four imperatives in this ethical teaching. Stassen notes that each of the four "resists evil by taking an action to oppose injustice, to stand up for human dignity and to invite to reconciliation." Paul echoed some of the same teaching on justice, "Do not repay anyone evil for evil. . . . Beloved, never avenge yourselves, but leave room for the wrath of God. . . . If your enemies are hungry, feed them; if they are thirsty, give them something to

---

73. Ibid., 135.
74. Ibid., 45.

drink.... Do not overcome evil by evil means, but overcome evil with good" (Romans 12:17–21).[75]

LOVE AND COMMUNITY

Traditional Righteousness	**Vicious Cycle**	**Transforming Initiative**
Matthew 5:43: You have heard that it was said: "You shall love your neighbor and hate your enemy."	Matthew 5:46–47: For if you love those who love you, what reward have you? Do not even the tax collectors do the same? And if you salute only your brethren, what more are you doing than others? Do not even the Gentiles do the same?	Matthew 5:44–45: But I say to you, *Love* your enemies and *pray* for those who persecute you, so that you may be sons of your Father who is in heaven; for he makes his sun rise on the evil and the good, and sends rain on the just and unjust.

Surprisingly, the transforming initiative comes second rather than third in the typical order of the text. Stassen explains that the change in the order is due to ending the first six triads that ends with a summary verse in 5:48: "Be perfect, therefore, as your heavenly Father is perfect." Stassen remarked that it would be odd for Jewish Christians or followers of Jesus to speak of God as morally perfect in a Greek idealist way. Rather, the word would mean "complete" or "all-inclusive" when completing this sixth triad in loving your enemy as well as your neighbor. The transforming initiative in Matthew 5:44–45 is to practice the kind of love that God gives to all the human family, whether friend or foe. God gives the warmth of sunshine on the evil and the good, and sends the showers of rain on the just and the unjust. Unlike the tax collectors and Gentiles who only love their friends, God's grace and God's love includes the entire circle of humankind to enemies as well as friends. So, the moral imperatives are to love your enemies and pray for those who persecute you. Love and pray are two practices that can turn persecutors and enemies into friends.[76]

The new *Dictionary of Scripture and Ethics* has an entree on "Just Peacemaking" that I found intriguing. Four book-length statements by well-known denominations and their leaders in the US stated that just war

---

75. Ibid., 137–38.
76. Ibid., 140–41.

and pacifism are outdated in guiding the public interest in war and peace and called for a new paradigm. The US Conference of Catholic Bishops (*The Challenge of Peace*), Methodists (*In Defense of Creation*), Presbyterian (*Peacemaking: The Believer's Calling*), and the United Church of Christ (*The Just Peace Church*) issued a similar call. The works that have developed on faith-based *Just Peacemaking* cited in this essay need to gather public and church discussion about these practices that aim at preventing war and creating peace.[77] Given the pacifist beginnings of the AG through two world wars and the shift in position on military service in 1967 which supports the individual conscience of each church member to choose to serve as a combatant, non-combatant, or conscientious objector, the AG could well serve the members of the church. By providing teaching on the three paradigms that inform the Christian social ethics on peace and war. There is no written position paper describing the options of pacifism, just war theory, and just peacemaking. Perhaps the time has come.

A Concluding Postscript

I recall when I was a student in social ethics in the Graduate School of Religion. A major flap occurred with the Faculty over Paul Ramsey's book, *Who Speaks for the Church: a Critique of the 1966 Geneva Conference of the Church*.[78] I remember the consternation of some Faculty who took offense with Ramsey's view that the church should not be in the business of creating social proclamations on public policy issues. He really tweaked the noses of those who championed "social justice" in the late 1960s and early 1970s when he argued that Christians and the church should be speaking more about social order in this time to balance the voices of social justice. Ramsey's view was critiqued as a commitment to the status quo.

As I wrote this chapter I recalled Ramsey's voice when I was researching, writing, and learning about the justice issues in which the AG leadership was speaking for the church on racial justice, immigration reform, and human trafficking. These "documents" gave me a sense of appreciation that my AG denomination was publically stating the church's position on correcting social injustices. When the justice issues are coupled with the Compassion Ministries, it is apparent that the AG has made a strong commitment to evangelism, social concern, and social action. Now the AG needs to develop another document that describes the three paradigms for the Christian ethics of peace and war: pacifism, just war theory, and just peacemaking theory.

77. Stassen, "Just-Peacemaking Theory," 442–45.
78. Ramsey, *Who Speaks for the Church?*

Bibliography

AG Disaster Relief Fund. http://ag.org/disaster/. Accessed Dec. 31, 2013.

AG Health Care Ministries. http://healthcareministries.org/faq/. Accessed Jan. 20, 2014.

AG Health Care Ministries. http://healthcareministries.org/team-members/expanding-hcm/. Accessed Jan. 20, 2014.

"Assemblies of God endorses NAE immigration resolution." *AG News*, August 4, 2011. http://ag.org/top/News/index_articledetail.cfm?Process=DisplayArticle&targetBay=c97d4. Accessed Jan. 20, 2014

Assemblies of God. The General Council of the Assemblies of God Statement of Fundamental Truths, Articles 10 and 11. http://ag.org. Accessed Jan. 19, 2014.

Beatty, Jerome. "Nile Mother." *Assemblies of God Heritage* 4, no. 4 (1984–85) 1, 3–6.

Birch, Bruce C., and Larry L. Rasmussen. *Bible and Ethics in the Christian Life*. Rev. and exp. ed. Minneapolis: Augsburg, 1989.

Brubaker, Pamela, et al. "Introduction: Just Peacemaking as the New Ethic for Peace and War." In *Just Peacemaking; the New Paradigm for the Ethics of Peace and War*, edited by Glen H. Stassen, 1–40. Cleveland, OH: Pilgrim, 2008.

Bueno, John. "Lord, Let Me Hold Their Hands." *Mountain Movers* 31 (1989) 7, 30.

Calcutta Mercy Ministries. "Who We Are: Our History." http://www.buntain.org/who-we-are/our-history. Accessed 12/31/2013.

Calcutta Mercy Ministries. "Who We Are: Our Mission." http://www.buntain.org/who-we-are/our-mission. Accessed 12/31/2013.

Clemmons, Ithiel. "Mason, Charles Harrison." In *The New International Dictionary of Pentecostal and Charismatic Movements*, edited by Stanley M. Burgess and Eduard M. Van Der Maas, 865–67. Grand Rapids: Zondervan, 2002.

———. "Racial and Spiritual Unity in the Body of Christ." *Advance* (Assemblies of God) (1995) 66–68.

Compact Family Services. http://www.compactfamilyservices.org/ministries. Accessed Dec. 13, 2013.

Compact Family Services, Highlands Maternity Home. http://www.compactfamilyservices.org/ministries/highlands-maternity-home. Accessed Dec. 13, 2013.

Compact Family Services, Hillcrest Children's Home. http://www.compactfamilyservices.org/ministries/hillcredt-childrens-home. Accessed Dec. 13, 2013.

Convoy of Hope; "Disaster Response, Hunger Relief & Community Outreach." http://www.convoyofhope.org/go/what/disaster_response. Accessed Dec. 31, 2013.

Dalton, Adele Flower. "Mama Lillian's Answer." *Mountain Movers* 31 (1989) 14–15.

Dempster, Murray W. "Christian Social Concern in Pentecostal Perspective." Presidential Address at the Twenty-First Annual Meeting of the Society for Pentecostal Studies (SPS) in Lakeland, Florida. November 8, 1991. 48 pages.

———. "Christian Social Concern in Pentecostal Perspective: Reformulating Pentecostal Eschatology." *Journal of Pentecostal Theology* 2 (1993) 53–66.

———. "Social Concern in the Context of Jesus's Kingdom Mission and Ministry." *Transformation: An International Dialogue on Mission and Ethics* 16 (1999) 43–53.

———. "Pentecostal Social Concern and the Biblical Mandate of Social Justice." *Pneuma* 9, no. 2 (1987) 129–53.

———. "The Old Testament Foundations of Christian Social Concern." Latin American ChildCare conference, San Salvador, El Salvador, May 21–26, 1985.

Division of Foreign Missions, Assemblies of God. "All About Missions: A Guide to Foreign Missions Ministries." 1989.

———. *All About Missions: A Guide to Foreign Mission Ministries.* 1988.

"Funeral Services Held for Mark Buntain." *Division of Foreign Missions Happenings* 5 (1989) 1.

Grant, David and Beth. *Beyond the Soiled Curtain: Project Rescue's Fight for the Victims of the Sex-Slave Industry.* Springfield, MO: Onward, 2007.

The Hope Supply: Philippines Typhoon Response. http://blog.convoyof hope.org/features/disaster-response/philippines-typhoon-response/. Accessed Jan. 5, 2014.

Hogan, J. Philip. "Because Jesus Did." *Mountain Movers* 31 (1989) 10–11.

"Human Trafficking: A Resource Document." http://ag.org. Accessed Jan. 20, 2014.

Ketcham, Maynard and Wayne Warner. "When the Pentecostal Fire Fell in Calcutta." *Assemblies of God Heritage* 3, no. 3 (1983) 5–6.

Latin America ChildCare. 30th Aniversary. http://lacc4hope.org/30th-anniversary-celebration. Accessed Dec. 31, 2013.

———. "Is There Hope for Tomorrow's Child?" *Mountain Movers* 31 (1989) 30.

———. "LoveIs to Care." A brochure. Division of Foreign Missions, Assemblies of God.

———. What We Do. http://lacc4hope.org/our-mission/what-we-do. Accessed Dec. 31, 2013.

———. Who We Are. http://lacc4hope.org/our-mission/who-we-are. Accessed Dec. 31, 2013.

"A Letter to AG News Readers." *AG News.* 3 pages. http://ag.org/top/News/index_articledetail.cfm?Process=DisplayArticle&targetBay=c97d4. Accessed Jan. 20, 2014.

Lovett, Leonard. "The Present: The Problem Racism in the Contemporary Pentecostal Movement." *Cyberjournal for Pentecostal-Charismatic Research* 14 (2015). http://www.pctii.org/cyberj/cyber14.html. Accessed September 30, 2016.

MacRobert, Iain. *The Black Roots and White Racism of Early Pentecostals in the USA.* New York: St. Martin's, 1988.

"Mark Buntain Honored by World Relief." *Mountain Movers* 31 (1989) 8.

Maston, T. B. *Biblical Ethics.* Waco, TX: Word, 1967.

Miller, Donald W., and Tetsunao Yamamori. *Global Pentecostalism: The New Face of Christian Social Engagement.* Berkeley: University of California Press, 2007.

National Association of Evangelicals. http://www..nae.net/government-relations/policy-resolutions/354-immigration-2009. Assessed Jan. 20, 2014.

National Association of Evangelicals. http://www.nae.net/government-relations/for-the-health-of-the-nation/human-rights/immigration. Assessed Jan. 20, 2014

The National Report on Domestic Minor Trafficking: America's Prostituted Children. May 2009. http://www.sharedhope.org/Resources/TheNationalReport.aspv. Accessed September 30, 2016.

Nelson, Jack A. *Hunger for Justice: The Politics of Food and Faith.* Maryknoll, NY: Orbis, 1980.

"Pentecostals Experience a 'Miracle in Memphis.'" *Memphis Commercial Appeal,* Oct. 20, 1994, A1-10.

Petersen, Douglas. "The Kingdom of God and the Hermeneutical Circle: Pentecostal Praxis in the Third World." In *Called and Empowered: Global Mission in Pentecostal Perspective,* edited by Murray W. Dempster, Byron D. Klaus, and Douglas Petersen, 44–58. Peabody, MA: Hendrickson, 1991.

"Racial Reconciliation Manifest" http://pctii.org/manifesto.html. Accessed Feb. 4, 2014.

Ramsey, Paul. *Who Speaks for the Church? A Critique of the 1996 Geneva Conference on Church and Society*. Norwich, Scotland: Saint Andrew, 1969.

Reynolds, Barbara. "Oregon Voters Can Learn from the Memphis Miracle." *USA Today*, Oct. 28, 1994, 11A.

Robeck, Cecil M., Jr. "Azusa Street Revival." In *The New International Dictionary of Pentecostal and Charismatic Movements*, edited by Stanley M. Burgess and Eduard M. Van Der Maas, 344–50. Grand Rapids: Zondervan, 2002.

———. "The Past: Historical Roots of Racial Unity and Division in American Pentecostalism." *Cyberjournal for Pentecostal-Charismatic Research* 14 (2015) http://www.pctii.org/cyberj/cyber14.html. Accessed September 30, 2016.

Rosenior, Derrick R. "The Rhetoric of Pentecostal Racial Reconciliation: Looking Back to Move Forward." In *A Liberating Spirit: Pentecostals and Social Action in North America*, edited by Michael Wilkinson and Steven M. Studebaker, 53–84. Eugene, OR: Pickwick, 2010.

Shemeth, S. "Buntain, Daniel Mark (1923–89)." In *The New International Dictionary of Pentecostal and Charismatic Movements*, edited by Stanley M. Burgess, 449. Grand Rapids: Zondervan, 2002.

———. "Trasher, Lillian Hunt." In *The New International Dictionary of Pentecostal and Charismatic Movements*, edited by Stanley M. Burgess, 1153. Grand Rapids: Zondervan, 2002.

"Sidetracked," *Mountain Movers* 31 (1989) 3.

Stassen, Glen H. *Just Peacemaking: The New Paradigm for the Ethics of Peace and War*. Cleveland, OH: Pilgrim, 2008.

———. *Just Peacemaking: Transforming Initiatives for Peace and Justice*. Louisville, KY: Westminister John Knox, 1992.

———. "Just-Peacemaking Theory." In *Dictionary of Scripture and Ethics*, edited by Joel B. Green, 442–45. Grand Rapids: Baker Academic, 2011.

———. *Peacemaking: Ten Practices for Abolishing War*. 2nd ed. Cleveland, OH: Pilgrim, 2004.

Stassen, Glen H., and David P. Gushie. *Kingdom Ethics: Following Jesus in Contemporary Context*. Downers Grove, IL: InterVarsity, 2003.

"Statement on Human Trafficking." July 2011. http://ag.org. Accessed Jan. 20, 2014.

Synan, Vinson. "The Future: A Strategy for Reconciliation." *Cyberjournal for Pentecostal-Charismatic Research* 14 (2015). http://www.pctii.org/cyberj/cyber14.html. Accessed September 30, 2016.

———. *The Holiness-Pentecostal Tradition: Charismatic Movements in the Twentieth Century*. 2nd ed. Grand Rapids: Eerdmans, 1997.

———. "Memphis 1994: Miracle and Mandate." http://www.pccna.org/about_history.htm. Accessed Jan. 27, 2014.

Teen Challenge USA. http://teenchallengeusa.com. Accessed Jan. 5, 2014.

Turner, William. "The Ideal: The Biblical Pattern of Unity, Endeavoring to Keep the Spirit's Unity." *Cyberjournal for Pentecostal-Charismatic Research* 14 (2015). http://www.pctii.org/cyberj/cyber14.html. Accessed September 30, 2016.

"United Pentecostal Church, District and Leadership." http://www.upci.ca/districts.html. Accessed Oct. 12, 2013.

"United Pentecostal Church, International." *Encyclopedia of Protestantism*, http://protestatism.enacademic.com/613/United_Pentecostal_Church_International. Accessed Oct. 12, 2013.

West, Russell. "That His People May Be One: An Interpretive Study of the Pentecostal Leadership's Quest for Racial Unity." PhD diss., Regent University, Virginia Beach, VA, 1997.

Wood, George O. "AG and COGIC Leaders Gather in Historic Meeting." AG NEWS Special Report, sent by e-mail from "General Superintendent's Office" agmin_coo@ag.org on Wednesday, November 27, 2013, 1:00 PM.

———. "A Vital Step Forward: The GCAG and UPCAG Unite." From the Desk of the General Superintendent Dr. George O. Wood, sent by e-mail from "General Superintendent, George O. Wood." agmin_coo@ag.org on Friday, February 14, 2014, 5:00 PM.

Pentecostal Theology and History

11

Tongues as Evidence of the Character of Spirit's Empowerment in Acts[1]

Craig S. Keener

IT IS A GREAT privilege for me to dedicate this article to Gary McGee, one of my mentors both in Bible college and in seminary. He continued to correspond with me as a friend after I left Springfield, Missouri to do my PhD. Although his strength was church history, his Bible classes were so informative that I audited some with him that I had earlier unknowingly taken with another professor. The information I learned remains valuable to me to this day.

Because of McGee's influence in the study of initial evidence,[2] I thought that, of all my prior work, the most useful to develop here would be an article I published several years ago in the *Journal of Pentecostal Theology*. Non-Pentecostals often object to the Pentecostal association of tongues with baptism in the Holy Spirit. They often rightly note that love is the dominant expression of the Spirit's activity in Pauline theology (e.g., Rom 5:5; 15:30; Gal 5:22; Col 1:8). They often further object that tongues, which appears just three times in Acts and as one gift of the Spirit among many in 1 Corinthians, is too obscure to play such a vital role in Spirit baptism.

Pentecostals, in turn, rightly point to the function of baptism in the Spirit for empowering believers for the central mission described in Acts, and that tongues is the one sign that accompanies it in each case where any sign is specified. But often Pentecostals have failed to address the question of *why* Luke associates tongues with baptism in the Spirit.

---

1. This article is adapted from Craig S. Keener, "Why Does Luke Use Tongues as a Sign of the Spirit's Empowerment?" *Journal of Pentecostal Theology* 15, no. 2 (2007) 177–84, courtesy of Brill (Used by Permission). I also addressed Luke and glossolalia in Keener, *Acts*, 1:806–31.

2. E.g., McGee, *Initial Evidence*.

Luke does not present tongues as a sign of Spirit baptism merely arbitrarily, but because it is logically connected to the purpose of baptism in the Spirit. Luke emphasizes baptism in the Spirit as power to testify for Christ cross-culturally; what better sign to evidence this particular empowerment of the Spirit than inspiration to speak in the languages of other cultures?[3]

The Focus of Luke's Pneumatology

Different New Testament writers focus on different aspects of the Spirit's activity in the life of the church, some of which correspond to emphases in contemporary Jewish literature (especially prophetic activity), whereas others move beyond these.[4]

Prophetic Speech in Acts 1:8; 2:4, 17–18

A survey of uses in Luke-Acts reveals, as Pentecostal scholars have often noted, that Luke's focus is on prophetic activity, that is, prophecy or other activities associated especially with prophets in the Old Testament (e.g., Luke 1:15–17, 67; 2:26; 4:18; 12:12; Acts 4:8, 25, 31; 7:51, 55; 21:4, 11).[5]

This prophetic focus is particularly evident in view of Joel 2:28–32 as a programmatic text for Luke's second volume[6]: God's people will prophesy (Acts 2:17–21, esp. 2:17–18). Such an observation does not imply that Luke would have rejected other early Christian emphases, but simply observes that, more than other NT writers, he maintains a frequent focus on a particular aspect of the Spirit's activity.[7]

---

3. I noted this point (much more briefly) in Keener, *Gift & Giver*, 180; and Keener, *3 Crucial Questions about the Holy Spirit*, 69.

4. For discussion of samples, see Keener, *The Spirit in the Gospels and Acts*, esp. 8–13; with a more diverse range of activities, Turner, *The Holy Spirit and Spiritual Gifts*, 1–18; with a fuller focus specifically on prophecy, see Menzies, *The Development of Early Christian Pneumatology*. For one mediating approach, see Cho, *Spirit and Kingdom in the Writings of Luke and Paul*.

5. See esp. Menzies, *Development*, esp. 205–77; also Stronstad, *The Prophethood of All Believers*.

6. Cf. e.g., L. T. Johnson, *The Literary Function of Possessions in Luke-Acts*, 41; scholars often parallel Jesus's opening speech in Luke's Gospel (Luke 4:18–27) with Peter's opening speech in Acts (Acts 2:17–40; e.g., Zehnle, *Peter's Pentecost Discourse*, 128.)

7. John's "baptism in the Spirit" undoubtedly included the entire sphere of the Spirit's eschatological activity, in contrast with the eschatological fire baptism and John's own baptism (Luke 3:16). But Luke's use of "baptize in the Holy Spirit" and "receive the

This programmatic text in 2:17–18 coheres naturally with the earlier programmatic passage in Acts 1:8, where the earliest witnesses[8] will bear witness to Christ by the Spirit's power. Both instances deal with inspired speech for God; indeed, the prophetic dimension of 1:8 is inescapable if we read "power" in the sense in which Luke frequently means it, which often associates it with healing or other signs (Luke 4:36; 5:17; 6:19; 8:46; 9:1; Acts 6:8; 10:38; cf. 3:12; 4:7).[9] This association would certainly fit subsequent narratives, in which healings and other signs are the most common (albeit not the exclusive) method of drawing attention to the gospel (e.g., 3:11–13; 4:14; 5:12–16; 8:6, 13; 13:12; 15:12; esp. 4:29–30; 14:3). Elijah and Elisha provide models for many of the miracles in Luke-Acts[10]; it is therefore likely that Luke construed such signs as prophetic activity.[11]

It is also not difficult to see the connection between these two programmatic statements about Luke's purpose in Acts and the manifestation of the promised outpouring in 2:4. The focus of Luke's pneumatology in general is prophetic, and in 2:4 the believers engage in inspired speech.

Cross-Cultural Inspired Speech in Acts 1:8; 2:4

What Acts 2:4 adds, however, is that the immediate result of the Spirit's empowerment to speak for God was manifested in inspired speech in languages

---

Spirit" focuses on the dimension of empowerment, explaining how it can sometimes occur subsequent to conversion (8:12–17). Because I have treated this elsewhere, see Keener, *Gift & Giver*, 137–69; and Keener, "Spirit, Holy Spirit," 491–93, I note it only in passing here.

8. The eleven and those with them (Luke 24:33; see Dillon, *From Eye-Witnesses*, 291.) The term "witness" may apply in Acts especially to the Twelve as a group (Luke 24:48; Acts 2:32; 3:15; 4:33; 5:32; 10:39, 41; 13:31), who were with Jesus from the beginning of his public ministry (1:21–22); but application to Paul (Acts 22:15, 18; 23:11; 26:16, 22) and others (22:20; cf. 10:43) shows that their witness function is paradigmatic (see Keener, *Acts*, 1:525, 689, 695–96). Luke narrates not disinterested history, but a paradigm for mission based on history; thus the power of the Spirit is given to all believers (2:38–39), and, despite Luke's emphasis on the movement's leaders, he occasionally narrates the evangelistic activity of others (8:4; 11:19–21).

9. Cf. also Brown, *Israel's Divine Healer*, 218–20.

10. E.g., Jesus heals leprosy (Luke 5:12–13), like Elisha (2 Kgs 5:14; Luke 4:27); he raises the dead (Luke 7:14–15; 8:51–55) in manners reminiscent of Elijah and Elisha (1 Kgs 17:19–23; 2 Kgs 4:32–35); he multiplies food (Luke 9:16–17) as Elijah and Elisha did (1 Kgs 17:16; 2 Kgs 4:3–7, 42–44).

11. See Stronstad, *The Charismatic Theology of St. Luke*, 43–45; Brodie, "Luke-Acts as an Imitation and Emulation," 78–85; Keener, *Gift & Giver*, 59–64; more generally, Keener, "Spirit, Holy Spirit," 484–96, esp. 493.

that the speakers had not learned. What is the significance of such a distinction for Luke's overall theme?

The theme of Acts is the church's cross-cultural mission. Whereas Luke's Gospel embraced the church's heritage, beginning and ending in Jerusalem, Acts shows the transition from heritage to mission, moving from Jerusalem to Rome. The focus of Luke's prophetic pneumatology in Acts is how this mission comes about; the Spirit repeatedly leading God's agents across cultural, ethnic, and geographic barriers to bring the gospel to everyone. With this in view, we may revisit 1:8, which explicitly lays out this theme.

Scholars have often identified Acts 1:8 as a key programmatic statement introducing the subject of Acts, and even providing a very rough (and asymmetrical) outline for Acts. Ancients did often provide a thesis statement close to the beginning of their work, as well as, at times, an outline of what would follow, not only in speeches (where they are most conventional) but even in works of historiography.[12] Acts 1:8 not only speaks of prophetic speech (as in 2:17–18), but emphasizes that it will ultimately cross cultural barriers—exactly as speaking other cultures's languages does.

For Luke, this empowerment represents a crucial step forward in salvation history. Acts 1:8 draws on two major lines of OT pneumatology. First, its connection with the ascension recalls Elijah passing on a double portion of the Spirit to Elisha before his ascension (2 Kgs 2:1–14); Jesus similarly prepares to empower the church to carry on his ministry after his ascension.[13] The language of "Spirit," "witnesses," and "the ends of the earth," however, evokes Isaiah's prophecies of the eschatological remnant of Israel sustained by God's Spirit announcing the true God to the nations.[14]

Luke's use of such biblical background demonstrates that, for him, the Spirit's empowerment to cross cultural boundaries is not simply an afterthought, but grounded in the heart of God's promises to his people, now being fulfilled because the Lord's Messiah has been enthroned (Acts 2:33–36). As a sign that God had empowered his people to cross cultural barriers, the inspiration to worship God in unlearned languages becomes a significant marker of God carrying out this long-range plan.

---

12. See e.g., Thucydides, 1.23.6; Dionysius of Halicarnassus, *Thuc.* 19; Lucian, *Hist.* 53; cf. Pliny, *N.H.* pref. 33; Polybius, 3.1.7; 11.1.4–5.

13. With e.g., Zwiep, *The Ascension of the Messiah*, 194.

14. See fully Pao, *Acts and the Isaianic New Exodus* (on the use of Isa 49:6 here, see esp. pp. 85, 92).

Other Tongues as a Sign of the Universal Mission

Many, perhaps most, scholars recognize Luke's depiction of Pentecost in Acts 2:5–13 as either a reversal or recapitulation of Babel.[15] As Genesis follows its table of nations (Gen. 10:1–32) with its narrative of God scattering the languages (Gen. 11:1–9), so here Luke associates his summary of locations with a scattering of languages (Acts 2:4, 8–13).[16] But whereas in Genesis God scatters the nations for judgment, here God unites his church around the common worship of God (2:11) and (in the *lingua franca* of most of the Jews gathered on Pentecost) their common message (2:14–41).

Most recognize in this narrative a proleptic foreshadowing of the "Gentile mission."[17] After this narrative, God scatters the church for mission (8:1, 4; 11:19–21), and the Spirit at each step leads the church into its cross-cultural mission (e.g., 8:29, 39; 10:19; 11:12; 16:7; 19:21). Luke also illustrates that Jesus continues to fill new believers with the Spirit (8:17; 9:17; 10:44; 19:6), in two cases mentioning specific manifestations, which in both instances include tongues (19:6; see esp. 10:44–46, where it specifically functions as a sign of having received the Spirit as at Pentecost). The purpose of the empowerment and the sign is presumably the same as at Pentecost: empowerment to proclaim Christ cross-culturally (cf. 2:38–39 with 1:8).

Many interpreters of this passage, including myself, point to its implications for ethnic reconciliation or cultural sensitivity today.[18] Luke's goal

---

15. For reversal, see e.g., Chéreau, "De Babel à la Pentecôte," 19–36; Dominy, "Spirit, Church, and Mission," 34–39; Hill, *New Testament Prophecy*, 95; Moule, *Christ's Messengers*, 23; Smith, "What Hope After Babel?," 169–91; and Spencer, *Acts*, 32–33; for a recapitulation, e.g., González, *Acts*, 39; and Wagenaar, "Babel, Jerusalem and Kumba," 406–21. Early Pentecostals also read their experience as a reversal of Babel, Anderson, *An Introduction to Pentecostalism*, 44. Some scholars demur, e.g., Dunn, *The Acts of the Apostles*, 24, but they seem to miss the connection implied by the table of nations.

16. Cf. Goulder, *Type and History in Acts*, 158. For the table of nations tradition in Second Temple Judaism, see Scott, "Luke's Geographical Horizon," 483–544, esp. 507–22; in Acts, Scott, "Luke's Geographical Horizon," 525–27.

17. See e.g., Dibelius, *Studies in the Acts of the Apostles*, 106; Dupont, *The Salvation of the Gentiles*, 58; Foakes-Jackson, *The Acts of the Apostles*, 11; and Robinson, *Twelve New Testament Studies*, 167.

18. E.g., Keener, "Day of Pentecost, First Lesson: Acts 2:1–21," 524–28, esp. 526–27; Park, *Racial Conflict & Healing*, 130–32; Venter, *Doing Reconciliation*, 155, 170; and Yong, *The Spirit Poured Out on All Flesh*, 94, 169–73; see also Bediako, "Jesus in African Culture," 93–121, esp. 120, for translation in the vernacular. It was so applied at Azusa Street; see Robeck, *The Azusa Street Mission & Revival*, 88, 137–38; and Yong, *The Spirit Poured Out on All Flesh*, 183.

for such reconciliation is the church's multicultural unity, achieved through the church's multiethnic mission to bring all humanity to recognize its rightful Lord, Jesus Christ. Other kingdoms, such as the empires of Alexander or Rome, sought to unite diverse cultures under a common rule[19]; but Jesus alone is humanity's rightful Lord (cf. 2:34–36).

It is precisely the disciples's worship in languages they have not learned that draws attention to this multilinguistic paradigm. Granted, tongues are not specifically noted as intelligible to anyone present on the subsequent occasions of 10:46 and 19:6; in fact, they likely were not understood by those present. (Compare the need for Spirit-inspired interpretation in Paul's approach to tongues.) Luke is explicit, however, that the essential phenomenon is the same (10:45–47), and that Acts 2 provides the paradigm through which we should read the later accounts (10:47; 11:16–17). In other words, it is impossible to disconnect Luke's use of tongues from the cross-cultural mission that 2:5–13 foreshadows.

Theological Ramifications

These observations have ramifications for understanding Luke's theology, hence some ramifications for Pentecostal theology today. Luke emphasizes tongues because this experience signifies cross-cultural empowerment.[20]

I should, however, begin by warning against construing more from the above argument than it is intended to bear. Granted that Luke uses tongues as a sign of cross-cultural empowerment, and granted that (as many scholars have argued) Luke's narrative is paradigmatic, it need not follow that Luke expected every individual who receives the Spirit in the Lukan sense to speak in tongues.[21] Luke uses ability to speak under inspiration in unlearned languages to evidence the *purpose* of Spirit baptism; that he does not

---

19. E.g., early empires, Plutarch, *Themist.* 27.2-3; 3 Macc. 6.5; for the Persians, perhaps Ps.-Callisthenes, *Alex.* 1.23; for Alexander, see e.g., Seneca, *Ep. Lucil.* 94.63; Plutarch, *Alex.* 45.1-3; 47.3; Dio Chrysostom, *Or.* 4.49; *Num. Rab.*, 13:14; for Rome, e.g., Polybius, 39.8.7; Vitruvius, *Arch.* 1. pref. 1; Dio Chrysostom, *Or.* 3.6-7; Menander, *Rhetor* 2.12, 422.22–23; less favorably, Rev 13.7.

20. Although earlier readers may have held various understandings of what tongues was, many did see this connection, as I did not yet recognize when I first wrote the earlier version of this article: Chrys., *Hom. 1 Cor.* 35.1, see Bray, *1-2 Corinthians*, 138; Leo the Great, *Sermons* 75.2, see Martin, *Acts*, 23; Bede, *Comm. Acts* 2.3A, see Martin, *Acts*, 22; Packer, *Acts of the Apostles*, 27; and Wesley, *Explanatory Notes*, 396, cited in McGee, *Miracles, Missions, & American Pentecostalism*, 61.

21. Granted, given the point of this empowerment in the Lukan sense, this empowering would presumably need to be expressed sooner or later in forms of Spirit-led speech honoring Christ.

narrate that evidence in every instance of Spirit baptism, however, makes it more difficult to argue that his agenda is to teach that each *individual* who receives cross-cultural empowerment must speak in tongues.[22] Scholars might argue for or against that conclusion, but it need not logically follow from the connection we have noted above.

What does logically follow is that glossolalia is *logically* connected with Luke's emphasis on baptism in the Spirit as empowerment for mission. It is not an arbitrary sign, but the one sign, of any Luke might have narrated, which most effectively communicates the purpose of baptism in the Spirit as an empowerment for universal mission.

This observation has theological ramifications for Pentecostalism. The earliest Pentecostals often believed that tongues would function as missionary languages, so they could testify of Christ in local languages without having first learned them. On reaching the mission field, most quickly discovered that this was not the case, yet proceeded with their missions task unabated, while continuing to pray in tongues.[23] The early Pentecostals were able to survive this transition in their understanding of tongues fairly smoothly because it did not affect their basic, and correct, insight into the nature of tongues. Even if speaking in tongues did not normally provide missionary languages, it did attest the Spirit's empowerment for the church's global mission.

The remarkable global expansion of Pentecostalism in the past century[24] suggests that the early Pentecostals had this basic insight correct. Non-

---

22. This issue was debated even among some early Pentecostal leaders; see e.g., Robeck Jr., "William J. Seymour," 81–89; S. Burgess, "Evidence of the Spirit," 33–34; McGee, "Early Pentecostal Hermeneutics," 107–10; McGee, *Miracles, Missions, & American Pentecostalism*, 135 (Abrams); Wacker, *Heaven Below*, 41; Opp, *The Lord for the Body*, 152 (on Bosworth); Williams, "The Acts of the Apostles," 219 (on Seymour); Alexander, *Black Fire*, 130–31 (Seymour); Hudson, "Strange Words and Their Impact on Early Pentecostals, 67; R. Burgess, "Pandita Ramabai," 195; cf. Jacobsen, *Thinking in the Spirit*, 10; Kalu, *African Pentecostalism*, 20 (on Abrams); and Robeck Jr., *Azusa Street Mission & Revival*, 178. Some argue that Seymour played down the role of tongues rather than denied their inclusion in Spirit baptism, Jacobsen, *Thinking in the Spirit*, 78; and Tarr, *The Foolishness of God*, 379–80.

23 See Anderson, *Introduction to Pentecostalism*, 190; Goff, "Initial Tongues," 64–65; McGee, "Early Pentecostal Hermeneutics," 102; McGee, "The Radical Strategy," 52–53; McGee, *People of the Spirit*, 77–78; Jacobsen, *Thinking in the Spirit*, 25, 49–50, 74, 76, 97; and Robeck Jr., *Azusa Street Mission & Revival*, 41–42, 236–37, 243, 252; esp. see Anderson, "Signs and Blunders,"195–99; McGee, "Shortcut to Language Preparation?," 118–23; and McGee, "Taking the Logic 'a Little Further,'" 99–125. For this view in the church fathers, see esp. Parmentier, "Das Zungenreden bei den Kirchenvätern,"376–98; also Talbert, *Reading Corinthians*, 90, though he notes that this was less common than the glossolalia interpretation.

24. See e.g., Anderson, *Introduction to Pentecostalism*, 11; and Yong, *The Spirit*

Pentecostals have often wondered how a movement apparently centered on tongues would fulfill late nineteenth-century aspirations to holiness and missions, but they have missed the focus of Pentecostal empowerment. Those who object to the centrality of tongues may be correct, in that the focus of the Pentecostal anointing is not tongues, but cross-cultural mission. Yet tongues is a logical, and not arbitrary, sign of the church's cross-cultural anointing for mission. This logical connection confirms an insight of early Pentecostalism that undergirds the history of the entire movement.

This connection also has theological implications for both non-Pentecostal and Pentecostal practice today. It invites non-Pentecostals interested in the church's mission and recognizing their need of the Spirit's empowerment not to despise the logical sign of that empowerment as articulated in Acts. Cross-cultural mission is not the sole domain of those who pray in tongues, but tongues is not simply an arbitrary interest of Pentecostals. The connection also invites Pentecostals to remember the empowerment to which tongues points. To pray in tongues, yet fail to be involved in the biblical task of cross-cultural, global evangelism, is to neglect the purpose of the anointing to which, in Luke's narrative, glossolalia bears eloquent witness.

Bibliography

Alexander, Estrelda Y. *Black Fire: One Hundred Years of African American Pentecostalism.* Downers Grove, IL: InterVarsity, 2011.

Anderson, Allan. *An Introduction to Pentecostalism: Global Charismatic Christianity.* Cambridge: Cambridge University Press, 2004.

———. "Signs and Blunders: Pentecostal Mission Issues at 'Home and Abroad' in the Twentieth Century." *Journal of Asian Mission* 2, no. 2 (2000) 193–210.

Bediako, Kwame. "Jesus in African Culture: A Ghanaian Perspective." In *Emerging Voices in Global Christian Theology*, edited by William A. Dyrness, 93–121. Grand Rapids: Zondervan, 1994.

Berger, Peter L. "Four Faces of Global Culture." In *Globalization and the Challenges of a New Century: A Reader*, edited by Patrick O'Meara, Howard D. Mehlinger, and Matthew Krain, 419–27 Bloomington: Indiana University Press, 2000.

Bray, Gerald, ed. *1–2 Corinthians.* Ancient Christian Commentary on Scripture: New Testament 7. Downers Grove, IL: InterVarsity, 1999.

Poured Out on All Flesh, 33–80; cf. similarly Berger, "Four Faces of Global Culture," 425; Johnson, Barrett, and Crossing, "Christianity 2010," 36; Mullin, *A Short World History of Christianity*, 211; Sanneh, *Disciples of All*, 275; Sweeney, *The American Evangelical Story*, 153; and Tomkins, *A Short History of Christianity*, 220. It should be noted, however, that many of these estimates include many groups that classical Pentecostals would not deem orthodox.

Brodie, Thomas L. "Luke-Acts as an Imitation and Emulation of the Elijah-Elisha Narrative." In *New Views on Luke and Acts*, edited by Earl Richard, 78–85. Michael Glazier. Collegeville, MN: Liturgical, 1990.

Brown, Michael L. *Israel's Divine Healer*. Studies in Old Testament Biblical Theology. Grand Rapids: Zondervan, 1995.

Burgess, Ruth Vassar. "Pandita Ramabai: A Woman for All Seasons: Pandita Ramabai Saraswati Mary Dongre Medhavi (1858–1922)." *Asian Journal of Pentecostal Studies* 9, no. 2 (2006) 183–98.

Burgess, Stanley M. "Evidence of the Spirit: The Medieval and Modern Western Churches." In *Initial Evidence: Historical and Biblical Perspectives on the Pentecostal Doctrine of Spirit Baptism*, edited by Gary B. McGee, 20–40. Peabody, MA: Hendrickson, 1991.

Chéreau, Georgette. "De Babel à la Pentecôte. Histoire d'une bénédiction." *Nouvelle Revue Théologique* 122, no. 1 (2000) 19–36.

Cho, Youngmo. *Spirit and Kingdom in the Writings of Luke and Paul: An Attempt to Reconcile These Concepts*, foreword by Robert P. Menzies, Paternoster Biblical Monographs. Waynesboro, GA: Paternoster, 2005.

Dibelius, Martin, *Studies in the Acts of the Apostles*. Translated by M. Ling, edited by H. Greeven. New York: Scribner's Sons, 1956.

Dillon, Richard J. *From Eye-Witnesses to Ministers of the Word*. Analecta Biblica 82. Rome: Biblical Institute, 1978.

Dominy, Bert B. "Spirit, Church, and Mission: Theological Implications of Pentecost." *Southwestern Journal of Theology* 35, no. 2 (1993) 34–39.

Dunn, James D. G. *The Acts of the Apostles*. Valley Forge, PA: Trinity, 1996.

Dupont, Jacques. *The Salvation of the Gentiles: Essays on the Acts of the Apostles*. Translated by J. R. Keating. New York: Paulist, 1979.

Foakes-Jackson, F. J. *The Acts of the Apostles*. Moffatt New Testament Commentary. London: Hodder & Stoughton, 1931.

Goff, James R., Jr. "Initial Tongues in the Theology of Charles Fox Parham." In *Initial Evidence: Historical and Biblical Perspectives on the Pentecostal Doctrine of Spirit Baptism*, edited by Gary B. McGee, 57–71. Peabody, MA: Hendrickson, 1991.

González, Justo L. *Acts: The Gospel of the Spirit*. Maryknoll, NY: Orbis, 2001.

Goulder, M. D. *Type and History in Acts*. London: SPCK, 1964.

Hill, David. *New Testament Prophecy*. Atlanta: Knox, 1979.

Hudson, Neil. "Strange Words and Their Impact on Early Pentecostals: A Historical Perspective." In *Speaking in Tongues: Multi-disciplinary Perspectives*, edited by Mark J. Cartledge, Studies in Pentecostal and Charismatic Issues, 52–80. Waynesboro, GA: Paternoster, 2006.

Jacobsen, Douglas. *Thinking in the Spirit: Theologies of the Early Pentecostal Movement*. Bloomington: Indiana University Press, 2003.

Johnson, Luke Timothy. *The Literary Function of Possessions in Luke-Acts*. Society of Biblical Literature Dissertation Series 39. Missoula, MT: Society of Biblical Literature, 1977.

Johnson, Todd M., David B. Barrett, and Peter F. Crossing. "Christianity 2010: A View from the *New Atlas of Global Christianity*." *International Bulletin of Missionary Research* 34.1 (2010) 29–36.

Kalu, Ogbu. *African Pentecostalism: An Introduction*. Oxford: Oxford University Press, 2008.

Keener, Craig S. *3 Crucial Questions about the Holy Spirit*. Grand Rapids: Baker, 1996.

———. *Acts: An Exegetical Commentary*. 4 vols. Grand Rapids: Baker Academic, 2012–2015.

———. "Day of Pentecost, Years A, B, C. First Lesson: Acts 2:1–21." In *The Lectionary Commentary: Theological Exegesis for Sunday's Texts*, edited by Roger E. Van Harn, 1:524–28. Grand Rapids: Eerdmans/London: Continuum, 2001.

———. *Gift & Giver: The Holy Spirit for Today*. Grand Rapids: Baker, 2001.

———. "Spirit, Holy Spirit, Advocate, Breath, Wind." In *The Westminster Theological Wordbook of the Bible*, edited by Donald E. Gowan, 484–96. Louisville: Westminster John Knox, 2003.

———. *The Spirit in the Gospels and Acts: Divine Purity and Power*. Peabody, MA: Hendrickson, 1997.

———. "Why Does Luke Use Tongues as a Sign of the Spirit's Empowerment?" *Journal of Pentecostal Theology* 15, no. 2 (2007) 177–84.

Martin, Francis, ed., in collaboration with Evan Smith. *Acts*. Ancient Christian Commentary on Scripture: New Testament 5. Downers Grove, IL: InterVarsity, 2006.

McGee, Gary B. "Early Pentecostal Hermeneutics: Tongues as Evidence in the Book of Acts." In *Initial Evidence: Historical and Biblical Perspectives on the Pentecostal Doctrine of Spirit Baptism*, edited by Gary B. McGee, 96–118. Peabody, MA: Hendrickson, 1991.

———. *Miracles, Missions, & American Pentecostalism*. American Society of Missiology 45. Maryknoll, NY: Orbis, 2010.

———. *People of the Spirit: The Assemblies of God*. Springfield, MO: Gospel, 2004.

———. "The Radical Strategy." In *Signs and Wonders in Ministry Today*, edited by Benny C. Aker and Gary B. McGee, foreword by Thomas E. Trask, 47–59. Springfield, MO: Gospel, 1996.

———. "Shortcut to Language Preparation? Radical Evangelicals, Missions, and the Gift of Tongues." *International Bulletin of Missionary Research* 25, no. 3 (2001) 118–23.

———. "Taking the Logic 'a Little Further': Late Nineteenth-Century References to the Gift of Tongues in Mission-Related Literature and Their Influence on Early Pentecostalism." *Asian Journal of Pentecostal Studies* 9, no. 1 (2006) 99–125.

McGee, Gary B., ed. *Initial Evidence: Historical and Biblical Perspectives on the Pentecostal Doctrine of Spirit Baptism*. Peabody, MA: Hendrickson, 1991.

Menzies, Robert P. *The Development of Early Christian Pneumatology*. Journal for the Study of the New Testament Supplement 54. Sheffield, UK: Sheffield Academic, 1991.

Moule, C. F. D. *Christ's Messengers: Studies in the Acts of the Apostles*. New York: Association, 1957.

Mullin, Robert Bruce. *A Short World History of Christianity*. Louisville: Westminster John Knox, 2008.

Opp, James. *The Lord for the Body: Religion, Medicine, and Protestant Faith Healing in Canada, 1880–1930*. Montreal: McGill-Queen's University Press, 2005.

Packer, J. W. *Acts of the Apostles*. Cambridge Bible Commentary. Cambridge: Cambridge University Press, 1966.

Pao, David W. *Acts and the Isaianic New Exodus*. Wissenschaftliche Untersuchungen sum Neuen Testament 2/130. 2000. Reprint, Grand Rapids: Baker, 2002.

Park, Andrew Sung. *Racial Conflict & Healing: An Asian-American Theological Perspective*. Maryknoll, NY: Orbis, 1996.
Parmentier, Martin. "Das Zungenreden bei den Kirchenvätern." *Bijdragen* 55, no. 4 (1994) 376–98.
Robeck, Cecil M., Jr. *The Azusa Street Mission & Revival: The Birth of the Global Pentecostal Movement*. Nashville: Thomas Nelson, 2006.
———. "William J. Seymour and 'The Bible Evidence.'" In *Initial Evidence: Historical and Biblical Perspectives on the Pentecostal Doctrine of Spirit Baptism*, edited by Gary B. McGee, 72–95. Peabody, MA: Hendrickson, 1991.
Robinson, John A. T. *Twelve New Testament Studies*. Studies in Biblical Theology 34. London: SCM, 1962.
Sanneh, Lamin. *Disciples of All Nations: Pillars of World Christianity*. New York: Oxford University Press, 2008.
Scott, James M. "Luke's Geographical Horizon." In *The Book of Acts in Its Graeco-Roman Setting*, edited by D. W. J. Gill and C. Gempf, 2:483–544. Grand Rapids: Eerdmans: Paternoster, 1994.
Smith, David. "What Hope after Babel? Diversity and Community in Gen 11:1–9; Exod 1:1–14; Zeph 3:1–13 and Acts 2:1–13." *Horizons in Biblical Theology* 18, no. 2 (1996) 169–91.
Spencer, F. Scott. *Acts*. Sheffield: Sheffield Academic, 1997.
Stronstad, Roger, *The Charismatic Theology of St. Luke*. Peabody, MA: Hendrickson, 1984.
———. *The Prophethood of All Believers: A Study in Luke's Charismatic Theology*. Journal of Pentecostal Theology Supplemental Series 16. Sheffield, UK: Sheffield Academic, 1999.
Sweeney, Douglas A. *The American Evangelical Story: A History of the Movement*. Grand Rapids: Baker Academic, 2005.
Talbert, Charles H. *Reading Corinthians: A Literary and Theological Commentary on 1 and 2 Corinthians*. New York: Crossroad, 1987.
Tarr, Del. *The Foolishness of God: A Linguist Looks at the Mystery of Tongues*. Foreword by Jack Hayford. Springfield, MO: Access, 2010.
Tomkins, Stephen. *A Short History of Christianity*. Grand Rapids: Eerdmans, 2005.
Turner, Max. *The Holy Spirit and Spiritual Gifts*. Rev. ed. Peabody, MA: Hendrickson, 1998.
Venter, Alexander. *Doing Reconciliation: Racism, Reconciliation and Transformation in the Church and World*. Cape Town, SA: Vineyard International, 2004.
Wacker, Grant. *Heaven Below: Early Pentecostals and American Culture*. Cambridge, MA: Harvard University Press, 2001.
Wagenaar, Hinne. "Babel, Jerusalem and Kumba: Missiological Reflections on Genesis 11:1–9 and Acts 2:1–13." *International Review of Mission* 92, no. 366 (2003) 406–21.
Wesley, John. *Explanatory Notes upon the New Testament*. 1754. Reprint, London: Epworth, 1966.
Williams, Demetrius K. "The Acts of the Apostles." In *True to Our Native Land: An African American New Testament Commentary*, edited by Brian K. Blount, with Cain Hope Felder, Clarice J. Martin, and Emerson Powery, 213–48. Minneapolis: Fortress, 2007.

Yong, Amos. *The Spirit Poured Out on All Flesh: Pentecostalism and the Possibility of Global Theology*. Grand Rapids: Baker, 2005.

Zehnle, Richard F. *Peter's Pentecost Discourse: Tradition and Lukan Reinterpretation in Peter's Speeches of Acts 2 and 3*. Society of Biblical Literature Monograph 15. Nashville: Abingdon, 1971.

Zwiep, Arie W. *The Ascension of the Messiah in Lukan Christology*. Novum Testamentum Supplement 87. Leiden: Brill, 1997.

12

1 Corinthians 12:13 Revisited—
A Pentecostal Reading

Donald A. Johns

Pentecostal Approaches to 1 Corinthians 12:13

It was in a volume edited by Gary B. McGee that I first suggested that the clause in 1 Cor 12:13a related directly to being baptized in the Spirit in the classical Pentecostal sense.[1] It is appropriate now, in a volume dedicated to the appreciation of his life, ministry, friendship, and scholarship, to investigate the matter more in-depth.

The "A" in the title of this brief essay is an indication that Pentecostals do not agree on the meaning of the two main clauses in 1 Cor 12:13. Thus, this study cannot arrive at "the" Pentecostal reading. Much less, given the complexity of the problem, can it claim to arrive at *the correct* reading. At best, it can suggest a way of looking at the text that is truly Pentecostal, that well accounts for the data, and that makes good rhetorical sense within the wider context of 1 Cor 12–14 and the letter as a whole.

The text reads as follows:

> καὶ γὰρ ἐν ἑνὶ πνεύματι ἡμεῖς πάντες εἰς ἓν σῶμα ἐβαπτίσθημεν, εἴτε Ἰουδαῖοι εἴτε Ἕλληνες, εἴτε δοῦλοι εἴτε ἐλεύθεροι, καὶ πάντες ἓν πνεῦμα ἐποτίσθημεν.
>
> *Kai gar en heni pneumati hēmeis pantes eis hen sōma ebaptisthēmen, eite Ioudaioi eite Hellēnes, eite douloi eite eleutheroi, kai pantes hen pneuma epotisthēmen.*[2]

---

1. Johns, "Some New Directions," 160–61.
2. From this point forward, Greek will be transliterated.

> For we were baptized *en* one Spirit *eis* one body, whether Jews or Greeks, slaves or free persons, and we were all given one Spirit to drink.[3]

Note that in this article, the two critical prepositions will usually be transliterated, not translated, so as to allow the reader to see the texts in a fresh way and keep exegetical options open for as long as possible.

Decades ago, James D. G. Dunn suggested that Pentecostals had tried to interpret this verse in such ways that their interpretations would align with Pentecostal theology. Dunn identified two basic approaches Pentecostals had used.[4]

"Baptized by One Spirit"

The first approach focuses on the meaning of *en* and takes Paul's statement as a reference to a third type of baptism in addition to Christian baptism in/with water and baptism in the Holy Spirit. This approach reads *en* as introducing instrument or agency, "we were all baptized *by* the one Spirit. . . ." Then, *eis* is taken as meaning "into," with the resultant full meaning being that the Spirit places a new believer into the body of Christ at the time of conversion. Thus, the expression here becomes a synonym for conversion. Dunn specifically mentions Ralph Riggs as holding this view[5] and it has continued to have followers. One could note, for example, such Pentecostal authors as Michael Dusing, Stanley Horton, Timothy Jenney, Gordon Lindsay, Anthony Palma, Roger Stronstad, George O. Wood.[6]

This approach has the advantage of not needing to reconcile the "we all" part of Paul's statement with the present reality that not all believers are baptized in the Spirit in the traditional Pentecostal sense, because (in this view) 1 Corinthians 12:13 does not refer to being baptized in the Spirit in that sense.

---

3. Unless otherwise noted, all translations are the author's own.
4. Dunn, *Baptism in the Holy Spirit*, 127–28.
5. Ibid., 127–128; and Riggs, *The Spirit Himself*, 57–59.
6. Dusing, "The New Testament Church," 534; Horton, *1 & 2 Corinthians*, 118–19; Horton, *What the Bible Says*, 214–16; Jenney, "The Holy Spirit and Sanctification," 416; Lindsay, *The Baptism of the Holy Spirit*, 6–7; Palma, *The Holy Spirit*, 102–3; Stronstad, *Spirit, Scripture and Theology*, 190; and Wood, *Living in the Spirit*, 53–55.

Eis ≠ "into"

The second approach is to suggest a meaning for *eis* other than "into"; for example "in," "for the sake of," or "with a view to." This view has the advantage of acknowledging that *eis* has a wide range of meanings.[7]

Two Spirit-Baptisms

A third approach is adopted by Howard M. Ervin,[8] who reads the text as being baptized "in" the one Spirit, but in a sense different from its meaning in the Gospels and Acts. Thus, Ervin concludes, being baptized in the one Spirit in 1 Cor 12:13 is a reference to being placed into the realm or sphere of the Spirit's operation and is a reference to the conversion complex of events. But the similar phrase spoken by John the Baptist, the resurrected Lord, or the apostle Peter means something different. Being given the one Spirit to drink then refers to "the outpouring of spiritual gifts" and connects with the gift of the Spirit at Pentecost.[9]

This approach has the benefit of interpreting the *en* in its natural sense with *baptizein*, but by suggesting that the NT knows of two types of Spirit-baptism, it could weaken the traditional Pentecostal doctrine that Spirit-baptism is separate from and at least logically subsequent to conversion.[10] A further result of Ervin's approach is that the phrase "baptized in one Spirit" in 1 Cor 12:13 would mean something quite different from the similarly worded phrase "baptize(d) in the Holy Spirit" found in the Gospels and Acts, while a very different phrase "given one Spirit to drink" in 1 Cor 12:13 would mean what "baptize(d) in the Holy Spirit" means in the Gospels and Acts. It is possible, but it is unlikely.

---

7. Dunn argues that with a verb of motion such as *baptizein*, *eis* must always have the sense of "movement toward so as to be in." However, this betrays a too-prescriptive grammar and over-interprets *baptizein* simply as a verb of motion, neglecting it's naming of a complete, specific action. This complete action is an "immersion," Dunn's own terminology (*Baptism in the Holy Spirit*, 5), which is itself temporary, though having lasting results.

8. Ervin, *Conversion-Initiation*, 98–102; Ervin, *Spirit Baptism*, 28–37; and Ervin, *These Are Not Drunken As Ye Suppose*, 45–50.

9. Ervin, *These Are Not Drunken As Ye Suppose*, 46.

10. Cf. Dunn, *Baptism in the Holy Spirit*, 129; On the other hand, we might note that Ervin's approach does comport well with the methodology of NT theology advocated by Dunn himself, that "a NT biblical theology should . . . allow each of the NT writers to speak with his own voice." Dunn, *New Testament Theology*, 7.

Spirit-Baptism at Conversion, Fully Experienced Only Later

A fourth, somewhat similar approach, is followed by Craig Keener, Larry Hart, and Frank Macchia. Keener speaks of receiving "full access" to the power of the Spirit at conversion, "though not always the full experience."[11] Hart speaks of two senses of being baptized in the Spirit: the Pauline initiatory sense, and the Lukan sense of empowerment for ministry, citing Keener's exposition.[12] And in *Baptized in the Spirit*, Macchia writes approvingly of the charismatic movement's "theological definition" of being baptized in the Spirit as initiatory, and its experiential definition as being an "empowerment for life and service."[13] He connects 1 Cor 12:13a with the initiatory aspect, and both parts of the verse with later experience(s): "we are in a real sense baptized into this Spirit as we are renewed in a drinking from the Spirit of Christ."[14]

In this approach, there is one baptism in the Spirit, but it has two aspects. The first connects with conversion-initiation[15] and places the convert into the church, the body of Christ. The second is concerned with experience of the reality and empowerment that the experience entails, which, occasionally in Acts and most often now, follows some period of time after conversion-initiation.

The Questions

Summarizing to this point, in my judgment the interpretation of 1 Cor 12:13 resolves itself into the answers to several closely related questions:

- Does *baptizein en . . . pneumati* have a consistent meaning in the New Testament?
- What is the force of *en* here? That is, is it "by" or "in"?
- What is the force of *eis* in *baptizein eis heni sōmati*?
- How does the second clause in the verse relate to the first?

---

11. Keener, *Gift and Giver*, 168; cf. Keener, *3 Crucial Questions about the Holy Spirit*, 34; Keener, *Gift and Giver*, 157–58; and Keener, *1–2 Corinthians*, 103.
12. Hart, *Truth Aflame*, 403–4.
13. Macchia, *Baptized in the Spirit*, 16.
14. Ibid., 202; see also 167, 201.
15. To use the term coined by Dunn, *Baptism in the Holy Spirit*, 5–7.

- How well does the resulting interpretation fit in with, and contribute rhetorically to, Paul's goals in this section of his letter?

Does *baptizein en . . . pneumati* have a Consistent Meaning in the New Testament?

THE PHRASE, BAPTIZEIN EN *pneumati hagiō*, is a metaphor picturing the Holy Spirit as a liquid in which the baptizing takes place. The phrase appears 6 times in the NT, in Matt 3:11; Mark 1:8; Luke 3:16; John 1:33; Acts 1:5; 11:16. The four instances in the Gospels are spoken by John the Baptist;[16] the first instance in Acts is spoken by the resurrected Jesus, and the second by Peter, quoting Jesus. We can note that in the NT, the phrase always occurs with the *baptiz-* root in a verb form, never in a noun form.

The three occurrences in the Synoptics use the future indicative active, "he [the coming one] will baptize you in the Holy Spirit" (with Matthew and Luke adding, "and in fire"). In Acts 1:5, the resurrected Lord uses the future passive, "you will be baptized in the Holy Spirit." And Peter, in Acts 11:16, quotes Jesus with only a minor difference in word order.

It should also be noted that in the Gospels and Acts, this phrase is always used in contrast with John's baptism "in water," and almost certainly triggers the use of the "in water." We can note Dunn's comment that *baptizein* in itself does not refer to "*water*-baptism"[17]; however, we can also observe that there is such a thing as an unmarked meaning of a word. That is, if there are no qualifiers or other pointers in the context, the unmarked meaning is that meaning which can be assumed.[18] The "unmarked meaning" of *baptizein* involves a physical ceremony performed using water.[19] Gordon Fee states that if Paul had omitted the reference to the Spirit, the reference would have "almost certainly have implied 'with water.'"[20] Further, metaphorical uses such as in Mark 10:38 and Luke 12:50 do not contradict this conclusion, since the metaphorical sense is made clear by the context, and metaphor is itself a form of marking. So, when baptism is being spoken

---

16. In John 1:33, John the Baptist uses the phrase in a quotation of "the one who sent me to baptize in water," a reference to God. Thus, the Baptist attributes the origin of the phrasing to God.

17. Dunn, *Baptism in the Holy Spirit*, 129.

18. Black, *Linguistics*, 124; and de Waard and Nida, *From One Language to Another*, 140.

19. And, I would argue, ideally "immersion in" water, but that subject is far outside the scope of this brief study.

20. Fee, *God's Empowering Presence*, 179.

about, whether that performed by John, the disciples of Jesus, or by Paul, "in water" is made explicit only when baptism in water is being distinguished and contrasted with baptism in something else, namely, in the Holy Spirit.

On the other hand, *baptizein en pneumati hagiō* is not the only term used to refer to the experience to which it points. For example, in Acts 11:16 and its immediate context, such other phrases as "the Holy Spirit fell on them," and "if God gave the same gift to them" are used. And in the narrative of Acts 10 to which Peter refers, the reader finds that "the Holy Spirit fell on all those who heard the message," and "the gift of the Holy Spirit had been poured out" on, and was "received" by, the Gentiles (Acts 10:44, 45, 47).

In Acts 2, while the events of the Day of Pentecost are obviously the fulfillment of the risen Lord's prophetic statement recorded in 1:5, Luke's description of that fulfillment uses different language: "they were all filled with the Holy Spirit." Peter connects the event with God's promise through Joel that He would "pour out [His] Spirit on all flesh" (2:16, 18).[21]

It seems reasonable to conclude, then, that *baptizein en pneumati hagiō* is not a technical term in the Gospels and Acts. We Pentecostals have adopted this biblical term to name our systematic theological doctrine, and to do so is appropriate. We can note that this study is written from a classical Pentecostal perspective, and the context and purposes of the present volume do not allow a full exposition or defense of the doctrine.

Still, we can observe that in the Gospels and Acts the term *baptizein en pneumati hagiō* does play a particularly important role given its use by John the Baptist (and by God, who commissioned him), its use later by Jesus in pointing forward to the pouring out of the Spirit that began on the Day of Pentecost, and its use by Peter in recalling that event and connecting it with what took place at the house of Cornelius. When the term is used, it always points to the same spiritual reality. While it may not reach the level of being a technical term, it does have a consistency of usage in the Gospels and Acts that makes it reasonable to suggest that the phrase *baptizein en heni pneumati* in 1 Cor 12:13a points to the same spiritual reality that Pentecostals posit concerning the phrase *baptizein en pneumati hagiō* in the Gospels and Acts. But in order to evaluate that suggestion, we must examine how prepositional phrases with *en* and *eis* are used with the verb *baptizein*. The interpretation of the two phrases in 1 Cor 12:13 introduced by those prepositions will profoundly shape the meaning adopted for the whole verse.

---

21. It should be noted that the "pouring out" in Acts 2 and 10 is also a metaphor that pictures the Spirit as a liquid.

En in 1 Corinthians 12:13

The types of prepositions used with *baptizein* and the meanings they convey with that specific verb are part of what is called "collocational" or "syntagmatic" relationships.[22] That is, any given word in a language will "collocate" or form "syntagmatic relationships with," or in more understandable terms, "be used with" a range of other words. The range may be small or large, but it is finite, and native speakers can sense when an inappropriate collocation is made. Beekman and Callow specifically mention "prepositional collocations," collocations of a verb with one or more prepositions.[23] The meaning of a verb often changes based on the preposition with which it is used.

Baptizein en as Agency?

It was mentioned above that many Pentecostal writers hold that *en* here means "by." Grammatically, *en* plus the dative case would be functioning as a pleonasm, or expanded equivalent for the simple dative case used in an instrumental sense. That is, the phrase would mean "by one Spirit." Based on anecdotal evidence, I suspect it probable that most contemporary Pentecostals take the same approach.

Perhaps the most important observation against this interpretation of *en* is that elsewhere in the NT, agency with passive of *baptizein* is never expressed by *en*, always by *hupo*.[24]

Baptizein en as Denoting the Element in which Baptism is Done

In other NT texts, the most common use of *en* with *baptizein* is to give the element in which the baptism is done. The simple dative case has the same function. We have noted that [*en*] *hudati* or "in water" is assumed with *baptizein* and is explicitly used only when a contrast is being made with being baptized in the Spirit.[25]

---

22. Beekman and Callow, *Translating the Word of God*, 162–63; Cotterell and Turner, *Linguistics and Biblical Interpretation*, 155–56; and Silva *Biblical Words and Their Meaning*, 119, 141–43.

23. Beekman and Callow, *Translating the Word of God*.

24. See the following texts: Matt 3:6, 13, 14; Mark 1:5, 9; Luke 3:7; 7:30.

25. For the dative *hudati*, see Mark 1:8; Luke 3:16; Acts 1:5; 11:16; for *en hudati*, see Matt 3:11; John 1:26, 31, 33.

Other "elements" in (*en*) which a baptism is done are "the cloud" and "the sea" (1 Cor 10:2). The full sentence is instructive, because it also contains *eis ton* Moses. Here, we can see that *en* gives the element in which the "baptism" is taking place, and *eis* does something else. While we should not assume the function of the *eis* is the same as it is in 1 Cor 12:13, the construction is the same as in Rom 6:3a and Gal 3:27, that is, *eis* plus the name of a person.

Other uses of *en* with *baptizein*

We should note that *en* is also used with *baptizein* in ways that are less relevant to the text being studied. *En* can give the geographical area or location in which the baptizing is taking place: "in the desert," Mark 1:4; "in the Jordan River," Matt 3:6; "in/at Ainon near Salim," John 3:23. It can also specify in whose name the baptism was performed, "in (*en*) the name of Jesus Christ," Acts 10:48. This last may relate to the invocation of the name of Jesus, as is indicated by *epi tō onomati Iēsou Christou* ("in/upon the name of Jesus Christ") in Acts 2:38 and *epikalesamenos to onoma autou* ("calling upon his name") in Acts 22:16, or may be more or less equivalent to the use "to baptize *eis* the name of" someone, discussed below. Or, tracing back to the OT usage of the Hebrew *bᵉsēm*, "in the name of," it may relate to the authority of the one commissioning the baptizing.[26]

Conclusion regarding *en* with *baptizein*

En with *baptizein* most commonly specifies the element in which the baptizing is performed, and never elsewhere in the NT specifies the agent performing the baptism. It is therefore reasonable to conclude that in 1 Cor 12:13a, the phrase *baptizein en heni pneumati* is to be taken as being baptized "in the one Spirit." However, that conclusion does not in itself specify either reception of the Spirit as a central component of conversion-initiation or reception of Spirit-baptism in the traditional Classical Pentecostal sense.

Eis in 1 Corinthians 12:13

The Greek preposition *eis* is used with the verb *baptizein* in various ways. Similar texts are grouped together for the sake of discussion.

---

26. Bietenhard, "*onoma*," 258-261.

Baptizein eis Repentance and Forgiveness

It is certain that this study cannot hope to resolve the meaning of *eis* in the first three of the following texts; too much is tied up in the theologies of baptism held by interpreters.

- *Baptizein eis* repentance, Matt 3:11
- *Baptisma*[27] *eis* forgiveness of sins, Mark 1:4
- *Baptizein eis* forgiveness of your sins, Acts 2:38

In the context of Matt 3:11, Matthew reports that the people being baptized were "confessing their sins," and where there was no repentance, John demanded it and announced judgment upon those who would refuse (3:7–10).

Mark 1:4, while not technically connecting the verb with the preposition *eis*, does connect the baptizing activity of John with his preaching of "a baptism of repentance[28] *eis* the forgiveness of sins," and in the next verse, the people are baptized by John, "confessing their sins." That one evangelist uses the verb and one the noun does not seem to radically change the meaning of the prepositional phrase.

Acts 2:38 is the Christian equivalent of the first two texts, since Peter's instruction was to "repent and be baptized . . . *eis* the forgiveness of your sins." Murray Harris concludes that is "wiser" to speak of the relationship expressed as "concomitance" rather than "causation."[29] "Causation" would indeed claim too much. But given G. R. Beasley Murray's discussion on "The Nature of Early Christian Baptism"[30] and the common use of *eis* to designate the goal of an action, it seems probable that at least some sort of goal-directedness is in view in each of these texts, even if one cannot take it as far as does Beasley-Murray.

Baptizein eis the Name of [Someone]

- *Baptizein eis* the name of the Father and the Son and the Holy Spirit, Matt 28:19
- *Baptizein eis* the name of the Lord Jesus, Acts 8:16; 19:5

27. *Baptisma*, "baptism," is the noun form of *baptizein*.

28. Cf. Acts 19:4, where Paul characterizes John's baptizing as a "baptism of repentance."

29. Harris, *Prepositions and Theology in the Greek New Testament*, 227–28.

30. Beasley-Murray, *Baptism in the New Testament*, 99–104.

- *Baptizein eis* the name of Paul, 1 Cor 1:13
- *Baptizein eis* my [Paul's] name, 1 Cor 1:15

Matt 28:19 is quite instructive and was chronologically the first in its utterance, though it is not found in the earliest of these three documents. In Matt 28:19, the two present participles further define the action of the main verb, "make disciples of." How is it that one makes disciples? By baptizing them and then instructing them in the teachings of their Lord. Thus, Harris's conclusion that baptizing "*eis* the name of" has to do with "the establishment of a relationship of belonging and possession"[31] may well be in the right direction, though the brief suggestion of Zerwick "to the worship and service of" preserves the discipleship overtones more in Matt 28:19.[32] The other two texts in Acts are "*eis* the name of the Lord Jesus," and these two likewise fit well with the meaning seen in Matt 28:19.

Examination of the two texts in 1 Cor 1 is also helpful. In 1 Cor 1:12, Paul chides the Corinthian believers for dividing into factions named after apostles or preachers. The identification with the person championed is expressed in the statement "*I* am of Paul, *I* [am] of Apollos"[33] and so on. Paul then focuses on the group that identifies with him, posing the rhetorical questions "was Paul crucified for you? Or were you baptized *eis* the name of Paul?" It is clear that they were not worshipping Paul, just following him as a preferred teacher, so Zerwick's "to the worship and service of" suggestion will not work here.

The NIV and ESV translations of the slogans of v. 12, "I follow Paul . . . I follow Apollos," and so on, captures the discipleship-establishing connotations of baptism. If any believers at Corinth had been baptized in Paul's name, they might have had reason to say "I follow Paul" that is, "I am a disciple of Paul"; but he is not the savior crucified for them, they were not baptized in his name, and so they have no such reason.

In narrative such as in Acts the situation is different. Frankly, it is difficult in a narrative text to discern much difference between the use of *en* in Acts 10:48 ("*en* the name of Jesus Christ") and the similar use of *eis* in 8:16 and 19:5.

Summarizing, *baptizein eis to onoma* [of a person] seems connected with establishing the relationship of the disciple to the teacher. The meaning,

---

31. Harris, *Prepositions and Theology in the Greek New Testament*, 228.
32. Zerwick, *A Grammatical Analysis of the Greek New Testament*, 99.
33. Emphasizing the pronoun "I" follows the suggestion of Zerwick, though not his rendering of the genitive by "for," that is, "*I am for Paul*," Zerwick, *A Grammatical Analysis of the Greek New Testament*, 499.

while not directly relevant to the interpretation of 1 Cor 12:13, is definitely goal-directed, and that, at least, is relevant.

Baptizein eis [Name of Someone]

- *Baptizein eis* Christ, Gal 3:27
- *Baptizein eis* Christ Jesus, Rom 6:3a
- *Baptizein eis* Moses, 1 Cor 10:2

In these three texts, there is no "in the name of" formula, just *eis* plus the name itself. Harris notes that the first two could just mean that the baptism is "with reference to Christ." Although it could be read as a shorter way of saying "into the body of Christ," he prefers to take it as a shorter way of saying "into the name of Christ."[34] We can note that baptism "*eis* the body of Christ" does not occur in the New Testament, and itself is an expanded construct based on the very text whose meaning we are investigating. Harris is on firmer ground with *eis* "the name of Christ," and this interpretation would fit well with the discipleship overtones discussed above. Caution is needed, though, because Paul could have said "*eis* the name of Christ," but did not.

Paul's parallel construction in 1 Cor 10:2 using the name of Moses should caution the interpreter against reading participatory meaning into the grammatical construction itself—that type of meaning must therefore come from the way it is used in the context. Fee, citing Beasley-Murray and Dunn, would like to make as little as possible of the reference to the Israelites being baptized *eis* Moses in 1 Cor 10:2.[35] On the other hand, Dunn would like to make rather much of the construction in Rom 6:3a, seeing it as referring to an act of God placing the believer in Christ and which is then "imaged by the ritual act."[36]

In Gal 3:27, participatory overtones are present in the context, but so are connotations of possession in v. 29. Similarly, Paul's introduction of participatory burial-resurrection symbolism into Christian baptism in Rom 6:3-4 almost overpowers the cleansing connotations of *baptizein*. It would be well, then, to move to the somewhat different uses in Rom 6:3b-4.

---

34. Harris, *Prepositions and Theology in the Greek New Testament*, 239.

35. Fee, *The First Epistle to the Corinthians*, 444-46; see Beasley-Murray, *Baptism in the New Testament*, 184-85; and Dunn, *Baptism in the Holy Spirit*, 126-27.

36. Dunn, *Romans 1-8*, 311.

Baptizein with *eis* and "death"

- *Baptizein eis* his [Christ's] death, Rom 6:3b
- *Baptisma*[37] *eis ton thanaton*, Rom 6:4

The first use of *baptizein* in Rom 6:3, already mentioned above, could easily be taken as simply a reference to Christian baptism. But the two instances listed here identify the baptism experience as related to the death of Christ. The relationship to "that death," *ton thanaton*, comes from the verb "buried with," the acted-out image of burial and raising up that Paul applies to the ceremony of baptism, and the parallel of Jesus being raised to life and the believer experiencing new life. While *eis* is an appropriate, or better, the preposition to use in the context of such statements, it can hardly carry that much freight in itself.

What Kind of Baptism?

- *Baptizein eis* what? Acts 19:3a
- [*Baptizein*] *eis* the baptism of John, Acts 19:3b

These two texts show how little the construction *baptizein eis* means in itself. The NLT translates v.3 using regular English as,

> "What baptism did you experience?" he asked.
> And they replied, "The baptism of John."

The GNT renders it,

> "Well, then, what kind of baptism did you receive?" Paul asked.
> "The baptism of John," they answered.

It was a "John-baptism," not a "Jesus-baptism." No big theological point is being made by the construction itself.

Baptizein eis with a Location

- *Baptizein eis* the Jordan, Mark 1:9

This usage is an equivalent of "*baptizen en* the Jordan River," Matt 3:6, mentioned above. It does not seem relevant to the interpretation of 1 Cor 12:13,

---

37. *Baptisma*, "baptism," is the noun form of *baptizein*, and is significant here since it directly follows an instance of *baptizein* and refers back to it.

except to note once again that, in itself, meaning carried by the construction *baptizein eis* is minimal.

Conclusion regarding *baptizein eis*

Given the range of usage of *baptizein eis*, one thing is certain: *baptizein eis hen soma* in 1 Cor 12:13 does not have to mean baptized "so as to form one body," or "so as to become part of one body." These readings often proceed by extrapolation from the translation of *eis* as "into." But the construction *baptizein eis* does not in itself carry heavy theological freight—that must come from the context, the object of the preposition *eis*, and one's theology of baptism. On the other hand, the preposition *eis* does often indicate some sort of movement in a direction or toward a goal.

Being Given One Spirit to Drink

How does the final clause in 1 Cor 12:13 relate to the first, to being "baptized *en* one Spirit"? The options are two: either the two clauses refer to the same Spirit-related experience, or they don't. In any given Pentecostal reading, the choice of an option will be strongly influenced, though not necessarily determined, by how the reader interprets "baptized *en* one Spirit." Ervin, for example, takes parallel metaphors to be in a synthetic relation, not synonymous; that is, the baptism metaphor refers to conversion, and the drinking metaphor refers to Spirit-baptism in the traditional Pentecostal sense.[38] Macchia takes the baptism as referring to conversion, but the drinking as "an ongoing renewal, a continual drinking of the Spirit."[39] Fee, on the other hand, argues that the Semitic parallelism and the importance of the common experience of the Spirit in both clauses points toward both referring to the same experience, which he takes as reception of the Spirit in the conversion complex of events.[40]

In my estimation, Fee is probably correct in evaluating the parallelism between being baptized in the Spirit and being given the Spirit to drink as synonymous. If so, then both metaphors point toward the same spiritual reality. However, it does not follow that one must rule out Spirit-baptism in the traditional Pentecostal sense as that very reality.

---

38. Ervin, *Conversion-Initiation*, 101–2; Ervin, *Spirit Baptism*, 32–33; and Ervin, *These Are Not Drunken As Ye Suppose*, 46.

39. Macchia, *Baptized in the Spirit*, 202; cf. 203.

40. Fee, *The First Epistle to the Corinthians*, 604–5.

The Proposed Interpretation

In proposing a Pentecostal reading, I draw on the common use of *en* with *baptizein* and to the consistent use of the terminology *baptizein en pneumatic hagiō* to suggest that the reading should begin "We were all baptized in one Spirit," taking the clause as referring to Spirit-baptism in the traditional Pentecostal sense. This experience was indeed the norm in apostolic Christianity.[41]

For the final clause in the verse, I draw on the usual goal-directedness of *eis*. While I disagree with their final interpretation of the verse, Robertson and Plummer's grammatical explanation is worded well: "the one body is the end to (εἰς) which the act is directed."[42] The nature of that goal-directedness is not inclusion into the body, or formation of the body, but the unity of the body or, perhaps even better given the immediate context, the well-being of that one body. Finally, taking the second clause as a synonymous parallel with the first, being given one Spirit to drink is another metaphor referring to Spirit-baptism.

Rhetorical Contribution to 1 Corinthians 12–14

The final task is to see if the proposed interpretation fits the context and contributes to the rhetorical goals of 1 Cor 12–14. The essential problem prompting Paul to write 1 Corinthians was that the church at Corinth was fractured by multiple issues including factions around preferred preachers/teachers, socioeconomic status, scruples[43] (knowledge, strong versus weak, and so on), and the exercise of spiritual gifts when they came together, including valuing certain (perhaps more spectacular?) gifts over others.

In chapters 12–14, Paul takes up the issue of spiritual gifts. In 12:4–7, he speaks of the variety or diversity of gifts, services or ministries, and activities, but then he emphasizes that each of these is the manifestation of the same Spirit, and each is given for the common good. In vv. 8–11, he lists nine such manifestations. As he begins the list, he explicitly states that it is the "same" Spirit, the "one" Spirit, who gives the manifestation/gift; then he ends the list by reiterating that it is "the one and the same Spirit" who is at work in each manifestation.

---

41. Ervin, *Conversion-Initiation*, 102.

42. Robertson and Plummer, *First Epistle of Paul to the Corinthians*, 272.

43. Witherington, *Conflict and Community*, 28, suggests that "the diversity of socioeconomic levels and religious and ethnic backgrounds" was a significant factor in the issues Paul addressed in 1 Corinthians.

Verse 12 then opens the section that extends to v. 26 or perhaps v. 27, in which Paul uses the body imagery. Commentators who see 12:13a as somehow referring to conversion and becoming part of or forming the body of Christ emphasize that it is the common experience of the Spirit in conversion-initiation, whether baptized "in" or "by," that brings people who are diverse into unity in the one body. And indeed, Paul does give a nod to socioeconomic status in the central phrase of v. 13.

However, the conversion-initiation interpretation does not really contribute much rhetorically to Paul's main goal in the section. Paul's image in vv. 12–27 concerns function,[44] and in 1 Cor 12, function relates to spiritual gifts, which are manifestations and gifts of "the one and the same Spirit." Paul's argument by analogy is not based on how one gets into the body[45]; rather, it is based on the recognition that different body parts have different functions, each of which is necessary to the well-being of the whole. Likewise, in the body of Christ, each person has been gifted by the Spirit to contribute a manifestation of the Spirit for the common good.[46]

How are these gifts, these manifestations, bestowed? By "being baptized in the one Spirit," by drinking in the one Spirit. Thus, the proposed reading comes to a different conclusion than Robert P. Menzies, who states that Paul never "alludes to Pentecost or the Pentecostal gift."[47] Under this proposed reading, Paul even mentions the Pentecostal gift outright as the basis for the variety of giftings comprising the manifestations of the Spirit.

Bibliography

Beasley-Murray, G. R. *Baptism in the New Testament*. Grand Rapids: Eerdmans, 1962.
Beekman, John, and John Callow. *Translating the Word of God*. Grand Rapids: Zondervan, 1974.
Bietenhard, Hans. "onoma." In *Theological Dictionary of the New Testament*, edited by Gerhard Friedrich and Gerhard Kittel, translated and edited by Geoffrey W. Bromiley, 5:242–83. Grand Rapids: Eerdmans, 1967.
Black, David Alan. *Linguistics for Students of New Testament Greek: A Survey of Basic Concepts and Applications*. Grand Rapids: Baker, 1988.
Bruner, Frederick Dale. *A Theology of the Holy Spirit*. Grand Rapids: Eerdmans, 1970.
Cottrell, Peter, and Max Turner. *Linguistics and Biblical Interpretation*. Downers Grove, IL: InterVarsity, 1989.

---

44. Schatzmann, *A Pauline Theology of Charismata*, 46–47.

45. Though I would not press the detail, the body parts that are given voice are already parts of the body.

46. Even the manner in which these manifestations are to be exercised must contribute to the well-being of the assembly, 1 Cor 14: 3, 4, 5, 12, 26.

47. Menzies, "The Spirit of Prophecy," 69, 71.

de Waard, Jan, and Eugene A. Nida. *From One Language to Another: Functional Equivalence in Bible Translating.* Nashville: Nelson, 1986.

Dunn, James D. G. *Baptism in the Holy Spirit.* Philadelphia: Westminster, 1970.

_____. *New Testament Theology: An Introduction.* Library of Biblical Theology. Nashville: Abingdon, 2009.

_____. *Romans 1–8.* Word Biblical Commentary 38A. Dallas: Word, 1988.

Dusing, Michael. "The New Testament Church." In *Systematic Theology*, edited by Stanley M. Horton, 525–66. Springfield, MO: Logion, 2007.

Ervin, Howard M. *Conversion-Initiation and the Baptism in the Holy Spirit.* Peabody, MA: Hendrickson, 1984.

_____. *Spirit Baptism: A Biblical Investigation.* Peabody, MA: Hendrickson, 1987.

_____. *These Are Not Drunken As Ye Suppose.* Plainfield, NJ: Logos, 1968.

Fee, Gordon D. *The First Epistle to the Corinthians.* New International Commentary on the New Testament. Grand Rapids: Eerdmans, 1987.

_____. *God's Empowering Presence: The Holy Spirit in the Letters of Paul.* Peabody, MA: Hendrikson, 1994.

Harris, Murray J. *Prepositions and Theology in the Greek New Testament: An Essential Reference Work for Exegesis.* Grand Rapids: Zondervan, 2012.

Hart, Larry D. *Truth Aflame: Theology for the Church in Renewal.* Rev. ed. Grand Rapids: Zondervan, 2005.

Horton, Stanley M. *1 & 2 Corinthians.* Springfield, MO: Logion, 1999.

_____. *What the Bible Says about the Holy Spirit.* Springfield, MO: Gospel, 1976.

Hunter, Harold H. *Spirit-Baptism: A Pentecostal Alternative.* Lanham, MD: University Press of America, 1983.

Jenney, Timothy P. "The Holy Spirit and Sanctification." In *Systematic Theology*, edited by Stanley M. Horton, 397–421. Springfield, MO: Logion, 2007.

Johns, Donald A. "Some New Directions in the Hermeneutics of Classical Pentecostalism's Doctrine of Initial Evidence." In *Initial Evidence: Historical and Biblical Perspectives on the Pentecostal Doctrine of Spirit Baptism*, edited by Gary B. McGee, 145–67. Peabody, MA: Hendrickson, 1991.

Keener, Craig S. *1–2 Corinthians.* New Cambridge Bible Commentary. Cambridge: Cambridge University Press, 2005.

_____. *3 Crucial Questions about the Holy Spirit.* Grand Rapids: Baker, 1996.

_____. *Gift and Giver: The Holy Spirit for Today.* Grand Rapids: Baker Academic, 2001.

Lindsay, Gordon. *The Baptism of the Holy Spirit.* Dallas: Voice of Healing, 1964.

Macchia, Frank D. *Baptized in the Spirit.* Grand Rapids: Zondervan, 2006.

Menzies, Robert P. "The Spirit of Prophecy, Luke-Acts and Pentecostal Theology: A Response to Max Turner." *Journal of Pentecostal Theology* 15 (1999) 49–74.

Palma, Anthony D. *The Holy Spirit: A Pentecostal Perspective.* Springfield, MO: Logion, 2001.

Pretlove, John L. "Baptism *en pneumati*: A Comparison of the Theologies of Luke and Paul." PhD diss., Southwestern Baptist Theological Seminary, 1980.

Riggs, Ralph. *The Spirit Himself.* Springfield, MO: Gospel, 1949.

Robertson, Archibald, and Alfred Plummer. *A Critical and Exegetical Commentary on the First Epistle of Paul to the Corinthians.* International Critical Commentary. 2nd. ed. Edinburgh: T. & T. Clark, 1914.

Schatzmann, Siegfried S. *A Pauline Theology of Charismata*. Peabody, MA: Hendrickson, 1987.
Silva, Moisés. *Biblical Words and Their Meaning: An Introduction to Lexical Semantics*. Grand Rapids: Zondervan, 1983.
Stronstad, Roger. *Spirit, Scripture and Theology: A Pentecostal Perspective*. Baguio City, Philippines: Asia Pacific Theological Seminary Press, 1995.
Witherington, Ben, III. *Conflict and Community in Corinth: A Socio-Rhetorical Commentary on 1 and 2 Corinthians*. Grand Rapids: Eerdmans, 1995.
Wood, George O., with Randy Hurst. *Living in the Spirit: Drawing Us to God; Sending Us to the World*. Springfield, MO: Gospel, 2009.
Zerwick, Max. *A Grammatical Analysis of the Greek New Testament*, 5th ed., edited and translated by Mary Grosvenor. 2 vols. Rome: Editrice Pontifico Istituto Biblico, 1996.

13

Understandings of the Gift of Tongues in Reformation Protestantism and Catholicism

GREGORY J. MILLER

Introduction

IT HAS BEEN TYPICAL for a Pentecostal understanding of Church history to emphasize the first century and the last century, with little attention paid to the long in-between. When Pentecostals have mentioned Martin Luther, John Calvin, or medieval Catholics at all, it often has been in denigration. Appreciation of Luther is sometimes given, but as a "partial" reformer, a first step in the right direction of the true reform of the Church. Calvin appears mainly as Luther's dour side-kick. Medieval Catholics fare even less well.

This position was expressed in a short book on the Pentecostal movement's place in history done in conjunction with the 1968 USA General Council's Committee on Advance. In it David Womack wrote:

> For centuries the truth of the NT religion was lost to the masses, for the Bible was buried in incomprehensible Latin and there were few copies in circulation.... Some writers have attempted to prove that the charismatic experiences of the baptism in the Holy Spirit and the prophetic gifts continued among true believers throughout medieval times. However such a theory lacks historical evidence. There may possibly have occurred isolated instances of the baptism in the Holy Spirit from time to time; but if so, any records of such spiritual happenings during the Dark Ages unfortunately have remained undiscovered. The idea that there existed a continuous line of apostolic Christianity from the first century to the present time is unfounded. There were

certain mystic movements within the Roman Catholic Church that emphasized the union of the devotee with Christ through meditation and self-afflicted suffering, but the elements of these movements were based more on Aristotelian philosophy than on any understanding of apostolic patterns.[1]

Fortunately these attitudes are changing. In part this has been the result of an increased openness to ecumenical dialogue.[2] Over the last three decades Pentecostals have been involved in a number of intra-faith dialogues with the Lutheran Institute for Ecumenical Research, the World Alliance of Reformed Churches, and the Vatican.[3] To date, these dialogues have been introductory and exploratory.[4] It makes sense that they have not yet deeply engaged the writings of Luther and Calvin or the experiences of medieval Roman Catholics. However, in contrast to restorationist Pentecostalism, events in the history of the church during the sixteenth century are central to these dialogue partners. It is understood that there is a wide array of Reformation and late-medieval thinkers who portrayed this phenomenon from both a biblical perspective and their contemporary practices, yet these were selected for this essay to present an overview of understanding. It is hoped that an exploration of pneumatological commonalities and divergences between Pentecostals and these early modern Christians may allow Pentecostals to become better dialogue partners as well as to provide fruitful soil for deepening the dialogue. This essay is a brief exploration of these points of contact and distinctives.

1. Womack, *The Wellsprings of the Pentecostal Movement*, 73.

2. There is still significant resistance to ecumenism. At the 2005 Assemblies of God General Council, Bylaws Article IX: "Doctrines and Practices Disapproved" was modified in an effort to modestly open possibilities for ecumenical exchange, but even this modification did not occur without a great deal of intense debate. The modification went to secret ballot and was approved by a margin of only 899–767.

3. The Pentecostal leader most important in the earliest phases of these dialogues was David du Plessis. His mantle is now being carried by Cecil M. Robeck Jr., Veli-Matti Kärkkäinen, and others. Gary B. McGee was a participant in the fifth phase of the Pentecostal-Catholic dialogue from 1998–2006 (see the essays on Ecumenism, Roman Catholic-Pentecostal Engagement in this volume). According to Robeck Jr., "Most Pentecostal leaders have a very limited vision for the potential benefits that engagement with the larger church might bring to them and to their evangelistic concerns." The quote is from his *cri de coeur* on Pentecostals and ecumenism, "Pentecostals and Christian Unity," 307–38.

4. The outcomes have been published as "Lutherans and Pentecostals in Dialogue," "Word and Spirit, Church and World," and "On Becoming a Christian." For important surveys of these dialogues, see for example Kärkkäinen, *Ad ultimum terrae*; Kärkkäinen, "The Holy Spirit and Justification," 26–39; and Wainwright, "The One Hope of Your Calling?" 7–28.

Primary Reformers on the Holy Spirit and the Gift of Speaking in Tongues

For Martin Luther, as for all Christians of the Reformation period, Pentecost was a major event in Church history and one of the most important feast days in the Church calendar. Luther frequently used sermons for Pentecost Sunday to teach about the Holy Spirit. He described the outpouring of the Holy Spirit this way:

> The Holy Spirit descended from heaven and filled all the assembled multitude, and they appeared with parting, fiery tongues and preached so unlike they were wont to do that all men were filled with amazement. The Spirit came pouring into their hearts, making them different beings, making them creatures who loved and willingly obeyed God. This change was simply the manifestation of the Spirit himself, his work in the heart. . . . They became new creatures, aware of possessing altogether different minds and different tendencies.[5]

This outpouring was not a one-time event. According to Luther, when the Holy Spirit comes to the believer he brings the gifts. Among these is an empowerment for service: "he [the Holy Spirit] inflames them with love unto boldness in preaching Christ—unto free and fearless utterance. . . . so that man may rejoice before God, filled with love for him and ready, in consequence, to serve his fellows gladly."[6] According to Luther, the Holy Spirit is also the sanctifier: "Here we should be intelligent and know that in one sense all is not accomplished when the Holy Spirit is received. The possessor of the Spirit is not at once entirely perfect, pure in all aspects. . . . We do not preach the doctrine that the Spirit's office is one of complete accomplishment, but rather that it is progressive; he operates continuously and increasingly. . . ."[7]

Luther also described how the Holy Spirit came into the life of the believer, and here modern Pentecostals part ways with the Reformer. Luther did not hold to a distinct, second experience after salvation with the evidence of speaking in tongues, in which the Holy Spirit is received in a special way. Rather, for Luther, the Holy Spirit is given to believers over and over through the preaching of Jesus Christ the Lord.[8] Therefore the Word of God and the Spirit of God are intimately linked (this is typical for the

---

5. Luther, "Pentecost," 331.
6. Ibid., 332.
7. Ibid., 334.
8. Ibid., 332.

Reformers overall). However, Luther adds that the Holy Spirit is not given to the proud or self-reliant, but only to those who need comfort, assurance, and power in the midst of their struggles and helplessness. In fact, Luther is clearly concerned in his discussion of the outpouring of the Spirit at Pentecost with those proud fanatics who "arrogantly and presumptuously boast possession of the Holy Spirit."[9] According to Luther, this prideful arrogance and boasting is a sure sign that the person does not have the Spirit.

Luther also preached several sermons on 1 Corinthians 12 and we therefore have no lack of material concerning his views on the charismata.[10] It is important to emphasize that Lutheran theology is fundamentally incarnational. That is, God always reveals himself through the physical world. So for Luther, the gifts are not some attempt at individualistic pietism or super-spiritualism, but are part of the working out of God's will in the everyday things of this world. Luther always emphasized that God revealed himself to humankind most perfectly in a baby who had dirty diapers, a man whose feet needed to be washed, and above all, on the cross.

When Luther discussed the spiritual gifts, he intentionally included the most basic kinds of things right next to the spectacular to emphasize that we should not value the more dramatic over the more mundane or to be impressed with spiritual fireworks. For example, Luther wrote "The Spirit who has given to one (the gift of) preaching and to you (the gift of) listening, and who has raised dead people through still another, this same Spirit has given to another the gift of comforting people. Before God there is no difference."[11] For Luther, the list of gifts by Paul in I Corinthians is only partial and incomplete. Every member has been gifted by the Spirit for the mutual edification of the body of Christ and the advancement of the Kingdom.

Perhaps then it should not be surprising that the gift of tongues for Luther was the ability to speak or use another language. The gift of "interpretation of tongues" was understood to be translating. In case anyone might think that this was less of a gift than "miracles" or "healings," Luther wrote: "It is a gift of God when one language is being translated into another. I can tell you a tale about that!"[12]

In Luther's advice concerning the reformation of worship, he cited I Corinthians 14 in support of always having someone read the lesson (in

9. Ibid.

10. This passage was the epistle lesson for the 10th Sunday after Trinity. The primary German edition of Luther's works, the Weimar Edition, contains transcripts of at least four sermons dealing with the passage, from 1524, 1531, 1535, and 1536.

11. Quoted in Froelich, "Charismatic Manifestations," 154.

12. Quoted in ibid., 153.

the language of the people), "thereupon the preacher, or whoever has been appointed shall come forward and interpret a part of the same lesson so that others may understand and learn it, and be admonished." Luther continued, "the former is called by Paul in I Corinthians 14 'speaking in tongues.' The other he calls 'interpreting' or 'prophesying' or 'speaking with sense or understanding.' If this is not done, the congregation is not benefited by the lesson, as has been the case in cloisters and in convents, where they only bawled against the walls."[13]

This interpretation of tongues is consistent through all of Luther's voluminous writings. He was oblivious to the distinctions that are important to Pentecostal theology, such as xenoglossy (the miraculous ability to speak and/or understand other human languages) and so-called "devotional tongues" as a private prayer language. The scriptural texts which describe all of those types were consistently interpreted by Luther simply to mean a divinely given aptitude for, and actualization of ability with human languages.

The understanding of the other central magisterial reformer, John Calvin, is similar. Material on the Holy Spirit abounds in Calvin's writings. In his discussion of the outpouring of the Holy Spirit on the day of Pentecost, he emphasized the importance of the miraculous physical signs that were present first for the disciples themselves and then for all of those who were present in Jerusalem on that day. According to Calvin, all Christians need physical signs: "For such is our slothfulness to consider the gifts of God, that unless he awake all our senses, his power shall pass away unknown."[14] And so Calvin interpreted the mighty wind and the fire as symbols of purity and empowerment.[15] Tongues were seen as a reversal of Babel:

> But God doth furnish the apostles with the diversity of tongues now, that he may bring and call home, into a blessed unity, men which wander here and there. These cloven tongues made all men to speak the language of Canaan, as Isaiah foretold (29:18). For what language soever they speak, yet do they call upon one Father, which is in heaven, with one mouth and one spirit (Rom 15:6).[16]

Thus speaking in tongues at Pentecost was a sign of the universality of the Church and of the gift of the gospel to every tribe and people.

---

13. This is found in Luther's 1523 tract, "Concerning the Order of Public Worship," 7–14.
14. Calvin, *Commentary upon the Acts of the Apostles*, 74.
15. Ibid., 76.
16. Ibid., 75.

Like Luther, Calvin did not interpret Acts 2 to ordain a normative, second experience after salvation for every believer with the evidence of speaking in tongues. But that does not mean that he saw this outpouring only as a one-time historical event. As already inferred by his discussion of the signs of Pentecost above, Calvin emphasized the continuing, essential work of the Holy Spirit in the Church. This is particularly clear when one examines his theological masterpiece, *The Institutes of the Christian Religion*.

The Holy Spirit is mentioned so often in the *Institutes* that the famous nineteenth and early twentieth-century American theologian Benjamin B. Warfield called Calvin the "theologian of the Holy Spirit."[17] A very brief summary of the role of the Holy Spirit in Calvin must include the following essential points. First, the Holy Spirit is essential in receiving faith.[18] Second, the Holy Spirit cleanses us and makes us Christ-like.[19] Luther emphasized the paradoxical nature of the Christian life in its struggle with sin and was fearful of any kind of works-righteousness. Within Calvin's theological system there is much more emphasis on holy living as a sign of the presence of the Spirit, and therefore of salvation. Third, the Spirit brings empowerment for Christian service, especially fearless preaching.[20] Finally, for Calvin the Holy Spirit plays an absolutely essential role in the daily life of the believer in giving both an assurance of the authority of Scripture and the salvation of the believer.[21] Concerning the Spirit as authenticator of Scripture, Calvin wrote:

> They who strive to build up firm faith in Scripture through disputation are doing things backwards ... The testimony of the Spirit is more excellent than all reason. For as God alone is a fit witness of himself in his Word, so also the Word will not find acceptance in men's hearts before it is sealed by the inward testimony of the Spirit.... Let this point therefore stand: that those whom the Holy Spirit has inwardly taught truly rest upon Scripture, and that Scripture indeed is self-authenticated; hence, it is not right to subject it to proof and reasoning. And the certainty it deserves with us, it attains by the testimony of the Spirit.[22]

17. The phrase appears in an essay titled "John Calvin the Theologian," which originally appeared in a booklet published by the Presbyterian Board of Education in 1909. Warfield, "John Calvin."

18. Calvin, *Institutes of the Christian Religion*, 466.

19. Ibid., 463.

20. Ibid., 82.

21. This theme and more all examined by Chung, "Calvin and the Holy Spirit, 40–55, esp. 43.

22. This is taken from the Calvin, *Institutes of the Christian Religion*, I.7: "The

In opposition to most medieval theologians, for whom "love" was the central focus, Calvin as Luther centered Christianity upon "faith." And Calvin's definition of faith, the cornerstone of his entire theological system, was based on the assurance that comes from the Holy Spirit in the hearts of believers. "We shall now have a full definition of faith," Calvin wrote, "if we say that it is a firm and sure knowledge of the divine favour toward us, founded on the truth of a free promise in Christ, and revealed to our minds and sealed on our hearts by the Holy Spirit."[23]

This does not mean that the believer never struggles with doubts—he or she struggles continually. But through the power of the Holy Spirit the believer will always gain the victory. For Calvin, therefore, the Spirit who was poured out on the believers at Pentecost must be the constant, comforting companion of every believer in all ages. I know of no other Reformer who put the Spirit at the very center of the daily Christian life as did Calvin. In the historical context in which he wrote, the importance of this doctrine is clear. The Protestants had separated themselves from the sacramental system of the Roman Catholic church, and were surrounded by those who told them that they were cut off from salvation. How could Pastor Calvin assure his listeners that they were indeed saved? Ignore the tempting voices, Calvin would say, Christian, look within and you will find the spirit of adoption by whom you cry out to God, "Abba father." Cling to the Spirit and you will know that you will be saved.

Calvin's position concerning the gift of tongues was almost identical to Luther's. In his commentary on I Corinthians he stated "There was a difference between the *knowledge* of tongues, and the *interpretation* of them, for those who were endowed with the former were, in many cases, not acquainted with the language of the nation with which they had to deal. The *interpreters* rendered foreign tongues into the native language."[24] Speaking of the time of the New Testament, Calvin writes: "These endowments they did not at that time acquire by labour or study, but were in possession of them by a wonderful revelation of the Spirit."[25]

The interpretation of the gift of tongues as seen here in Luther and Calvin was the norm among early modern Protestant leaders.[26] It seems to

---

Testimony of the Spirit Necessary to Give Full Authority to Scripture," 68–73.

23. Ibid., 475.

24 Calvin, *Commentary on I Corinthians*, 403; italics in original.

25. Ibid.

26 Although phenomena more similar to Pentecostalism can be found in fringe figures of the Reformation such as the "Zwickau Prophets" and possibly the radical Reformer Thomas Müntzer, this understanding of the gift of tongues was predominate across all leaders of early Protestantism from Ulrich Zwingli to Menno Simons. On

me that this understanding of the gift of tongues was so engrained in these Reformers, that it would have required an enormous leap of the imagination to understand the gift of tongues in the Pentecostal sense. It is almost painful to read Calvin's commentary on I Corinthians 14 because of the exegetical gymnastics he has to do to make sense of the gift of tongues as the ability to speak a foreign language. The summary picture in Calvin's mind of Paul's correction of the Corinthian church must be that someone was not only speaking an untranslated foreign language during worship, but doing it badly—no wonder he thought Paul didn't want it in church.

Luther on Drunkenness and "Sighs Which Cannot Be Uttered"

Although one certainly cannot imagine John Calvin using this kind of metaphor, Luther spoke of being "drunk in the Spirit." He used it as shorthand for a reckless, fearless confidence in God which produces exuberant joy and praise. During his lectures on Genesis, as professors (and preachers) are accustomed to do, he went off on a tangent about this kind of drunkenness. The section is so fascinating that it bears quoting at length. After quoting Eph 5:18-20 ("don't be drunk with wine, but be filled with the Spirit,") and Acts 2:4, Luther added:

> In this way the godly are filled with the Holy Spirit, so that they cannot keep from breaking forth into thanksgiving, confession, glorifying God, and teaching and proclaiming the Word of the gospel.[27]

After discussing how this drunkenness in the Spirit enabled the early church to laugh at the majesty and power of the Roman Empire, he continued:

> This happened in the early days of the martyrs. But it is also necessary today for the whole church and for us, too, to be made drunk with the Holy Spirit and not to fear the pope and the ragings of all the tyrants and devils. Christ has called us and has tied us with a most pleasing bond to His vineyards, that is, to His spiritual gifts, with which He fills us, so that we fear none of all the things that can harm us.[28]

---

glossolalia among some radicals, see Williams, *The Radical Reformation.*
27. Luther, "Lectures on Genesis," 249.
28. Ibid., 251.

Luther had particular need of this kind of exuberant joyfulness. It is clear that he suffered from bouts of spiritual attacks which he called "*Anfechtungen.*" He believed these attacks to be a necessary, but difficult part of one's spiritual development. For Luther it was essential that we have the help of the Holy Spirit in our infirmities interceding for us with "sighs that cannot be uttered" (Rom 8:26).[29] Several Pentecostal scholars have made linkages between this phenomenon from Romans 8 and glossolalia.[30] It should be emphasized that Luther held that outward miraculous manifestations of the Holy Spirit such as a dove descending on Jesus, the tongues of fire, and the miracle of speaking languages one has not learned at Pentecost were used by God to establish the Church as signs to the unbelievers (citing I Cor 14:22), but were no longer used by God once the Church had been established.[31] Nevertheless, according to Luther, it was through the intercession of the Holy Spirit that victory comes to all believers, and this intercession is connected for him with "sighs" or "groanings."[32]

Roman Catholic Jubilation

If we want to find more extensive experiences similar to modern Pentecostalism in the Age of the Reformation, however, we must turn from Protestantism. Throughout the history of the Church there has been an important minority tradition that is classified under the general heading of "mysticism."[33] Critics of the mystic tradition have been concerned about its wandering around in the mists of theological abstraction, its focus on individual spiritual experience over the community or service, and its propensity to be a divisive force in the life of the church. However, there is

---

29. Melanchthon's commentary on Romans 8:26–27 reads: "Meanwhile the Holy Spirit brings it about that we in some part obey and call on God. The obedience and invocation Paul calls 'sighs too deep for words.'" *Commentary on Romans by Melanchthon*, 181.

30. Among others, Macchia is in support of the connection of glossolalia to the "groaning" of Rom 8:26. See Macchia, "Sighs Too Deep for Words," 47–73, esp. 59–60. Also Bertone, "The Experience of Glossolalia and the Spirit's Empathy," 54–65; and Fee, *God's Empowering Presence*, 577.

31. Froelich, "Charismatic Manifestations," 173.

32. Luther, "Lectures on Galatians," 381, 384–85.

33. On the history of the Christian mystic tradition, see especially the work of McGinn, particularly the three volumes of his Presence of God series: *The Foundation of Mysticism*, *The Growth of Mysticism*, and *The Flowering of Mysticism*.

much that is valuable and vibrant here, and I believe it is important for Pentecostals to understand their connection to this long-standing tradition.[34]

The mystics of the Medieval and Early Modern Church claimed to experience marvelous things. Many of their experiences are familiar to Pentecostals.[35] But they neither called them "speaking in tongues" nor connected them to the gifts of the Holy Spirit in Corinthians or Acts. Rather they called these experiences "jubilations" and linked them to Psalms such as 95, 98, and 100 ("make a joyful noise" Psalms).[36] Perhaps the best definition is from John Ruysbroeck, a Dutch/Flemish mystic (died 1381), who links jubilation with spiritual drunkenness:

> Spiritual inebriation is this; that a man receives more sensible joy and sweetness than his heart can either contain or desire. Spiritual inebriation brings forth many strange gestures in men. It makes some sing and praise God because of their fullness of joy, and some weep with great tears because of their sweetness of heart. It makes one restless in all his limbs, so that he must run and jump and dance; and so excites another that he must gesticulate and clap his hands. . . . the satisfaction are so great, that the heart cannot bear them, but breaks out with a loud voice in cries in joy. And this is called the jubilus or jubilation, that is, a joy which cannot be uttered in words.[37]

One example is Philip Neri (1515–1595). He was born in Florence to a family of the minor nobility and served as a tutor in Rome where he became overwhelmed by the spiritual needs of the many pilgrims to the city. His greatest accomplishment was the foundation of the organization known as

---

34. Chan is one of the theologians who have seen commonalities between the Christian mystic tradition and Pentecostalism. See Chan, *Pentecostal Theology*, 74. However, most Pentecostal exploration has been in the context of the early Church rather than medieval or early modern manifestations.

35. While Chan likens "glossolalia-like responses" to the Pentecostal experience, he does so as an equivalent within different cultural-linguistic systems; however, it seems to me that the actual experiences themselves have important elements of equivalence. Ibid., 62.

36. Burgess calls this Ensley's "jubilation as tongues" thesis and does not examine it in detail as it is not specifically linked to Spirit baptism (Burgess, "Evidence of the Spirit," 24) but later Burgess gives a fuller description and linkage (Burgess, "Holy Spirit," 759–60).

37. Ruysbroeck, *The Adornment of the Spiritual Marriage*, II.19, 24, 69, 78. It is important to note that many theologians who have written about glossolalia understand the Greek use of "tongues" in Acts and 1 Corinthians to require at a minimum a language-like speech-act that would exclude inarticulate sounds. See Sullivan, *Charisms and the Charismatic Renewal*, 124.

the Priests of the Oratory, which became a center for moral reform and prayer among the clergy.

The fundamental spiritual experience of his life occurred in the context of the feast of Pentecost in 1544. While at prayer pleading with the Holy Spirit to bestow His gifts upon him, Neri felt himself filled with the power of the Holy Spirit to such a degree that his heart began to palpitate, and he was overcome by the sensation of inner fire. Late in his life he described to a confidant that this was experienced as a "ball of fire" entering his mouth and resting in his heart, filling him with a sense of God's love and great joy.[38] Among the many miracles attributed to Neri, was the *jubilus*, with dramatic physical manifestations of trembling and heart palpitations. He would often be so overcome that he threw himself down on the ground, roll about, and cry out to God.[39] Quite literally, Neri was a "holy roller."

It is with Teresa of Avila in Spain (1515–1582) that we find descriptions of the phenomena that most closely resemble Pentecostalism. After she became a nun she experienced a time of serious illness. During this period she began to practice internal prayer, and this gradually evolved into visions and other deep spiritual experiences. Her depth of insight and skill in communication have made her one of the most important of the mystics. Her books *The Interior Castle* and the *Way of Perfection* remain among the classic texts of the Christian experience of God.

She was noted as having experienced frequent *jubilus* in ways that sound very close to speaking in tongues: "Many words are spoken, during this state, in praise of God, but, unless the Lord himself puts order into them, they have no orderly form. The understanding, at any rate, counts for nothing here; the soul would like to shout praises aloud, for it is in such a state that it cannot contain itself—a state of delectable disquiet. . . ."[40]

And even more directly from the *Interior Castle*:

> In the midst of these experiences that are both painful and delightful together, our Lord sometimes gives the soul feelings of jubilation and a strange prayer it doesn't understand. I am writing about this favor here so that if He grants it to you, you may give Him much praise and know what is taking place. It is, in my opinion, a deep union of the faculties; but our Lord nonetheless

---

38. According to the early biography by Antonio Gallonio published in 1600, "Every day Philip used to pray to the Holy Spirit, with all the ardor at his disposal, to endow him with His holy gifts. No day was suffered to pass without calling on the Spirit's aid. And this was not without result." Gallonio, *The Life of Philip Neri*, 16–17. See also Türks, *Philip Neri: The Fire of Joy*, 16–17.

39. See Bacci, *The Life of Philip Neri*, 23–29; and Trevor, *Apostle of Rome*, 40–44.

40. Quoted in Ensley, *Sounds of Wonder*, 95.

leaves them free that they might enjoy this joy—and the same goes for the senses—without understanding what it is they are enjoying or how they are enjoying. What I'm saying seems like gibberish, but certainly the experience takes place in this way.[41]

This is similar to a theophanic understanding of glossolalia perhaps best articulated by the Pentecostal theologian Frank Macchia as "a freeing of the spirit to respond to the immediate presence of the living God."[42] Pentecostals (and Protestants) step back from some of the intense bridal mysticism that Teresa experienced. But there is no doubt that she knew what it was to be passionately in love with God with the accompanying physical manifestations common to Pentecostals.

Conclusions

As a result of this brief sketch, some tentative conclusions can be offered. First, it will be obvious to any Pentecostal that there is considerable overlap in Luther's and Calvin's views of the role of the Holy Spirit in the life of the believer with Pentecostal understandings. In fact, Pentecostals potentially can have their theology of the Holy Spirit deepened through an engagement with the rich pneumatology of Calvin. Second, Luther and Calvin differ significantly with Pentecostals in their understanding of glossolalia. This is in large part because of the fundamental assumption that the pertinent scriptural texts concerning "speaking in tongues" (Acts 2:4; I Cor 12, 14, etc.) all described speaking in actual human languages. However, one potentially fruitful connection between Pentecostals and Lutherans is in Luther's understanding of "sighs which cannot be uttered" (Rom 8:26). Third, in the lives of some Roman Catholics there has been significant congruence with Pentecostal experiences of the charismata, including glossolalia. The connection is often missed because Catholics sometimes have used the descriptor "jubilation" rather than "speaking in tongues" for them. In particular, one potential locus for Pentecostal-Catholic dialogue concerns understanding charismata to be a theophanic response, a natural physical manifestation when humans encounter the Almighty God.

As I have done here, some other Pentecostal scholars are beginning to advocate paying more attention to the *entire* history of Christianity. Theologian Simon Chan is at the forefront of this movement. According to Chan:

---

41. St. Teresa of Avila, *The Interior Castle*, 141–42.
42. See Macchia, "Sighs Too Deep for Words," 52.

> It ought to give Pentecostals no small comfort when they realize that what they had been practicing spontaneously in a rather unreflective manner is remarkably akin to something which has a long history in the Christian tradition. . . . If Pentecostals can locate the logical function of glossolalia within the larger Christian tradition it would provide a surer basis for its use and ensure that it will have a significant place in their own devotional life.[43]

I contend that it is entirely possible, and even necessary, to maintain important Pentecostal distinctives *while at the same time* recognizing connections to much larger movements within the history of the Church, movements which predate Pentecostalism by centuries. We do a disservice to the Holy Spirit when we fail to recognize that He is active not only today, but that He was also at work in the spiritual drunkenness of Luther and the dancing and clapping of Teresa of Avila.

Bibliography

Bacci, Pietro Giacomo. *The Life of Philip Neri*. Vol. 1. St. Louis: Herder, 1903.

Bertone, John. "The Experience of Glossolalia and the Spirit's Empathy: Romans 8:26 Revisited." *Pneuma* 25, no. 1 (2003) 54–65.

Burgess, Stanley "Evidence of the Spirit: The Medieval and Modern Western Churches." In *Initial Evidence: Historical and Biblical Perspectives on the Pentecostal Doctrine of Spirit Baptism*, edited by Gary B. McGee, 20–40. Peabody, MA: Hendrickson, 1991.

———. "Holy Spirit, Doctrine of: The Medieval Churches." In *The New International Dictionary of Pentecostal and Charismatic Movements*, edited by Stanley M. Burgess and Eduard M. Van Der Maas, 746–63. Grand Rapids: Zondervan, 2002.

"Bylaws of the General Council of the Assemblies of God, Article IX.B, List of Doctrines and Practices Disapproved, Section 11 The Ecumenical Movement." *Minutes of the 51st Session of The General Council of the Assemblies of God, with revised Constitution and Bylaws 51st General Council, Denver, Colorado, August 2–5, 2005*, 125. Springfield, MO: General Secretary's Office, 2005.

Calvin, John. *Commentary on the Epistles of Paul the Apostle to the Corinthians*. Vol. 1. Translated by John Pringle. Grand Rapids: Eerdmans, 1948.

———. *Commentary upon the Acts of the Apostles*. Vol. 1. Translated by Christopher Fetherstone. Grand Rapids: Eerdmans, 1957.

———. *Institutes of the Christian Religion*. Vol. 1. Translated by Henry Beveridge. Grand Rapids: Eerdmans, 1989.

Chan, Simon. *Pentecostal Theology and the Christian Spiritual Tradition*. London: Sheffield Academic, 2003.

Chung, Paul. "Calvin and the Holy Spirit: A Reconsideration in Light of Spirituality and Social Ethics." *Pneuma* 24, no. 1 (2002) 40–55.

---

43. Chan, *Pentecostal Theology*, 82.

Ensley, Eddie. *Sounds of Wonder: Speaking in Tongues in the Catholic Tradition*. New York: Paulist, 1977.

Fee, Gordon. *God's Empowering Presence*. Peabody, MA: Hendrickson, 1994.

Froelich, Karlfried "Charismatic Manifestations and the Lutheran Incarnational Stance." In *The Holy Spirit in the Life of the Church*, edited by Paul D. Opsahl, 136–57. Minneapolis: Augsburg, 1978.

Gallonio, Antonio. *The Life of Philip Neri*. Translated by Jerome Bertram. San Francisco: Ignatius, 2005.

Kärkkäinen, Veli-Matti. *Ad ultimum terrae: Evangelization. Proselytism and Common Witness in the Roman Catholic-Pentecostal Dialogue (1990–1997)*. Frankfurt: Peter Lang, 1999.

———. "The Holy Spirit and Justification: The Ecumenical Significance of Luther's Doctrine of Salvation." *Pneuma* 24, no. 1 (2002) 26–39.

Luther, Martin. "Concerning the Order of Public Worship." In *Luther's Works*, edited by Jaroslav Pelikan, 53:7–14. Minneapolis: Fortress, 1965.

———. "Lectures on Galatians." In *Luther's Works*. Vol. 27, *Lectures on Galatians 5–6, 1535*. Edited by Jaroslav Pelikan. St. Louis: Concordia, 1964.

———. "Lectures on Genesis." In *Luther's Works*. Vol. 8, *Lectures on Genesis Chapters 45–50*, edited by Jaroslav Pelikan. St. Louis: Concordia, 1966.

———. "Pentecost." In *Sermons of Martin Luther*, edited by John Nicholas Lenker, 7:329–36. Grand Rapids: Baker, 2000.

"Lutherans and Pentecostals in Dialogue." Strasbourg, France: Institute for Ecumenical Research, 2010. http://www.strasbourginstitute.org/en/dialogues/lutheran-pentecostal-dialogue/

Macchia, Frank. "Sighs Too Deep for Words: Toward a Theology of Glossolalia." *Journal of Pentecostal Theology* 1 (1992) 47–73.

McGinn, Bernard. *The Flowering of Mysticism*. New York: Crossroads, 1998.

———. *The Foundation of Mysticism*. New York: Crossroads, 1991.

———. *The Growth of Mysticism*. New York: Crossroads, 1994.

Melanchthon, Philip. *Commentary on Romans by Melanchthon*. Translated by Fred Kramer. St. Louis: Concordia, 1992.

"On Becoming a Christian: Insights from Scripture and the Patristic Writings with Some Contemporary Reflections: Report of the Fifth Phase of the International Dialogue Between Some Classical Pentecostal Churches and Leaders and the Catholic Church (1998–2006)." http://www.vatican.va/romancuria/pontifical councils/chrstuni/eccl-comm-docs/rcpcchrstunidoc20060101becoming-a-christianen.html. Accessed September 30, 2016.

Robeck, Cecil M., Jr. "Pentecostals and Christian Unity: Facing the Challenge." *Pneuma* 26, no. 2 (2004) 307–38.

Ruysbroeck, John. *The Adornment of the Spiritual Marriage*. Translated by C. A. Wynschenk. Edited by Evelyn Underhill. London: Watkins, 1951.

Sullivan, Francis. *Charisms and the Charismatic Renewal: A Biblical and Theological Study*. Ann Arbor, MI: Servant, 1982.

Teresa of Avila. *The Interior Castle*. Translated by Kieran Kavanaugh. Mahwah, NJ: Paulist, 1979.

Trevor, Meriol. *Apostle of Rome: A Life of Philip Neri*. London: Macmillan, 1966.

Türks, Paul. *Philip Neri: The Fire of Joy*. Translated by Daniel Utrecht. New York: Alba House, 1995.

Vondey, Wolfgang, ed. *Pentecostalism and Christian Unity: Ecumenical Documents and Critical Assessments*. Eugene, OR: Pickwick, 2010.

Warfield, Benjamin. "John Calvin the Theologian." In *Calvin and* Augustine, edited by Samuel Craig, 484. Philadelphia: Presbyterian and Reformed, 1956.

Wainwright, Geoffrey. "The One Hope of Your Calling? The Ecumenical and Pentecostal Movements after a Century." *Pneuma* 23, no. 1 (2003) 7–28.

Williams, George H. *The Radical Reformation*. Kirksville, MO: Truman State University Press, 2000.

Womack, David A. *The Wellsprings of the Pentecostal Movement*. Springfield, MO: Gospel Publishing House, 1968.

"Word and Spirit, Church and World: Final Report of the International Dialogue Between Representatives of the World Alliance of Reformed Churches and some Classical Pentecostal Churches and Leaders: 1996–2000." In *Pentecostalism and Christian Unity: Ecumenical Documents and Critical Assessments*, edited by Wolfgang Vondey, 199–227. Eugene, OR: Pickwick, 2010.

14

"This is Our Story"

Early Pentecostal Historiography and the Spiritual Politics of a Movement's Memory

EDWARD J. K. GITRE

History in Question

EARLY PENTECOSTALS HAD A problem with history. The *Apostolic Herald* in 1909 did not pull a punch: "No great human leader or radical reformer is at the head of this movement directing its forces or manipulating its ecclesiastical mechanism. Instead of this visitation being a reform, or strictly a movement, it is rather a breaking forth of centuries of overdue power; the praying down of heaven's Pentecost; the retrievement of the sad history of the past."[1] This acidic view of church history did not tact outside the mainstream of early Pentecostal thinking, but very much held the center. Even when it came time to write their own histories and biographies, Pentecostals maintained their disdain. Anti-historicism provided Carl Brumback the basic premise of his nearly four-hundred-page history of the Assemblies of God, *Suddenly . . . from Heaven*, published in 1961: "[w]e Pentecostalists regard the absence of a progenitor of our own Movement as an indication that this mighty revival was begotten directly by an extraordinary outpouring of the Holy Spirit."[2] Academic historians have had a field day with this "primitive" historiography.[3] Even the sympathetic historian Grant Wacker,

---

1. "Concerning This Movement," 3.

2. Brumback, *Suddenly . . . from Heaven*, quoted in Cerillo, "The Beginnings of American Pentecostalism," 3.

3. See Cerillo, "Beginnings of American Pentecostalism"; Creech, "Visions of

himself of Pentecostal lineage, has written of the title (*Suddenly . . . from Heaven*) in italics that it could hardly "have been more non-historical, if not antihistorical, in intent."[4]

At first glance, one might suppose that in denying human agency Pentecostals, such as Brumback and the editors of the *Apostolic Herald*, wished to subjugate history to belief. The utter rejection is, still, more than a little quizzical. The pages of church history, the history of radical evangelicalism included, are chock full with unqualified accolades to individuals of heroic faith; the Wesley brothers, D. L. Moody, Charles Finney, Evan Roberts, George Whitefield—these men received their due. Why did early Pentecostals take such a dim view of history? Certain theological commitments absolutely animated this predilection. Yet to be perfectly honest, so did politicking. An observant outsider I. G. Martin noted, as early as 1906, a scattering of the Pentecostal flock as a result of discord among influential pastors and jockeying for spiritual leadership. "We found on investigation that there were already divisions among [Pentecostals], and that one meeting had become three. For, while some were saying, 'We are with Seymour,' others are saying, 'We are with Parham'; and still others, 'We are with Bartleman.'"[5] While proclaiming the unmediated anointing of the Spirit, early Pentecostals were not jettisoning history in *toto*. Rather, they were rejecting claims of a "progenitor," a "human leader or radical reformer . . . at the head of this movement directing its forces or manipulating its ecclesiastical mechanism." This disavowal applied especially to Charles Parham, the one minister of the three with a legitimate claim to have had a strong, initial hand in steering forces and engineering mechanisms. To understand how history became suspect, we need to examine the cheap, widely circulated newspapers that were so crucial in forging a collective Pentecostal identity. By commemorating the testimonies of divine visitation; providing preachers a platform to augment their pulpits; advertising camp meetings, conventions, and conferences; chronicling the latter rain's advance across the U.S. and around the world; and establishing "correct" full-gospel doctrine, these papers not only documented Pentecostalism's unfolding history—they helped make it.[6]

Glory"; Wacker, "Are the Golden Oldies Worth Playing?"; and Wacker, "Biography and Historiography."

4. Wacker, "Are the Golden Oldies Worth Playing?," 96.
5. Martin, "Los Angeles Letters"; cf. Vanzandt, *Speaking in Tongues*, 37–38.
6. See Stephens, "There is Magic in Print."

Bible Evidence

Arthur. T. Pierson, who wrote in *Forward Movement of the Last Half Century* published in 1905, stated: "Of all the important spiritual movements of the half century not one compares in importance with the revival working and out-working of the Spirit of God." And "[t]his may be called the Pentecostal Movement, since the bestowment [sic] of the Spirit for fuller activity in and through the believer, dates from Pentecost. But by this name is now meant the general movement, peculiar to our day, in the direction of new emphasis upon the work of the Spirit of God, in three aspects—*sanctifying, enduing, and filling*."[7] When Pierson wrote this he had in mind not the Pentecostal movement as we know it, but the Higher Life Movement radiating out of Keswick, England. An appreciation of the spiritual effervescence of late Victorian-era Christianity, and its blooming affinity for "religious *experiences*," helps to illuminate the finer distinctions of what might look to one person as the (divisive) scattering and to another as the (expansive) consolidation of a prodigious religious flock. "Few would doubt that the central impulse of the higher life movement was its determination to recover the theology and presence of the Holy Spirit." Wacker, in agreement with other historians, has commented on the flourishing of religious experience. "Indeed, the whole nineteenth-century evangelical movement, Wesleyan as well as Reformed, might well be defined as historic Protestant orthodoxy spiced with a tingling expectation that the power of the Holy Spirit, lost since the days of the apostles, was about to be restored."[8] The acuity of this burgeoning, but very deliberate, affinity for this member of the Trinity—particularly the Spirit's omnipresence and more ecstatic attributes, like speed and power, expressed through the popular metaphors of "wind" and "fire"—suited itself with remarkable congeniality to the principle forces of Euro-American modernity—chief among them the technology-driven acceleration and compression of time and space.[9]

Within this milieu, the Methodist-turned-holiness evangelist Charles Parham found himself attracted to and honed in on the one spiritual gift he reckoned to have the greatest potential to spread the "full gospel" around the entire globe in the shortest period of time; the capacity to speak in unknown tongues under the Spirit's unction. By this he meant not truly unknown languages but what he called "missionary tongues"; God would give believers the ability to speak actual, foreign tongues instantaneously, thus bypassing

---

7. Pierson, *Forward Movements of the Last Half Century*, 137.
8. Wacker, "The Holy Spirit and the Spirit of the Age," 54.
9. See Kern, *The Culture of Time and Space*.

the customary, more time-consuming path of missionaries taking formal language training.[10] A small group of students at the makeshift Bethel Bible school in Topeka, Kansas, had reached a problem in their study when they came upon the second chapter of Acts. Parham, their teacher, explained:

> I had felt for years that any missionary going to the foreign field should preach in the language of the natives. That if God has ever equipped His ministers in the way he could do it today. I believed our experience should tally exactly with the Bible, and neither sanctification nor the anointing that abideth taught by Stephen Merritt and others tallied with the 2nd Chapter of Acts. Having heard so many different religious bodies claim different proofs as the evidence of their having the Pentecostal baptism, I set the students at work studying out diligently what was the Bible evidence of the baptism of the Holy Ghost, that we might go before the world with something that was indisputable because it tallied absolutely with the Word.[11]

Only after this concerted scriptural examination did his student Agnes Ozman receive her "foreign tongues," reputedly Chinese, during a New Year's Day 1901 prayer meeting some would describe as spiritual mayhem, but Parham would confidently call divine perfection. "There was no chattering, jabbering, or stuttering. Each one[12] spoke clearly and distinctly in a foreign tongue, with earnestness, intensity and God given unction."[13] The centrality of Parham's leadership in this totally independent recovery of Acts 2 has been established as "too pat to be true"[14]—I personally remember in the mid-1990s Gary B. McGee's ebullient fascination with reports he had uncovered of a Miss Jennie Glassey speaking in tongues in St. Louis, Missouri, in 1895—but he nevertheless "framed the chief doctrinal distinctive of classical Pentecostalism," later taught by Bartleman and Seymour, that speaking in tongues was "the requisite sign or 'Bible evidence' of the baptism in the Holy Spirit" and that through this baptism God would distribute "among

---

10. Cf. Charles Parham, "Free-Love," 4–5.
11. Sarah Parham, *The Life of Charles F. Parham*, 51–52.
12. See also McGee, "'The Latter Rain,'" 648–65.
13. Sarah Parham, *The Life of Charles F. Parham*, 55.
14. Anderson, *Vision of the Disinherited*, 54; see also, 52–57. Cf. Goff, *Fields White Unto Harvest*, 66–72. For the inconsistency of the accounts of the events at Parham's school, cf. Charles Parham, "Birth of the Apostolic Faith"; and LaBerge, *What God Hath Wrought*, 29; and Ozman, "Where the Latter Rain First Fell," 2. For evidence of Parham having heard of speaking in tongues before January 1, 1901, cf. J. C. Vanzandt, *Speaking in Tongues*, 31; and Shumway, "A Critical Study of 'The Gift of Tongues,'" 158.

the saints every intelligible language to expedite world evangelization in the ends times."[15]

This sustained assertion that speaking in tongues was, in the parlance of later Assembly of God doctrine, the "initial physical evidence" established Parham's ministry as the theological lynch pin between Anglo-American missions and a United States-based circuit of radical evangelical preachers in the holiness camp. To be sure, in no small measure does he owe this distinction to the inauspicious ministerial career of yet another student, William J. Seymour. This part of the story has been well represented by others. In the fall of 1905, in another of Parham's makeshift Bible schools, this one in Houston, Texas, Seymour learned the new Bible evidence doctrine. Shortly thereafter, with Parham's apparent blessing, he left, traveling westward to establish a ministry in Los Angeles through local contacts—this despite having yet to receive the Bible evidence himself.[16] At the other end of his arduous excursion, relations with the holiness mission that was to receive him turned icy; Seymour was physically locked out. A reluctant member took him in, a Bible study ensued and one member received their Bible evidence. Following the Topeka pattern, this Spirit baptism was quickly followed by a host of others, attracting reporters and, as a consequence, a lot of local attention.[17] With their Bonnie Brae Street bungalow bursting at the seams, Seymour and the others soon encamped themselves in an abandoned Methodist church. And, in a move inspired by an electrifying revival taking place halfway around the world in Wales, the newly christened Apostolic Faith Mission set no order of service and eschewed the customary ecclesiastic authority of a minister ruling behind a pulpit. Embracing a radical egalitarian rule of order would, they believed, set the Spirit free. Men, women, and children alike took advantage of the stipulation of participation that anybody could sing, testify, prophecy, exhort, or expound on Scripture under the Spirit's unction. The unbridled enthusiasm that followed shook the beams of the old, wood-clad building as the faithful proclaimed their deliverance from infirmities spiritual and physical, mortal and demonic. The curious and the seekers flowed into the building packed in tightly as rumors and reports proliferated, "[s]cenes transpiring here are what Los Angeles churches have been praying for for years." One rapturous Methodist testified, "[w]e prayed that the Pentecost might come to the city of Los Angeles. . . . God almighty says He will pour out of His Spirit upon

---

15. McGee, "'The Latter Rain,'" 650; cf. Goff, *Fields White unto Harvest*, 16.

16. Robeck, "William J. Seymour," 74.

17. For the most detailed accounts of Seymour's ministry in Los Angeles, see Nelson, "For Such a Time As This."

all flesh. This is just what is happening here."[18] The latter rain had come to the City of Angels.

That autumn, Seymour and his band of leaders would have good cause to align themselves in even closer proximity to the revival blanketing the mine-pocked Welsh countryside. The Apostolic Faith Mission's embrace of radical, Welsh-inspired egalitarianism suited a teeming port city populated by migrants; however, it did not endear the mission to the father of Bible evidence, Parham. Learning of the outpouring, Parham visited in October 1906 prepared to assume the mantel of leadership, although what he encountered at the mission utterly astounded him. He was appalled by such sordid display of what he labeled "free-love"—men and women praying uninhibitedly together, embracing, swooning, catching each other as they fell overwhelmed by the Spirit. The sexualization of religious enthusiasm commingled in Parham's vexed mind with that particularly well-honed American fear of racial (anti-egalitarian) bastardization through the mere contact of skin. He was provoked to utter repulsion by the sight of blacks and whites "mingling" in worship, writing later of of how damningly frequently "a white woman, perhaps of wealth and culture, could be seen thrown back in the arms of a big 'buck nigger,' and held tightly thus as she shivered and shook in freak imitation of Pentecost. Horrible, awful shame!"[19] He certainly aimed to do something about the bedlam, but was never granted the opportunity. The interracial council of men and women running the mission severed the relationship with him, marking their disassociation by inserting into their name a geographical amendment that henceforth they were to be known not as the Apostolic Faith Mission but the *Pacific* Apostolic Faith Mission. Next they would expunge Parham's name from the record book of history.

Crying Wolf

The Pacific Apostolic Faith Mission was from the start ambivalent about church history. In September 1906, the mission began printing its own newspaper, greatly increasing its visibility, titled *The Apostolic Faith*. Editors of the paper offered readers two divergent perspectives on history. The one was progressive, the other revolutionary. The appellation, the "latter rain" outpouring often affixed to the movement, best conveys the second perspective. Its predecessor, the "former rain," referred not to various outpourings of the past, but to the New Testament outpouring of the Holy Spirit

---

18. *Apostolic Faith* (Los Angeles), November 1906.

19. Charles Parham, "Free-Love" 4. See also Shumway, "A Critical Study of The Gift of Tongues," 178.

on the day of Pentecost. The Pacific Apostolic Faith Mission promulgated the eschatological conviction of mainstream premillennialists, that in advance of Jesus's Second Coming, God would visit upon the earth one great and final "latter rain" outpouring. D. Wesley Myland's hymn, entitled "'The Latter Rain' Song: Pentecost Has Come," articulated well their eschatological vision: "There's a Pentecost for all the sanctified, Heaven's witness, true, which cannot be denied, And the Spirit's gifts are being multiplied In God's holy church today / Oh, I'm glad the promised Pentecost has come, And the 'Latter Rain' is falling now on some; Pour it out in floods, Lord, on the parched ground, Till it reaches all the earth around."

For the most part, *The Apostolic Faith* propounded to the disjunctive latter rain motif, emphasizing the mission's distinct, God-ordained position. Copying Parham's recollection of the Topeka New Year's Day outpouring, for instance, the paper's inaugural issue told the story of how the students at Bethel had independently discovered the "Bible evidence" after "searching through the country everywhere" for a sure answer, but finding none. Looking near and far, they had been quite unable "to find any Christians that had the true Pentecostal power. So they [Parham and the students] laid aside all commentaries, and notes and waited on the Lord."[20] The paper did, however, admit that history was not entirely bereft of spiritual power. That same inaugural issue showcased various charismatic outpourings dating at least as far back as the Enlightenment. "At the beginning of the Eighteenth century, among the French Protestants, there were wonderful manifestations of the Spirit power accompanied by the Gift of Tongues."[21] Citing the second volume of the Bishop John Fletcher Hurst's massive, new *History of the Christian Church,* the paper then authenticated the same gift among the Quakers and Irvingites, and during an early 1840s revival in Sweden, and another in Ireland in 1859. The second issue sustained both this progressive historiography as well as the more radical approach. An article demonstrating a more revolutionary perspective, "The Pentecostal Baptism Restored: The Promised Latter Rain Now Being Poured Out on God's Humble People," opens nonetheless with a progressive interpretation: "All along the ages men have been preaching a partial Gospel. A part of the Gospel remained when the world went into the dark ages. God has from time to time raised up men to bring back the truth to the church."[22] The author commended the ministries of Martin Luther, John Wesley, and Charles Cullis of the "faith-healing" movement.

20. "The Old-Time Power," 1.
21. "The Promise Still Good," 1.
22. "The Pentecostal Baptism Restored," 1.

After Parham's curt departure, God's story became markedly easier for the Pacific Apostolic Faith Mission to discern. Issue number three, the next issue in the series, published after his visit, offered readers yet another history of the Los Angeles "latter rain" outpouring in an article entitled "Pentecost With Signs Following: Seven Months of Pentecostal Showers. Jesus, Our Projector and Great Shepherd." The paper reported, "[m]any are asking how the work in Azusa Mission started and who was the founder. The Lord was the founder and He is the Projector of this movement."[23] The same issue addressed Parham's claim of precedence rather pointedly.

> Some are asking if Dr. Chas. F. Parham is the leader of his movement. We can answer, no he is not the leader of this movement of Azusa Mission. We thought of having him to be our leader and so stated in our paper, before waiting on the Lord . . . We can be rather hasty when we are very young in the power of the Holy Spirit. . . . But the Lord commenced settling us down, and we saw that the Lord should be our leader. So we honor Jesus as the great Shepherd of the sheep.[24]

The revolution had succeeded.

All subsequent accounts of the movement's origin written for *The Apostolic Faith* would display this radical historiography. "The real Pentecost that has been hidden for all these centuries, the Lord is giving back to the earth through some real humble people that have no better sense than to believe God."[25] "[T]here was a time when we were fed upon theological chips, shavings, and wind, but now the long, long night is past. We are feeding upon the Word which is revealed by the Holy Ghost—this whole Word and nothing but the Word."[26] The mission had made a "clean sweep of the past"—and of Parham. Future references to the Pentecostal outpouring dated the movement not to 1901 but to 1906, establishing the primacy of the mission. "The wonderful sign in 1906 is the restoration of tongues, which foretells the preaching of the pure gospel to all nations, which must be done before the Gentile Times end. (Matt 24:14),"[27] read a 1907 issue, quoting *The Prophetic Age*. Another piece in the same issue, "Speaking in Tongues. Is this of God?" also postdates the outpouring: "[i]n the spring and summer

---

23. "Pentecost with Signs Following," 1.

24. Ibid. The majority of *The Apostolic Faith* papers in circulation today are from a collection reprinted by Fred Corum (1981). The December issue, the post-Parham-break issue, in this reprint collection is missing part of a page containing this quote.

25. *The Apostolic Faith* (Los Angeles), Feb.-Mar. 1907, 6.

26. *The Apostolic Faith* (Los Angeles), April 1907, 3.

27. *The Apostolic Faith* (Los Angeles), May 1907, 1.

of 1906, God began to answer the very prolonged cry of some of His hungry children, a cry for a Pentecost with scripture evidence."[28] So successful was this erasure that when *The Apostolic Faith* printed a later testimony of the "Latter Rain falling" in of all places, Topeka, no mention of Parham or Ozman was ever made, nor needed.[29]

If the discredited evangelist's position was not precarious enough as a result of the Pacific Apostolic Faith's decision, events in Texas not many months later well sealed his fate: he was charged with sodomy. Though the charge was dropped, as a minister of the gospel he was a marked man. The Apostolic Faith movement in Texas disfellowshipped him early in the summer of 1907. He had relocated his ministry to the state and counted fellow workers there among his closest friends; and now he was utterly abandoned. The ex-Methodist Field Director Warren Carothers who had entered the Pentecostal fold under Parham's ministry, had not only deserted the man but had lobbied against him. In a letter to Howard Goss, another leader in the area, Parham wrote that his one-time lieutenant was now "trying to get all the Movement to follow him in revolt." To Goss he lamented of the betrayal: "He has failed me in my greatest trial and is trying to turn all my support away as though he thought he could starve me out . . . He is trying to gain the hearts of the workers and get control of Texas."[30] The disfellowshipped evangelist's post-expulsion escapades did little to repair the damage or to stench the defection. Rumors circulated in the southern Pentecostal press that he and his remaining "descendants" were drumming up support to lead a foul's errand to Palestine to recover the Ark of the Covenant. A German Azusa Street convert, and recently minted missionary to Northern China, reported to the Atlanta *Bridegroom's Messenger* that he had received a paper with the preposterously blasphemous claim that Parham was the actual "sixth angel John saw at Patmos," trumpeting the Second Woe of the Great Tribulation.[31]

Parham's refusal to go quietly garnered the ultimate reproach that he was an agent of the Devil, a devouring wolf dressed in sheep's clothing. G. B. Cashwell, who was a *Bridegroom's Messenger* correspondent, fretted over the confusion this devouring wolf dressed in sheep's clothing was reeking in the field through his "poison of false teaching." "I warn all of God's saints against such teachers and leaders, and those who exhibit a spirit of

28. "Speaking in Tongues: Is This of God?," 1.

29. Not only does the article not mention Parham's work, but the person who brought back the Pentecostal message to Topeka came from Los Angeles. Foster, "Los Angeles Campmeeting," 1.

30. Charles Parham, letter to Howard Goss.

31. Junk, "From Bros. Thomas Junk," 1.

organizing and consolidating and putting themselves up as leaders of God's people. It is purely of self and the Devil," he alerted readers.[32] In the fall of 1913 the Arkansan *Word and Witness* brimmed with reports of latter rain outpourings in foreign fields and fields closer to home, such as Sheldon, Iowa; Cumberland, Maryland; and Menominee, Michigan, among others. A young man who had attended the West Texas Camp Meeting the year before had received his Bible evidence and upon returning home shared the good news, inspiring eighteen conversions. But without a shepherd, the newborns allowed into their midst a "wolf in sheep's clothing," teaching "the damnable heresy of Parham's no-Hellism and Annihilation." The editor E. N. Bell, an early Assembly of God stalwart, used the report to exhort flocks afield. "Brethren, the word says, 'If there come any unto you and bring not this doctrine (the true doctrine of Christ, as the context shows) receive him not into your house, neither bid him God speed, for he that biddeth him God speed is a partaker of his evil deeds,' 2 John 9–11."[33] Parham had a history of entertaining rather unorthodox beliefs, however, now there was absolutely no mercy. Pentecostals were told to turn the reproached evangelist out completely and literally. A brief note from Carothers printed in *Word and Witness* in 1912 might well have served as an epitaph to the founder's exiled career: "Separated from Parham and God is blessing."[34]

Barring Parham from the pulpit was one matter, scrubbing his memory from the Apostolic Faith's history was another. Proponents of the initial "Bible evidence" of the Spirit baptism, who soon after these events came to occupy, with Bell, the executive councils of the new Pentecostal denominations and fellowships, could not utterly expunge the evangelist's contribution. Yet like the Pacific Coast *Apostolic Faith*, when it came time to write the latter rain's history, they artfully omitted his name.[35] Soon after his fallout with Parham, Carothers penned a history of the nascent movement for the Houston-based *Apostolic Faith*. It took readers on a quick tour of "the light" of apostolic teaching through history before landing on the opening act of the Pentecostal outpouring, 1901 New Year's Day. While attributing the Apostolic Faith's birth to Ozman's receiving the gift of tongues, Carothers delicately elided Parham's leadership and omitted his name. "At this juncture the students in a Bible school in Topeka, Kansas, during the winter that closed the nineteenth and ushered in the twentieth century, came to the conclusion that speaking in tongues would accompany the real baptism

32. Cashwell, "Letter from Bro. Cashwell," 4.
33. "Revival News in Home Land," 3.
34. "More Good News," 2.
35. See, for example, Taylor, *The Spirit and the Bride*, 92.

as it did in Bible days."³⁶ Apparently, in Carother's telling, the students at the Kansas Bible school were not only Spirit-led, but self-taught. In his narrative the disfellowshipped evangelist had nothing whatever to do with Seymour or the Azusa Street mission. "Brother W. J. Seymour, an African preacher of Houston, became interested in the meetings in Houston, and fully accepted the new teaching," he wrote. "We were arranging to send him out with the message among the African population in Texas when he suddenly announced that he was called of God to go to California."³⁷ A plurality of Spirit-led ministerial authority replaced the compromised singularity of Parham's role, extracting a noticeable link in the unfolding chain of Pentecostal precedence.³⁸

In the mid-1910s, B. F. Lawrence wrote the most comprehensive and thus defining history in the early years of the burgeoning Pentecostal movement, *The Apostolic Faith Restored*, published as a small book and serialized in the Pentecostal press. He, too, like Carothers, adopted the perspective of the Topeka students. They had finished their regular studies but had a little time left before the winter holidays, so the question "What is the Bible evidence of the baptism in the Holy Spirit?" that had agitated the mind of many in those days "was given them to study over in these remaining days," Lawrence wrote, neglecting their teacher's name. "As a result of their study and experience, they declared that the speaking in tongues was a part of the baptism in the Spirit in the sense that it invariably accompanied it. This was a bold stand for a little, unknown company of people to take, and it resulted in much persecution. However, many thousands now agree with them." Again no mention of Parham; only a couple of paragraphs later in a brief notice "[u]nsuccessful meetings" held elsewhere in Missouri does his name appear burrowed as the mere "head of the Bible School in Topeka where the work broke out."³⁹ To tell the story of the Apostolic Faith in Texas, Lawrence leaned heavily if not entirely on Carother's editorialized reconstruction. This is where and when "The Movement" truly became "a movement"—where, Lawrence maintained, "Order and harmony prevailed" under the watchful eyes of "Field Directors and State Encampments" who "helped to preserve the integrity of the movement and to repress lawlessness." Might this be a veiled reference to one especially pernicious wolf? Perhaps, though the author again elected to bury Parham's name in an easy-to-miss reference in a later paragraph. Not only did he ignore his expulsion, but when address-

36. Carothers, "History of Movement," 1.
37. Ibid.
38. Cf. Shumway, "A Critical Study of 'The Gift of Tongues,'" 164.
39. Lawrence, "Apostolic Faith Restored: Article VI," 4.

ing the Apostolic Faith's first schism—the Parham-Azusa Street debacle—he deferred entirely, through quotation, to Carother, the Texas Field Director who believed it simply too "painful to write" and therefore wouldn't.[40]

While Parham's star plummeted, the reputation of the Pacific Apostolic Faith Mission rocketed, leading others to adopt the mission's radical historiography. In some instances, simply noting the year 1906 established Los Angles, as opposed to Topeka, as the birthplace of the latter rain Pentecost.[41] While most accounts elaborated in far greater detail, few could top the verve of the evangelist Aimee Semple McPherson. "The name 'AZUSA' has become that of an international shrine. All that it stands for has become a guiding star, a signpost in a wilderness of modernism, a beckoning light house to urge men back to the power of Apostolic days."[42] The city she, too, called home "held the beacon light of Pentecost so high that it flashed across the continent and leaped across the tossing billows of the sea until the lights of its Holy Ghost fire reached even the hearts of those who lived in darkest India and Africa and Ceylon and the islands of the sea."[43] Stanley Frodsham's write up in the April 1909 edition of the English paper *Victory!* is but slightly more subdued. "A little over four years ago, in a little tumble-down building in Los Angeles, California, the Holy Ghost fell on a company of despised coloured people. This was the beginning of a world-wide Revival, which we feel sure is the greatest Revival the world has ever seen."[44] And later in his more detailed history, *With Signs Following*, he also would write only of the students, and not Parham, when discussing the 1901 New Year's Day prayer meeting.[45] To be sure, most Pentecostals selected the late dating and the radical historiography with no thought of Parham, because of their personal identification with the movement through the mission. The Pacific *Apostolic Faith* contains testimonies from a host of visitors who helped shape the future of the Pentecostal movement, among them Florence Crawford, Glen Cook, Charles Mason, G. B. Cashwell, and William Durham.[46] Still, the effect was the same.

40. Lawrence, "Apostolic Faith Restored: Article VII," 4.

41. See, for instance Kinne, "Tongues Movement," 14. See also "Last Great Outpouring of the Spirit," 1.

42. Corum, *Like as of Fire*, (1981), reprint of a note written by Aimee Semple McPherson, given to the author while editor of *Word and Work*, April 30, 1936.

43. Ibid.

44. Frodsham, "The Latter Rain," 1. Cf. "The Pentecostal Outpouring," 5. See also Huffman, "The Story of Pentecost," 1.

45. Frodsham, *With Signs Following*.

46. *Apostolic Faith* (Azusa Street) Glen Cook 1:3, November 1906, 2.4; Charles Mason 1:6, Feb.-Mar. 1907, 7.1–2; William Durham, 1:6, Feb.-Mar. 1907, 4.1–3; G. B.

A Movement Born

"THIS MOVEMENT, which had its beginning in the City of Los Angeles, in that year 1906 is unlike any other movement in many respects," the Ottawa, Canada, *Good Report*[47] declared. The paper's latter rain historiography, dating the Apostolic Faith movement to 1906 and to the city of Los Angeles, suggests an important, wholly neglected convergence in the collective identity and history of Pentecostalism. Note how in the absence of a progenitor these radical evangelicals committed themselves to Pentecostalism as an outward focused, forward-moving "MOVEMENT." The elision, the conscious decision to whitewash Parham's role and influence, ironically and unintentionally dovetailed with the Pacific Apostolic Faith Mission's espousal of radical egalitarianism. The *Apostolic Faith* (Los Angeles) trumpeted,

> This outpouring of the Spirit has circled the globe, and is bringing the children of God into one Spirit . . . Missionaries go out trusting God alone for their support. The Spirit is being poured out upon the people of God everywhere they will receive Him. God's word is studied as never before, the Blood of Jesus exalted. Satan is enraged. God is sifting His people. He is gathering out a company of overcomes for His bride. Is not this the latter rain?[48]

Pentecostals in and around Azusa Street, and elsewhere, too, were motivated to look afield and to the future for their collective meaning and identity, not entirely for theological reasons, but because they believed Jesus's Second Coming was fast approaching. Parham's disgrace had given them good reason not to gaze too long into the past. History was better left forgotten. But, then again, history's loss has been the gain of a "MOVEMENT" that has, over the century, truly encircled the globe.

Bibliography

Periodicals

The Apostolic Faith (Baxter Springs, Kansas)
The Apostolic Faith (Houston, Texas)
The Apostolic Faith (Los Angeles, California)
The Apostolic Herald
Bridegroom's Messenger

Cashwell, 1:4, December 1906, 3.1–2; T. B. Barratt, 1:4, December 1906, 3.2.
  47. "Apostolic Faith Movement," 4.
  48. "The Promised Latter Rain," 1.

Household of God
The Latter Rain
The Pentecostal Messenger
Word and Witness
Weekly Evangel

Other Sources

Anderson, Robert Mapes. *Vision of the Disinherited: The Making of American Pentecostalism*. Peabody, MA: Hendrickson, 1979.
"Apostolic Faith Movement." *Good Report* (1911) 4.
Brumback, Carl. *Suddenly . . . from Heaven*. Springfield, MO: Gospel, 1961.
Carothers, W. C. "History of Movement: A Brief Statement of the Origin and Spread of the Present Pentecostal and Accompanying Movement." *Apostolic Faith* (Houston, Texas) (1908) 1.
Cashwell, G. B. "Letter from Bro. Cashwell." *Bridegroom's Messenger* 1 (1908) 4.
Cerillo Jr., Augustus. "The Beginnings of American Pentecostalism: A Historiographical Overview." In *Pentecostal Currents in American Protestantism*, edited by Edith L. Blumhofer, Russell P. Spittler, and Grant Wacker, 229–59. Chicago: University of Illinois Press, 1999.
"Concerning This Movement." *Apostolic Herald* (1909) 3.
Corum, Fred T. *Compilen, Like as of Fire*. Npo; Nd, 1981.
Creech, Joe. "Visions of Glory: The Place of the Azusa Street Revival in Pentecostal History." *Church History* 65, no. 3 (1996) 405–24.
Foster, C. E. "Los Angeles Campmeeting of the Apostolic Faith Missions." *Apostolic Faith* (Los Angeles) (1907) 1.
Frodsham, Stanley H. "The Latter Rain." *Victory!* 10 (n.d.) 1
———. *With Signs Following: The Story of the Pentecostal Revival in the Twentieth Century*. Rev. ed. Springfield: Gospel, 1946.
Goff, James R., Jr. *Fields White Unto Harvest: Charles F. Parham and the Missionary Origins of Pentecostalism*. Fayetteville: University of Arkansas Press, 1988.
Huffman, John. "The Story of Pentecost." *Pentecostal Herald* (1919) 1.
Junk, Thomas. "From Bros. Thomas Junk." *Bridegroom's Messenger* 1 (1909) 1.
Kern, Stephen. *The Culture of Time and Space, 1880–1918*. Cambridge, MA: Harvard University Press, 1983.
Kinne, S. D. "Tongues Movement." *The Household of God* (1909) 14.
"Last Great Outpouring of the Spirit." *The Household of God* (1910) 1.
Lawrence, B. F. "Apostolic Faith Restored: Article VI.—Incidents of the Spirit's Work from 1901 to 1904." *Weekly Evangel* (St. Louis, MO), 12 Feb. 1916, p. 4.
———. "Apostolic Faith Restored: Article VII.—Houston, Texas and W. J. Seymour." *Weekly Evangel* (St. Louis, MO), 19 Feb. 1916, p. 4.
LaBerge (née Ozman), Agnes. *What God Hath Wrought*. Chicago: Herald, n.d.
Martin, I. G. "Los Angeles Letters." *Pentecostal Messenger* (1906).
"More Good News." *Word and Witness*, 20 Oct. 1912, p. 2.
McGee, Gary B. "'The Latter Rain' Falling in the East: Early-Twentieth-Century Pentecostalism in India and the Debate over Speaking in Tongues." *Church History* 68, no. 3 (1999) 648–65.

Nelson, Douglas. "For Such a Time As This: The Story of Bishop William J. Seymour and The Azusa Street Revival." PhD diss., University of Birmingham, 1981.
"The Old-Time Power." *Apostolic Faith* (Los Angeles) (1906) 1.
Ozman, Agnes. "Where the Latter Rain First Fell: The First One to Speak in Tongues." *Latter Rain Evangel* (1910) 2.
Parham, Charles F. "Birth of the Apostolic Faith, or Latter Rain Pentecostal Movement." *The Apostolic Faith* supplement (1912).
———. "Free-Love." *The Apostolic Faith* (Baxter Springs, KS) (1912) 4–5.
———. Letter to Howard Goss, January 31, 1907. Flower Pentecostal Heritage Center, Springfield, Missouri.
Parham, Sarah. *The Life of Charles F. Parham: Founder of the Apostolic Faith Movement.* 1930. Reprint, New York: Garland, 1985.
"Pentecost With Signs Following: Seven Months of Pentecostal Showers. Jesus, Our Projector and Great Shepherd." *Apostolic Faith* (Los Angeles) (1906) 1.
"The Pentecostal Baptism Restored: The Promised Latter Rain Now Being Poured Out on God's Humble People." *Apostolic Faith* (Los Angeles) (1906) 1.
"The Pentecostal Outpouring." *Victory!* (1909) 5.
Pierson, Arthur T. *Forward Movements of the Last Half Century.* 1905. Reprint, New York: Garland, 1984.
"The Promise Still Good." *Apostolic Faith* (Los Angeles) (1906) 1.
"The Promised Latter Rain." *Apostolic Faith* (1908) 1.
"Revival News in Home Land." *Word and Witness*, November 20, 1913, no. 3.
Robeck, Cecil M., Jr. "William J. Seymour and 'The Bible Evidence.'" In *Initial Evidence: Historical and Biblical Perspectives on the Pentecostal Doctrine of Spirit Baptism*, edited by Gary B. McGee, 72–95. Peabody, MA: Hendrickson, 1991.
Shumway, C. W. "A Critical Study of 'The Gift of Tongues.'" AB thesis, University of Southern California, 1912.
"Speaking in Tongues: Is This of God?" *Apostolic Faith* (Los Angeles) (1907) 1.
Stephens, Randall J. "There Is Magic in Print. The Holiness Pentecostal Press and the Origins of Southern Pentecostalism." *Journal of Southern Religion* 5 (2002). http://jsr.fsu.edu/2002/Stephens.htm. Accessed 9 November 2013.
Taylor, G. F. *The Spirit and the Bride.* 1907?. Reprint, New York: Garland, 1985.
Vanzandt, J. C. *Speaking in Tongues.* Portland, OR: privately published, 1926.
Wacker, Grant. "Are the Golden Oldies Worth Playing? Reflections on History Writing among Early Pentecostals." *Pneuma* 8, no. 2 (1986) 81–100.
———. "Biography and Historiography of Pentecostalism (U.S.)." In *Dictionary of Pentecostal and Charismatic Movements*, edited by Stanley Burgess, Gary B. McGee, and Patrick H. Alexander, 65–76. Grand Rapids: Zondervan, 1988.
———. "The Holy Spirit and the Spirit of the Age in American Protestantism, 1880–1910." *Journal of American History* 72, no. 1 (1985) 45–62.

15

Healing in the Early Pentecostal / Charismatic Tradition
A Historical Perspective[1]

Vinson Synan

Jesus is my healer in my room
Jesus is my healer in my room
He writes out my prescriptions
He gives me all my medicine
He heals me of my sickness
Jesus is my healer in my room

—Black Pentecostal Spiritual

During the Twentieth Century the Pentecostal Movement grew from a small and persecuted handful of believers to become, along with their charismatic cousins, a major Christian tradition. Although mostly known for their distinctive practice of speaking in tongues, perhaps in the public eye they may be better known for their teaching and practice of divine healing.

---

1. Recent broad surveys on Pentecostalism include Synan, *Century of the Holy Spirit*; Synan, *The Holiness-Pentecostal Tradition*; and Hollenweger, *Pentecostalism: Origins and Developments*. An indispensable general source is Burgess, McGee, and Alexander, *Dictionary of Pentecostal and Charismatic Movements*; and the more recent version, Burgess, and Maas, *International Dictionary of Pentecostal and Charismatic Movements*. The statistics are taken from Barrett, Kurian, and Johnson, *World Christian Encyclopedia*.

In fact the popularity of their massive public healing crusades may account more for their worldwide growth than speaking in tongues.

Just who are these "Pentecostal/Charismatics" anyway? Following the great Roman Catholic charismatic scholar, Kilian McDonnell, the broadest theological definition might be those Christians who stress the baptism in the Holy Spirit and the gifts of the Spirit toward the proclamation that Jesus Christ is Lord, to the Glory of God the Father.[2]

This category would include all Christians who have been called "Classical Pentecostals" (Assemblies of God, Church of God in Christ, Pentecostal Holiness Church, the Churches of God (Cleveland, TN), International Church of the Foursquare Gospel, etc.), and both Protestant and Catholic Charismatics. Altogether Pentecostal/Charismatic accounted for over 600,000,000 members in the world in 2013 and are by far the second largest family of Christians in the world after the Roman Catholic Church.

Even though speaking in tongues as evidence of the baptism in the Holy Spirit is the most original contribution of the Pentecostal Movement, actually the emphasis on divine healing has a much longer history than tongues in the Holiness/Pentecostal tradition and has caused not only spectacular growth, but at times resulted in confusion and turmoil within the churches. While tongues came to the fore in 1901 with the ministries of Charles Parham in Topeka, Kansas, and William J. Seymour in the Azusa Street revival in Los Angeles, the emphasis on healing goes back to the mid-nineteenth century when efforts were made to restore New Testament signs and wonders to the church.[3]

Before this time, most Christians had seen no contradiction between faith and medicine. Most would have agreed with Sirach in the intertestamental book *Ecclesiasticus* when he advised:

> Cultivate the physician in accordance with the need for him, for him also hath God ordained. It is from God that the physician getteth wisdom and from the king receiveth gifts. The skill of the physician lifteth up his head, and he may stand before nobles. God hath created medicines out of the earth, and let not a discerning man reject them. Was not the water made sweet by the wood that He might make known to all men His power? And He gave men discernment that they might glory in His mighty works. By means of them the physician assuages pain.

---

2. McDonnell and Bittlinger, *The Baptism in the Holy Spirit*, 47–48.

3. For the development of the healing movement in the Holiness Movement see Chappell, "Healing Movements," 353–74. Also see Dayton, *Theological Roots of Pentecostalism*, 115–41; and Faupel, *The Everlasting Gospel*, 115–86. A more recent book on Pentecostals and divine healing is Alexander, *Pentecostal Healing*.

And likewise the apothecary prepareth confection that his work may not cease nor health from the face of the earth. My son, in sickness, be not negligent. Pray unto God for He can heal. Turn from iniquity and purify thy hands and from all transgressions cleanse thy heart. Give a meal offering with a memorial. And offer a fat sacrifice to the utmost of thy means. And to the physician also give a place; nor should he be far away, for of him there is a need. For there is a time when successful help is in his power; for he also maketh supplication to God to make his diagnosis successful and the treatment that it may promote recovery. (Sirach 38:1–14)[4]

This was written in a time when many devout Jews refused to see a doctor or take medicine because medical treatment might imply a lack of faith in God. So what I will say today is not so new in religious history.

The roots of all modern healing movements lie in Europe, where healing in answer to prayer was first taught by Presbyterian Edward Irving in London (1830), by Lutheran Johann Christoph Blumhardt in Germany (1843), by Dorothea Trudel in Switzerland (1851), and by Otto Stockmayer in Switzerland (1867). These teachers developed not only the idea of the "healing home" (a hospital-like retreat where prayer was administered instead of medicines), but also a theology of healing which was to affect many in America and lead to the Pentecostal doctrine of divine healing "as in the atonement." The most influential book coming out of Europe in this period was Stockmayer's *Sickness and the Gospel,* which pioneered the idea that physical healing for the body was included in the over-all atonement.[5]

Building on the pioneering work of Blumhardt, Trudel, and Stockmayer in Europe, a long list of American leaders in both the Holiness and Pentecostal movements added a flood of books on healing. They also pioneered more and more radical views of healing that eventually excluded the use of medicines or doctors in favor of prayer alone.

Charles Cullis

Although divine healing had been practiced in America by George Fox, founder of the Quakers; Joseph Smith, founder of the Mormons; and Elizabeth Mix, the Black Holiness evangelist; the first person to bring healing to the attention to the American general populace was Charles Cullis of

4. See Charles, *The Apocrypha and Pseudepigrapha,* 448–50.
5. For early European developments see Chappell, "Healing Movements," 355–66; on Stockmayer, see Chappell, "Healing Movements," 356.

Boston, Massachusetts. Cullis, already a medical doctor, began his ministry in 1864 when he opened his first free faith home for consumptives where the sick could receive "the comforts of a warm home and complete medical care." His first efforts were quite similar to the ministry of Mother Teresa's "home of the destitute and dying" in Calcutta.[6]

By 1870, however, Cullis added prayer to his ministry of care-giving and traditional medicine after seeing a patient, Lucy Drake, instantly healed of a debilitating brain tumor after the laying-on of hands. This led Cullis to turn his homes into "healing homes," where the patients would be treated with loving care and minus medicine and prayer.[7] By the 1880s, Cullis was conducting annual healing conventions in Old Orchard, Maine, as well as holding healing conventions around the nation. By 1885, the message of healing had become international when William Boardman convened the first "International Conference on Divine Healing and True Holiness" in the Great Agricultural Hall in London where 2000 persons gathered to advance the cause of divine healing around the world.

After this event a stream of books on healing flowed from Holiness and Evangelical presses extolling the power of healing in answer to prayer. These included Boardman's 1881 book *The Lord that Healeth Thee*, and Kelso Carter's 1884 book titled *The Atonement for Sin and Sickness: or a Full Salvation for Soul and Body*. These books brought healing beyond the level of anecdotal testimonies and into the arena of theological discourse and debate.[8]

Adoniram J. Gordon

The man who elevated divine healing to the level of the atonement was A. J. Gordon, the popular Boston pastor who eventually founded the seminary that bears his name today. Through his association with Cullis, Gordon became a staunch believer in divine healing, so much so that in 1882 he published his famous book, *The Ministry of Healing*, in which he asserted that healing for the body was part of the atonement. Using Psalm 103:3 KJV "who forgiveth all thine iniquities, who healeth all thy diseases" and Matthew 8:17 "He himself took our infirmities and carried away our diseases," Gordon concluded that Divine healing for the body was included in the atonement side by side with the forgiveness of sins.

6. Quote from Chappell, "Healing Movements," 358; see also Chappell, "Healing Movements," 358–60; and Dayton, *Theological Roots in Pentecostalism*, 122–25.

7. Chappell, "Healing Movements," 359–60.

8. Ibid., 360–61.

After many other teachers added their agreement to Gordon's formulation, including A. B. Simpson, founder of the Christian and Missionary Alliance, a host of teachers and churches asserted their belief in divine healing "as in the atonement." Decades later when the Pentecostal denominations were formed, they added this phrase to their statements of faith.[9]

Alexander Dowie

By the turn of the century, the idea of "healing homes," where the sick could be cared for without cost and where the treatment would be prayer instead of traditional medical treatment, had spread far and wide. It was Alexander Dowie, the fire-breathing healing evangelist from Scotland and Australia, who made a complete break from medical treatment. Denouncing doctors as "agents of Satan," he called on his followers to trust God completely for their healing. His distrust for the medical profession may have come from his years as a surgical assistant in Scotland where at the same time he studied theology at Edinburgh University. Later, after serving as a Congregationalist Pastor in Sydney, Australia, Dowie left his denomination to found an independent holiness church in Melbourne before immigrating to the United States in 1888.[10]

After two years of itinerant healing ministries on the West Coast where he organized local chapters of his "International Divine Healing Association," Dowie settled in Chicago where in 1893 he set up a wooden tabernacle outside the entrance to the Chicago World's fair. Soon the inside walls of the building were covered with the crutches and braces of those who claimed healing at the hands of the balding evangelist.

Shortly afterward, Dowie bought the Imperial Hotel in Chicago and converted it into a healing home. In these "golden years," Dowie was lionized by the public, spoke to the largest audiences in the history of Chicago, and was received by Presidents McKinley and Theodore Roosevelt.

It was not long, however, before the ecclesiastical and medical establishments in Chicago began a concerted attack on Dowie and his healing claims, with many vicious anti-Dowie articles appearing in the Chicago newspapers. By 1895, Dowie had been arrested for practicing medicine without a license and had spent 120 days in court answering over 100 arrest warrants, partly for his vociferous attacks on the corrupt politics of the

---

9. Dayton, *Theological Roots in Pentecostalism*, 127–30.

10. Two biographies on Dowie are Harlan, *John Alexander Dowie*; and Lindsay, *The Life of John Alexander Dowie*. A major recent source for Dowie is Faupel, *Everlasting Gospel*, 116–35.

city government. In response, Dowie in April 1895 published his first but not last volley against the medical establishment. His vitriolic article titled, "Doctors, Drugs, and Devils, or the Foes of Christ the Healer" appeared in *Physical Culture* magazine. In it he made the following statements:

> I want to say today that doctors as a profession, are directly inspired by the devil. There is not an atom of foundation for science in medicine. All doctors are "poisoners-general and surgical butchers" and "professional destroyers. "They are monsters who hold in their hands deadly poisons and deadly surgical knives, and in the name of the law demand that you lie down upon the altar of their operating tables, that they may deprive you of your consciousness and make you a living sacrifice.[11]

With the immense popularity gained at the Chicago World's Fair and in response to such articles, Dowie in 1896 proclaimed the founding of a new last days church for all true believers, the "Christian Catholic Church," and called on all his followers to join with him in a holy war against the religious establishment. By 1900 he began construction of "Zion City" on 6,500 acres 20 miles north of Chicago. Planned for 200,000 residents, Zion was to be a center of commerce and government as well as religion. In short order Dowie constructed homes, banks, schools, a hotel, and a wooden tabernacle that would seat no less than 8,000 persons. Those who took the commuter train from Chicago for Sunday services were greeted with large signs stating that Zion was "the only place where it is easy to do right and difficult to do wrong." They were also told that in Zion there would be:

> No Profanity, No vulgarity, No sorcerers, No medical poisoners, No cut throat competition, No saloons or beer gardens, No intoxicating liquors, No surgical butchers, No cigarette or tobacco stores, No vaccination: the foulest of all the foul inventions of the Devil and some dirty doctors, No drugs, No theaters, No dance halls, No opium joint, No gambling establishment, No house of ill fame assignation, No pharmacy, No apothecary's shop, or drug store, No place for the manufacture or sale of drugs or medicines of any kind, No place or office of residence of a practicing physician or surgeon. As well as No unclean food or oysters, that scavenger of the sea, or swine, that scavenger of the earth. No place for holding secret meetings or assemblies of any oath bound society.[12]

11. Dowie, "Doctors, Drugs and Devils," 81–86.

12. This passage was supplied to me by Terryl Todd of Libertyville, IL who copied them from a contemporary photograph.

Indeed, Zion would be a place where holiness and healing would be in and everything else would be out!

A sad footnote on Dowie's ministry was that in 1901, he suddenly proclaimed himself to be "Elijah the Restorer" in fulfillment of Scripture and announced plans to set up new Zion communities all over the world. On top of this, in 1905 he suffered a stroke that made him a living vegetable, leading to power struggles over control of his vast religious empire. He died in disgrace in 1907, ignored by those who formerly adored him.[13]

Dowie's stern position against all medicine and doctors, however, took root in many sectors of the Holiness movement and became the majority view of the Pentecostals when the movement began in 1901 in Topeka, Kansas.

Charles Fox Parham and William J. Seymour

Although Parham is known as the man who formulated the doctrine that speaking in tongues was the "Bible evidence" of the baptism in the Holy Spirit, he was first widely known as a healing evangelist. As a Methodist pastor and later as a Holiness teacher, Parham adopted Wesleyan language to describe divine healing. He once said that sickness is instantly "cleansed away root and branch" in answer to prayer. [14]

In 1898, after a visit to Dowie's Zion City, Parham established his "Bethel Healing Home" in Topeka, Kansas, where the sick could come and rest in a "spiritual hospital" where Prayer and Bible reading took the place of doctors and medicine. It was only after he opened his "Bethel Bible School" that he and his students discovered the connection between tongues and the baptism in the Holy Spirit (on January 1, 1901, the very first day of the Twentieth Century). After this event, Parham preached a "five-fold gospel" emphasizing the new birth, second blessing sanctification, the baptism in the Holy Spirit evidenced by tongues, divine healing "as in the atonement," and the instant rapture of the church. In this schema everything happened in an instant, including divine healing.[15]

When Pentecostalism exploded on the world scene at Azusa Street in 1906 under the African American pastor William J. Seymour, his teaching on healing was essentially the same as his teacher Charles Parham. This included divine healing as in the atonement. In one article on healing,

---

13. See Lindsay, *John Alexander Dowie*, 193–275; and Faupel, *Everlasting Gospel*, 118–33.

14. The definitive biography of Parham is Goff, *Fields White unto Harvest*, 32–70.

15. Goff, *Fields White unto Harvest*, 90.

Seymour lamented that "many Christians will take a doctor before Jesus. They put a doctor between them and the atonement . . . the doctor gives you poison and you die because you dishonor the atonement."[16]

When someone wrote a letter to Seymour's *Apostolic Faith* asking "Do you teach that it is wrong to take medicine?" The answer was as follows: "Yes . . . medicine is for unbelievers, but the remedy for the saints of God we find in Jas. 5:14. . . ." In another note on healing Seymour stated that "a sanctified body is one that is cleansed from all sickness and disease. The Lord gives you power over sickness and disease. . . ."[17]

For the next decade the Pentecostals generally held to Parham's and Seymour's "atonement" view that taking medicine or going to a doctor showed a lack of faith in God. Under the fiery preaching of the Pentecostals, healing was now taken out of the residential "healing homes" and preached from the roof-tops. Healing evangelists laid hands on the sick in gospel tents, in school houses, and in whatever church would allow them a hearing.

In this period, many Pentecostal saints vowed that they would never touch another pill for the rest of their lives while "trusting God for their bodies." The standard testimony was as follows:

> I praise God that I am saved, sanctified, filled with the Holy Ghost, looking for Jesus to come, and I have trusted God for my body for 40 years" (or however many years since they had taken their last medicine).

In 1920, for instance, Sam Page, one-time head of the Pentecostal Holiness Church reported that he had been "saved and healed for 27 years." In the first church I pastored in Virginia, there was an elderly lady of 94 years, Sister Gayle, who testified that she had "trusted God for her body for 50 years." One preacher, W. J. Noble, after promising not to take any medicine or see a doctor "until death" testified:

> "He has healed me of many diseases such as broken bones, tonsillitis, lagrippe, influenza, indigestion, diptheria, ingrown toenails, cancer, and tuberculosis in the last stage." Theirs was indeed a heroic faith.[18]

If there were any sick people among them, many Pentecostals felt that either there was sin in the body, or the person lacked the faith to be healed. If anyone suffered from depression or any other mental or emotional disorder, they were generally thought to be demon possessed. Instead of psychiatry

---

16. Seymour, "Salvation and Healing," 2.
17. Seymour, "Questions and Answers," 2, 4.
18. Synan, *The Old-Time Power*, 166–71.

or psychoanalysis, exorcisms were the order of the day for those who were "oppressed of the devil." In any case, the sick often lay in their beds in a darkened sickroom for weeks, praying for a healing touch while often enduring agonies of pain while refusing any kind of medicines or visits from physicians. In this case, Jesus and Jesus alone was the caregiver and healer.

Confusion and Schism over "Remedies"

For several decades Pentecostals made news in many communities over their views and practices on divine healing. In the period from Azusa Street to World War II some Pentecostal preachers were not only arrested for "practicing medicine without a license," but were accused of "murder" for allowing family members to die without medical aid. Some even looked on this as a mark of distinction and suffering for the faith. Francis Marion Britton of the Pentecostal Holiness Church, for instance, allowed his first wife to die "unaided," although fifty neighbors threatened to have him tried for "murder" because of a lack of medical attention. Not only did his wife die "without drugs," but also two of their children.[19]

In the Church of God, Walter Barney, a pastor in Wytheville, Virginia, was tried and convicted of "manslaughter" in 1915 for refusing medical care for a daughter who later died. His conviction was later overturned with a pardon by the Governor of Virginia. To many Pentecostals, people like Britton and Barney were heroes of healing who were gladly persecuted for their faith. But, to other Pentecostals, they seemed to be fanatics who gave Pentecostalism a bad name.[20]

The only schism among Pentecostals over the use of medicine divided the Pentecostal Holiness church when, in 1919, a furor erupted in the church when a Georgia preacher, Hugh Bowling, wrote in the church paper *The Advocate* that it was no sin at all to take "remedies" and that going to a doctor implied no lack of faith in the patient. To some leaders, this position seemed to be a compromise from the heroic stand for divine healing that many had taken over the years. One letter to the editor exhorted:

> Beloved, let us never lower the standard, for if we fail to preach this wonderful truth, we are a fallen church, and if our ministers advocate drugs and doctors, something is wrong . . . you are not preaching the full gospel.[21]

---

19. Ibid., 166.
20. *Church of God Evangel*, Dec. 1, 1910, 1–2; Jan. 23, 1915, 2.
21. Synan, *Old-Time Power*, 167.

After this, a great struggle ensued with charges and counter-charges on each side. In a later article in *The Advocate* Bowling explained his position:

> I do not believe that those who get sick and use no remedies and drag around for weeks and after so long a time get well, are divinely healed, but that nature alone restored them ... I do not believe in lying about divine healing.
>
> I do not believe that sickness is evidence of unbelief.
>
> I do not believe that healing is paralleled with salvation in the atonement.[22]

This was the last straw! Leaders of the denomination made charges against Bowling and his friend, Watson Sorrow. In the end, Bowling was given his day in an ecclesiastical court, but was expelled from the church when he failed to appear for the hearing. He and some friends thereafter organized the "Congregational Holiness Church" in 1921. In time the controversy was largely forgotten, but in later years the very men who criticized Bowling for advocating medicine, themselves died in hospitals using the best doctors and medicines available.[23]

Oral Roberts and the City of Faith

The famous healing evangelist Oral Roberts was only three years old in Oklahoma when his denomination was torn with controversy over divine healing. In fact, in some places divine healing almost faded from the life of the churches. In his book *Expect a Miracle*, Roberts says that faith for healing was at a low ebb in the Pentecostal Churches where his father and mother served as pastors. His miraculous healing from tuberculosis as a sixteen year old boy, however, was destined to change his life and the life of the American church in the decades to come. After his healing, young Oral answered the call to preach. The first few years of his ministry saw Roberts struggling as a traveling evangelist and pastor of small Pentecostal Holiness churches.[24]

In 1947, while pastoring a small church in Toccoa, Georgia, Oral saw a man instantly healed after a motor had fallen on his foot, crushing it to the

22. Ibid.
23. Ibid., 169–71.
24. Of the many autobiographies of Oral Roberts, the best and most recent one is *Expect a Miracle*. The most important biography of Roberts is Harrell, *Oral Roberts: An American Life*.

bone. Impressed with this unexpected miracle, Roberts began to fast and pray for the gift of healing to be released in his ministry. After returning to Oklahoma, he pastored other churches while studying in Phillips University and helping to found Southwestern College in Oklahoma City.[25]

During a time of fasting and prayer in his Enid, Oklahoma church, Roberts heard the Lord commission him to bring God's healing power to his generation. His first healing crusade in his hometown of Ada, Oklahoma in 1948 was so successful that he immediately launched a tent-healing crusade ministry that eventually made him a household name throughout the world. A major breakthrough came in 1953 when he began televising his healing lines on national television. This brought divine healing into the very living rooms of the nation. In doing this, Roberts created a new media genre-that of the "televangelist." The income generated by his television ministry ultimately led Roberts to found his own university in 1965 in Tulsa. Here, he planned to train young people to take divine healing to the furthermost nations and peoples of the world.[26]

On top of his sensational and wildly successful healing ministry, in 1980 Roberts dedicated his 77-story hospital in Tulsa, which he dubbed the "City of Faith." Here, he said, would be celebrated a "marriage between prayer and medicine, the supernatural and the natural, in the treatment of the whole person." The hospital included plans for a Medical school where future doctors could minister healing through medicine and prayer. After an initial period of euphoria and success, however, the dream of a Pentecostal hospital ran aground on the rocks of financial disaster. Although his partners gave tens of millions of dollars to the project, few were willing to travel to Tulsa for treatment, even after the City of Faith hospital offered free plane tickets to anyone who would come. By 1990 it was clear that even Roberts's staunchest supporters would rather trust in Oral's prayers for healing than come to his hospital.[27]

With the closing of the City of Faith in 1989, the circle was complete. The healing movement had begun in the 1860s with Charles Cullis ministering prayer in a public hospital in Boston. Afterwards, the "healing home" movement saw people abandoning hospitals in favor of entering healing homes for rest and prayer. Then, in the most radical phase, the Dowie era, people denounced all "doctors, drugs and devils" in favor of prayer alone. But, by the 1990s, Pentecostals and Charismatics had generally settled on

---

25. Roberts, *Expect a Miracle*, 54–56.

26. Ibid., 64–100.

27. It is interesting that Roberts did not mention the City of Faith in his last autobiography, evidently putting stress on his highly successful university.

a position in which a sick person would still ask for prayer first and trust God for healing, and then go to the doctors for regular medical care. If they got well, whether with medical treatment or without it, they claimed their healing to be a miracle from God.

In the end, most Pentecostals would agree with the final position of Oral Roberts on the question of healing. After laying hands on over one million sick folk in his crusades, he concluded that all miraculous healing comes from God, whether from natural processes, as the result of prayer with the laying on of hands, or through the ministry of doctors and medicine. Gone were the days when children were left to die in agony "without drugs or doctors." Still, as the century came to an end, there were those faith teachers like Kenneth Hagin who could say," "I took my last aspirin in 1934 when I had my last headache." He made a point that he had received no medicine or medical care in the 63 years since. That, by the way, was the year in which I was born.[28]

Concluding Observations

In summary, the story of healing in the Pentecostal/Charismatic movement came down to the question of who was in the sickroom. Before Cullis, the only healer in the house was the medical doctor. In his first healing homes, there were now two healers in the house, the doctor and Jesus. In his later years, there was only one healer in the house—Jesus.

Under Dowie, doctors and drugs were not only totally excluded, they were demonized. Later, under such Pentecostal evangelists as Aimee Semple McPherson and Oral Roberts, the healing homes were abandoned in favor of evangelistic healing crusades under tents and in large city auditoriums.

With the creation of the City of Faith, prayer and medicine were again joined together. Now, Jesus and the doctor were in the same room ministering to the sick and giving God the glory for any healing that took place, whether from natural processes, from medicine or surgery, or from prayer. In the end, the long-term effect of Pentecostal/Charismatic caregiving was to invite Jesus back into the sickroom where He could add his healing touch to that of the doctors and nurses.

Indeed, by the 1990s medical science was confirming the fact that religious faith and prayer make a measurable scientific difference in the healing process. In 1998, for example, the Templeton Foundation was sponsoring classes on religion, healing, and prayer in the major medical schools of the nation. Not only this, but by the mid-1990s there was a veritable flood of

28. Synan, "The Faith of Kenneth Hagin," 62–70; and Riss, "Kenneth E. Hagin," 345.

magazine articles, TV specials, and scholarly studies announcing "discoveries" about prayer and healing that Christians in general, and Pentecostals in particular had known for decades.

One of the most important media breakthroughs was the June 1996 issue of *Time Magazine* with a cover story titled, "Faith and Healing: Can Spirituality promote Health? Some Surprising Evidence." This story told of Aids patients who were studied in a controlled experiment where one-half were treated with drugs alone and the other half with drugs and prayer. The results were significantly better for those who received prayer. It was also stated that "according to a 1995 study at Dartmouth, one of the strongest predictors of survival after open heart surgery is the degree to which patients say they draw strength and comfort from religion." The article concluded with a sidebar titled "Ambushed by Spirituality" which reported that 82% of Americans "believe in the healing power of personal prayer."[29]

The story of faith and healing was also carried prominently in the USA on national network television in March 1998, when Peter Jennings of the American Broadcasting Company (ABC) aired a series on faith and healing called "A Closer Look." He reported that in recent times "the relationship between faith and the physical is taken more seriously." He also reported on research that proves that "people with strong religious faith live longer than others" and that "faith is an essential ingredient for survival." In medical schools, he reported, religious faith and spirituality is now "a legitimate field of study." In fact, 30 American medical schools now teach courses on spirituality because "you cannot teach medicine in a spiritual vacuum." Dr. Tim Johnson, the medical reporter for ABC who is also an ordained minister of the Gospel, said of these developments, "this is a sea change in my lifetime."[30]

Looking back, a strong case could be made for giving credit to the Pentecostals for this "sea change" in public attitudes. Perhaps Oral Roberts was truly a prophet ahead of his times when he built a "City of Faith" where there would be a "marriage between prayer and medicine." The unexpected difference was that this marriage was celebrated not in just one hospital, but in hundreds more around the world. Now science is again admitting Jesus back into the sickroom where God can use the ministry of doctors and medicine, while also answering the prayer of faith for miraculous healing.

---

29. Wallace, "Faith and Healing," 58–62.

30. Jennings, Wehmeyer, and McFadden, "A Closer Look," *ABC Nightly News*, ABC, March, 1998.

Bibliography

Alexander, Kimberly Ervin. *Pentecostal Healing: Models in Theology and Practice*. Blandford Forum. Dorset, UK: Deo, 2006.
Barrett, David, George T. Kurian, and Todd M. Johnson, eds. *World Christian Encyclopedia: A Comparative Survey of Churches and Religions AD 30–AD 2200*. New York: Oxford University Press, 2000.
Burgess, Stanley, Eduard M. Van Der Maas, eds. *New International Dictionary of Pentecostal and Charismatic Movements*. Grand Rapids: Zondervan, 2002.
Burgess, Stanley M., Gary B. McGee, and Patrick H. Alexander, eds. *Dictionary of Pentecostal and Charismatic Movements*. Grand Rapids: Zondervan, 1988.
Chappell, Paul. "Healing Movements." In *Dictionary of Pentecostal and Charismatic Movement*, edited by Stanley M. Burgess, Gary B. McGee, and Patrick H. Alexander, 353–74. Grand Rapids: Zondervan, 1988.
Charles, R. H. *The Apocrypha and Pseudepigrapha of the Old Testament*. Vol. 1. London: Clarendon, 1913.
Dayton, Donald. *Theological Roots of Pentecostalism*. Grand Rapids: Francis Asbury, 1987.
Dowie, Alexander. "Doctors, Drugs and Devils, or, the Foes of Christ the Healer." *Physical Culture* (1895) 81–86.
Faupel, William. "The Everlasting Gospel: The Significance of Eschatology in the Development of Pentecostal Thought," *Journal of Pentecostal Theology Supplemental* Series 10. Sheffield, UK: Sheffield Academic, 1996.
Goff, James. *Fields White unto Harvest: Charles Fox Perham and the Missionary Origins of Pentecostalism*. Fayetteville: University of Arkansas Press, 1988.
Harlan, R. *John Alexander Dowie and the Christian Apostolic Church in Zion*. Evansville, WI: Antes, 1906.
Harrell, David. *Oral Roberts: An American Life*. Bloomington, IN: Indiana University Press, 1985.
Hollenweger, Walter J. *Pentecostalism: Origins and Developments Worldwide*. Peabody, MA: Hendrickson, 1997.
Lindsay, Gordon. *The Life of John Alexander Dowie*. Shreveport, LA: Voice of Healing, 1951.
McDonnell, Kilian, and Arnold Bittlinger. *Baptism in the Holy Spirit as an Ecumenical Problem*. South Bend, IN: Charismatic Renewal Services, 1972.
Riss, Richard M. "Kenneth E. Hagin." In *Dictionary of Pentecostal and Charismatic Movement*, edited by Stanley M. Burgess, Gary B. McGee, and Patrick H. Alexander, 345. Grand Rapids: Zondervan, 1988.
Roberts, Oral. *Expect a Miracle: My Life and Ministry: Oral Roberts, an Autobiography*. Nashville: Nelson, 1995.
Seymour, William J. "Questions and Answers." *Apostolic Faith* (Los Angeles) (1908) 2.
———. "Salvation and Healing." *Apostolic Faith* (Los Angeles) (1906) 2, 4.
Synan, Vinson. *The Century of the Holy Spirit*. Nashville: Nelson, 2001.
———. "The Faith of Kenneth Hagin." *Charisma* 15 (1990) 62–70.

———. *The Holiness-Pentecostal Tradition: The Charismatic Movement in the Churches.* Grand Rapids: Eerdmans, 1997.

———. *The Old-Time Power: A History of the Pentecostal Holiness Church.* Franklin Springs, GA: Advocate, 1973.

Wallace, Claudia. "Faith and Healing." *Time Magazine* 147, no. 26, June 24, 1996, pp. 58–62.

16

Pentecostal Origins in Scandinavian Pietism on the Great Plains

Darrin J. Rodgers

REVIVALS AT TOPEKA AND Azusa Street may have been two of the most visible focal points of early twentieth-century American Pentecostalism, but prior revivals, including those among Scandinavian settlers in the northern Great Plains, provided precedents and leaders for the emerging movement. The first chroniclers of modern Pentecostalism documented these Scandinavian enthusiasts in Minnesota and the Dakotas, but later histories often minimized or omitted these revivals, discounting their significance or deeming them unverifiable oral history. However, evidence discovered within the past fifteen years verifies these early accounts and suggests that these approximately two dozen or more pre-Azusa Scandinavian congregations that practiced tongues-speech and healing may have made a greater impact on the Pentecostal movement than previously thought.[1] This essay aims: 1) to document pre-Azusa Scandinavian evangelicals who practiced tongues-speech and healing in the northern Great Plains; and 2) to address related historiographical issues.

Scandinavian settlers in Minnesota and the Dakotas experienced a spiritual awakening in the late 1890s and early 1900s, spawning a number of congregations that practiced speaking in tongues and healing. While some of these revivals predated the Topeka and Azusa Street revivals, many of these plains enthusiasts soon identified with the larger Pentecostal movement, including Carl M. Hanson, an evangelist who witnessed glossolalia in a revival in Grafton, North Dakota in 1895, and John Thompson, pastor of the Moorhead (Minnesota) Swedish Free Mission, which experienced several protracted revivals in the late 1890s and early 1900s. The Moorhead

---

1. Portions of this paper were adapted from Rodgers, *Northern Harvest*.

congregation yielded Mary Johnson, the earliest-known missionary from America to venture overseas, who participated in the twentieth-century revivals that featured tongues-speech. Several regional networks of congregations that practiced tongues-speech and healing emerged, including the Scandinavian Mission Society and a largely unorganized group of Scandinavians who embraced a form of evangelical universalism, some of whom chartered under the legal name of Assembly of God Missionary Fellowship.

Forgotten Pentecostal History

Claims of an early Pentecost on the plains should be backed up by hard evidence. The earliest Pentecostal historians cataloged numerous oral histories of early glossolalic revivals.[2] Pentecostal journalist Stanley Frodsham, in his 1946 history, assembled a list of at least 11 claims of tongues-speech in the U.S. between 1850 and 1900, occurring in New England, Ohio, Minnesota, South Dakota, North Carolina, Tennessee, and Arkansas. Frodsham recounted stories of turn-of-the-century revivals told long after their occurrence, and did not cite any sources pre-dating the Azusa Street revival.[3] Carl Brumback and William Menzies, in their respective 1961 and 1971 histories of the Assemblies of God, repeated Frodsham's list, providing little additional evidence.[4] Menzies, minimizing the importance of the revivals recorded by Frodsham, remarked, "These were all isolated, however, and did not seem to have more than local significance."[5] Edith Blumhofer omitted these early revivals in her 1989 history of the Assemblies of God.[6]

The first significant research on these early Scandinavian revivals was published in the 2003 book, Darrin Rodgers, *Northern Harvest: Pentecostalism in North Dakota*. Responding to the research, Blumhofer acknowledged the existence of these glossolalic Scandinavian-American revivals in the context of "the dense overlapping networks in which early Pentecostalism arose." But she questioned whether they could be characterized as Pentecostal because they originated separately from Parham and because participants viewed tongues as a gift, but not necessarily as a uniform evidence

---

2. Lawrence, *Apostolic Faith Restored*, 46–47; also published in serial form as "Apostolic Faith Restored" [Article V] *Weekly Evangel*, January 29 and February 5, 1916, 4. See also, Ness, *Demonstration of the Holy Spirit*, 6–7.

3. Frodsham, *With Signs Following*, 9–17.

4. Brumback, *Suddenly from Heaven*, 12–17; and Menzies, *Anointed to Serve*, 29–33.

5. Menzies, *Anointed to Serve*, 29.

6. Blumhofer did not refer to the revivals recounted by Frodsham in her two histories of the Assemblies of God (USA): *The Assemblies of God*, and *Restoring the Faith*.

of Spirit baptism.[7] Gary B. McGee, in his 2004 history of the Assemblies of God, drew upon this research and prominently featured the stories of these Scandinavian believers, whom he characterized as Pentecostal.[8] McGee, in his later and seminal *Miracles, Missions, and American Pentecostalism*, provided more extensive treatment of the Scandinavian pietists, clarifying that they were "Pentecostal," though not necessarily "Classical Pentecostal."[9]

Despite the mixed treatment by historians, early published sources both verify that speaking in tongues among the Scandinavians was practiced prior to Azusa Street, and identify these pre-Azusa tongues as existing in continuity with post-Azusa tongues. The Azusa Street periodical, *Apostolic Faith*, printed a 1906 letter making this claim. A. O. Morken, a Norwegian from Audobon, Minnesota, noted that Pentecost in Audobon predated Azusa by two years:

> A copy of the Apostolic Faith has been sent to us, and were much blest when we read and saw that God baptized his children with the Holy Ghost exactly the same way as He has done here. It is two years ago since God began to baptize His children in this place and some are talking with tongues, some have the gift of prophecy, etc.[10]

Morken testified of this early instance of tongues-speech in a February 25, 1904 letter to a Norwegian-language evangelical newspaper, *Folke-Vennen*:

> Praise our God – He has also blessed us abundantly with all spiritual blessings in Christ, as some did in the apostolic times, the gift of grace appeared among us when a portion received grace to speak in divers tongues. It was perceived that it was not common speech, but rather angelic language; those under the Spirit's effect, gripped in a power that seized them completely in the endeavor. What they tell is incomprehensible for themselves and for the others, but the Spirit Himself has given [the interpreters] a share, so that all indicate an encouragement and

---

7. Blumhofer, "Response to: Rediscovering our Diverse Roots."

8. McGee, *People of the Spirit*, 25, 69, 88.

9. McGee, *Miracles, Missions, and American Pentecostalism*, 91–92. For the purpose of this article, I will consider the Scandinavians in Minnesota and the Dakotas who practiced tongues-speech and healing, without connection to Parham and without a doctrine of uniform evidentiary tongues, to be "Pentecostal" or "Proto-Pentecostal," but not "Classical Pentecostal."

10. *Apostolic Faith* (Los Angeles) (December 1906) 3. For additional information on the Audobon congregation, see Gordon and Linda Bakken, *Bakkens in America*, 8, 16–17; and Rodgers, *Northern Harvest*, 5–6, 58–60.

admonition to the children of God who will be staying awake and imploring that Jesus comes soon.[11]

Morken proceeded to note the outpouring was not confined to Audobon: "but we hear that at the main places are the same blessings."[12] Descendants of Morken date the revival as beginning in 1902 or 1903.[13]

According to later accounts, these Proto-Pentecostals were located in west central Minnesota (Alexandria, Audobon, Detroit Lakes, Evansville, Fergus Falls, Lake Eunice, Moorhead, and Tordenskjold), northwest Minnesota (Argyle, Fosston, Hallock, Holt, Karlstad, Lake Bronson, Stephen, Thief River Falls, and Warren),[14] eastern North Dakota (Grafton and Hillsboro),[15] and southeast South Dakota (Greenfield).[16] This list included both organized churches and unorganized home meetings. The history of this network or networks is sketchy, and it is likely that additional, undocumented Proto-Pentecostal groups existed.

Carl M. Hanson

It is unknown where the Pentecostal fire first fell, but evangelist Carl M. Hanson, apparently spirit-baptized in 1899, had some influence among these groups. Carl M. "Daddy" Hanson, was a spiritual father to many early Pentecostals on the northern Great Plains. His brand of radical Scandinavian pietism prefigured the emerging Pentecostal movement, in which he became an early leader. Hanson traversed Minnesota and the eastern

---

11. Morken, "Fra vor egen Loesekreds," 4. (Translated) Erik L. Williamson

12. Ibid., 5.

13. For a 1902 claim, see Johnson, "A Godly Heritage," 26–27. For a 1903 claim, see Gordon and Linda Bakken, *Bakkens in America*, 8.

14. Ness, *Demonstration of the Holy Spirit*, 6–7; Vagle, "When Pentecost Fell in Minnesota," 9–11. For a history of the early Pentecostal movement in northwest Minnesota, see Rodgers, *Northern Harvest*, 58–62, 181–82. For west central Minnesota, see Rodgers, *Northern Harvest*, 216–18.

15. See Rodgers, *Northern Harvest*, 58–62, 154–55, 177.

16. Ness, *Demonstration of the Holy Spirit*, 7. Frodsham repeated Ness's account in *With Signs Following*, 16. Ness wrote, "Another remarkable outpouring of the Spirit took place at Greenfield, South Dakota, in the First Methodist Church where Rasmus Kristensen was pastor. This was in 1896. As Brother Kristensen was preaching the power would fall, the people being filled with the Holy Ghost and speaking in other tongues; and many other wonderful manifestations of God being witnessed." Rasmus Christiansen of Greenfield, South Dakota (I assume this is the same person, despite spelling differences) wrote two pre-Azusa articles: "De aandelige Gaver [spiritual gifts]," 1 (the article, which has not been translated, contains numerous references to 1 Cor 12–14); *Folke-Vennen*, March 8, 1906, p. 5 (untitled, untranslated letter).

Dakotas during the late 1890s and early 1900s, spreading glossolalic revival even before the Topeka and Azusa Street revivals. Hanson, born in 1865 in Minnesota to Norwegian immigrants, converted to Christ as a student in the college preparatory program at Augsburg Seminary, a Lutheran school in Minneapolis.[17]

Shortly after being healed of blood poisoning in 1895, Hanson set out as an evangelist. He recounted how, that year, he received his "anointing to preach":

> I commenced to witness for the Lord and after a series of meetings – we had had a cottage meeting in our home – as I arose to testify the Spirit of God came upon me in such a way that I became unconscious of a single word spoken. But the result was that the whole audience was moved. Some cried, others rejoiced, while others exclaimed, "The Lord has spoken." I myself realized such a joy in my soul and a keenness in my spirit to know the condition of things, and received an anointing to preach, and revivals followed.[18]

Hanson recorded how his understanding of water baptism and spirit baptism evolved during that first year of ministry:

> Soon after (receiving an anointing to preach) I became aware there was much more for me and that I needed it, as I realized in studying the Word that Jesus required the same works to be done now as in the days of the Apostles given by Jesus. Matt. 10, etc.
>
> It was also made plain that if we came to the place the Apostles were (Acts 1 and 2), the same power would fall. This brought me to pray for the Baptism in the Holy Spirit, and searching the scriptures I soon found I was not baptized in water according to the Word. Also many false doctrines had to be cleansed out. My hunger became so great at times I made up my mind to go home and wait until I was endued, but had to go out again and again.[19]

Hanson also recorded that he witnessed a small girl speak in tongues in one of his meetings during that first year of ministry:

---

17. C. M. Hanson, 1900 MN census records; Hankin, phone conversation; and "Rev. C. M. Hanson at Home with the Lord," 2, 7.

18. C. M. Hanson, "My Personal Experiences."

19. Ibid.

> In 1895, while holding meetings and preaching the full gospel, as I saw it, with a full consecration, sanctification and Baptism in the Holy Spirit, one came clear through and spoke in tongues, as in Acts 2.[20]

Significantly, the tongues-speech witnessed by Hanson occurred a decade prior to the Azusa Street revival. The 1895 instance of tongues took place during services he held on the H. N. Russum farm near Grafton, North Dakota, and the person to speak in tongues was a small girl. Hanson initially declared, "this must be that which was spoken by the prophet Joel." After searching Scripture, he became convinced the experience was of God, but had not yet connected tongues to spirit baptism.[21] G. Raymond Carlson, former General Superintendent of the Assemblies of God, traced the origins of his own family's Pentecostal faith to that meeting.[22]

Hanson continued to thirst for more of God and questioned whether he was truly spirit-baptized. In a 1906 tract he wrote:

> While there [in Grafton] I met a Brother whom I thought had more than I had. I then thought that I had the Baptism in the Holy Spirit, but that he had the fire also. I asked him to pray for me, and I received a wonderful anointing, so that I was laid out under the Power a long time, being filled with exceeding joy. I had also gone through a wonderful cleansing before, and was clear in my spirit, but was struggling over Baptism in the Holy Spirit. With all this and many other blessings and administrations of the Holy Spirit I could not get satisfied.[23]

Hanson wrote that two years later (apparently in 1897) he prayed for a woman who, shortly after being spirit-baptized, "leaped, shouted, and praised God, sang and prophesied and spoke in other tongues."[24] In another two years (apparently in 1899), Hanson also received this experience:

> But with all this, and many other wonderful experiences, I was not satisfied until two years later, while laboring in the country, I was led to get alone with the Lord. Opportunity was given, and as I knelt down to pray I fell backwards to the floor and all at once, like a mighty rushing wind, the Spiritual atmosphere was cleared up and my whole inward soul was enlightened.

20. Ibid.

21. Carlson, "When Pentecost Came to the Upper Midwest," 3.

22. Ibid. For additional information on the Grafton outpouring, see: Rodgers, *Northern Harvest*, 154–55.

23. C. M. Hanson, "My Personal Experiences."

24. Ibid.

The atoning blood justifying me before God made everything clear. The Holy Spirit then, as a person, took possession of His Temple, speaking in other tongues, while I realized myself as a listener and an instrument in the hands of the Almighty. Oh, the joy that filled my soul; and how unworthy I felt as it now became clear that the Holy Spirit had come in to dwell, and I knew Him as a person, not merely as an influence or a blessing.[25]

Hanson continued to itinerate as an evangelist, preaching the Word and sharing with others how he was saved, healed, and baptized in the Holy Spirit. Hanson's daughter recounted, "my father began giving testimony wherever doors were open to him: in churches, schoolhouses, homes, and missions. The response was amazing. Everywhere people were saved. This was usually followed by a consuming desire for more of God's power in their lives."[26] Hanson was Norwegian, while the Scandinavians to whom he ministered were mostly Swedes. Hanson primarily preached in the Swedish and English languages, causing some Norwegian listeners to mistake him for a Swede.[27]

Hanson received this experience in 1899. Hanson continued to itinerate as an evangelist. In 1900, Hanson and his family moved from Lemond, Minnesota to Minneapolis, where Hanson attended Zion Tabernacle, a congregation pastored by Frederick A. Graves and affiliated with faith healer John Alexander Dowie.[28]

Hanson itinerated as a Free Mission evangelist in Minnesota, the Dakotas, Wisconsin, and Iowa, preaching his brand of radical evangelicalism,

---

25. Ibid. See also Berg, "Early Days of the Pentecostal Renewal in Minnesota," 5; Brumback, *Suddenly from Heaven*, 14; Carlson, "When Pentecost Came to the Upper Midwest," 3; Frodsham, *With Signs Following*, 16; Menzies, *Anointed to Serve*, 30–31; and Ness, *Demonstration of the Holy Spirit*, 7. Historians differed on the dates of these events. Hanson and Berg wrote that the Grafton revival occurred in 1895. Frodsham and Brumback concurred with Hanson and Berg. Carlson and Menzies dated the revival at 1896, and Ness placed it at 1898. According to a careful reading of Hanson's 1906 tract, his spirit-baptism occurred four years after the Grafton revival (apparently in 1899). Berg, Frodsham, Brumback, and Menzies wrote Hanson was spirit-baptized two years after the Grafton revival, Ness dated the spirit-baptism to 1899, and Carlson wrote that it occurred "shortly after" the Grafton revival.

26. Berg, "Early Days of the Pentecostal Renewal in Minnesota," 5.

27. Hankin, phone conversation.

28. Carlson, "When Pentecost Came to the Upper Midwest," 3; "Anna C. Berg," 13; Berg, interview by Wayne Warner. According to Anna, the Hansons attended Graves's mission for four years. Articles from Dowie's periodical placed Graves in Chicago in late 1902, where he served as an elder in Central Zion Tabernacle, then in Minneapolis as early as March 1903 through at least June 1905. *Leaves of Healing* (December 6, 1902) 223; (March 7, 1903) 635; and (June 24, 1905) 349.

making converts, and seeking funds and workers for a rescue mission he had opened in St. Paul in late 1904. In late February and early March 1905, Hanson held meetings in the Gotland neighborhood near Fergus Falls, Minnesota. Seizing upon local gossip, a reporter wrote:

> Several young people have been attending these meetings and it is reported that they work themselves into a perfect frenzy, rolling on the floor, endeavoring to climb up the walls, tossing chairs about and talking oddly in what is supposed to be ancient or peculiar languages, imagining that they have the gift of tongues.[29]

Ostensibly sympathizing with one emotive 18-year-old participant (whom the reporter freely named), the article continued, "One of the meetings came to a climax Thursday evening when a young girl named Miss Olga Nelson appeared to lose her reason entirely, and became so violent that the family was finally compelled to take her to the county jail. She quieted down to some extent there, but does not appear to be very materially improved today, as she walks up and down in the jail, singing hymns and imagining she is going to Africa. It is hoped that she will come out all right in a few days."[30] The next day, the newspaper reported that Hanson planned to take five or six young female converts to Minneapolis to help them find positions as domestics or to engage in mission work.

The irate father of one of the young people at Hanson's meeting swore out a warrant for Hanson's arrest on charges of disorderly conduct.[31] At the hearing, several boys testified that Hanson seemed to hypnotize his converts. According to the reporter:

> [Hanson] claimed the testimony was somewhat exaggerated, although cheerfully admitting that he and his converts roll about on the floor whenever the spirit so moves them. He vehemently denied any insinuations as to hypnotic influence, and claims that the violent actions just described are the results of the working of spirits either of good or evil, and in some instances of the conflicts of the powers of light and darkness as described in the Scriptures. He also states that converts are frequently given the gift of tongues, as they were of old, and that they talk in whatever language the spirit directs. He claims further that he knew one lady who had no knowledge whatever of German who

---

29. "Too Much Excitement," 3.
30. Ibid.
31. "Fined $35," 3.

has able to talk this language when thus moved, and that the converts know exactly what they are doing at all times.³²

Despite the controversy, some converts apparently stuck by Hanson and paid his fine.³³ In a November 1905 letter to *Folke-Vennen*, Hanson recounted opposition he faced, referred to his critics as false prophets, and reiterated his call to minister to youth.³⁴ Hanson's daughter recalled angry mobs interrupting her father's services: "Eggs, tomatoes, and even stones were thrown. In tent meetings the ropes were sometimes cut and at times burned."³⁵

In a February 1905 letter, Hanson discussed the relationship between salvation and spirit-baptism: "With the New Birth one has the opportunity to see the Kingdom of God, but with the Spirit Baptism one comes into the Kingdom, into the Ark, into the Father's House."³⁶ He further claimed that with spirit-baptism, "the sin of mankind is annihilated and Christ is glorified in us."³⁷ Describing those Christians without spirit-baptism, Hanson wrote, "Without the power of the Holy Spirit the work became defective," and "their missions are not perfect for God."³⁸ Addressing the apparent novelty of his doctrines, he explained, "the question about spirit baptism has been buried in God's Word together with the teaching of baptism and the laying on of hands and recovery for the body, etc." These teachings, he claimed, were obscured by church leaders who kept the masses in the dark.³⁹ In 1906, Hanson printed a tract, in which he testified to having already lived with the Pentecostal blessing for over seven years.⁴⁰

C. M. Hanson soon identified with the emerging Pentecostal movement in Chicago, which had roots in the Azusa Street revival.⁴¹ On Sep-

---

32. Ibid.

33. Ibid.

34. Hanson, letter, *Folke-Vennen* (November 30, 1905) 5.

35. Berg, "Early Days of the Pentecostal Renewal in Minnesota," 5.

36. Carl Hanson, letter (trans. Erik L. Williamson), *Folke-Vennen*, (February 2, 1905) 5.

37. Ibid.

38. Ibid.

39. Ibid.

40. C. M. Hanson, "My Personal Experiences."

41. It is unknown when Hanson identified with the Chicago Pentecostals. He may have been influenced by his close friend and former pastor, Frederick A. Graves, who had moved to Zion City, IL in 1905 or 1906 and became an early Pentecostal. In a 1908 letter, Hanson recounted a trip to Detroit Harbor, Wisconsin, during which he apparently met with Chicago Pentecostals. Carl Hanson, untranslated letter, *Folke-Vennen* (September 24, 1908) 5. For another account of Hanson's trip, see John Ommundsen,

tember 25, 1909, Chicago Pentecostal leader William Durham ordained Hanson as a minister with the Full Gospel Assembly.[42] Durham served as pastor of the North Avenue Mission, where F. A. Sandgren, editor of *Folke-Vennen*, was an elder.[43] Hanson transferred his ordination to the Assemblies of God (AG) on September 11, 1917. Participants at the 1922 organizational meeting of the North Central District Council (AG) unanimously elected "Daddy" Hanson, revered as one of the region's Pentecostal pioneers, to serve as the District Council's first Chairman (1922–23).[44]

Scandinavian Mission Society

The Swedish Free Mission in Moorhead was a leading congregation in the Scandinavian Mission Society of Minnesota (*Det Skandinaviska Missionssällskapet i Minnesota*), a small association of Scandinavian free church congregations in Minnesota and the Dakotas. The Scandinavian Mission Society emerged among Scandinavian pietists who opposed the 1885 organization of the Covenant Church (now Evangelical Covenant Church). The largest group to oppose the organization was the Free Mission Friends, colloquially known as "the Free," and now known as the Evangelical Free Church of America.

The Scandinavian Mission Society was organized in 1889 by August Davis and other radical Free Missions Friends—known as "the Free-Free"—who promoted holiness, divine healing services, and the contemporary practice of biblical spiritual gifts such as speaking in tongues.[45] Throughout most of the 1890s, congregations in the Scandinavian Mission Society did not have permanent pastors. Instead, a plurality of elders, including Moorhead pastor John Thompson, rotated between the various churches.[46]

The Moorhead congregation experienced one or more protracted periods of revival. At some point during this period of revival, believers began to manifest Pentecostal gifts. Thompson's son wrote:

> God graciously poured out His Spirit with signs following. Many received the glorious Baptism in the Holy Ghost speaking

---

untranslated letter, *Folke-Vennen* (November 12, 1908) 4.

42. C. M. Hanson, ministerial file.
43. Riss, "William H. Durham," 594–95.
44. "Minutes of meeting held at Brainerd, Minn., November 10, 1922."
45. *Golden Jubilee*, 37–40; and Olson, *The Significance of Silence*, 151.
46. *1883–1958, Diamond Jubilee*; and John Thompson, interview by author. For one critic's view of the Scandinavian Mission Society, see Lindberg, *Looking Back Fifty Years*, 61–66.

in other tongues as the Spirit of God gave utterance. At that time we had not heard of any other places having received a like experience, but later we heard of people in California and Winnipeg, Canada, having received a like precious outpouring of the Holy Spirit . . . Praise God, the spirit of revival was manifested in every service.[47]

The chronology of this revival is uncertain. Henry H. Ness wrote that the revival began in 1892.[48] Several historians repeated Ness's account, which did not distinguish between the beginning of the protracted period of revival, which lasted years, and when Pentecostal gifts began to be manifested.[49] Likewise, Thompson's grandson believed the revivals started in the 1890s and was uncertain when people started speaking in tongues.[50] Some evidence suggests that the Pentecostal gifts, and speaking in tongues in particular, began occurring in about 1903. Thompson's son wrote in 1937 that "the Latter Rain outpouring as on the day of Pentecost" in Moorhead occurred "thirty-four years ago," "in the beginning of this century."[51] If Pentecostal manifestations began occurring in Moorhead at about the same time as they did in other pre-Azusa revivals in Minnesota and the Dakotas, then it is unlikely the Moorhead manifestations began as early as 1892. In Minnesota and the Dakotas, scattered reports of tongues-speech exist from 1895 to 1899, followed by documentation of more than a dozen tongues-speaking congregations from 1899 to 1906.

The Scandinavian Mission Society wielded some influence in the northern Great Plains, or as one pioneer noted, it was the "controlling power" among Scandinavian free churches in Minnesota at the turn of the twentieth century.[52] August Davis, who served as an early Society Chairman, endorsed Fredrik Franson's training courses for women ministers.[53] One critic of female ministers lamented that the Society's "many groups and churches" had only four resident pastors, and that about fifty women were preaching in the pulpits. The critic derided the Society as not well-organized, charging that "the women evangelists and a few others" controlled the elec-

47. P. Thompson, "Pentecostal Outpouring," 8.
48. Ness, *Demonstration of the Holy Spirit*, 6–7.
49. Brumback, *Suddenly from Heaven*, 14; and Menzies, *Anointed to Serve*, 30.
50. John Thompson, interview by author.
51. P. Thompson, "Pentecostal Outpouring," 8. Citing Thompson's article, historian Wayne Warner concluded the revival occurred in 1903. Warner, "Pentecostal Revival," 27.
52. Lindberg, *Looking Back Fifty Years*, 61.
53. Ibid., 58.

tion of officers at the annual meetings. Davis was succeeded as Chairman by John Thompson, pastor of the Moorhead Swedish Free Mission.[54]

The Scandinavian Mission Society published a monthly periodical, *Bref-dufvan* (The Letter Dove), from 1909 to 1933. *Bref-dufvan* published articles about John Thompson, Mary Johnson, and other Scandinavians who practiced tongues-speech and healing.[55] It is not known how widespread Pentecostal gifts were among Scandinavian Mission Society congregations. However, the practice of rotating elders between the various congregations must have spread Pentecostal teachings across the fellowship, since some of the elders (including Thompson) practiced speaking in tongues and healing.

Assembly of God Missionary Fellowship

Another small network of Scandinavian-speaking pietists embraced both Pentecostal gifts and a form of evangelical universalism. The origins of this network, of which two congregations later adopted the name Assembly of God Missionary Fellowship (AGMF), are sketchy. While some members of these early Pentecostal churches were Swedes, most were Norwegians, many of whom had Haugean Lutheran backgrounds.

In Norway, Haugean believers attended the state church on Sunday and held their own evangelical home prayer meetings during the week. In America, some Haugean immigrants continued holding evangelical meetings separate from the Lutheran Sunday services, while others brought their fervent prayer and evangelical preaching into the regular services. Free from the supervision of church hierarchy, these Haugean believers sometimes developed their own theological beliefs as they sought to restore biblical faith.

By the late 1890s and early 1900s, scattered Scandinavian evangelicals in Minnesota and the Dakotas had begun to experience tongues-speech and healing, gifts that spread to other Scandinavian fellowships across the northern Great Plains. While many of the region's early Scandinavian Pentecostals treasured independence and resisted organization, a number of overlapping networks of congregations emerged. One of these networks, including congregations in North Dakota (Hillsboro and Reynolds), Minnesota (Bemidji, Fosston, and Leonard), and South Dakota (Victor), fostered theological innovations that set it apart from other early Scandinavian believers.

54. Ibid., 61–63.

55. See, for instance: *Bref-Dufvan* (April 1918) 4, a lengthy account by editor William Melin on Mary Johnson's and Ida Andersson's missionary efforts.

This network of congregations did not adopt a name, although in later years the Hillsboro and Bemidji congregations incorporated under the name Assembly of God Missionary Fellowship. It is thought that believers chose this name because they referred to their congregations in Norwegian as *guds forsamling*, meaning "God's assembly." The leader of the Reynolds Assembly, Peter Haugen, additionally identified the name of the church universal to be the Church of Jesus Christ, although this name was not universally agreed upon by the various congregations.[56]

The first congregation in what became the AGMF may have been in Fosston, where members claimed John Hoiden, in 1892, was the first to preach the "Full Gospel."[57] Hoiden, a carpenter, had emigrated from Norway in 1889 at age 29.[58] Another Norwegian immigrant, Jens Bengaard, apparently was also involved in the early Fosston congregation. Bengaard, the owner of a Fosston shoe store, was born in Norway in 1859. While Fosston Pentecostals trace their origins to Hoiden and possibly to Bengaard, there is no known evidence whether these two men specifically taught healing and tongues-speech. However, according to oral history, miracles and tongues occurred among the Fosston believers prior to 1900.[59]

Hoiden and Bengaard apparently met in Fosston, but by the early 1900s, most Pentecostal activity seemed to have shifted to meetings held in the rural area near Fosston. Evidence suggests that Pentecost did not come to rural Fosston until between 1900 and 1903. A handful of Norwegian and Swedish families from rural Fosston withdrew from their Lutheran churches, primarily because of disagreement over the practice of tongues, and formed a Pentecostal congregation. Located ten miles north of Fosston, the church eventually became known as the Hill River Gospel Tabernacle.[60]

The date of the congregation's formation is uncertain, but burial of family members in a Lutheran cemetery in 1900 and in a new Pentecostal cemetery, Mamre Cemetery, in 1903, suggests that the congregation formed between those two dates. Believers met in homes, at times led by elder Jacob Bakken of Audobon. Bakken, according to his descendants, came into Pentecost in about 1902 or 1903. In 1905, Bakken baptized in water a number of Hill River believers, including the Carlson, Hanson, Matson, Nystrom,

---

56. In the absence of published sources, this history of the AGMF relied heavily on oral history.

57. "Hill River Gospel Tabernacle," 44.

58. Hoiden, 1920 MN census records.

59. Heckman, "History of the Fellowship of Christian Assemblies," 46; and Nystrom, "100 Years of Pentecostal Blessings in Fosston."

60. Nystrom, "100 Years of Pentecostal Blessings in Fosston."

Sandeen, and Ulseth families. Bakken ordained Andrew Matson and Christ Ulseth as elders to lead the Pentecostals in the Fosston area.[61]

The believers in rural Fosston initially held services in various homes. About 1905, several families, including the Andrew Matsons and Victor Nystroms, built large homes that served as meeting places for the Pentecostals. The Fosston believers identified with the revival emanating from Azusa Street in 1906 or 1907. A second congregation, Queen Assembly, was formed in Queen Township in 1907. While the distance between members of the two congregations was not great—perhaps less than ten miles—it was enough to make separate home meetings convenient. The two groups maintained close fellowship. Olaf Ophus served as elder in the Queen Assembly for a number of years until his death in 1940. Hill River Gospel Tabernacle eventually organized, and in 1933, erected a building located on the Fosston-Trail Road. Hill River Gospel Tabernacle held annual June conventions, which several hundred Pentecostals of various backgrounds regularly attended. After members of the older generation who objected to organization passed away, Queen Assembly organized as Queen Pentecostal Assembly in 1945.[62]

In the late 1940s, the two congregations increasingly associated with different groups of churches. Hill River Gospel Tabernacle continued to associate with AGMF congregations, while Bethel Assembly leaned toward the Independent Assemblies of God (IAG), led by Duluth minister Elmer C. Erickson. In 1948, Hill River Gospel Tabernacle suffered a split due to disagreements over various doctrinal and organizational issues. Some members withdrew and joined with Queen Pentecostal Assembly to form a new organization, Bethel Assembly, which completed construction of a new church in Fosston in 1949. In time, Hill River Gospel Tabernacle closed and members began attending Bethel Assembly. In 1969 members moved the old Hill River Gospel Tabernacle building to Sand Hill Lake Bible Camp, an IAG camp in rural Fosston. Despite having membership in the IAG, which did not accept the "eternal restoration" teaching (see below), many members continued to hold that belief and to fellowship with AGMF believers. AGMF members sometimes attended Lake Geneva Bible Camp (an AG camp near Alexandria, Minnesota), but resisted efforts by the AG to organize their congregations.[63]

61. Ibid.

62. Ibid.; and "The Ancestors and Descendants of Victor Nystrom and Lydia Sophia (Carlson) Nystrom."

63. Heckman, "Bethel Pentecostal Assembly," 14; Matson, Obituary, *Herald of Faith*, July 1941, p. 15; Nystrom, phone interview by author; Nystrom, "100 Years of Pentecostal Blessings in Fosston"; Clara and Victor Matson, phone interview. Several

The Hillsboro congregation, an early Norwegian Haugean group, was started in the 1890s by Lars Overmoe. The Hillsboro saints, who had become Pentecostal by at least 1908, fellowshipped with the early Pentecostal believers in Minnesota. The Hillsboro congregation incorporated as The Assembly of God Missionary Fellowship in 1945.[64] A November 1908 missions conference at Hill River included the following leaders: Andrew Matson and John Hoiden of Fosston, Lars Overmoe of Hillsboro, Jacob and Ole Bakken of Audobon, and Ole Nygaard of Underwood, Minnesota.[65]

The Bemidji congregation, formed in 1918, had its origins in earlier prayer meetings held by three women: Junia Beckstrand, Molly Vaughn, and Harriet (last name unknown). For years, they met together and prayed that men would accept Christ. Finally, several men did accept Christ and were ordained as elders. The Bemidji congregation, also known as the Nymore Assembly, was incorporated in 1944 as The Assembly of God Missionary Fellowship. The Leonard congregation formed in the early 1900s, but merged with the nearby Nymore Assembly in about the late 1940s.[66]

Additional believers in the Bagley and Clearbrook areas were involved in the Fosston and Leonard assemblies, and may have also met in their own communities for fellowship. It is uncertain whether separate congregations ever emerged in Bagley and Clearbrook.[67] The Reynolds Assembly grew out of a Haugean fellowship and, from 1916 to 1950, was led by elder Peter Haugen, a reflective man whose doctrines at times stirred debate. The final congregation in this network to form, located just over the South Dakota state line between Hankinson, North Dakota, and Victor, South Dakota, consisted primarily of members of the Swanson family.[68]

Congregations in this network, most of which thought paid clergy to be unscriptural, recognized local leaders as elders, who had teaching authority and served in pastoral roles. Elders included: Andrew Matson of Fosston; Christ Ulseth of Fosston; Olaf Ophus of Fosston; Peter Haugen (ordained in 1912 when he lived in nearby Bagley, and moved to Reynolds in 1916);

Fosston believers submitted letters to early Pentecostal periodicals, including: Anderson, *Apostolic Faith* (Los Angeles) (June 1908) 4; Andrew Hanson, *Apostolic Faith* (Los Angeles) (January 1908) 1; Andrew Hanson, *Household of God* (January 1909) 5; A. Hanson, *Folke-Vennen* (February 13, 1908) 5; (July 2, 1908) 5; (August 13, 1908) 5; and (December 10, 1908) 5.

64. For more information on the Hillsboro congregation, see Rodgers, *Northern Harvest*, 177.
65. Andrew Hanson, "Fra Missionsmødet i Hill River," 5.
66. Parks, "Church History of the Assembly of God Missionary Fellowship."
67. Vaughn, phone interview; and Nystrom, correspondence.
68. See for Reynolds Assembly, Rodgers, *Northern Harvest*, 60–62, 245–46.

Selmer Sondreal of Reynolds; Molly Vaughn of Bemidji; Lowell Vaughn of Bemidji (who spent time studying with Abraham Heidal in Washington); Eldon Vaughn of Bemidji; Clarence Stenlund of Leonard; Lars Overmoe of Hillsboro; and Joseph Overmoen of Hillsboro.

Great diversity regarding doctrine and practices existed among the congregations. Elders were sober, reflective men and women who took the study of Scripture very seriously. Believing existing denominations to have corrupted Christ's teachings, they set out to restore true doctrine. According to elder Eldon Vaughn of Bemidji, "truth was revealed to us throughout the years." Over time, they discovered additional truths and modified or discarded previous beliefs. Vaughn explained, "we never nailed anything down too hard [so] that we couldn't take it back up again." The absence of a central authority to define orthodoxy and set boundaries gave rise to numerous competing beliefs. It is difficult to speak of "AGMF beliefs," as scriptural interpretations varied from person to person, and as individuals often changed their minds over time.[69]

Elders developed many innovative doctrines, including a form of evangelical universalism called "eternal restoration" or "restitution of all things." The origin of this doctrine, which gained wide acceptance in the network, is uncertain. Andrew Matson of Fosston, according to his descendants, was an early proponent. Matson, struggling with the idea that a good God would send people to an eternal damnation, diligently studied Scripture. He seriously considered turning from God should he be unable to resolve this dilemma. Finally, he determined that all creation eventually would be restored to God. According to this doctrine, in the afterlife non-Christians would be subjected to tremendous punishment commensurate with their sins, but eventually there would be an "eternal restoration" of fallen creation to God. This revelation brought great joy to Matson, who led many others to accept this belief.[70]

Peter Haugen of Reynolds also taught a form of "eternal restoration," wherein those who accept Christ while alive would become "sons of God" and reside in heaven, the unsaved would be resurrected, go through the tribulation, and live on earth for 1,000 years in a literal Kingdom of God.[71] Many in the network were influenced by the Concordant Publishing Concern, a nondenominational teaching ministry formed in Los Angeles in 1909. While Concordant taught a similar form of universalism, it is unknown whether Concordant was the origin of the "eternal restoration" be-

69. Vaughn, phone interview.
70. Nystrom, phone interview.
71. Sondrol, interview.

lief among AGMF congregations.[72] Also influential in this group were late nineteenth-century evangelical universalist authors Andrew Jukes and A. P. Adams and early twentieth-century Pentecostal universalists Charles H. Pridgeon and A. E. Saxby.

Peter Haugen, perhaps the most controversial elder, introduced several new doctrines to the group and stirred debate. In a 1917 tract, Haugen outlined his "doctrine of baptisms." He argued that four different water baptisms existed in Scripture: 1) "baptism to Moses," when one entire nation (Israel) was baptized at once (Exod 14:21–22; 1 Cor 10:1–2); 2) "baptism of John," a baptism of repentance and preparation toward Christ (Matt 3:5–6, etc.); 3) "baptism in the name of Jesus," the baptism of grace for Christians (Acts 2:38, etc.); and 4) "baptism of the nations," a baptism which will occur after the "snatching away" (rapture) of the church and employ the Trinitarian formula, when nations will be baptized and a literal Kingdom of Christ set up on earth (Matt 28:18–20).[73]

Whereas it is unknown whether Haugen was influenced by the Oneness movement, which was emerging about the same time, and also promoted baptism in the name of Jesus rather than using the Trinitarian formula, Haugen did not, however, deny the doctrine of the Trinity.[74] Haugen also identified the existence of different heavens, callings, and futures for Christians, depending on whether a person was baptized in the name of Jesus. Haugen published another tract in which he clarified roles within God's family. He claimed that Israel, not the church, is the "bride of Christ," and that Christians really are God's adopted children.[75]

Some elders eschewed formal liturgies. In the Reynolds Assembly, Haugen rejected a prepared order of worship, the song service always proceeding on an impromptu basis, "as the spirit led." Services did not include an expository sermon. Instead, an elder led a Scripture lesson with interactive discussion. At Hill River, the typical service followed a pattern: singing, congregational prayer during which everyone would kneel, testimonies, and a sermon or biblical exposition. Haugen strictly prohibited published Sunday school lessons, deeming the Bible the only book appropriate for religious education. Members of the Hill River, Bemidji, and Hillsboro assemblies, however, often used published curriculum in their fellowships.[76]

---

72. Vaughn, phone interview.
73. Haugen, "Doctrine of Baptisms."
74. Ibid.
75. Haugen, "The Bride of Christ."
76. Sondrol, interview; and Nystrom, correspondence.

Nymore Assembly in Bemidji is the only remaining AGMF congregation. As members died or moved away, the Reynolds and Hillsboro congregations slowly declined until they largely ceased functioning by the 1970s. Some continued to fellowship together, but attended other Pentecostal and evangelical churches. Former AGMF members often retained their distinctive beliefs, which at times became points of contention in their new congregations.

Early Missionaries

McGee has written extensively about the intertwining of missions with early American Pentecostalism.[77] Charles Parham and various other Pentecostal pioneers believed the restoration of speaking in tongues was for use on the mission field—allowing missionaries to supernaturally bypass the necessity of language school. It took six years for this theory to be put to the test. A. G. Garr, the first foreign missionary from North America with Parham's understanding of the missionary nature of tongues, left the Azusa Street Mission for India. Garr, upon his arrival in Calcutta in early 1907, quickly discovered that he would have to learn the language by more traditional methods.

It was not by accident that the two major Scandinavian Proto-Pentecostal networks of churches mentioned in this article—the Scandinavian Mission Society and the Assembly of God Missionary Fellowship—including variations upon the word "missions" in their names. The Scandinavian pietists in the Dakotas and Minnesota, themselves immigrants, placed great emphasis on pushing the gospel beyond their national borders. Mary Johnson, one of the prominent life-long missionaries to emerge from this group, is also the earliest-known person in the twentieth century who spoke in tongues and left North America to serve overseas as a missionary. She set sail for Africa approximately two years prior to A. G. Garr's departure for India.

Mary Johnson was raised in the Swedish Free Mission in Moorhead. Johnson was born on July 5, 1884, in Harwood, North Dakota, a small farming community located several miles north of Fargo. Her parents, Karl and Karin, were recent Swedish immigrants and struggled to provide for their four children. Feelings of isolation, loneliness, language difficulties, and financial pressures took their toll on Karl, who suffered a nervous breakdown soon after Mary's birth. He was placed in a sanitarium, leaving Karin to raise the children. After two of Mary's older sisters succumbed to sickness and died, Karin became very protective of Mary, also a sickly child.

77. For instance, McGee, *Miracles, Missions, and American Pentecostalism.*

The family frequently attended services at the Moorhead Swedish Free Mission, where Mary surrendered her life to Christ at age 14 during the church's annual missions festival. Swedish women evangelists, associated with *Helgelseförbundets* (Swedish Mission Friends), often visited the Moorhead congregation. One of the evangelists, Ida Andersson, stayed with the Johnson family when Mary was sixteen years old. Mary, longing to experience the joy that Andersson exuded, met with her several times over the next few years. At age nineteen, Johnson began traveling with Andersson. Andersson previously traveled with itinerant evangelist Gustaf Jonsson. Andersson and Johnson headed to Texas, where Jonsson asked them to pastor a group of converts. Johnson sang and played instruments in services, while Andersson preached and mentored her younger companion.

The two women sensed God was calling them as missionaries to South Africa. In November 1904, they returned to Minnesota to attend the annual Free Mission missionary society meeting at Lake Eunice, located southwest of Detroit Lakes. Andersson had been an evangelist in The Swedish Mission Friends missionary society for thirteen years. At the meeting, Johnson was spirit-baptized and spoke in tongues. Andersson had the experience several years later. Participants at the Lake Eunice meeting encouraged Johnson and Andersson to heed God's call and go to South Africa. The two women set out in faith, without a definite budget or amount of support, and arrived in Durban, Kwa-Zulu Natal on January 16, 1905.[78]

According to the son of the Moorhead pastor, Johnson and Andersson reported back to America that they initially "did not believe the heathen Christians would understand the Baptism with the Holy Spirit, so they did not instruct them in the same." However, "God put them to shame by baptizing these Kafirs in the Holy Spirit. They spoke in other tongues, just as we did in Moorhead."[79] Johnson and Andersson worked at several Kwa-Zulu Natal missions, where they studied the Zulu language. In 1908 they moved to Filipi, where they established a mission station consisting of a school and a church. The two women devoted their lives to ministry to the people of Kwa-Zulu Natal. The mission associated with non-Pentecostal Scandinavian Free Mission groups. Johnson and Andersson did maintain contact with and receive regular support from early Scandinavian-American Pentecostals, including members of Fargo Gospel Tabernacle and Kulm Gospel

---

78. An eight-part serialized biography of Mary Johnson, see Reinholdz, "En Guds plöjerska"; and Mary Johnson, Obituary, *Trons Segrars*, July 5, 1968, 13.

79. P. Thompson, "Pentecostal Outpouring," 8.

Tabernacle. Andersson returned to Minneapolis in 1949, where she died in 1964. Johnson remained in Filipi, where she died in the late 1960s.[80]

Significantly, Johnson, the earliest known tongues-speaking missionary from America to venture overseas in the twentieth century, did not hail from Parham's Apostolic Faith band or from the later Azusa Street revival, but was a product of Scandinavian pietism.[81] Additionally, while some early missionaries from Azusa Street believed that the gift of tongues eliminated their need to study languages,[82] there is no known evidence that Johnson and Andersson expected to preach using the gift of tongues. The Moorhead congregation later sent out additional missionaries, including: Augusta Johnson, the first person to be spirit-baptized and speak in tongues in the Moorhead congregation; Florence Bergstrom, who married missionary Ephraim Anderson; and Standia Thompson.[83]

Abraham Heidal emerged as one of the best-known leaders in the Assembly of God Missionary Fellowship. He was born in Queen Township in 1891 to Norwegian immigrants with a Haugean Lutheran background. His family moved to Saskatchewan, where they homesteaded near Eagle Creek in 1905. In March 1909, friends from Minnesota who had become Pentecostal traveled to Eagle Creek, where they held Pentecostal services in which Heidal accepted Christ and was spirit-baptized. Heidal served as a missionary in Kaoyi, Hopei, China from about 1914 until 1941, when he was taken as a Japanese prisoner of war. He was repatriated to Canada the following year, and continued in ministry as an evangelist in Canada and the U.S. until his death in 1969. Heidal ministered among the AGMF congregations, helping to formulate their emerging doctrine.[84] Heidal also maintained contact with the Concordant Publishing Concern and submitted letters to its periodical, *Unsearchable Riches*.[85] Another AGMF missionary to China and

---

80. Ida M. Andersson, Obituary, *Minneapolis Star*, August 20, 1964, 13D.

81. I was unable to find evidence that Johnson and Andersson had any contact with Parham's Apostolic Faith band, which operated primarily in Kansas, Missouri, and Texas. Moreover, Parham's group did not grow significantly until 1905, after the two women had already arrived in South Africa. Parham attracted sizable crowds in 1901 in Kansas, but by 1902 had lost most followers. Parham next found success in a fall 1903 revival in Galena, Kansas, followed by a February 1904 revival in Baxter Springs, Kansas. He moved to Texas in April 1905, where he found significant support in Orchard, Houston, and Galveston. Goff, *Fields White Unto Harvest*, 87–100.

82. McGee, "'Latter Rain Falling in the East,'" 648–65.

83. P. Thompson, "Pentecostal Outpouring," 8.

84. Abraham Heidal, "My Childhood and Conversion"; and Hilma Livinia Heidal, Obituary.

85. For example: *Unsearchable Riches* 31 (1940) 133–34; 32 (1941) 98; 33 (1941) 245–46, 278; and 36 (1944) 251–62.

native of Fosston, Minnesota, Joseph Matson, also maintained links with the Apostolic Church of Pentecost of Canada (ACOP).[86] The AGMF and the ACOP were similarly sympathetic to Oneness views.

It is conceivable that another Norwegian-American Pentecostal missionary to China, Bernt Berntsen, was influenced by the theological trajectories of the AGMF. Berntsen immigrated from Norway to the United States in 1893 and in 1904 joined with a large group of missionaries who left for China with the non-denominational South Chihli Mission. Upon reading about the Azusa Street Revival in the Apostolic Faith newspaper, he returned to America in 1907 and visited the revival in Los Angeles, where he was baptized in the Holy Spirit. He returned to China as a Pentecostal missionary, later became a founding member of the Assemblies of God, but by about 1916 identified with the Oneness movement. He was an important catalyst that led to the founding of the True Jesus Church, a Oneness Pentecostal denomination that is one of the largest indigenous Protestant churches in China.[87]

Historians have not yet determined the influences that caused Berntsen to embrace Pentecostalism in 1907, or its Oneness variant a decade later. However, it is quite likely that Berntsen was aware of the Scandinavian-American pietists in Minnesota and the Dakotas who were practicing tongues-speech before Azusa Street, and who had embraced a form of "Jesus Only" doctrine by the 1910s. Broad networks of radical Scandinavian pietists, facilitated by globe-trotting evangelists and widely-circulated periodicals, almost ensured that the Berntsen would be familiar with the Pentecostal claims on the Great Plains.[88]

Historiography

Importantly, the revivals in Minnesota and the Dakotas testify to Pentecostalism's roots in Scandinavian pietism. This genesis, separate from the Topeka and Azusa Street revivals, underscores the plural nature of the movement. Early Scandinavian Pentecostals hailed from pietist traditions, such as the Haugean movement in Norway[89] and the Awakened and Laestadian

86. Joseph Matson, *Chopsticks*.

87. Tiedemann, "The Origins and Organizational Developments," 108–46.

88. I have discussed this theory at length with True Jesus Church researchers R. G. Tiedemann and J. Gordon Melton.

89. In Norway, Hans Nielsen Hauge pioneered a revival movement at the turn of the nineteenth century. Hauge's experience of a spiritual awakening in 1796, identified by several Lutheran historians to be a "baptism of the Spirit," led him to begin preaching. In Norway, Haugean believers attended the state church on Sunday and held

movements in Finland[90] and Sweden.[91] Early Scandinavian Pentecostals often emphasized continuity with their pietist heritage, recalling instances of miracles, tongues, and other spiritual gifts that occurred in previous centuries in Scandinavia.[92]

By the 1870s and 1880s, a trans-Atlantic revival among Scandinavians in Europe and America resulted in the formation of networks of Scandinavian "free church" congregations, many of which later joined what became the Evangelical Free Church of America and the Evangelical Covenant Church of America. Many leaders in this revival, perhaps most notably Fredrick Franson, drew heavily from American evangelicalism. However, historian Frederick Hale warned against regarding Scandinavian free churches "merely as an outgrowth of American Christianity."[93] Scandinavian free churches were the product of a "complex tapestry" with "innumerable threads to the pattern," including both Scandinavian and American influences.[94] Similarly, Scandinavian pietists in Minnesota and the Dakotas who practiced tongues-speech and healing prior to Azusa

---

evangelical home prayer meetings during the week. In America, some Haugean immigrants continued holding evangelical meetings separate from the Lutheran Sunday services, while others brought their fervent prayer and evangelical preaching into the regular services. Free from the supervision of church hierarchy, these Haugean believers sometimes developed their own theological beliefs as they sought to restore biblical faith. Some of these new churches were explicitly Lutheran and formed organizations such as the Hauge Synod. Others affiliated with networks of free churches, some of which became Pentecostal. Nodtvedt, *Rebirth of Norway's Peasantry*, 105; Aarflot, *Hans Nielsen Hauge*, 15–43; Lee, *A New Springtime*; and Lee (President of the Association of Free Lutheran Congregations), phone interview.

90. The pietistic "Awakened Movement" in Finland, led by Paavo Ruotsalainen, paralleled the rise of the Haugean movement in Norway. Like Hauge, Ruotsalainen experienced an awakening in 1796. Unlike Hauge, historians record that Ruotsalainen spoke in tongues. Recent Finnish Pentecostal scholarship describes early nineteenth-century Finns as experiencing "a general spiritual unrest in Finland," in which "[p]eople were expecting the end of the world and spontaneous revivals sprang up with people speaking in tongues, falling into a trance, preaching in trance, prophesying and having dreams and visions." Meller, "Early Pentecost in Lutheran Finland." See also Ahonen, "Awakened," 343; and Ahonen, *Missions Growth*, 8–9.

91. In Småland, Sweden, newspapers in the early 1840s published numerous stories of odd religious manifestations. One ecstasy, termed "preaching sickness," affected people who attended meetings held by powerful revivalists. Critics mocked the spasms, jerks, and emotionalism of those affected, but also conceded that many involved were converted, gave up alcohol, and returned stolen property. Nyvall, *The Swedish Covenanters*, 36–38; Olsson, *By One Spirit*, 60–64; and Stephenson, *The Religious Aspects of Swedish Immigration*, 24–48.

92. Rodgers, *Northern Harvest*, 30–34.

93. Hale, *Trans-Atlantic Conservative*, 13.

94. Ibid., 1.

Street should not be viewed simply as converts to American evangelicalism. Perhaps the most obvious Pentecostal origin is American evangelicalism, but Scandinavian pietism also provided the Pentecostal movement with leaders and precedents.

Pre-Azusa Scandinavian Pentecostals did have contact with English-speaking evangelicals. *Folke-Vennen* published articles by Hauge and Rosenius next to translations of articles by American Holiness leaders. Faith healer John Alexander Dowie also may have wielded some influence, as Carl M. Hanson, several years after receiving the gift of tongues, began attending a Minneapolis mission associated with Dowie. However, I was unable to find evidence that Pentecostal practices among Scandinavians in Minnesota and the Dakotas originated with English-speaking evangelicals. I did not find any evidence that the Scandinavians from Minnesota and the Dakotas had contact with Parham's Apostolic Faith band, which operated primarily in Kansas, Missouri, and Texas. Parham's group did not grow significantly until 1905, well after the Scandinavian Proto-Pentecostal congregations had formed on the northern Great Plains.[95] The Scandinavian Pentecostals themselves testified to a separate origin. Peter Thompson, recalling the outpouring at the Swedish Free Mission in Moorhead, stated, "At that time we had not heard of any other places having received a like experience."[96]

The pre-Azusa Scandinavian Pentecostals figured prominently in the origins of the Evangelical Free Church of America and the Evangelical Covenant Church of America. Minnesota, a hotbed of Scandinavian free church activity at the turn of the twentieth century, was home to a number of pre-Azusa Scandinavian Pentecostal congregations. Evangelical Free Church historian Arnold T. Olson wrote that he doubted "that all of the pioneers would be accepted in our churches today. Some preached 'a second blessing' and some even practiced speaking in tongues."[97]

A 1934 history of the Swedish Evangelical Free Church of America recounted:

> The so-called "tongues movement" had also a short but lively chapter in our history. If the writer recalls rightly, this movement had its beginning in one of our churches in South Dakota. A small group within this church was affected by it. They thought

---

95. As noted above in note 81, Parham attracted sizable crowds in 1901 in Kansas, but by 1902 had lost most followers. Parham next found success in a fall 1903 revival in Galena, Kansas, followed by a February 1904 revival in Baxter Springs, Kansas. He moved to Texas in April 1905, where he found significant support in Orchard, Houston, and Galveston. Goff, *Fields White Unto Harvest*, 87–100.

96. P. Thompson, "Pentecostal Outpouring," 8.

97. Olson, *The Significance of Silence*, 151.

it was from God and that they were divinely gifted with a special language and therefore called as missionaries to Africa.[98]

While this account did not identify the years these phenomena occurred, they likely took place in the 1890s or 1900s, the period documented by the chapter in which the paragraph was located. The statement, "if the writer recalls rightly, this movement had its beginning in one of our churches in South Dakota," is subject to multiple interpretations. The author may have intended to identify the earliest-known instance of tongues-speech among the Scandinavian free churches (but not necessarily elsewhere). A more tantalizing interpretation is that, from the perspective of the author of the 1934 history, the Pentecostal movement seemed to have its origins, not in Topeka or Los Angeles, but in South Dakota.

The latter interpretation is supported by a similar account of a revival in South Dakota reported by B. F. Lawrence in his 1916 history, *Apostolic Faith Restored*:

> Between 1900 and 1903, the Spirit fell in South Dakota upon a band of people, who afterward went to Africa. I have not been able to get in touch with the man who could give me full information concerning this work, but I think that these people were Norwegians. I know that the man who accompanied them to Chicago was, and that he afterward preached in La Grange, Illinois. His name was Bakke. These people, at least Mr. Bakke, did not believe that tongues were the evidence of the baptism, but regarded them as gifts given in the sovereignty of God.[99]

Lawrence's account, in the first published history of the Pentecostal movement written by an insider, demonstrates that early Pentecostals were aware of the early glossolalic revivals among the Scandinavians in Minnesota and the Dakotas, and that at least some viewed them as a precedent to what later happened at Topeka or Azusa Street.

Early Scandinavian Pentecostals in Minnesota and the Dakotas, recent immigrants to America whose primary tongue was not English, maintained significant connections to their roots in Scandinavian pietism. Judging from a number of letters to *Folke-Vennen* from Carl M. Hanson, A. O. Morken, and others, that periodical had some influence among early Pentecostals. *Folke-Vennen*, a Norwegian-language non-denominational evangelical periodical, was published weekly in Chicago. Its articles reflected a broad spectrum of influences in Scandinavian pietism, ranging from Martin Luther's sermons,

---

98. *Golden Jubilee*, 40.
99. Lawrence, *Apostolic Faith Restored*, 46–47.

to devotionals by Norwegian revivalist Hans Nielsen Hauge and Swedish pietist Carl Olof Rosenius, to translations of writings by American Holiness leaders such as A. B. Simpson. Stanley H. Frodsham reported that evangelist F. A. Sandgren was spirit-baptised in 1907, after which he spread the news of the Pentecostal outpouring through the columns of *Folke-Vennen*.[100] However, the periodical printed testimonies of tongues-speech as early as February 1904 (Audobon, Minnesota).[101] *Folke-Vennen* began publishing news of the revival stemming from Azusa Street in 1906, including articles by Norwegian Pentecostal leader Thomas B. Barratt,[102] early Pentecostal missionary to India, Minnie Abrams,[103] and Chicago Pentecostal leader William H. Durham.[104] Durham served as pastor of the North Avenue Mission, where F. A. Sandgren was an elder.[105] Further study of *Folke-Vennen* would be a valuable addition to the study of Pentecostal history.

It is possible that early Pentecostals in Chicago first became aware of contemporary tongues-speech, not from news of Azusa Street, but from news of prior glossolalic revivals in Minnesota and the Dakotas. Durham and Sandgren may have read about pre-Azusa tongues in *Folke-Vennen* as early as 1904. Likewise, Frederick A. Graves, an early Pentecostal and noted musician in Zion City, IL,[106] must have been aware that his friend, Carl M. Hanson, claimed to possess the gift of tongues when Hanson attended Graves's Minneapolis mission for several years at the turn of the twentieth century.[107] These multiple connections between Chicago Pentecostal leaders and pre-Azusa glossolalic revivals on the Great Plains point to the need to further study Pentecostalism's diverse roots. Azusa Street may have been

100. Frodsham, *With Signs Following*, 42. Sandgren served as pastor of the North Avenue Mission in Chicago in 1917 and later affiliated with the Pentecostal Assemblies of the USA. Sandgren, communication to E. N. Bell.

101. Morken, "Fra vor egen Loesekreds," 4.

102. *Folke-Vennen* (December 13, 1906) 1; (January 16, 1908) 2; (July 2, 1908) 2.

103. *Folke-Vennen* (February 20, 1908) 4; (February 27, 1908) 2; (March 5, 1908) 2; (March 12, 1908) 2; (June 25, 1908) 3; and (September 3, 1908) 5.

104. *Folke-Vennen* (March 26, 1908) 4.

105. Riss, "William H. Durham," 594–95. Blumhofer, in an excellent biographical essay on William H. Durham, noted that Sandgren and Durham had been friends since 1903. Blumhofer, "William H. Durham," 127, 131.

106. Gardiner, *Out of Zion*, 41–42; and Jones, "Frederick A. Graves," 680.

107. Berg, interview. According to Berg, her father, Carl M. Hanson, attended Graves's mission for four years. As noted above in note 28, articles from John Alexander Dowie's periodical placed Graves in Chicago in late 1902, where he served as an elder in Central Zion Tabernacle, then in Minneapolis as early as March 1903 through at least June 1905, *Leaves of Healing* (December 6, 1902) 223; (March 7, 1903) 635; and (June 24, 1905) 349.

the focal point of early Pentecostalism, but prior revivals, including those in Minnesota and the Dakotas, provided precedents and leaders for the emerging movement.

The genesis of the pre-Azusa Scandinavian revivals in the northern Great Plains, separate from the Topeka and Azusa Street revivals, underscores the plural nature of the Pentecostal movement. This study challenges the historiographic assumption that the modern Pentecostal movement began on January 1, 1901 in Topeka, Kansas, and augments the growing body of scholarship identifying Pentecostalism's non-American roots, in order to better tell the full story of the full gospel.

Bibliography

Periodicals

The Apostolic Faith (Los Angeles, CA)
Bref-Dufvan
Folke-Vennen
Leaves of Healing
Trons Segrars
Unsearchable Riches
Weekly Evangel

Other Sources

1883–1958, Diamond Jubilee, Evangelical Free Church, Moorhead, Minnesota. Moorhead, MN: Church, 1958.

Aarflot, Andreas. *Hans Nielsen Hauge: His Life and Message*. Minneapolis: Augsburg, 1979.

Ahonen, Lauri. "Awakened." In *New International Dictionary of Pentecostal and Charismatic Movements*, edited by Stanley M. Burgess and Eduard M. Van Der Maas, 343. Grand Rapids: Zondervan, 2002.

Ahonen, Lauri. *Missions Growth: A Case Study on Finnish Free Foreign Mission*. Pasadena, CA: William Carey Library, 1984.

"The Ancestors and Descendants of Victor Nystrom and Lydia Sophia (Carlson) Nystrom, Fosston, Minnesota." 2002. Manuscript found in Flower Pentecostal Heritage Center.

Andrew J. Matson. Obituary. *Herald of Faith* (1941) 15.

"Anna C. Berg." In *Historical Sketches of the Minneapolis Gospel Tabernacle*, 13. Minneapolis: Church, 1930.

Bakken, Gordon and Linda. *Bakkens in America*. Wichita, KS: Author, 1995.

Berg, Anna Hanson. Interview by Wayne Warner, September 23, 1980, audio recording.

Berg, Anna. "Early Days of the Pentecostal Renewal in Minnesota: A Pioneer Minister and Missionary Reminisces." *Assemblies of God Heritage* 16, no. 4 (1996-97) 5-6, 27.

Blumhofer, Edith. *The Assemblies of God: A Chapter in the Story of American Pentecostalism*. Springfield, MO: Gospel Publishing House, 1989.

———. "Response to: Rediscovering our Diverse Roots, by Darrin Rodgers." Annual meeting of the Society for Pentecostal Studies, Milwaukee, Wisconsin, March 2004. Flower Pentecostal Heritage Center.

———. *Restoring the Faith: The Assemblies of God, Pentecostalism, and American Culture* Urbana, IL: University of Chicago Press, 1993.

———. "William H. Durham: Years of Creativity, Years of Dissent." In *Portraits of a Generation: Early Pentecostal Leaders*, edited by James R. Goff and Grant Wacker, 123-42. Fayetteville: University of Arkansas Press, 2002.

Brumback, Carl. *Suddenly from Heaven: A History of the Assemblies of God*. Springfield, MO: Gospel Publishing House, 1961.

Carlson, G. Raymond. "When Pentecost Came to the Upper Midwest." *Assemblies of God Heritage* 4, no. 1 (1984) 3-5, 10.

Christiansen, Rasmus. "De aandelige Gaver" (spiritual gifts). *Folke-Vennen*, May 12, 1904, p. 1.

"Fined $35," *Fergus Falls Daily Journal*, March 11, 1905, p. 3.

Frodsham, Stanley H. *With Signs Following*. Rev. ed. Springfield, MO: Gospel Publishing House, 1946.

Gardiner, Gordon P. *Out of Zion: Into All the World*. Shippensburg, PA: Companion, 1990.

Goff, James R., Jr. *Fields White unto Harvest: Charles F. Parham and the Missionary Origins of Pentecostalism*. Fayetteville: University of Arkansas Press, 1988.

Golden Jubilee: Reminiscences of our Work under God, Swedish Evangelical Free Church of the U.S.A., 1884-1934. Minneapolis: Church, 1934.

Hale, Frederick. *Trans-Atlantic Conservative Protestantism in the Evangelical Free and Mission Covenant Traditions*. New York: Arno, 1979.

Hankin, Irene. Phone conversation with author, October 1, 2002.

Hanson, Andrew "Fra Missionsmødet i Hill River." *Folke-Vennen*, December 10, 1908, p. 5.

Hanson, Carl M. 1900 MN census records, E. D. 105, sheet 16, line 97.

———. Ministerial file in Flower Pentecostal Heritage Center.

———. "My Personal Experiences of the Graces of Salvation, Healing and Baptism in the Holy Spirit." Tract, 1906.

Haugen, Peter. "The Bride of Christ." Tract, Reynolds, ND, c. 1940.

———. "Doctrine of Baptisms." Tract, Reynolds, ND, December 1917.

Heckman, Warren L. "History of the Fellowship of Christian Assemblies." MA thesis, Olivet Nazarene University, 1994.

Heckman, Warren. "Bethel Pentecostal Assembly." *Conviction* (1965) 14.

Heidal, Abraham. "My Childhood and Conversion." Typewritten manuscript, 6 pages.

"Hill River Gospel Tabernacle." In *Centennial History of the Thirteen Townships*. Gonvick, MN: Richards, 1983.

Hilma Livinia Heidal. Obituary, *Tacoma News Tribune*, April 16, 1962.

Hoiden, John. 1920 MN census records, Fosston, Polk Co., E. D. 207, sheet 14, line 38.

Ida M. Andersson. Obituary, *Minneapolis Star*, August 20, 1964, p. 13D.

Johnson, M. Earl. "A Godly Heritage: The Family of Earl and Darliene Johnson." *Assemblies of God Heritage* 20, no. 3 (2000) 26–27.
Jones, Charles Edwin. "Frederick A. Graves." In *New International Dictionary of Pentecostal and Charismatic Movements*, edited by Stanley M. Burgess and Eduard M. Van Der Maas, 680. Grand Rapids: Zondervan, 2002.
Lawrence, B. F. *Apostolic Faith Restored*. St. Louis, MO: Gospel, 1916.
Lee, Robert. *A New Springtime: Centennial Reflections on the Revival in the Nineties among Norwegian-Americans*. Minneapolis: Heirloom, 1997.
———. Phone interview by author, February 19, 1996.
Lindberg, Frank Theodor. *Looking Back Fifty Years: Over the Rise and Progress of the Swedish Evangelical Free Church of America*. Minneapolis: Franklin, 1935.
"Mary Johnson." Obituary. *Trons Segrars*, July 5, 1968, p. 13.
Matson, Clara and Victor. Phone interview by author, September 10, 2002.
Matson, Joseph. *Chopsticks: An Exciting Adventure of Love and Faith, Trial and Triumph*. Trail, MN: Taiwan Full Gospel Mission, 1994.
McGee, Gary B. "'Latter Rain Falling in the East': Early-Twentieth-Century Pentecostalism in India and the Debate over Speaking in Tongues." *Church History* 68, no. 3 (1999) 648–65.
———. *Miracles, Missions, & American Pentecostalism*. American Society of Missiology 45. Maryknoll, NY: Orbis, 2010.
———. *People of the Spirit: The Assemblies of God*. Springfield, MO: Gospel, 2004.
Meller, Leo. "Early Pentecost in Lutheran Finland." Unpublished manuscript summarizing recent Finnish Pentecostal scholarship, 2004.
Menzies, William W. *Anointed to Serve: The Story of the Assemblies of God*. Springfield, MO: Gospel, 1971.
"Minutes of meeting held at Brainerd, Minn., November 10, 1922 for the purpose of forming a District Council." Minnesota District Council (AG) Archives, Minneapolis, Minnesota.
Morken, A. O. "Fra vor egen Loesekreds." Translated by Erik L. Williamson. *Folke-Vennen* (1904) 4–5.
Ness, Henry H. *Demonstration of the Holy Spirit as Revealed by the Scriptures and Confirmed in Great Revivals of Wesley, Finney, Cartwright, Whitfield, Moody, etc.* Seattle: Hollywood Temple, 1940s?.
Nodtvedt, Magnus. *Rebirth of Norway's Peasantry: Folk Leader Hans Nielsen Hauge*. Tacoma, WA: Pacific Lutheran University Press, 1965.
Nystrom, Lowell. "100 Years of Pentecostal Blessings in Fosston." Roseville, MN: Author, 2003.
———. "100 Years of Pentecostal Blessings in Fosston." In 50th Anniversary booklet, Fosston, MN: Bethel Assembly, 1999.
———. Correspondence with author, December 21, 2002.
———. Phone interview by author, September 10, 2002.
Nyvall, David. *The Swedish Covenanters: A History*. Chicago, IL: Covenant Book Concern, 1930.
Olson, Arnold T. *The Significance of Silence*. Minneapolis: Free Church, 1981.
Olsson, Karl A. *By One Spirit*. Chicago, IL: Covenant, 1962.
Parks, Iris. "Church History of the Assembly of God Missionary Fellowship, Bemidji, MN, [and] the Assembly of God, Hill River, MN." N.p.: Author, 1993.

Reinholdz, Naemi. "En Guds plöjerska: Mary Johnsons liv och verksamher." *Trons Segrars*, August 9, 1968–September 27, 1968.

"Rev. C. M. Hanson at Home with the Lord." *North Dakota District Echoes*, July-August 1954, pp. 2, 7.

Riss, Richard M. "William H. Durham." In *New International Dictionary of Pentecostal and Charismatic Movements*, edited by Stanley M. Burgess and Eduard M. Van Der Maas, 594–95. Grand Rapids: Zondervan, 2002.

Rodgers, Darrin J. *Northern Harvest: Pentecostalism in North Dakota*. Bismarck, ND: North Dakota District Council of the Assemblies of God, 2003.

Sandgren, F. A. Correspondence from Chicago to E. N. Bell, Springfield, MO, November 19, 1921, Flower Pentecostal Heritage Center.

Sondrol, Leroy. Interview by author, Grand Forks, ND, December 1999.

Stephenson, George M. *The Religious Aspects of Swedish Immigration*. Minneapolis, MN: University of Minnesota Press, 1932.

Thompson, John. Interview by author, June 1998, Springfield, MO, transcript of audio recording.

Thompson, Peter B. "Pentecostal Outpouring of Thirty-four Years Ago." *Pentecostal Evangel*, November 27, 1937, p. 8.

Tiedemann, R. G. "The Origins and Organizational Developments of the Pentecostal Missionary Enterprise in China." *Asian Journal of Pentecostal Studies* 14, no. 1 (2011) 108–46.

"Too Much Excitement." *Fergus Falls Daily Journal*, March 10, 1905, p. 3.

Vagle, Anna. "When Pentecost Fell in Minnesota." *Full Gospel Men's Voice*, September 1960, pp. 9–11.

Vaughn, Eldon. Phone interview by author, December 1999.

Warner, Wayne. "Pentecostal revival stirs Swedish church." *Pentecostal Evangel*, April 21, 1996, p. 27.

17

Power in your Mouth
Pentecostalism and Orality[1]

Del Tarr

Avant Propos

This essay purports to link two conceptual ideas for the reader: First, introducing perhaps a little known "spiritual gift" of the person this volume honors, the charismatic gift of prophecy in public meetings. Second, linking prophecy to the topic of the oral/aural world of communication as existed and practiced by the ancient cultures and historical settings of the Bible. Westerners (First-World peoples of the last two hundred years), especially, know little of the pre-literate world that still exists as the majority population. Our culture of wild digital electronic marvels all but prohibits this understanding.

My administrative position as Dr. Gary B. McGee's President for many years allowed me to observe and encourage his known capacity as a word smith and teacher, and to observe that added grace of the prophetic oral inspiration of the Holy Spirit for the benefit of student, faculty, and the greater church world. The topic of "oralness" on which this essay is centered would not have been possible for me but for the privilege of having learned and employed in ministry two preliterate vernacular languages of West Africa during a 20-year period, namely *Mori* of Burkina Faso and *Eve* of Togo.

---

1. Part of this essay is drawn from the author's book: *The Foolishness of God*, chapter 4, 101–96.

Gary McGee's Journey to Orality's Power

McGee is known as an author of renown. While this volume is a tribute to his writing and teaching skills, the reader should know of another "gift" he manifested: the gift of prophecy as defined in the Apostle Paul's writings to the Corinthian Church (1 Cor 12–14).

Upon accepting the presidency of the Assemblies of God Theological Seminary (1990 to 1999) I had come with the intense desire to accelerate the Seminary's emphasis on a distinctive most other seminaries could not or would not emphasize. This related to the world of Pentecostalism. Upon suggesting the motto of "Knowledge on Fire" to describe AGTS as a theological institution, the faculty was challenged to explore and engage in the Apostle's challenge: "Follow the way of love and eagerly desire spiritual gifts, especially the gift of prophecy" (1 Cor 14:1). A number of the faculty did indeed join in my own search and expectation for us all. It was Gary McGee who, in a few months, began to electrify our chapel services from time to time with a growing surrender to the heart of God in both foretelling and forth telling that best describe this gift. I honor McGee for both his gifts of writing and Spirit-inspired oralness that seldom are exhibited in one person to the extent we witnessed.

Spoken Words and Visual Symbols

A visual demonstration of "showing" and auditory "speaking" are equally communicative. An example of this is depicted every time the Table of the Lord is observed in worship and obedience. In essence, when the bread and the cup are displayed and made visible/available in public and observable by anyone and everyone present, the scene represents a visual illustration of God's loving sacrifice and presence. The visible demonstration of the Eucharist is saying: "This is what our God is like." "Our creator God who wants to redeem us as well as partner with us . . . *is like this. . .*"

Symbols and Words

The rather magical story of Moses holding up the "rod of the Lord" over his head with the help of Aaron and Hur seems strange until one perceives the symbolism of that piece of wood (rod) in that scene as representing the power of God. "The rod of the Lord" symbolized: *This is what our God is like* (like the elements of Communion). The miraculous piece of wood was to become a snake, eat up the other snakes, be waved in the air to produce lice, flies, frogs, and even cause the death angel's plague to definitively define God's power to deliver His people from the hand of Pharaoh. In fact, how else can we justify the severe punishment of the Lord on Moses's latter misuse of that rod when he struck the rock twice instead of speaking to the rock for water in the desert as he was commanded? That surprising punishment deprived him of entering into the land to which he had painfully led the Israelites for over 40 years! Surprising, no? Unless we understand that the Lord must have seen the misuse of the rod as: *This is NOT what your God is like.*

People's Words and Symbols can Bring God's Blessings

Remember the words of Jesus to Peter in Matt 16? "Blessed are you, son of Jonah . . . " after he had identified, for the first time from the mouths of the apostles, the true and proper identity of the Messiah, "You are the Christ, the Son of the living God." I believe we can demonstrate that God loves it when humans properly identify Him—and to the contrary He punishes those who take His name in vain.

Let's study this closely: When Peter responds for the disciples to answer Jesus's question: "Who do you say that I am?" Peter was saying, "You, Jesus, are not just a man, like were all the prophets. You are the incarnate God-Man like no other!" And perhaps neither the apostles, nor any historian, nor we in this advanced age where knowledge has increased to an unprecedented degree can yet totally comprehend the mystery of the Incarnation!

So what have we seen? Humanity's physical symbols to which he attributes the meaning of words (the elements of communion), *or* the old rod of Moses used to symbolize God's power of deliverance, *or* the very spoken words of a man properly describing God's essence results in blessing and deliverance when true, or punishment when misused.

Speech more than Writing

When the Bible speaks about the mouth and tongue, it almost always refers to oral speech (language), not written words. Speech used to mean something much more powerful than it means in our "literate" world. Because of Gutenberg's printing marvel which changed the world as significantly as any invention until the computer, oral speech has become downgraded to "hearsay." Today, we don't just want someone's *word*, we want it in print and hopefully signed and witnessed by a notary public! But when Jesus said: "For by your words you will be acquitted, and by your words you will be condemned" (Matt 12:37), He was referring to the gravity of oral speech. A man's words used to be his bond, often sealed with a handshake. The thesis of this essay is that God's Word (oral and sometimes later written) should be seen from the context of the world in which it was spoken and later compiled. God's Word was first heard as oral speech (inspiration), seldom, if ever, read from a manuscript or book until later. There is a strong predisposition to what is oral/aural in the Bible relating to a prophet's inspiration in God's dealings with mankind. This paper submits that hyper-literate, textual societies and cultures have lost, by default, the very idea of *oralness* since the predominance of what is written has displaced God's use of both oral and written means of communication. That is not because He discredits things in print—no. He even commanded that certain things be written down (Exod 17:14; Deut 17:18; Jer 30:2, etc.). Rather, it's because the majority of the people living in the culture of biblical inspiration were basically illiterate (our definition), and even more importantly, God has always wanted His people to have fresh, extemporaneous, non-textbook contemporary inspiration even when they *have* written texts available, which I hope to show below. *Is it possible God still lays more importance on speech than we do today?*

Modern Communication Theory and the prophetic gifts of the Spirit as spoken by the prophet Isaiah give us insight and biblical precision to our thesis. "As for me, this is my covenant (promise) with them, says the Lord. My Spirit, who is on you, and my words that I have put in your mouth, will not depart from your mouth, or from the mouths of your children, or from the mouths of their descendants from this time on and forever, says the Lord." (Isa 59:21)

For the ancient pre-literate world, the mouth was understood to be the source of social power because human speech is at the top of the communication chain. In every culture from time immemorial, a clan's spokesperson or "wordsmith," whose speech could not be ignored, was recognized as one of the most powerful individuals and often to be feared. Every African chief or Indian Mogul had his "interlocuteur" that demanded the attention of the masses. The "mouth person" spoke *for* the titular head of the clan or city or state. Even if the political leader was a good speaker, he deferred to the expert because of his command of the language that exploited every idiom and nuance of the words he chose. *The prophecy above from Isaiah is about a covenant from God to oralness and speech. It is something superior in its communicative power by its extemporaneous directness.*

Not Just Old Testament Prophecy

One must not relegate this covenant to just an Old Testament dispensation and therefore disregard it in today's world and theological era called "grace" of the New Testament. How is that? Because this is the indisputable scriptural essence that the apostle Peter cited in the New Testament on the day of Pentecost in Acts 2:17–18; 39. He was standing in the temple witnessing God's miracle, exactly as Jesus had recently predicted noticing that people's mouths were *being very busy!* "The promise is for you and your children and for all who are far off – for all whom the Lord our God will call," relating to the *"in your mouth and mouths of your children, and from this time on and forever, says the Lord"* of the Isaiah passage.[2] Theologians in the early middle ages and the Reformed Theologians after them, rejected an important prophecy and thus refused to embrace the *second half* of John the Baptist's duel prophetic pronouncement in John's gospel chapter one: First, "Look, the Lamb of God who takes away the sins of the world" (John 1:29). And second: " . . . He is the one who will baptize with the Holy Spirit" (John 1:33) ("and with fire" Luke 3:16). *Why has the Christian world largely embraced the first prophetic words and neglected the second?* He will baptize you with the Holy Spirit and with fire.

A major part of the answer, I submit, is related to oral communication sometimes inspired by God's Spirit, and sometimes via the memory banks of the human mind, and sometimes both, in timing and context.

Bible times, like today's "two-thirds world," had vast areas where illiterate people outnumbered those who could read and write. Our "first world" culture now has five centuries of print literacy (since Guttenberg) in the West that *blinds* us to a cultural orientation of the Bible. (It's amazing how many valuable texts on hermeneutics ignore this fact.) The ancient Hebrew world, during the time of the Old Testament writings, was not literate like we know today. It was only slightly better during New Testament times. (A "scribe" was someone of rare and unusual skills who made his living by writing for those who could not read or write.)

The Difference

Oral communication and written communication are quite *dis*similar in some respects, even when they originate from the same person! I'm not talking about grammar or punctuation, obviously, but something much

---

2. For a full explanation of this theme, see Ruthven, *What's Wrong With Protestant Theology?*

more significant and powerfully important. Mono-linguistic people (like Anglos in the USA), who know no pre-literate people or their languages may have difficulty perceiving this contrasting dimension of reality. We are today an expanding "textual," "literate," people of books, newspapers, street signs, magazines, Kindles, smart phones, and, in spite of the recent electronic media of all descriptions, we are still dependent on reading. Our 500 years of "print literacy" is a very different world than the culture of the Bible.

From Oralness to Literacy

Before the marvels of communicating by electronics, the available channels of communication besides oral speech, were drums, smoke signals, reflecting mirrors, cannon shots, lantern signals, etc. and were subject to severe limitations. In *The Responsive Chord*, Tony Schwartz speaks of the problem of communications by a pre-technological society as we know it today. Napoleon established a network of 224 line-of-sight semaphore stations spanning over 1000 miles. The coded message using flags had to be repeated accurately at each station for the correct message to get through. The chance of an error was quite high.[3]

The West Ignores Oral-Education Literacy (What difference does it make?)

North Americans assume that print-literacy is the only definition of the term "literate" and the idea of "oral-literacy" (competency in speech) seems an oxymoron. It's because they confuse literacy with being educated in the Western model. Only that which is "in print" is the highest form of communication. We invest heavily in schools, books, and written records, and marginalize the non-literate. Those who insist on "literacy" over everything, find it difficult to accept the truth that people do not need to be literate before they can become Christian.[4]

In a chapter on "Cultural Assumptions of Western Missionaries," anthropologist Paul Heibert[5] describes how hundreds of years of print literacy makes us unconscious of how the other half of the world communicates. We assume they are like us. When we do, it affects the way we study the Word of God and the way we share it.

---

3. Schwartz, *The Responsive Chord*, 3.
4. Hiebert, *Anthropological Insights for Missionaries*, 135.
5. Ibid., 134–35.

We think that our studies of the Bible are unbiased, that our own interpretations of the Scriptures are the only true ones. It disturbs us, therefore, when we begin to discover that theologies are also influenced by culture... All human theologies are only partial understandings of Theology as God sees it. We see through a glass darkly.[6]

Important Difference

For hundreds of years up until now, anyone who was not "literate" according to this definition was the object of discrimination. This increased the way our society valued the linear process.[7] Our linear bias, I contend, makes it difficult to understand people from preliterate auditory cultures where the spoken word is still the only word. This is an issue few Bible scholars address.

Print Fosters Systems

Print literacy encourages an emphasis on systems. To organize (systematize, create retrieval engines and databases) requires systems. This in turn fosters rational thought by divorcing ideas from feelings! *Oral societies live with a constant direct tie to information and the emotional content of those they interact with. No printed page carries the emotional impact of an oral presentation because of the lack of the non-verbal elements of communication, which accompanies the oral medium* (such as *vocalics*—the impact of the voice on meaning; *kinesics*—the part that gestures and facial expression play on the total package; *occulesics*—the vivid effect of the use of the eyes in face-to-face dialogue; *haptics*—the communication of touch; *proxemics*—the communication of the use and abuse of personal space, etc.).[8] Almost *none* of these elements are available in written communication. In fact, the experts in human communication tell us that 65 percent of what we communicate in a dialogue is not related to words![9]

---

6. Ibid., 198; see also Tarr, *Double Image*.

7. Schwartz, *The Responsive Chord*, 10.

8. For an interesting and informative expose of this theory, see: Northrop, *The Meeting of East and West*; and F. H. Smith summarized in Perry, *The Gospel in Dispute*, 99–106. Oralness leads to concrete relational thinking as a first order. Plato and Aristotle set the West on a course of conceptual thinking as a priority. Oral thinkers organize their world of communication on proverbs, aphorisms, allegory and folk tales. See Tarr, *Double Image*, 11–15.

9. See Tarr, *The Foolishness of God,* Appendix 1, 397–98 for a list of some of the

Who Cares? What Difference does it Make? (Hang with me now!)

The difference is simple: Not understanding oralness restricts our understanding of the charismata, prejudices the illiterate oral peoples of the world (more than half), and distorts our receptivity to one of the important ways of how God wants to interact with us, His children! *Is that important or what?—You Think?!*

Paul Hiebert quotes Walter Ong explaining how this Western emphasis on a visual/print world has its roots in Greek philosophy:

> Plato's ideas launched the new world, the opposite of the old, which his attacks on the poets proscribed. The old [oral] world had made much of man's activities and of human struggle as the focus or axis of all reality. Where the old world had been warm and human, Plato's "ideas" or "forms" . . . were cold and abstract. The world had been mobile, and event-full, and its oral narrative was a swirl of exciting activity. In contrast, Plato's new ideas were motionless, a-historical; where the old view had held all knowledge in a concrete human setting, the new traced everything to the abstract, the other-worldly, the totally objective, the fixed, modeled on an immobile figure visualized on a motionless field.[10]

The crowning achievement of this predisposition was print literacy and, consequently, the attachment to the written word—whether in education, politics, law, or the religious world. Soon after Gutenberg's printing press changed the world, orality became suspect by the industrialized world. However, the majority of the world's population, even in the twenty-first century, is "illiterate" and lives in oral societies where what happens (real events) are the grist of cognition and social communicative interaction. This fact is hidden from North Americans in general. As a people, we have "bought into" the myth that literacy makes us superior people—a part of our extreme ethnocentricity.

I do not suggest that the oral extemporaneous Gifts of the Spirit replace or depreciate God's written Word! God wants and needs *both*. The Church (bishops, priests, pastors, leaders) cut off the in-breaking of the Spirit because He was too dangerous!! They couldn't predict and control the charismata—they couldn't fit the Spirit into the bulletin (!) *They* wanted control.

---

experts in non-verbal communications.

10. Ong, "World as View and World as Event," 642.

An Advantage of Oralness is Tying Message and Messenger

Oral societies are highly organized (surprise!) but in ways we can hardly fathom with the textual/literate mind. All peoples have similar building blocks to cognition, but they prioritize those blocks differently. The mode is highly interactive between speaker and listener. One can't talk to a book (and expect a response), but one can interact with concrete human experiences told verbally and in one's "hearing." (Today we call this "real time.") Communication in oral societies is not in abstractions, or in a monologue between reader and the printed page, but in dialogue form—consequentially so much more personal. *Writing divorces a message from the messenger.* (Why is that?) We read and trust even if we know nothing about the author/writer. Thus we use abstractions to form ideas and formulate dogma, independent of whether he/she who wrote the words is worthy of our trust. This happens rarely in oral societies where what is uttered is compared with the speaker's known personality and reputation. North Americans value print and assume it is the highest form of literacy.

And here lies one of the problems with "tongues and prophecy" and some other charismata. They are not literate! They are oral expressions in communication under the inspiration of the Holy Spirit. A modern society fixated on literacy has great difficulty accepting their legitimacy. A literate society encourages rational thought even at the expense of feelings—in fact, feelings are generally seen as suspect and should be divorced from ideas. This is why Jesus hit the scribes: " . . . His voice you have never heard, his form you have never seen; and you do not have his word abiding in you, for you do not believe him whom he has sent. You search the scriptures, because you think that in them you have eternal life; and it is they that bear witness to me" (John 5:37–39).

They had the velum manuscripts which they "searched," but they had abandoned and killed the prophets and resisted the Holy Spirit (Acts 7:51–52). *Priests never have liked prophets!* It only took 300 years after the resurrection before the apostolic church, too, no longer had "God putting words in their mouths, or their children's mouths"—even though God never wanted it to stop. *Look what Plato and Aristotle, and subsequently Thomas Aquinas, have done to the New Testament model of life in the Spirit which was almost totally oral/aural oriented.*

Evangelical Cessationist's Limitations

Listen to a missionary of a very conservative Evangelical denomination working with a remote African tribe who after 20 years has only one congregation of 120 members which he pastors himself. He writes to "scold" his Pentecostal sister in America:

> Lorraine, I hope you won't be offended by what I'm going to say next... We believe God has made it clear that all prophesies are contained in the Bible. There are no more 'new prophesies's or 'words from the Lord' coming to people today. When we say we received 'messages from God' we have by-passed His appointed means of communicating to us, the Bible alone.[11]

How sad to hear from this good brother, who is working in a country where a sister Pentecostal church is working and training African pastors and has found a constituency of over 200,000 believers, in less than 20 years. This Evangelical cessationist believes he is protecting the Scriptures: in fact he is choking them!

Paul the apostle said "not to put out the Spirit's fire" (I Thess. 5:19). Interesting this "fire" metaphor and how often it is repeated in the New Testament. Harvey Cox shows a good diversification between Evangelical Fundamentalists and Pentecostals relating to the issue of the "literate" mind:

> I also learned that it is a serious mistake to equate Pentecostals with Fundamentalists. They are not the same. Fundamentalists attach such unique authority to the letter of the verbally inspired Scripture that they are suspicious of the Pentecostals's stress on the immediate experience of the Spirit of God. This should not be surprising. Text-oriented believers in any religion tend to be scared of mystics. However, this does not mean that Pentecostalism does not embody a complex of religious ideas and insights. It does. The difference is that while the beliefs of the Fundamentalists, and of many other religious groups, are enshrined in formal theological systems, those of Pentecostalism are imbedded in testimonies, ecstatic speech, and bodily movement. But it is a theology, a full-blown religious cosmos, an intricate system of symbols that respond to the perennial questions of human meaning and value. The difference is that, historically, Pentecostals have felt more at home singing their theology, or putting it in pamphlets for distribution on street corners. Only recently have they begun writing books about it."[12]

11. From a Sept 3, 2010 Facebook exchange. Names changed and omitted.
12. Cox, *Fire From Heaven*, 15.

Pentecostals and Charismatics believe the renewal of the gifts of the Spirit in religious worship and mission is a return to the oralness of the original New Testament model. What part of that rejection is related to a misunderstanding about oralness by literate minded churchmen and women, even today?

A Plea to Re-Examine

No one would question the value of "fixating" communication in written form where it can be stored, comparatively unchanged after hundreds of years, while oralness may quite easily be redefined or shifted in content. (But let's be serious—written accounts of anything can and are often changed by political [read religious] "editors.") Yes, literacy is extremely valuable—we can't go back. But we can examine what it has done to a valuable language system, the part of human communication still used by the majority of the world's peoples. And we might look at how our literary predisposition may have produced a built-in bias against spontaneous prayer language found in Acts 2, 9, 11, and I Corinthians 12–14, plus many other accounts in the New Testament record. I argue in my recent book: *The Foolishness of God*[13] that cessationist Evangelicals are trapped when seeing through the lens of modern textual logic by making the Lord a totally reasonable God as in the words of John Stott stating that "it's illogical to believe that He would continue glossolalia past the age of the apostles."[14] There is a better way, the way our honoree found by running against the stream of our textual dominated system.

Pentecostals might do better to simply embrace the paradoxical nature of tongues-speech, says Rybarczyk:

> Praying with tongues is both very non-rational and non-linear . . . Something vibrant, authentic, and Spirit-inspired has been sacrificed over the near-century long attempt to explain and define the paradox of tongues as a rational and indeed 'normal' Christian phenomenon. It is not normal, anymore than was Jesus's death on a cross. And we should add, that is a good thing! . . . In their rabid rush to become rational Evangelicals, Pentecostals have forsaken the implications that a theology of tongues could have for the Church universal. In their historical debates with other Christians, Pentecostals have processed and

---

13. Tarr, *The Foolishness of God*, 53.
14. Stott, *Baptism and Fullness*, 113.

re-processed glossolalia mostly as a lone element in Christian spirituality.[15]

"Right on!" says James K. A. Smith:

> In this essay, I will argue that the early Christian community was a charismatic community which placed emphasis on *hearing* not reading. As such, early Christianity was not a religion of the Book, though it was certainly a religion of the Word. It was a community centered, not around scribes but prophets. In the history of the Christian community, a shift occurred whereby text received a privileged status and the original oral/aural and charismatic way of being was suppressed and oppressed and gradually declared to be defunct. This emphasis on writing(s) (or the privileged status of writings) confined revelation to a past epoch; 'scribalism'—the emphasis on the letter—planted the seeds which killed and quenched the ongoing revelatory ministry of the Spirit by silencing the prophets with the Canon ... realized nearly two thousand years later in Protestant fundamentalism and conservative evangelicalism—textual communities *par excellence*.[16]

The early Apostolic Church was a prophetic community. It was also a predominately oral/aural community. "Faith," Paul would insist, "comes by hearing" (Rom 10:17). He also asks: "How shall they call upon this one whom they have not believed? And how can they believe without hearing?" (Note, he didn't say reading). "Nor did he say 'How can they preach without a text?'"[17]

Colonialism's Crushing Effect

During the 30 years we lived in and associated with West Africa, we saw the destructive forces of French colonialism and their language on the rich oralness of the Mossi and Ewe of Burkina Faso and Togo, respectively. In I Corinthians 1, Paul asks: "Where is the scribe?" Evidently not in the Church, as time and again the early Christians were reviled for being illiterate (*agrammatos*) and ignorant (*idiotes*, Acts 4:13) as was Jesus Himself (John 7:15). But this lack of scribes only signaled the fact that for the Christian community, faith was *hearing* the Word, which is not only *about* Christ but *is*

---

15. Rybarczyk, "Expressing the Inexpressible."
16. Smith, "The Closing of The Book," 49–71; italics in original.
17. Ibid., 50

Christ. *"It is precisely this oral way of being which, I would propose, has been recaptured in the contemporary charismatic communities . . . Perhaps the oral nature of Pentecostalism is best captured in the emphasis on glossolalia, which cannot be written nor can it be repeated."*[18]

The Textualization of our Faith
(Now we're getting serious!)

James K. A. Smith, a Pentecostal Assembly of Canada scholar from Canada, asks the following pertinent question: "Is Christianity a religion of the book? That is, were the early Christians a people of the book or rather a people of the Spirit? Was the early Christian community a literate/textual/book community or rather an oral/aural community?"[19] Smith argues that the early Christian community was a charismatic community, which placed emphasis on *hearing,* not reading. It was a community centered not on scribes but on prophets. He argues that our literary bias has facilitated our acceptance of Fundamentalism and Evangelicalism's predisposition to consider the text and Canon of the Scriptures so important that it crowds out the necessity (or possibility) for God to supernaturally talk to us by His in-breaking gifts of the Spirit. He calls this exaggerated emphasis on *that which is in print: The Textualization of our faith.*[20]

> 'Speaking in Tongues's . . . is a practice which paradigmatically and dramatically underscores the oral-narrative character of Pentecostalism. Glossolalia became an integral element of Pentecostal 'oral-narrative liturgy' because that which is most characteristically human and constitutive of human community (i.e., language) required a new speech incapable of being co-opted by the routinizing of church bureaucracies or worldly regimes.[21]

Not Just Existence of Texts, but their Status

The paradigm shift in world-view impacted by a change from orality to literacy as a social value brought about momentous implications. In the historical study of how folks communicated a thousand years ago, texts were

18. Cartledge, "Charismatic Prophecy," 100; emphasis mine.
19. Smith, "The Closing of The Book," 49.
20. Ibid., 55–63. I'm greatly indebted to James Smith's article and his research.
21. Land, *Pentecostal Spirituality,* 26

not authoritative texts because the authority rested with the oral word of the emperor or sovereign. Even though texts existed, their status was derivative. *Texts were reminders of the power of the presence of the king.* About the eleventh century, states Smith, communities became "textualized" (Smith's term to describe what occurs in the shift from an oral/aural worldview to a literate/textual mode).[22]

Again—What Difference Does it Make?

This difference totally gutted the power of an 800-year social system of the Moro Nabas (emperors) of the Mossi in Burkina Faso, West Africa. The French colonialists came with the insistence of the superiority of their language to all others. (This exists to this day.) By the time I personally witnessed the power of "l'alphabetisation" it was 1960. Although only six percent of the whole population was "literate," that small group had all the political power, and had systematically deposed the real power structure of 800 years of emperor, paramount chiefs, sub-chiefs, and a great amount of the social place of elders. They didn't do this with guns, but with prejudicially distorted French educational values.

Jack Deere, a former professor at Dallas Theological Seminary and one-time proponent of ultra-dispensationalism, speaks of his own discovery of this "textualization" in his own life.

> In the process of getting theologically trained and becoming a seminary professor, I developed an intense passion for studying God's Word. I found myself loving the Bible more than I loved the author of the Bible. I was caught in this trap for more years than I would like to remember . . . It took me too long to learn that knowing the Bible is not the same thing as knowing God, loving the Bible is not the same thing as loving God, and reading the Bible is not the same thing as hearing God."[23]

Is it possible to hear from God apart from His Word? Many say no. An even larger percentage of believers today say yes. However, those who say yes quickly affirm that when God speaks today, He speaks to confirm Scripture or gives inspiration that agrees with, but never contradicts the Word of God as known in the Canon. In 1 Corinthians 12–14 there is a description of the expectations of a normal worship service in Corinth. In that context, the role of prophets was a part of that expectation, an important part. Those

---

22. Smith, "The Closing of The Book," 55
23. Deere, *Surprised by the Power of the Spirit*, 187.

with verbal gifts (tongues, interpretation of tongues, prophecy, words of wisdom and knowledge) played an essential role in the community, which waited to hear the Lord speak *from the mouths of the participants under the inspiration of the Holy Spirit* (all under the examination and judgment of the body of believers). Orality, then, as in much of the world today, was what the New Testament community practiced. This oral culture in which our Scriptures were first given by word of mouth and subsequently written down (sometimes scores of years later) is a world unknown to us and has been for hundreds of years.[24]

In the history of the Christian community, a shift occurred whereby texts (reading/writing/literature) received a privileged status and the original oral/aural and charismatic way of being was suppressed where the new emphasis was on the letter. Carthage and Smith believe the seeds of literalism were the seeds that killed and quenched the ongoing revelatory ministry of the Spirit by silencing the prophets with the Canon. "Protestant fundamentalism and conservative evangelicalism are textual communities *par excellence*."[25] The authors go even farther when they state: "It is precisely this textualism of evangelical theology which undermines the Pentecostal experience of continuing revelation."[26]

The more textual a society, the less its people can tolerate the high amount of indirection and ambiguity with which the Bible is so replete. I had to learn a "non-textual" vernacular language to discover this truth. If we had the space here, we could examine the linguistic etymology of the power of words from the chief or emperor in traditional Mossi culture where the word "*nore*", symbolized by a sharp knife, is the same word for mouth and authority/power.[27] With that perception, can you imagine the poignant symbolism for these believers internalizing John the Revelator's vision of the triumphant *King of Kings and Lords of Lords*? "Out of his mouth comes a sharp sword with which to strike down the nations!" (Rev 19:15).

Smith, drawing on Brian Stock, avows that our "literal" world and its high priority on print literacy has "stolen," by substitution, much of the

24. See Tarr, *Double Image*, 151–52, for an example of how oral speech, like drum-talk, can instruct us on this vital issue.

25. Cartledge, "Charismatic Prophecy," 62.

26. Smith, "The Closing of The Book," 58.

27. For a more detailed exposure of this principle see Tarr, *Double Image*, chapter 6, 149–79. Remember, the Mossi were totally "orally educated-literate" before the arrival of the French colonialists. I also know for the purist, to say one is "orally-educated literate" is an oxymoron because for them education cannot exist without reading/writing. I use it in the connotative sense of speech as a social skill highly valued, just like reading and writing is in a text-literate society. One must not naïvely believe that all who can speak are equal in an oral society, any more than all who can read and write are equal.

authority ("mouth") that exists in the Bible and transferred it all to the written text of the Bible, which he defines as "textualization."[28]

Mega Shift

This is what the French changed in Burkina Faso. Only now, those who had power of *written word* were those who had understanding of knowledge as pieces of information in a printed, fixed form with squiggles of ink following one another, left to right, on lines that proceed down a page. In this *shift, texts are no longer understood as records but as "sites" where facts are "embodied" rather than simply recorded.*[29] As in West Africa and over 50 percent of the world, when textualization happens, the non-literate become *illiterate*. And as literacy becomes identical with rationality, the illiterate become the irrational. All of life becomes a text, the oral/aural is pressed into service by writing ... viewed through the lens of a *text*.[30]

Now, *texts* become the authority instead of the words of the king! The people love the written 'laws's more than the earlier authoritative words of the ruler. Stock makes a final clarification:

> Texuality, then is something different than literacy; that is, a community may possess and use texts but not yet be a textual community ... the issue is not one of *use* but one of *status*. A textual community is one that accords primary status to texts and the lens through which all of life is viewed.[31]

Smith here submits that evangelicalism (via evangelical theology) is a textual community and, as such, marginalizes and suppresses the orality of the Pentecostal tradition. A Pentecostal evangelical theology is a house divided against itself. He claims the Bible is a testimony that the King is alive and is a magnificent reminder of the imperial presence, *not* a substitute for it. Smith believes that the evangelical world's need for "textualization" has frozen God's revelation in time.[32]

Looking through the lens of Communications Theory, I submit God still wants to use humankind in the *incarnational model of His part/Our part*. Today's minister, preacher, prophet, or simple layperson who understands this delicate incarnational balance can mature in the Spirit to have

---

28. Smith gives credit to Stock, *The Implications of Literacy*, 29–87.
29. Smith, "The People of the Book," 56.
30. Ibid., 57.
31. Brian Stock, *The Implications of Literacy*, 62.
32. Smith, "The People of the Book," 58–59.

singular *power in his/her mouth*! McGee grew to not only believe this, but practiced it and blessed the Body of Christ.

My individual world has been impacted by two preliterate vernacular languages. If revelation can *only* come from a "text," then a whole people (in particular the Mossi and the Ewe—and untold hundreds of others) are excluded from revelation until they can read in their own mother tongue (or—heaven forbid—they are taught a "sacred language" like Latin or Arabic or Geʿez or *English*). Think how parochial is that thought! I feel sad for many of my brothers and sisters in the Body of Christ who are stuck in an evolved print-literacy bias. They want no part of a Holy Spirit they cannot *predict and control*. Thank God for this age of Holy Spirit renewal sweeping so many into the Spirit's fullness that previously denied this potential empowerment! Like Jack Hayford puts it: "Jesus prophesied it, the Father intended it, the Holy Spirit enabled it, and the Church received it."[33]

Drum Talk

Many tribes on the West African savannah still use drums to communicate with each other. This writer has spent many hours conversing with drummers about their craft. I came to an amazing and disturbing discovery. I could not understand "drum talk" until I could shift my mind away from the literal, linear, print organized orientation of my European languages (English and French). I chafed at the drummer's inability to drum according to *my* rules. I found it *non-precise* in the extreme. I concentrated on the specifics and missed the *essence of the message*. I had made the same mistake of the disciples of Jesus when they took too literally the words of Jesus (Mark 8:14–21). L. M. Hussy describes the disciples's fault and, at the same time, defines much of Western man's weakness in understanding the realm of the Spirit of God: "The disciples set about to torture a literal significance from phrases first coined to blast utterly a literal intent."[34]

Drum talk is a lot like speaking a language under the inspiration of the Spirit of God. *And both are like using a piece of smoked glass to safely view an eclipse of the sun—it conceals in order to reveal.* I've slowly and painfully discovered that God loves ambiguity because it's intimately related to the journey of faith He prefers for us . . . or at least for me.

---

33. Hayford, *The Beauty of Spiritual Language*, 100.
34. Hussey, "The Wit of the Carpenter," 329–36.

Bibliography

Cartledge, Mark H. "Charismatic Prophecy: A Definition and Description." *Journal of Pentecostal Theology* 5 (1994) 79–120.
Cox, Harvey. *Fire from Heaven: The Rise of Pentecostal Spirituality and the Reshaping of Religion in the Twenty-First Century*. Reading, MS: Persus, 1995.
Deere, Jack. *Surprised by the Power of the Spirit*. Grand Rapids: Zondervan, 1993.
Hayford, Jack. *The Beauty of Spiritual Language: A Journey toward the Heart of God*. Dallas: Word, 1992.
Hiebert, Paul. *Anthropological Insights for Missionaries*. Grand Rapids: Baker, 1985.
Hussey, L. M. "The Wit of the Carpenter." *American Mercury* 5 (1925) 329–36.
Land, Steven. *Pentecostal Spirituality: A Passion for the Kingdom*. Journal of Pentecostal Theology Supplemental 1. Sheffield, UK: Sheffield Academic, 1993.
Northrop, F. S. C. *The Meeting of East and West*. New York, Macmillan, 1946.
Ong, Walter. "World as View and World as Event." *American Anthropologist* 71, no. 4 (1969) 634–47.
Perry, Edmund. *The Gospel in Dispute*. New York: Doubleday, 1958.
Ruthven, Jon. *What's Wrong With Protestant Theology?* Tulsa, OK: Word and Spirit, 2013.
Rybarczyk, Edmund. "Expressing the Inexpressible: Tongues as Apophatic Speech." The thirty-first annual meeting of the Society for Pentecostal Studies in Lakeland, Florida, 2002.
Schwartz, Tony. *The Responsive Chord*. Garden City, NY: Anchor, 1973.
Smith, James K. A. "The Closing of the Book: Pentecostals, Evangelicals, and the Sacred Writings." *Journal of Pentecostal Theology* 11 (1997) 49–71.
Stock, Brian. *The Implications of Literacy: Written Language and Models of Interpretation in the Eleventh and Twelfth Centuries*. Princeton: Princeton University Press, 1983.
Stott, John R. W. *Baptism and Fullness: The Work of the Holy Spirit Today*. Downers Grove, IL: InterVarsity, 1975.
Tarr, Del. *Double Image: Biblical Insights from African Parables*. Mahwah, NJ: Paulist, 1994.
———. *The Foolishness of God: A Linguist Looks at the Mystery of Tongues*. Springfield, MO: Access, 2010.

Questions for Lazarus

Kilian McDonnell, OSB

They gave a dinner for him [Jesus] and Lazarus was one of those at table with him ....It was because of him [Lazarus] that many of the Jews were deserting and were believing in Jesus. John 12:2, 11

it's me they want to see, Sheol's the cave of ashes
and black mist, where even worms
are fuzzy. No one returns,
but I've been there and back.

A crowd of Jews say they've come
to Bethany to dine with Jesus,
who named and called me
from the tomb. Truth be told,

it's me they want to see,
the one who does not smell of death
but of burial spices the way the sandal
tree has no fragrance until it's felled.

They call me friend, grasp my arm,
watch me drink the Syrian wine
and in between the toasts they pose
questions about what goes on up there.

What had I seen?
The glory of God as on Mt. Sinai?
Can one walk through
the shadow of God?

When Moses reads the Torah
does he bend back and forth
so God will notice him? We know
there's no outside to God

but did you see his face?
You who have tasted eternal life
and found it sweet, will you taste death
again and find it bitter

Index of Authors

Aarflot, Andreas, 322n89, 326
Abbot, Walter M., 48, 66, 68–69, 82, 96–99, 168–69
Ahonen, Lauri, 322n90, 326
Aker, Benny C., xix, 9, 31, 103–25, 236
Alexander, Estrelda Y., 184n58, 185, 187, 233n22, 234
Alexander, Kimberly Ervin, 287n3, 299
Alexander, Patrick H., xvii, 4, 12, 13n2, 30–31, 69, 190, 285, 286n1 299
Allen, John L., Jr., 159–60, 168
Anderson, Allan, 175n17, 181n42, 186n64, 187, 233nn23–24, 234,
Anderson, Gerald H., 88n22, 96, 152–53, 188–89
Anderson, Robert Mapes, 274n14, 284
Arias, Mortimer, 105n7, 107n19, 110n28, 122
Askew, Thomas, 140n60, 142n65, 151
Attansi, Katherine, 43n20, 48

Bacci, Pietro Giacomo, 266n39, 268
Bakken, Gordon and Linda, 303n10, 304n13, 326
Barrett, C. K., 103n1, 122,
Barrett, David B., 6, 12, 138, 151, 181, 187, 234n24, 235, 286n1, 299
Bauer, Walter, 121n62, 122
Beasley-Murray, G. R., 247, 253
Beatty, Jerome, 194n4, 220
Bediako, Kwame, 231n18, 234

Beekman, John, 245, 253
Bellofatto, Gina A., 71n4, 81
Benedict XVI, Pope, 83n1, 97, 160, 168
Berg, Anna Hanson, 307nn25–26, 309n35, 326–27
Berger, Peter L., 234
Best, Thomas, 57n10, 67–68, 106n15
Betrone, John, 264n30, 268
Bevans, Stephen B., xix, 9, 85n7, 88n22, 92n33, 93, 97–98, 155–69
Bietenhard, Hans, 246n26, 253
Birch, Bruce C., 203n38, 220
Bittlinger, Arnold, 287n2, 299
Black, David Alan, 243n18, 253
Black, Matthew, 103n1, 122
Blumhofer, Edith, 284, 302, 303n7, 325n105, 327
Boers, Hendrickus, 105n9, 122
Bonk, Jonathan J., xix, 9, 33, 126–54
Boring, M. Eugene, 103n1, 106–7, 122
Bornkamm, Günther, 105n6, 122
Bosch, David J., 94n45, 97, 156, 168, 182n46, 187
Bowers, Paul, 104, 105n5, 114n42, 118, 122
Bray, Gerald, 232n20, 234
Briggs, John, 68, 146n88, 151
Brodie, Thomas L., 229n11, 235
Brooks, O. S., Sr., 110n28, 123
Brown, Michael L., 229n9, 235
Brubaker, Pamela, 213n65, 220

Brumback, Carl, 271–72, 284, 302, 307n25, 311n49, 327
Bruner, Frederick Dale, 253
Bueno, John, 196n20, 220
Burgess, Ruth Vassar, 233n22, 235
Burgess, Stanley M., xv–xvii, xix, 3–12, 30–31, 69, 188–90, 220, 222, 233n22, 235, 265n36, 268, 285, 286n1, 299, 326, 329
Byrskog, Samuel, 107n21, 110, 114, 117n51, 120, 123

Cahill, Thomas, 151
Callow, John, 245, 253
Calvin, John, 260–63, 268
Carey, William, 128–29, 151
Carlson, G. Raymond, 306nn21–22, 307n25, 307n28, 327
Carothers, W. C., 280–82, 284
Cartledge, Mark H., 235, 342n18, 344n25, 347
Cashwell, G. B., 279, 280n32, 284
Castro, Emilio, 182n46, 187
Cerillo Jr., Augustus, 271nn2–3, 284
Chan Simon, 265nn34–35, 267–68
Chappell, Paul, 287n3, 288n5, 289nn6–8, 299
Charles, R. H., 288n4, 299
Chéreau, Georgette, 231n15, 235
Cho, Youngmo, 228n4, 235
Christiansen, Rasmus, 304n16, 327
Chung, Paul, 261n21, 268
Cleary, Edward L., 42n17, 49
Cleeton, Elaine R., 12
Clemmons, Ithiel, 205, 207n48, 220
Clifford, Catherine E., 84n4, 98
Comblin, José, 162, 163n30, 168
Coote, Robert T., 33, 188–89
Corum, Fred T., 184n59, 187, 278n24, 282nn42–43, 284
Corwin, Gary R., 31–32
Cottrell, Peter, 245n22, 253
Coulter, Dale M., 76, 79, 81
Cox, Harvey, 178n28, 182n48, 187, 339, 347
Cranfield, C. E. B., 104n1, 111n30, 116n47, 123
Creech, Joe, 271n3, 284

Crossing, Peter F., 181n41, 187, 234n24, 235,
Dalton, Adele Flower, 193n3, 194n4, 220
Dayton, Donald W., 186n65, 187, 287n3, 289n6, 290n9, 299
de Waard, Jan, 243n18, 254
Deere, Jack, 343, 347
Del Colle, Ralph, 58n12, 67
Delio, Ilia, 92, 94, 97
Dempster, Murray W., xix, 9–10, 33, 43n18, 49, 181, 182n48, 187, 189, 192–223
Dennis, James S., 127, 137–43, 151–52
D'Espine, Henri, 57n8, 67
Dibelius, Martin, 231n17, 235
Dichter, Thomas W., 150n102, 152
Dillon, Richard J., 129n8, 235,
Dominy, Bert B., 231n15, 235
Donfried, Karl P., 105n10, 123
Douglas, J. D., 184n56, 188
Dowie, Alexander, 291, 299
Dulles, Avery, 72n8, 81
Dunn, James D.G., 104n1, 110n29, 117nn49–50, 118n52, 123, 162, 168, 231n15, 235, 240, 241n7, 241n10, 242n15, 243, 249, 254
Dupont, Jacques, 231n17, 235
Dusing, Michael, 240, 254

Edwards, Denis, 92n33, 93–94, 97, 163, 168
Ellacuría, Ignacio, 91n29, 97, 168
Elliot, J. K., 105n9, 120, 123
Ensley, Eddie, 266n40, 269
Ervin, Howard M., 241, 251, 252n41, 254
Evans, Justin, 183, 188

Faggioli, Massimo, 86n15, 87n16, 91, 97
Faupel, D. William, 175n17, 188, 287n3, 290n10, 292n13, 299
Fee, Gordon D., 104n1, 119n56, 123, 243, 249–51, 254, 264n30, 269
Ferguson, Niall, 145n85, 152
Fieldhouse, D. K., 148n97, 152
Fitzmyer, Joseph A., 105n10, 118, 123

INDEX OF AUTHORS

Foakes-Jackson, F. J., 231n17, 235
Fortino, Eleuterio F., 87n21, 97
Foster, C. E., 279n29, 284
Francis, Pope, 62n21, 67, 96–98
Frere, Rt. Honorable Sir Bartle Edward, 135, 136n39, 152
Friedrich, Gerhard, 105n9, 123, 253
Frodsham, Stanley H., 282, 284, 302, 307n25, 326n100, 327
Froelich, Karlfried, 259nn11–12, 264n31, 269
Fuchs, Lorelei, 57n10, 67–68

Gaillardetz, Richard R., 84n4, 98
Galbraith, John Kenneth, 148, 152
Gallagher, Joseph, 48, 66, 68–69, 82, 96–99, 168–69
Gallonio, Antonio, 266n38, 269
Gardiner, Gordon P., 325n106, 327
Garlington, Don B., 115n44, 123
Gee, Donald, 175n16, 188
Gensichen, Hans-Werner, 127n2, 152
Gitre, Edward J. K., xix, 10–11, 271–85
Glasser, Arthur F., 172, 188
Goff, James R., Jr., 33, 233n23, 235, 274n14, 284, 292nn14–15, 299, 320n81, 323n95, 327
González, Justo L., 157n8, 168, 231n15, 235
Goodell, William, 130n11, 152
Goodpasture, H. McKennie, 137n43, 152
Goswell, Gregory, 122n63, 123
Goulder, M. D., 231n16, 235
Graham, Billy, 170n4, 188
Grant, David and Beth, 212, 221
Green, Matthew D., 33, 43n19, 49
Gros, Jeffrey, 37n1, 49–50, 57n10, 67–68, 87n19, 98
Gundry, Stanley N., 4–5
Gushie, David P., 215n68, 215n70, 216nn71–72, 217nn73–74, 218nn75–76, 222
Gusmer, Charles W., 39n6, 49

Hadden, Jeffrey, 182n48, 188
Hale, Frederick, 322nn93–94, 327
Hamalainen, Arto, 187–88

Hamon, Bill, 78–79, 81
Hanson, Andrew, 315n63, 315n65, 327
Hanson, Carl M., 305–9, 327
Harbison, E. Harris, 17, 30
Harlan, R., 290n10, 299
Harrell, David, 295n24, 299
Harris, Murray J., 247–48, 249n34, 254
Harrison, Everett F., 105, 106nn11–13, 114n42, 123
Hart, Larry D., 242, 254
Haugen, Peter, 317, 327
Hawthorne, Gerald F., 105n8, 123
Hayford, Jack, 346–47
Hearnshaw, F. J. C., 148n97, 152
Heasman, Kathleen., 146n88, 152
Heckman, Warren L., 313n59, 314n63, 327
Hedlun, Randy, 31
Heidal, Abraham, 320n84, 327
Hengel, Martin, 107n20, 109n25, 123
Herrin, Judith, 147n93, 152
Hiebert, Paul, 335, 336n6, 337, 347
Hill, David, 231n15, 235
Hocken, Peter, xix, 8, 70–82
Hocking, WIlliam Ernest, 146n87, 152
Hodges, Melvin L., 42n16, 49
Hogan, J. Philip, 194, 221
Hollenweger, Walter J., 5, 182n48, 188, 286n1, 299
Holmes, Pamela, 184n58, 188
Hoornaert, Eduardo, 147n92, 152
Horton, Stanley M., 32, 240, 254
Hubbard, Benjamin J., 104n1, 123
Hudson, Neil, 233n22, 235
Huffman, John, 282n44, 284
Hughson, Thomas, 84, 89, 92, 95, 98
Hunter, Harold H., 187–88, 254
Huntington, Samuel P., 148n97, 149, 152
Hurst, Randy, 240, 255
Hurtado, L. W., 107n20, 109n25, 112n36, 113n37, 114n41, 123
Hussey, L.M., 346–47

Itioka, Neuza, 175, 176n20, 188

Jacobsen, Doublas, 233nn22–23, 235
Jayasooria, Denison, 178n29, 188

Jenkins, Philip, 151n104, 152, 185n63, 188
Jenney, Timothy P., 240, 254
Jeremias, Joachim, 104n1, 123
Jewett, Robert, 104n1, 105n10, 114n42, 115n43, 116, 123–24
Jipp, Joshua W., 113n37, 124
John Paul II, Pope, 62n21, 68, 84, 92, 95, 98, 156–58, 160, 163n34, 164n38, 168
Johns, Donald A., xix, 10, 239–55
Johnson, Alan, 105n7, 122
Johnson, Elizabeth, 160, 163, 168
Johnson, Luke Timothy, 228n6, 235,
Johnson, M. Earl, 304n13, 328
Johnson, Todd M., 6, 12, 71n4, 81, 138n51, 153, 181n41, 187, 234n24, 235, 286n1, 299
Jones, Charles Edwin, 325n106, 328
Joyner, Rick, 78, 82
Junk, Thomas, 279n31, 284

Kähler, Martin, 155, 156n3, 169
Kalu, Ogbu, 233n22, 235
Kärkkäinen, Veli-Matti, 257n4, 269
Käsemann, Ernst, 104n1, 124
Kasper, Cardinal Walter, 57n11, 68, 86n12, 92, 98
Keener, Craig S., xx, 10, 106, 120, 124, 227–38, 242, 254
Kern, Stephen, 273n9, 284
Ketcham, Maynard, 196n15, 221
Kidd, Benjamin, 139, 152
Kim, Kirsteen, 156n6, 162, 165n47, 167, 169
Kinne, S. D., 282n41, 284
Klaus, Byron D., xi-xiii, 22n49, 23n58, 28, 30, 33, 43n18, 49, 155n1, 169, 182n48, 187, 189, 221
Kloppenburg, Bonaventure, 55n5, 68
Kraft, Charles H., 176n20, 188
Kreider, Alan, 147, 152
Kurian, George T., 138n51, 153, 286n1, 299,

LaBerge (neé Ozman), Agnes, 185n62, 189, 274n14, 284–85
Ladner, Gerhard B., 80n43, 82

LaGrand, James, 110n28, 113n38, 116n46, 124
Land, Steven, 342n21, 347
Lang, Joseph R., 84n3, 98
Latourette, Kenneth Scott, 130n11, 153
Laurie, Thomas, 131–34, 153
Lawless, Chuck, 104n1, 114n40, 124
Lawrence, B. F., 281, 282n40, 284, 302n2, 324, 328
Lee, Robert L., 322n89, 328
Lewis, Paul W., xv-xvii, xx, 3–12
Liggins, John, 135–36, 153
Lindberg, Frank Theodor, 310n46, 311nn52–53, 312n54, 328
Lindsay, Gordon, 240, 254, 290n10, 292n13, 299
Long, Charles Henry, 134n35, 153
Longenecker, Richard N., 119n56, 124
Lovett, Leonard, 206n46, 221
Lowe, Valerie G., 182n48, 189
Luter, A. Boyd, Jr., 105n8, 124
Luther, Martin, 258–60, 263–64, 269

Macchia, Frank, 75–76, 82, 242, 251, 254, 264n30, 267, 269
MacLeod, David J., 115n44, 124
MacMullen, Ramsay, 147, 153
MacRobert, Iain, 205n43, 221
Magnuson, Norris, 146n88, 153
Martin, Francis, 232n20, 236
Martin, I. G., 272, 284
Maston, T. B., 203n38, 221
Matson, Joseph, 321n86, 328
Matthey, Jacques, 87n17, 98, 169
May, Melanie A,, 57n8, 68
McBrien, Ricard, 84n6, 98
McClung, Grant, xx, 9, 170–91
McDonnell, Kilian, xx, 11, 25, 92n33, 98, 287, 299, 349–50,
McGee, Gary B., xi-xiii, xv-xvii, 3–5, 7–8, 12–33, 40–43, 46–49, 69, 92, 93n35, 98, 155, 169–70, 190, 227, 232n20, 233nn22–23, 235–37, 254, 268, 274, 275n15, 284–85, 286n1 299, 303, 318, 320n82, 328
McGinn, Bernard, 264n33, 269
Melanchthon, Philip, 264n29, 269

INDEX OF AUTHORS

Meller, Leo, 322n90, 328
Menzies, Robert P., 33, 228nn4–5, 236, 253n44, 254
Menzies, William W., 3, 12, 181, 190, 302, 307n25, 328
Meyer, Harding, 37n1, 49, 57n10, 67–68
Michel, Otto, 110n28, 124
Miller, Donald W., 202–3, 221
Miller, Gregory J., xx, 10, 256–70
Moo, Douglas J., 104n1, 124
Moreau, A. Scott, 31
Morken, A. O., 303–4, 325n101, 328
Morosco, Robert E., 104n1, 124
Motte, Mary M., xx, 8, 83–99
Moule, C. F. D., 231n15, 236
Müller, Father Karl, 40–41, 43–45, 48–49
Müller, U. B., 104n1, 106, 124
Mullin, Robert Bruce, 234n24, 236
Mundy, David Lee, 182n48, 190
Murray, John, 104n1, 124
Myer, Ron, 78, 82

Nelson, Douglas, 175n17, 285
Nelson, Jack A., 204, 221
Ness, Henry H., 302n2, 304n14, 304n16, 307n25, 311, 328
Newberry, Annette, xx, 7, 13–33
Newton, J. C. Calhoun, 139n53, 153
Nida, Eugene A., 243n18, 254
Nnyombi, Richard, 87n20, 98
Nodtvedt, Magnus, 322n89, 328
Northrop, F. S. C., 336n8, 347
Nystrom, Lowell, 313nn59–60, 314nn61–63, 328
Nyvall, David, 322n91, 328

Oleska, Michael J., 158, 169
Olson, Arnold T., 310n45, 323, 328
Olsson, Karl A., 322n91, 328
O'Malley, John, 84n4, 98,
Ong, Walter, 337, 347
Opp, James, 233n22, 236
Ozman, Agnes, *See* LaBerge (neé Ozman), Agnes

Packer, J. W., 232n20, 236
Palau, Luis, 180, 190

Palma, Anthony D., 240, 254
Palmer, Michael D., 182n48, 190
Pao, David W., 230n14, 236
Parham, Charles F. , 274, 276–77, 279, 285
Parham, Sarah, 274n11, 274n13, 285
Park, Andrew Sung, 231n18, 237
Parks, Iris, 615n66, 328
Parmentier, Martin, 233n23, 237
Paul VI, Pope, 43–45, 49, 54, 62n21, 68, 72, 82, 90, 98, 156–57, 160, 169
Payne, Ernest A., 128n6, 153
Pearlman, Myer, 41n11, 50
Pennoyer, F. Douglas, 176n20, 190
Perry, Edmund, 336n8, 347
Peters, George, 173, 190
Petersen, Douglas, 33, 43n18, 49, 182n48, 187, 189, 197n21, 221
Pfaff, William, 145n86, 153
Phillips, James M., 33, 188–89
Pierson, Arthur T., 127, 135, 153, 273, 285
Plummer, Alfred, 252, 254
Plummer, Robert L., 103–104, 105n6, 124
Pohill, John, 104n1, 124
Pousson, Edward K., 182n48, 190
Pretlove, John L., 254

Radano, John A., xx, 8, 54–69
Ramsey, Paul, 219, 222
Rasmussen, Larry L., 203n38, 220
Rausch, Thomas P., 76, 82
Rausch, William G., 87n19, 98
Rauschenbusch, Walter, 181, 190
Reddin, Opal L., 176n20, 190
Reinholdz, Naemi, 319n78, 329
Reyonlds, Barbara, 207n48, 222
Riggs, Ralph, 240, 254
Riss, Richard M., 297n28, 299, 310n43, 325n105, 329
Robeck, Cecil M., Jr., xx, 7–8, 37–50, 58nn13–14, 59, 60n18, 60n20, 65nn28–29, 69, 155n1, 169, 184n60, 187–88, 190, 206nn46–47, 222, 231n18, 233nn22–23, 237, 257n3, 269, 275n16, 285
Roberts, Oral, 295–96, 299

INDEX OF AUTHORS

Robertson, Archibald, 252, 254
Robinson, John A. T., 231n17, 237
Rodgers, Darrin J., xx, 11, 23n60, 27n71, 31, 301–29
Rosenior, Derrick R., 206, 222
Rusch, William G., 37n1, 49–50, 57n10, 67–68,
Ruthven, Jon, 334n2, 347
Ruysbroeck, John, 265, 269
Ryan, Tom, 86, 98
Rybarczyk, Edmund, 340, 341n15, 347

Sandidge, Jerry L., 39, 50
Sanneh, Lamin, 234n24, 237
Schatzmann, Siegfried S., 253n44, 255
Scherer, James A., 85n7, 98
Schleiermacher, Friederich, 156n4, 169
Schreiner, Thomas R., 104n2, 107, 113n38, 115n44, 118, 124
Schreiter, Robert J., 166, 169
Schroeder, Roger P., 88n22, 92n33, 97, 158, 161n26, 167n52, 168
Schwartz, Tony, 335, 336n7, 347
Scott, James M., 231n16, 237
Self, Charles, xvin2, xvii
Sellers, Ian, 146n88, 151
Seymour, William J., 293, 299
Shemeth, S., 194, 195nn10–13, 196, 222
Shibley, David, 186, 190
Shumway, C. W., 274n14, 276n19, 281n38, 285
Shupe, Anson, 182n48, 188
Silva, Moisés, 245n22, 255
Sivalon, John C., 90, 98
Smalley, Martha Lund, 131n22, 133n28, 153
Smith, David, 231n15, 237
Smith, James K. A., 11, 12, 341–45, 347
Smith, Susan, 95n47, 98
Smith, Sydney, 129, 153
Sobrino, Jon, 91n29, 97, 168
Soderlund, Sven K., 105n9, 124
Spencer, F. Scott, 231n15, 237
Spittler, Russell P., 4, 12, 181n46, 182n46, 186n65, 190, 284
Springer, Kevin, 176n20, 190
Stannard, David E., 134n34, 145n85, 154

Stassen, Glen H., 213–17, 218nn75–77, 220, 222
Stephens, Randall J., 272n6, 285
Stephenson, George M., 322n91, 329
Stock, Brian, 340n14, 344–45, 347
Stoeger, WIlliam R., 94, 98
Stott, John R. W., 180n36, 190, 340, 347
Strachan, Hew, 145, 154
Stronstad, Roger, 228n5, 229n11, 237, 240, 255
Sugden, Christopher, 179, 190
Sullivan, Francis, 265n37, 269
Sweeney, Douglas A., 234n24, 237
Synan, Vinson, xx, 3, 4n1, 11–12, 33, 175, 184–85, 190, 206, 207n48, 222, 286–300

Talbert, Charles H., 233n23, 237
Tarr, Del, xx, 11, 233n22, 237, 330–47
Taylor, Alva W., 145nn83–84, 154
Taylor, G. F., 280n35, 285
Teresa of Avila, 266, 267n41, 269
Thompson, Peter B., 310, 311n47, 311n51, 319n79, 320n83, 323, 329
Tiedemann, R. G., 321n87, 329
Tomkins, Stephen, 234n24, 237
Trevor, Meriol, 266n39, 269
Türks, Paul, 266n38, 269
Turner, Max, 228n4, 237, 245n22, 253
Turner, William, 206n46, 222

Vagle, Anna, 304n14, 329
van Beek, Huibert, 65n26, 69
van der Maas, Eduard, 5, 12, 30, 188–90, 220, 268, 286n1, 299, 326, 329
Vanzandt, J. C., 272n5, 274n14, 285
Venter, Alexander, 231n18, 237
Vischer, Lukas, 57n10, 68
Vondey, Wolfgang, 37n1, 50, 76, 82, 270,

Wacker, Grant, 27n71, 31, 33, 233n22, 237, 271, 272nn3–4, 273, 284–85, 327
Wagenaar, Hinne, 231n15, 237
Wagner, C. Peter, 43n19, 50, 78, 82, 176n20, 190
Wainwright, Geoffrey, 257n4, 270

Wallace, Claudia, 298n29, 300
Wallace, Daniel B., 108n22, 111n30, 124
Wallis, Arthur, 78n33, 82
Walls, Andrew, 137n44, 150, 154
Warfield, Benjamin, 261, 270
Warneck, Gustav, 103, 104n2, 124, 127, 150, 154
Warner, Wayne, 196n15, 221, 311n51, 329
Warren, William, 129-31, 133, 134nn33-34, 154
Webster, Donovan, 145n85, 154
Weigel, George, 73-74, 75n19, 82
Wesley, John, 232n20, 237
West, Russell, 207n48, 222
White, John, 176n20, 190
Whitsett, Christopher G., 108n23, 124
Wilkin, Robert Lewis, 147n94, 154
Williams, Demetrius K., 233n22, 237
Williams, Don, 176n20, 191

Williams, George H., 263n26, 270
Willitts, J., 125
Wimber, John, 176n20, 191
Witherington, Ben, 242n43, 255
Womack, David A., 256, 257n1, 270
Wood, George O., 207, 208nn50-51, 222, 240, 255
Wright, N. T., 105n9, 117n50, 124-25
Wright, Ronald, 134n34, 154
Wuellner, Wilhelm, 120, 125

Yamamori, Tetsunao, 202-3, 221
Yong, Amos, 43n20, 48, 75-76, 82, 95, 98, 159, 169, 231n18, 233n24, 238

Zehnle, Richard F., 228n6, 238
Zerwick, Max, 248, 255
Ziefle, Joshua R., 38n3, 46, 50
Zwiep, Arie W., 230n13, 238

www.ingramcontent.com/pod-product-compliance
Lightning Source LLC
Chambersburg PA
CBHW071147300426
44113CB00009B/1109